LORD GEORGE
BENTINCK

D0144967

The Library of Conservative Thought
Milton Hindus, Series Editor
Russell Kirk, Founding Series Editor

America's British Culture, by Russell Kirk
Authority and the Liberal Tradition, by Robert Heineman
A Better Guide than Reason, by M.E. Bradford
Burke Street, by George Scott-Moncrieff
The Case for Conservatism, by Francis Graham Wilson
Céline, by Milton Hindus
Character and Culture, by Irving Babbitt
*Collected Letters of John Randolph of Roanoke to
John Brockenbrough, 1812–1833*, edited by Kenneth Shorey
A Critical Examination of Socialism, by William Hurrell Mallock
Edmund Burke: Appraisals and Applications,
edited by Daniel E. Ritchie
Edmund Burke: The Enlightenment and Revolution, by Peter J. Stanlis
The Essential Calhoun, by John C. Calhoun
Foundations of Political Science, by John W. Burgess
Ghosts on the Roof, by Whittaker Chambers
The God of the Machine, by Isabel Paterson
A Historian and His World, A Life of Christopher Dawson 1889–1970,
by Christina Scott
Historical Consciousness, by John Lukacs
I Chose Freedom, by Victor A. Kravchenko
I Chose Justice, by Victor A. Kravchenko
Irving Babbitt, Literature, and the Democratic Culture, by Milton Hindus
The Jewish East Side, edited by Milton Hindus
Lord George Bentinck, by Benjamin Disraeli
The Moral Foundations of Civil Society, by Wilhelm Roepke
Natural Law, by Alexander Passerin d'Entréves
On Divorce, by Louis de Bonald
Orestes Brownson: Selected Political Essays, edited by Russell Kirk
The Phantom Public, by Walter Lippmann
*The Politics of the Center, Juste Milieu in Theory and Practice, France and
England, 1815–1848*, by Vincent E. Starzinger
Regionalism and Nationalism in the United States, by Donald Davidson
Rousseau and Romanticism, by Irving Babbitt
The Social Crisis of Our Time, by Wilhelm Roepke
Tensions of Order and Freedom, by Béla Menczer
We the People, by Forrest McDonald

A POLITICAL
BIOGRAPHY

LORD GEORGE BENTINCK

Benjamin Disraeli

with a new introduction by
Robert W. Kamphuis, Jr.

Transaction Publishers
New Brunswick (U.S.A.) and London (U.K.)

Library of Congress Catalog Number: 89-34108
ISBN: 1-56000-947-0
Printed in the United States of America

Library of Congress Cataloging-in-Publication Data

Disraeli, Benjamin, Earl of Beaconsfield, 1804–1881.
  Lord George Bentinck : a political biography / Benjamin Disraeli ; with a new introduction by Robert W. Kamphuis, Jr.
      p. cm. — (The library of conservative thought)
  Originally published: London : Archibald Constable and Co., 1905.
  Bibliography: p.
  ISBN 1-56000-947-0 (pbk. : alk. paper)
  1. Bentinck, George, Lord, 1802–1848. 2. Politicians—Great Britain—Biography. 3. Great Britain—Politics and government—1837–1901. I. Kamphuis, Robert W. II. Title. III. Series.
DA541.B3D57   1997
941.081'092   89-34108
[B]—DC20   CIP

TO

LORD HENRY BENTINCK

IS INSCRIBED

THIS POLITICAL BIOGRAPHY

OF

ONE FOR WHOM HE ENTERTAINED A DEEP AFFECTION

AND WHOSE TALENTS AND VIRTUES

HE SHARES

CONTENTS

INTRODUCTION TO
THE TRANSACTION EDITION

Lord George Bentinck is an account of high political drama—
among the best ever written. Lord George Bentinck, Benjamin Disraeli, and Sir Robert Peel are the stars, with Peel
as the antagonist and Bentinck the subject and Disraeli the
author as the protagonist team. "Although of perfectly different natures, they pulled together without any difficulty,"
a contemporary observed.[1] By temperament, skills, background, and resources, they were ideally matched and necessary to one another. Disraeli wrote this biography as a
tribute to his colleague, whose untimely death in 1848 left
Disraeli alone to lead the Conservative party in the House
of Commons.

Lord George Bentinck was well known in his day, even if
most history books pass him by. From the 1820s to the mid-
1840s he was a dominant figure in English horse racing, acknowledged by many as "king of the turf." In 1845 alone, his
horses won 82 races. Victories came about in part thanks to
Bentinck's close attention to every detail of the diet, care,
and training of his horses. As demonstrated in the events of
this book, he had a phenomenal capacity for facts and their
relations, and he was willing to put in as much effort as necessary to master them. He was a winner because he worked.

He was also known for his relentless integrity. Once, in a
storyline worthy of Dick Francis, he became convinced that
one of his own jockeys had thrown a race, and he pursued
the matter, and the hapless jockey, regardless of cost until
the Jockey Club was convinced and disqualified the rider.
At a time when racing was a passion of the ruling class,
Lord George Bentinck was one of the patricians.

Aside from his renown on the turf, family and fortune were enough to secure his standing in society's highest elite. Bentinck's father was the Duke of Portland, and both his grandfather and his uncle had been prime ministers. Bentinck himself was immensely rich. His contemporaries report that more than once he stood to gain or lose £150,000 on a race (he was proud to back his judgment), and in the fashion-conscious age of Beau Brummell, he never wore the same cravat twice. In short, "a vehement and imperious spirit, unflinching courage, a mind of great native vigor directed by a will that never knew submission, and the reputation for unbending rectitude that wins the confidence of men."[2]

Lord George was also a long-standing member of the House of Commons. Though a member of Parliament for 18 years prior to the start of the events in this book, he spoke only infrequently in debates. During his first eight years he said nothing at all. Viewing himself as nothing but a good judge of men and horses, he admitted that he had little attraction to politics, and was known to put in appearances at Westminster in a topcoat pulled over hunting regalia.

Disraeli's biography brings to life matters bigger than Bentinck's personality: enduring issues and principles by which to govern and to live. We really meet Bentinck only in flashes. Yet since his pride did not demand sycophancy, he would have applauded Disraeli's treatment. It took extreme provocation—"being sold" was Bentinck's term—at the hands of his party's leader, Sir Robert Peel, to move him off the back bench and track, into the forefront of national controversy and leadership. In 1845 he had clout, ability, indignation, and a determination to do something about it. What he and like-minded men needed was (and is) rare: an imagination powerful enough in depth and breadth to bring the full range of their convictions into focus and devise an effective program of action.

No word attaches more naturally to Benjamin Disraeli than imagination, though others may apply equally. The chronicle of his life and achievements is erratic, even wild.

Yet a unifying purpose may be found underlying his major successes and failures, especially as a statesman.[3] From his flamboyant, fervid youth to the full maturity of power, Disraeli strove to discern, articulate, and participate in the essence of English greatness. "My politics are described by one word," he said, "and that word is England." His apprehension of order is his greatest accomplishment and his enduring legacy.

But Disraeli was not a seer only. "I am only truly great in action," he once said of himself. Elsewhere he wrote, "Action may not always be happiness, but there is no happiness without action." Disraeli's compulsion to act boldly to defend and enhance English order was irresistible, perhaps as often as not precipitous. The tension between Disraeli's great gifts and the demands of the situations in which he placed himself may be the best key to understanding his failures. For those who govern, the present moment is always decisive, but imagination is seldom rushed to good effect.

The meaning and truth of this emerge in a contrast with Disraeli's and Bentinck's great antagonist in these events, Sir Robert Peel. "Though nearly two generations have elapsed since his death," wrote Moneypenny in 1912, "...he still suffers from the excessive praise, and in a less degree from the excessive blame, that fall to statesmen while they live." Moneypenny continues,

Mainly interested in finance and in practical measures of administration, he cared little for the imperial ideas of generations that had preceded and were to follow his own. But, as Mr. Gladstone once remarked, he was the best man of business who was ever Prime Minister; and he was that not only by virtue of what Disraeli called his "unrivaled powers of dispatching affairs," but also by his possession of many of the higher moral qualities of the ideal man of business. There was indeed a good deal more of egoism and ambition in his character than has often been recognized, but he was incapable of any petty or ignoble self-seeking; and in point of industry, rectitude, and devotion to public duty, he set an example which has served permanently to raise the standard of English government. That is a better title to fame than the dubious distinction, which Disraeli assigned him, of having been the greatest Member of Parliament that ever lived.[4]

Walter Bagehot, in his lucid 1856 essay "The Character of
Sir Robert Peel," cuts to the heart of Peel's strengths and
weaknesses:

A great administrator is not a man likely to desire to have fixed opinions,—his natural bent and tendency is to immediate action: the existing and pressing circumstances of the case fill up his mind; the letters
to be answered, the documents to be filed, the memoranda to be made,
engross his attention; he is angry if you distract him. A bold person
who suggests a matter of principle, or a difficulty of thought, or an
abstract result that seems improbable in the case "before the board,"
will be set down as a speculator, a theorist, a troubler of practical life.
To expect to hear from such men profound views of future policy, digested plans of distant action, is to mistake their genius entirely.... So
the brain of the great administrator is naturally occupied with the details of the day, the passing dust, the granules of that day's life; and his
unforeseeing temperament turns away uninterested from reaching
speculations, from vague thought, and from extensive and far-off plans.
Of course it is not meant that a great administrator has absolutely no
general views: some indeed he must have,—a man cannot conduct the
detail of affairs without having some plan which regulates that detail;
he cannot help having some idea, vague or accurate, indistinct or distinct, of the direction in which he is going and the purpose for which he
is traveling. But the difference is, that this plan is seldom his own, the
offspring of his own brain, the result of his own mental contention; it is
the plan of someone else.[5]

For one who assumes the burden of governing, "The necessary effect of all this labor is, that those subject to it have no
opinions," according to Bagehot. "It requires a great deal of
time to have opinions; belief is a slow process."[6] Unlike Peel,
Disraeli insisted both on governing, and on having opinions
that were his own. This was his quandary. Quick and in-
sightful, Disraeli's mind was amazingly gifted, but it is still
small wonder that the insistent "now" of the political moment
caught him on many occasions less than wholly prepared.

The "now" of *Lord George Bentinck,* however, found
Disraeli at his best; in a sense he had spent years preparing
for it. "Disraeli's personal contest with Peel is the dramatic
moment of his career," observes Paul Elmer More.[7] F. J.
Hearnshaw writes, "It was he personally who brought Peel
down, as clearly as it was David who brought down Goliath.

And the one event was scarcely less spectacular and sensational than the other."[8]

Disraeli was an exceptional practitioner of the art of politics, an art that in his day found its highest expression in Parliamentary debate. His early forays were failures. He lost his first four elections. Once he did win a seat, his maiden speech was a disaster: the derisive laughter of the House eventually drowned out his words. According to Lord Blake, the effort was so unfortunate that, "If Disraeli's peroration had been listened to in silence it might have blasted his Parliamentary reputation forever. As it was, he inspired a certain sympathy for his courage if for nothing else when, having been on his feet for precisely the time that he intended, he shouted in a voice heard high above the hubbub, 'I will sit down now, but the time will come when you will hear me.'"[9]

His talent matured into ability. *Weekly Chronicle,* a *Newsweek* of the nineteenth century, describes Disraeli in top form at the time of these events: "No report can give an idea of the effect produced in the House of Commons. The manner of delivery, the perfect intonation of the voice, the peculiar looks of the speaker—all contributed to a success that we believe to be perfectly unparalleled. No man within our recollection has wielded a similar power over the sympathies and passions of his hearers."[10]

He was heard indeed. Again according to *Weekly Chronicle:*

> For him to rise late, in a stormy debate, cool, even to iciness, amidst the fever-heat of party atmosphere around, was suddenly to arrest all passions, all excitement, all murmurs of conversation, and convert them into one absorbing feeling of curiosity and expectation. They knew not on whom to fix their watch—whether on the speaker, that they might not lose the slightest gesture of his by-play, or whether they should concentrate their attention on his distinguished victim, whom he had taught them almost to regard with levity. The power of the orator was more confessed, perhaps, in the nervous twitchings of Sir Robert Peel, and his utter powerlessness to look indifferent, or to conceal his palpable annoyance, than even in the delirious laughter with which the House accepted and sealed the truth of the attacks.[11]

Despite his dominant presence in the actual events, Disraeli is almost invisible in *Lord George Bentinck.* To understand this, remember that his esteem for Bentinck, his friend and colleague, was great and genuine. "Overwhelmed by a great calamity [in] the death of one to whom I was bound by personal ties, far stronger even than those political ties that knit us together," is how Disraeli described himself in a letter of 1848. "It is the greatest sorrow I have ever experienced," he wrote in another.[12] Disraeli also recognized the significance of Bentinck's complementary style and standing. As noted earlier, Bentinck had an encyclopedic mind for facts, and his own speeches were always closely and even tediously tied to the best available evidence. Because of his established credibility and minute attention to detail, Bentinck's words carried weight and provided a powerful foundation for Disraeli's attacks. In tribute to his friend and to his importance in these events, Disraeli stays in the wings offstage.[13]

Also revealing may be a comparison between Disraeli's treatment of Bentinck and his development of leading characters in the body of his other narrative prose, his novels. Disraeli wrote fiction of enduring interest. Several of his books remain in print, and for good reason. There is a gemlike quality about them: the best, including *Coningsby, Sybil,* and *Tancred,* sparkle brilliantly, though they can be rough and are not all equally well polished. In praise of Disraeli's literary talent, one critic of the time went so far as to ask, "May not I lament the degradation of a promising novelist into a Prime Minister?"[14] As a literary device, Disraeli commonly relies on a title character to maintain the unity of what otherwise threatens to break down into a series of vignettes, portraits, sketches, and comments. We meet them in flashes, just as we do Lord George. The title characters Coningsby and Sybil, for instance, are like punts that carry the reader along streams that wind through much of the social and political landscape of Victorian England. Similarly, Lord George carries us through the great events of 1845 to 1848.

Something of the essence of the Bentinck-Disraeli partnership—and something of the character of each man—may be seen in their responses to the issue of whether Jews might sit in the House of Commons. Removal of Jewish disabilities was brought up regularly by the Whigs, and rejected just as regularly by the Conservatives. In 1847—the year after the fall of Peel, when Disraeli and Bentinck needed to consolidate their leadership of the Conservative party—another round of this debate arose, and it is described in this book. Both Disraeli and Bentinck defied the pressure of political expedience to speak in support of a Whig proposal.

Disraeli's position was characteristically complex. Personal factors shaped his views in distinctive ways. His family was Jewish until a dispute over temple duties moved Isaac D'Israeli to have his children baptized when Benjamin was 13. Benjamin regarded Christianity as the fulfillment of Judaism. In *Lord George Bentinck* he asserts a view parallel to the traditional theological paradox of *felix culpa*— "the happy fall." Just as the fall in Eden made it possible for us to know God's grace in a rich way that would have been otherwise inconceivable, so, Disraeli argues, we know the fullness of God's grace in Christ only through the crucifixion. To what extent is it really appropriate, he asks, to condemn Jews who were the instrument of this unfolding of divine goodness? Was it not in fact among Jews that the Church first took root, so that we are all in this sense children of Abraham? Disraeli recognized the Jews as a people chosen and distinguished by God. That and their strength in adversity show them to be natural aristocrats of the highest order. Believing this gave him a sense of perspective on the social scene; as a scion of the Jewish race, he was free to be audacious and to reach for the heights.[15] He was also free to support removal of Jewish disabilities.

Views like these were quite unpopular in Britain, yet time and time again throughout his career Disraeli boldly asserted them.[16] His stance may also have been in part a reaction to the sedentary state of the religious life in which most early nineteenth-century Anglicans comfortably participated.[17] Many leading minds of the time, such as Newman and Coleridge, were dissatisfied religiously and searching for sources of vitality to invigorate Christian religion. It is not surprising that Disraeli would have sought to identify sources for vital religion, and given his propensity to form his opinions in his own idiosyncratic way, it is furthermore not surprising that he would have looked to his own heritage for such sources.

Bentinck did not share Disraeli's views. For the most part, he was indifferent to the issue and did not view it as a high-priority problem. "This Jewish question is a terrible annoyance," he wrote in a letter to a friend. "I never saw anything like the prejudice that exists against them. For my part I don't think it matters two straws whether they are in or out of Parliament."[18] Though not a matter of deep personal significance, Bentinck had in earlier debates and votes been a supporter of Jewish rights, though he based his support on a widely held, conventional principle of straightforward toleration rather than anything like Disraeli's theories. Loyalty and recognition of Disraeli's significance to the Conservative party pushed him to a bolder position on the issue than he might otherwise have chosen: "I don't like letting Disraeli vote by himself apart from the party otherwise I might give in to the prejudices of the multitude," he continued in his letter to his friend.

Thus, Bentinck stood by Disraeli in a difficult situation, in a manner consistent with his own convictions. Standing against the current led Bentinck to feel constrained (if not relieved) to step aside from formal leadership of the party. His outspoken support on this and other issues may be seen to have saved Disraeli from being dropped by the newly established Conservatives.

THE CORN LAWS AND THE FALL OF PEEL

Bentinck, Disraeli, and Peel—the main figures of the drama—are now introduced. On to the setting. When this book opens in 1845, Peel had been prime minister for four years with a commanding majority of 91. In describing his "mandate" Keir writes that, "The electorate of 1841 rallied to a party which stood for economy, remedy of abuse, and resistance to further organic change" in society.[19] But Peel lost sight of his mandate, and therein hangs the tale. "Peel by his tactless arrogance [though supremely competent, he was never warm or endearing] had seemed to invite a declaration of war," writes Moneypenny, "and war, if he sought it, he was now to have with a vengeance."[20] The gauntlet was thrown on a matter that may sound trivial and boring to any modern readers: the corn laws. Yet in reality the issues are surprisingly contemporary.

The "corn laws" were a tax on corn imported into England. The purpose was to protect British farmers from foreign competition that could force them to cut prices to less than what would be needed for a decent living. Ensuring reasonable income was in turn expected to ensure that the country was capable of self-sufficiency in agriculture. During the eighteenth century, protection for a great many British commercial activities had been the national policy. Through the first four decades of the nineteenth century, however, Parliament dismantled the protectionist edifice.

Peel and his party took part in this process. When he took office, protectionist duties remained on some 1200 goods. In an effort to update fiscal policies, consistent with his mandate, he revised 750 of these duties in 1842, including the corn law. By 1845, duties still covered 813 articles; Peel that year placed 430 on the duty-free list. He also turned against the corn law completely, prompted by a potato blight in Ireland that caused great suffering there. Because many Irish were cash-poor peasants, Peel judged that removal of the corn duty was necessary, so that grain prices might fall to levels that the Irish could afford.

But the corn laws were unique among protectionist measures. As McDowell observes, "the corn laws were not merely a section of the fiscal system, they were a symbol and a practical expression of the national determination to maintain the social and political supremacy of the landed interest."[21]

The agricultural interest already had been shaken by passage of the Reform Bill of 1832. A mordant journal entry by

Sir Walter Scott reveals the mood of despair among conservatives, or Tories, as they were called at the time: "It has fallen easily, the old Constitution.... It has been thrown away like a child's broken toy. Well, *transeat,* the good sense of the people is much trusted to; we shall see what it will do for us. The curse of Cromwell on those whose conceit brought us to this pass. *Sed transeat.* It is vain to mourn what cannot be mended."[22]

More than a century earlier, the Tory Lord Bolingbroke described the idea of the constitution. "By constitution we mean, whenever we speak with propriety and exactness, that assemblage of laws, institutions and customs, derived from certain fixed principles of reason, directed to certain fixed objects of public good, that compose the general system, according to which the community hath agreed to be governed." Disraeli spoke of the constitution in this sense as "the realized experience of the nation."[23]

In 1832, in 1845, and throughout much of the nineteenth century, this constitution—the assemblage of laws, institutions, and customs according to which the community had agreed to be governed—suffered hard knocks from a kind of "fixed principle" generally alien to previous British experience: a rationalistic abstraction promulgated with ideological fervor. "Freedom of enterprise was indeed the prevalent maxim of the whole century from the younger Pitt to Gladstone," according to Sir David Keir. "This was the age of *laissez-faire.*"[24] In this age, with its strong atomistic proclivity derived from or reflected in Benthamite utilitarianism, everything in Bolingbroke's assemblage was open to challenge. "Unfortunately," Holdsworth observes, "those principles [of individualism and free trade] were based not so much on their expediency in the conditions of the day, as on the ground that they embodied a set of truths which, being universally true, should be universally applied."[25] "Cold" and "calculating" are the words used by Sir Richard Vyvien, M.P., in 1842, in a letter to his constituents to describe the free trade view, advocates of which were prepared to sacrifice nearly any custom or institution on the altar of efficiency.[26]

Free trade sentiment crystallized for the undoing of the corn laws in the form of the Anti-Corn Law League, founded at Manchester in 1839. The League was a new phenomenon in British politics: a well-organized movement that made use of demagogic techniques to achieve a single, narrowly defined political objective. "The anti-corn law pressure is about to commence," wrote Sir James Graham at the beginning of the Irish potato blight, "and it will be the most formidable movement in modern times."[27]

Insofar as great political questions seldom can be reduced to black and white, there is much to be said for the position of the League. Evaluated in purely economic terms, the corn laws were, like import duties generally, crude instruments for achieving political goals. While gauging the effectiveness of tariffs in promoting domestic industry is often hard, certain effects are clear. Tariffs decrease trade in both a taxed commodity and, in generally unintended and undesired ways, in other goods and services dependent on that commodity. Moreover, they raise prices. These effects were evident in the history of the corn laws. On the matter of unintended side effects, it was argued that "the corn laws limited the overseas market for British goods. Agrarian countries were willing to buy our manufactures, but they could only pay for them with corn, and this we refused to receive. Remove the import duties on grain and immediately a great expansion of our export trade would follow. Industrial stagnation and unemployment would come to an end."[28] Thus, manufacturers, with increasing success as their economic power grew, tended strongly to oppose the corn laws. The duties were also intensely unpopular among consumers: passage of the 1815 version even caused riots in London.

Various versions of the corn laws, including Peel's of 1842, had the defect that they aimed at maintaining a specific price rather than at achieving a general effect. Because a sector of an economy, such as agriculture, involves an almost infinitely complex interaction of participants, decisions, and external factors, including in this case international factors, to find the optimum level for a tariff is notoriously difficult, and there is little reason for confidence that civil servants or a crowd of legislators will do the job right.

But these concerns were moot in any case in the 1840s. The high cost of transportation to Britain made imported corn considerably more expensive than domestically grown crops, even without the tariff. The reality of this natural protection, candidly acknowledged even by Richard Cobden, a guiding light of the League, removed the real issues in retention or repeal of the corn laws from the realm of expedience to that of symbol and vision.

Disraeli had long objected to the "cold and calculating" mind of the free trade ideologues. As early as 1835 he decried it in his *Vindication of the English Constitution:*

> We have before this had an *a priori* system of celestial mechanics, and its votaries most syllogistically sent Galileo to a dungeon, after having triumphantly refuted him.... And now we have an *a priori* system of politics. The schoolmen are revived in the 19th century, and are going to settle the State with their withering definitions, their fruitless logomachies, and their barren dialectics.... These considerations naturally lead me to a consideration of the great object of our new school of statesmen in general, which is to form political institutions on abstract principles of theoretic science, instead of permitting them to spring from the course of events, and to be naturally created by the necessities of nations. It would appear that this scheme originated in the fallacy of supposing that theories produce circumstances, whereas the very converse of the proposition is correct, and circumstances indeed produce theories.[29]

Disraeli was not alone in his disdain for such a distortion of market-oriented political economy to ideology. Nearly a century before, Adam Smith, the father of modern economics, wrote:

> The man of systems...is apt to be very wise in his own conceit, and is so often enamored with the supposed beauty of his own ideal plan of government, that he cannot suffer the smallest deviation from any part of it. He goes on to establish it completely and in all its parts, without any regard either to the great interests or to the strong prejudices which may oppose it: he seems to imagine that he can arrange the different members of a great society with as much ease as the hand arranges the different pieces upon a chess board; he does not consider that the pieces

upon the chess-board have no other principle of motion besides that which the hand impresses upon them; but that, in the great chess-board of human society, every single piece has a principle of motion of its own, altogether different from that which the legislature might choose to impress upon it.[30]

Peel, on the other hand, was won over by the logic of the League. In 1845 the facts about the potato blight and the state of British agriculture were quite unclear, which is hardly surprising given the limitations of economic analysis then and the deep ideological predispositions toward such evidence as there was. Despite these uncertainties, Peel abandoned protectionism. In Parliament he announced to members of his own party, "I wish to have the opportunity of frankly stating to those gentlemen who have honored me upon so many occasions with their confidence, that I can continue this contest no longer—that they must devolve the duty of maintaining protection upon other persons, who can adduce better arguments in its favor than I can."[31]

While "being sold" is what Lord George Bentinck termed such a change in policy, others are more sympathetic. A nineteenth-century biographer of Peel writes,

No man can venture to impugn the honesty of the motives by which Sir Robert Peel was actuated at this most important crisis of his public life. The course which he adopted involved the sacrifice of every object and every feeling most dear to a political leader; it was equally fatal to the reputation of the past, and the prospects of the future.... It was a political martyrdom of the noblest description; it was the voluntary submission to stings and tortures, infinitely more agonizing and more difficult to endure than "Luke's iron crown and Damien's bed of steel." Where a statesman has everything personally dear to lose, and nothing to gain, by a change of policy, it requires infinitely more than ordinary perversity of faction, to discredit his motives.[32]

Good intentions notwithstanding, only Peel himself seemed surprised and vexed when his party followed his advice and found others on whom to devolve the duty of maintaining protection, or, more accurately, their vision for England.

Disraeli's opposition was hardly a part of the surprise, even to Peel. From the beginning the two coexisted uneasily in the Conservative party. Peel was thoroughly in control, truly a "Goliath," as Hearnshaw observed. The expansion of the franchise in 1832, so lamented by Sir Walter Scott, brought with it a great electoral victory for the Whigs and complete disarray for the Tories. It was Peel who saved the party from disintegration, gave it the name "Conservative," and patiently labored to bring about the victory of 1841. Building on a program spelled out in his Tamworth Manifesto of 1834, he sought to forge a party that could win elections and meet the needs of the times—largely construed in terms of finances and administration. He succeeded.

Disraeli, on the other hand, had no such record of accomplishment, and indeed had been erratic in his politics. Aside from a virulent anti-Whiggism developed early, he had difficulty settling his political allegiances. Lord Blake chronicles his casting about as he sought to develop and articulate his own political vision: "Disraeli had first tried to get in with Whig consent,...then stood as a strong Radical, then as a Radical with a slightly Tory tinge,... then issued an address whose tone was near-Tory with a slight Radical tinge, and finally issued one as a strong Radical again." To justify this floundering Disraeli once even felt constrained to produce a pamphlet entitled "What is He?"[33]

Disraeli finally joined the Conservatives, though not unequivocally. His declarations of loyalty to the party were fulsome enough, and he was eager to be on Peel's good side, as is shown by the dedication of *Vindication* to him. Nonetheless, Disraeli remained quite prepared to vote against his party's leadership. In 1839, for example, he opposed Peel's initiative to centralize the administration of poverty relief through revision of the Poor Law, the framework for dealing with the problems of poverty. That year he was one of only three, and in 1840 one of only five, to oppose strong measures against Chartism, a populist reform movement originating in the difficulties of societal adjustment to rapid industrialization.

Relations were further strained in 1841 when Peel refused a direct request from Disraeli for a post in his administration. This rejection is quite understandable, in light of Disraeli's erratic record and bizarre mannerisms. It was also a mistake. Disraeli was supremely able, and equally ambitious. Peel's rebuff threatened to stall his career, and left him with nothing to lose in breaking ranks. By 1845 Disraeli was in open rebellion, opposing Peel repeatedly in Parliament, and publishing harsh criticism of the prime minister's program and leadership in the novels *Coningsby* and *Sybil.* In Book II of *Coningsby,* for instance, Disraeli fulminates that,

> The Tamworth Manifesto of 1834 was an attempt to construct a party without principles: its basis therefore was necessarily latitudinarianism; and its inevitable consequence has been Political Infidelity.... There was indeed considerable shouting about what they called Conservative principles; but the awkward question naturally arose, what will you conserve? The prerogatives of the Crown, provided they are not exercised; the independence of the House of Lords, provided it is not asserted; the Ecclesiastical estate, provided it is regulated by a commission of laymen. Everything in short that is established, as long as it is a phrase and not a fact.... Conservatism discards Prescription, shrinks from Principle, disavows Progress; having rejected all respect for Antiquity, it offers no redress for the Present, and makes no preparation for the Future.[34]

For Peel, in light of all this, the surprise was not Disraeli's final break, but that Bentinck and those like him (the backbone of the Conservative party) went with him. Mainly this can be accounted for by Disraeli's firm adherence in this crisis to the Burkean notion of party. As Bentinck and Disraeli understood it, and as Peel did not, a national party must be more than a mere amalgamation of power- and advantage-seeking individuals and interests, and more than its leaders. Instead it must be, as Burke described it, "a body of men united, for promoting by their joint endeavors, the national interest, upon some particular principle in which they are all agreed."[35] In rejecting the corn laws, Peel rejected the "particular principle" upon which he came to power.

DISCERNING ENGLISH ORDER

Drawing on Disraeli's speeches, novels, and political writings, one may discern his understanding of the British constitution. This is far from easy, however, for after his *Vindication* Disraeli never attempted to lay out his views systematically.[36] Nonetheless, four aspects of his politics are particularly relevant to the events recounted in *Lord George Bentinck*. First, society is an organic unity, not a mere aggregation of individuals and material interests. Second, society is best governed by an aristocratic principle that cannot be equated merely with the nobility and its material advantages. Third, historic institutions are vital to national greatness. And finally, the land is perhaps the most important of these institutions.

Throughout his career Disraeli affirmed the fundamental, organic unity of English society. He rejected simple dichotomies among classes or interests. For example, in *Coningsby* he lauds England's manufacturers: "rightly understood, Manchester is as great a human exploit as Athens.... It is the philosopher alone who can conceive the grandeur of Manchester, and the immensity of its future."[37]

Disraeli is often portrayed as a simple apologist for the nobility, motivated throughout his life by an intense, almost pathetic, longing for acceptance. That is a mistaken view, and not only in light of Disraeli's affirmation of fundamental unity in society.[38] In this book Disraeli articulates a positive vision of aristocracy:

> It is not true that England is governed by an aristocracy in the common acceptation of the term. England is governed by an aristocratic principle. The aristocracy of England absorbs all aristocracies and receives every man in every order and class who defers to the principle of the society, which is to aspire and excel.[39]

This Burkean "natural aristocracy" is also asserted in *Coningsby,* by Millbank, Disraeli's model of the best in the rising class of industrialists. "No sir," says Millbank, "you may make aristocracies by laws; you can only maintain them by manners. The manners of England preserve it from its laws. And they have substituted for our formal aristocracy an essential aristocracy; the government of those who are distinguished by their fellow-citizens."[40] Here "manners" are an outward expression or manifestation of inner character. What one does and how one does it are the distinguishing marks of the "essential" aristocrat, whatever some law might say about his status. Certain classes serve the common good. Fulfillment of such duty is a foundation of personal dignity and the proper basis of privilege.

The natural aristocracy must operate through institutions, Disraeli argues. "Individuals may form communities, but it is institutions alone that can create a nation," he says in *Vindication*:

> It is our institutions that have made us free, and can alone keep us so; by the bulwark which they offer to the insidious encroachment of a convenient and enervating system of centralization which, if left unchecked, will prove fatal to the national character. Therefore I have ever endeavored to cherish our happy habit of self government, as sustained by a prudent distribution of local authority.

In part it was recognition of the importance of institutions that led him to cast his lot with Peel's Conservatives, rather than attempt to succeed as an independent or a scarcely less isolated Radical. In a letter of the same year as *Vindication,* Disraeli expounds the true nature of Toryism and its relationship to institutions:

> I am still of the opinion that the Tory Party is the real democratic party of this country. I hold one of the first principles of Toryism to be that Government is instituted for the welfare of the many. This is why the Tories maintain national institutions, the objects of which are the protection, the maintenance, the moral, civil, and religious education of the great mass of the English people: institutions which whether they assume the form of churches, or universities, or societies of men to protect the helpless and to support the needy, to execute justice and to maintain truth, alike originated, and alike flourish for the advantage and happiness of the multitude.[41]

It was this concern for the vitality of institutions that led Disraeli to oppose Peel's 1839 revision of the Poor Law. Cen-

tralization subverts local institutions by shifting both responsibility and power out of the hands of those most closely
in touch with problems and the people they affect. Centralization may be cheaper, but it is not necessarily more effective, since "crystallizing" customs into national legislation
deprives communities of flexibility and the ability to "adapt
to all the circumstances of the moment and the locality." In
keeping with his commitment to the fundamental unity of
society, Disraeli objected to the way in which centralization
and the enervation of community result in the neglect of
the duty of every person to care for his neighbor. Speaking
specifically of lonely anonymity in big cities, but with more
general application, Disraeli observes that the inhabitants
"are not in a state of cooperation, but of isolation, as to the
making of fortunes; and for all the rest, they are careless of
neighbors. Christianity teaches us to love our neighbor as
ourself; modern society acknowledges no neighbor."[42]

Throughout his career Disraeli maintained the central
importance of the land. To understand this, one can start
by recognizing that people associate for many reasons:
shared work, principles, financial interests, likes or dislikes,
and more. There is a danger in such association, founded on
distinctiveness, difference, and exclusivity. Too often vision
narrows to the limited perspective of the group, and particular interest is pursued at the expense of others. Disraeli
recognized a significant impetus toward an inclusive perspective in the territorial constitution of England. Within a
given area one is likely to find a fairly broad cross-section of
the people—rich and poor, educated and uneducated, crafts-
men, laborers, professionals, and others—among whom
unity may be attained through the shared experiences,
achievements, responsibilities, and interests of living together. This is the essence of community.

The "squirarchy" that Disraeli defended were pillars in
the social structure that expressed and perpetuated this
territorial constitution. "This was the class which, in alliance with the clergy as junior partners, effectively governed
a great part of England," observes Lord Blake. "They were

unfashionable and cut no ice outside their own localities, but they were the solid backbone of rural England."[43] Even Gladstone, who built his career opposing Disraeli and the Conservatives after the fall of Peel, said in 1852, "I look to the sober-minded portion of that party as the most valuable raw material of political party in the country."[44]

Peel's repudiation of the corn laws struck at everything above; Disraeli had stronger reasons than mere ambition for opposing him. In Disraeli, Bentinck recognized a kindred spirit. Their alliance and their success made it possible for Stanley, the Conservative leader in the House of Lords, still to ask in 1850, "whether the legislative power is to rest with the land and those connected with it or with the manufacturing interests of the country." A hundred years later a Conservative could still maintain such views in these terms:

> The true English character is robust, independent, and adventuring. I stand convinced that the mainspring of these great qualities of the English people—the greatest qualities of the English people—is the land and soil of England. If the English character were to lose its robustness and independence, it would lose its very substance, and England would cease to be England. That is why I stand solid to my belief that before everything and above all things we must maintain a vigorous and secure agriculture and countryside ever to invigorate our national life.... I would have England turn again to Disraeli for inspiration, for that would be to return again to the land.[45]

Disraeli gave effective voice to convictions that were widely and deeply held. "Return me to Parliament—not because my broad lands stretch from Buckingham to Ayelsbury—" said Disraeli in an election speech shortly after the fall of Peel, "but because my public character and my Parliamentary reputation have shown you that I may be trusted, and, what is more, that I am capable.... No one has done more by his speeches or his pen to uphold these loftier influences which regulate society."[46]

"THE GREAT GAME"

Bentinck certainly recognized the accuracy of Disraeli's

words, but nearly all others in Parliament who agreed with the message mistrusted Disraeli the messenger. This problem plagued him throughout his career. Partial explanations may be found in his youthful mistakes, indiscretions, misadventures, quirks, and affectations, and later, of course, in partisan differences and odd positions such as we have discussed. Clearly Disraeli could not have prevailed in these events without the partnership of Lord George, and Bentinck's death surely slowed Disraeli's rise to national leadership.

Yet there remains a further dimension of Disraeli that put off many of his contemporaries. Perhaps an additional piece of this puzzle may be found in regarding him as an exemplar of Johan Huizinga's *homo ludens,* the man at play. Huizinga's thesis[47] is that play is a natural and important dimension of serious cultural phenomena such as knowing, law, art, and religion. In his provocative development of this idea Huizinga writes of the nineteenth century as an era in which,

> the great currents of its thought, however looked at, were all inimical to the play factor in social life. Neither liberalism nor socialism offered it any nourishment. Experimental and analytical science, philosophy, reformism, Church and State, economics, were all pursued in deadly earnest.... Never had an age taken itself with more portentous seriousness. Culture ceased to be "played."[48]

Walter Bagehot, who understood Peel so well, expresses this grave spirit of the era. Describing at their close Disraeli's years as a member of the House of Commons, he writes,

> after his fashion, he showed a high magnaminity and conscience in not opposing or hampering the ministry on great questions,—say of foreign policy, when his so doing would hurt the country; but this praise must end here. On all minor Parliamentary questions, Mr. Disraeli has simply no conscience at all: he regards them as a game.... His mode of regarding Parliamentary proceedings as a play and a game is incomprehensible to the simple and earnest English nature.[49]

What Water Bagehot and other earnest Victorians reproach, Huizinga celebrates:

Ever since the end of the 18th century, debates in the House of Commons have been conducted very largely according to the rules of a game and in the true play-spirit. Personal rivalries are always at work, keeping up a continual match between the players whose object is to checkmate one another, but without prejudice to the interests of the country which they serve with all seriousness.[50]

Just so Disraeli said late in life, "I have climbed to the top of the greasy pole," when for the first time he became prime minister with a commanding majority. A spirit of play permeated his career, and it permeates *Lord George Bentinck,* making the book a delight.

Robert W. Kamphuis, Jr.
March 1997

NOTES

1. Lord Malmesbury, as quoted in Moneypenny and Buckle, *Life of Benjamin Disraeli* (New York: Macmillan and Co., 1910–1920), vol. 3, p. 116. Hereafter referred to as Moneypenny and Buckle.
2. Moneypenny and Buckle, vol. 2, p. 359.
3. Analyzing Disraeli's late novel *Endymion* (1880), Moneypenny and Buckle observe that "[Disraeli's] own ambition, his belief in the power of will, and in the utilization of opportunity, find extreme and uncompromising utterance in Myra's words: 'a human being with a settled purpose must accomplish it,'" vol. 6, p. 560.
4. Moneypenny and Buckle, vol. 2, pp. 309–10.
5. Walter Bagehot, "The Character of Sir Robert Peel" (1856), reprinted in *The Works of Walter Bagehot* (Hartford, Conn.: The Travelers Insurance Company, 1891), vol. 3, pp. 21–22.
6. Bagehot, pp. 20–21.
7. Paul Elmer More, "Disraeli and Conservatism," in *Aristocracy and Justice: Shelbourne Essays,* Ninth Series (New York: Houghton Mifflin, 1916), p. 162.
8. F. J. C. Hearnshaw, *Conservatism in England* (London, 1933), p. 207.
9. Robert Blake, *Disraeli* (New York: St. Martin's Press, 1966).
10. *Weekly Chronicle,* March 23, 1845.
11. Ibid.
12. Moneypenny and Buckle, vol. 3, pp. 112–13.
13. Disraeli's abiding gratitude to the Bentinck family is revealed in the following incident, recounted by Harold Macmillan in 1962:

> a remarkable thing happened towards the end of Disraeli's life. There was another duke by now—the one who told me the story.

He was 23, and he had only just succeeded. He had been a young officer in the Blues, on £500 a year, and now he had come into all the vast Portland estates. He was inexperienced in public affairs and politics, and was quite unnerved one day when Disraeli's private secretary sent for him and said that Disraeli wanted to see him at Hughendon [the estate bought for Disraeli by the Bentincks]. To his horror he discovered that he was the only guest. He was asked to put on a white tie for dinner (he was to stay the night). When he came down to dinner there were just the three of them, Disraeli, the private secretary, and himself. Disraeli said good evening to him, and not a single word was spoken by anyone throughout that long Victorian dinner, not one single word. Disraeli sat there impassive, glittering with all his orders, wearing the lot—the Star of India and all the rest. His face was white, and tight like a drum; he was an old, old man. Then at the end of dinner he spoke, and he said: "My lord duke, I have asked you here tonight because I belong to a race that never forgives an insult and never forgets a benefit. Everything I have I owe to the house of Bentinck. I thank you."

Quoted in *The Oxford Book of British Political Anecdotes,* edited by Paul Johnson (New York: Oxford University Press, 1986), p. 136.

14. Sir Leslie Stephen, "Disraeli's Novels," in *Hours in a Library* (London, 1879), p. 140.
15. For further exploration of the influence of Judaism on Disraeli, see Isaiah Berlin, "Benjamin Disraeli, Karl Marx, and the Search for Identity," in *Against the Current: Essays in the History of Ideas* (New York: The Viking Press, 1980), pp. 252–86.
16. For example, at the time of the events covered in this book Disraeli published *Tancred* (1847) (Oxford: Oxford University Press, The World's Classics edition, 1982). The novel forms the third part of a trilogy begun with *Coningsby* and continued in *Sybil*. *Tancred* deals explicitly with religious themes.
17. See Claude Welch, *Protestant Thought in the Nineteenth Century* (New Haven: Yale University Press, 1972), vol. 1, pp. 109–10. See also *The Study of Anglicanism,* edited by Stephen Sykes and John Booty (London SPCK, 1988), especially the contributions by Perry Butler, A. M. Allchin, and Paul Elmen.
18. Letter to John Manners, quoted in Blake, p. 260.
19. Sir David Lindsay Keir, *The Constitutional History of Modern Britain Since 1485,* 9th edition (New York: W.W. Norton, 1969), p. 411.
20. Moneypenny and Buckle, vol. 2, p. 310.
21. R. B. McDowell, *British Conservatism: 1832–1914* (London: Faber and Faber, 1959), p. 45.
22. *Journal of Sir Walter Scott,* 1829–1832, pp. 154–155.
23. Henry St. John, 1st Viscount Bolingbroke, "A Dissertation Upon Par-

ties," in *Works of Lord Bolingbroke* (Philadelphia: Carey and Hart, 1841), vol. 2, pp. 5–172.

24. Keir, p. 368.

25. Sir William Holdsworth, *A History of English Law* (London: Methuen & Co., 1952), vol. 14, p. 8.

26. See McDowell, 35. Birnie's 1948 account of "the rise and decline of free trade" in nineteenth-century Britain seems remarkably similar to what one might observe about twentieth-century America. Birnie writes,

> With the close of the Napoleonic Wars, Britain was now the sole workshop of the world, and her manufacturers stood in no fear of foreign competition. They were prepared to sacrifice protection for themselves in the home market, in the hope that greater freedom of trade would assist them in establishing a foothold in foreign markets.... [By the 1880s, however,] to the man on the street, it seemed unjust that foreign goods should be admitted to Britain free, while British goods were taxed in other countries, and to this unfair treatment he was inclined to attribute the persistently unfavorable balance of trade which now began to excite anxiety. Worst of all, it had become clear that Britain could not hope to maintain the lead over her competitors which she had held during the early nineteenth century. She continued to make progress, it was true, but relatively her progress was less rapid than that of other nations, which were becoming industrialized and entering into competition with her in foreign markets. Between 1876 and 1885, Britain's share in world trade fell from 23 to 19 percent. It was inevitable that this relative decline should stimulate criticism of her fiscal policy. Protectionist sentiment revived, [and it was urged that] the weapon of retaliation should be used to induce other nations to lower their tariffs.

Arthur Birnie, *An Economic History of the British Isles* (London: Methuen & Co., 1948), pp. 294, 299.

27. Charles Whibley, "The Corn Laws: A Group," in *Political Portraits* (London: MacMillan & Co., 1917), p. 261.

28. Birnie, p. 297.

29. Benjamin Disraeli, "Vindication of the English Constitution" (1835), reprinted in *Whigs and Whiggism: Political Writings by Benjamin Disraeli,* edited by William Hutcheon (London: Kennikat Press, 1971), p. 119.

30. Adam Smith, *The Theory of Moral Sentiments,* 1795.

31. W. Cooke Taylor, *The Life and Times of Sir Robert Peel* (London: Peter Jackson, Lake Fisher, Son, & Co.), vol. 3, pp. 433–34.

32. Taylor, p. 423.

33. Disraeli, "What is He?" 1833. Reprinted in *Whigs and Whiggism,* pp. 16–22.

34. Disraeli, *Coningsby, or the New Generation* (1844) (Oxford: Oxford University Press, 1982), Book 2, chapter 5.
35. Burke, "Thoughts on Present Discontents," in *Select Works,* edited by E. T. Payne, vol. 1, p. 82.
36. Asked for advice by the editor of a new conservative journal, Disraeli was succinct: "Above all, no programme." This attitude is consistent with his rejection of the systematizing tendencies of Benthamites and free traders.
37. *Coningsby,* Book 4, chapter 1.
38. Disraeli's early years clearly demonstrate a strong element of social climbing, which is why the charge has enough validity to stick, despite his consistent growth toward deeper, more enduring concerns, and despite his abiding hostility toward the Whig "grandees" and "magnificoes," a group that included most of the nation's richest and most powerful families—people a mere climber would probably want to conquer.
39. *Lord George Bentinck,* p. 560.
40. *Coningsby,* Book 4, chapter 1.
41. The next sentences of this letter strikingly anticipate a contemporary political issue. Ours is a society characterized by governmental programs that benefit and are advocated by particular constituencies. Sam Peltzman has analyzed empirically "the necessary conditions for growth of government: a broadening of the political base that stands to gain from redistribution generally and thus provides a fertile source of political support for expansion of specific programs" (*Journal of Law and Economics* 23 [October 1980: 209–87]). Theodore J. Lowi analyzes this in terms of "interest group liberalism" in *The End of Liberalism,* 2d edition (New York: Norton, 1979). Foreshadowing Peltzman's observations, Disraeli writes,

> I deny that the Tories have ever opposed the genuine national or democratic spirit of the country; on the contrary, they have always headed it. It was the Tories who increased the constituency by the £50 tenancy clause; *a most democratic measure,* but one in my opinion, that has eminently tended to the salvation of the State. I deny that the Tories oppose short Parliaments or the ballot, because they will give too much power to *the people:* it is because they will give too much power to *the constituency;* a shrewd and vast difference. (Emphasis original.)

Quoted in Gertrude Himmelfarb, *Marriage and Morals Among the Victorians and Other Essays* (New York: Vintage Books, 1987), p. 187.

42. Benjamin Disraeli, *Sybil, or the Two Nations,* 1845 (Oxford: Oxford University Press, 1981), Book 2, chapter 5.
43. Blake, p. 279.

44. Quoted in J. B. Conacher, *The Peelites and the Party System: 1846–52* (Newton Abbot, Devon, England: David and Charles, Ltd., 1972), p. 130.
45. Sir R. George Stapledon, *Disraeli and the New Age* (London: Faber and Faber, Ltd., 1943), p. 5.
46. Speech at Aylesbury to his constituents before the General Election of 1847. Found in *Selected Speeches of the Late Right Honorable the Earl of Beaconsfield,* edited by T.E. Kebbel (London: Longmans, Green & Co., 1882), vol. 1, p. 179.
47. Johan Huizinga, *Homo Ludens* (Boston: Beacon Press, 1950).
48. Huizinga, p. 192.
49. Bagehot, "Mr. Disraeli as a Member of the House of Commons" (1876), reprinted in *The Works of Walter Bagehot,* vol. 3, pp. 446–50.
50. Huizinga, p. 207.

INTRODUCTION

I

The Life of Lord George Bentinck is in a sense the most serious of Disraeli's works. It was composed at a time when he had abandoned fiction for the more sternly engrossing pursuit of politics. During the years, which had passed since the writing of his novels, he had devoted himself with all his inspired energy to the business of the House of Commons, and *Sybil* and *Tancred* were but interludes in a life of affairs. 'Literature he has abandoned for politics,' wrote Mrs. Disraeli to Peel as early as 1841, and when, in 1852, he essayed in *Lord George Bentinck* the portraiture of an English worthy, Disraeli was already better known as a statesman than as a novelist. His brilliant and pitiless campaign against Peel had overshadowed the victories won in another field; and his political biography was received with a respect not always shown to those who have practised successfully the art of fiction.

And it deserved all the respect accorded to its sound judgment and well-balanced style. Fashioned after the best models, it is embellished, like the works of Livy and Thucydides, with deftly-drawn characters and authentic speeches. The biographer, moreover, was writing of what he had seen and heard: not merely were all the documents ready to his hand; he himself had taken a foremost part in the events which he chronicled. But nowhere in his book will you find the taint of journalism. On every page there is a sense of great issues and lofty purposes. Though Disraeli was removed but a year or two from the battles of wit and reason, which are the matter of his history, his imagination allowed him to see the immediate past in a just perspective, and his one defect, amiable and deliberate, is to underrate with a true modesty the importance of his own part. So gravely does he consider the personages in his drama, that they might have been ancient Romans, or the subjects of a despotic doge. And then how skilful is the narrative, how right the feeling of proportion! None but a master could interweave pages of *Hansard*, 'the *Dunciad* of Downing Street,' into the substance of his book, and make every chapter interesting. Sternly political though it be, the biography is always dramatic, and the two chief actors in the drama, Lord George Bentinck and Sir Robert Peel, are brilliantly disengaged from the dingy background of the House of Commons. Of these he writes in the true spirit of romance. The picture of Peel sitting unmoved and unconscious in the deserted House can never be forgotten. 'The benches had become empty,' thus runs the passage, 'the lights were about to be extinguished; it is the duty of the clerk of the House to examine the chamber before the doors are closed, and to-night it was also the strange lot of this gentleman to disturb the reverie of a statesman.'

But, while Disraeli saw even the arch-enemy through the softening mist of imagination, Lord George, as he drew him, seems to have stepped straight out of the pages of fiction. 'One man alone brooded over the unexampled scene,' says he at the outset, and you are reminded straightway of *Henrietta Temple* or *The Young Duke*. Again, he tells us that, to make his first speech, 'Bentinck rose long past the noon of night.' It is such touches as this that make the book acceptable to those who do not regard politics as the end of life, and his admirers will surprise the true Disraeli upon every page. Like all great men, he rises with the occasion, and the description of Lord George's death is the work of a true artist. With the noble extravagance, characteristic of his style, he takes leave of his hero 'upon the *perron* of Harcourt House, the last of the great hotels of an age of stately manners, with its wings, and courtyard, and carriage portal, and huge outward walls.' And when he tells the last sad tale in a few pages of admirable dignity, he is inspired to quote the *Ajax*—Ὦ Θάνατε, Θάνατε, νῦν μ' ἐπίσκεψαι μολών—though Greek quotations seldom came from his pen. In brief, the whole work is cast in the mould of fancy, and, accurate and impartial though it be, it never sinks to the arid prose of conventional biography.

Disraeli, moreover, being always sincere, does not suppress his own qualities, even in so impersonal an affair as biography. The narrative sparkles with humour, and is alive with wit. The Sugar question, not a lively one, is an excuse for a jest, that has not yet lost its point. 'Strange,' says he, 'that a manufacture which charms infancy and soothes old age, should so frequently occasion political disaster.' And, while he gives free play to his wonderful gift of irony, he does not mitigate his stern convictions. Though he proclaims with enthusiasm the fortunate truth that 'the history of England is the history of reaction,' he admits that 'progress and reaction are but words to mystify the million. They mean nothing, they are nothing; they are phrases, and not facts. All is race.' So he returns to the gospel preached with eloquent sincerity in his novels; and it may be said of him, as of few men, that, whatever may be the subject of his discourse, he is always honestly and candidly himself. He conceals nothing, he attenuates nothing; he deals not in 'ifs' and 'ans'; and thus he presents the strongest contrast to the politician who in after years was his fiercest opponent and most dangerous rival.

His *obiter dicta* are always sound. He is equally wise in the discussion of men and manners. Whether he writes of Hume, who 'never once lost his temper,' or of the aristocracy, which does not 'yield its confidence grudgingly,' he finds the right word for the sane thought. But it is Lord George Bentinck's loyal championship of religious equality, his stout advocacy of the admission of Jews to Parliament, that excuses his longest and most eloquent digression. This digression is an echo, subdued to a deeper note, of the pæan sung to Judaism by Sidonia in the pages of *Coningsby*. But it is something else than a pæan: it is an argument as well; and, though it was written by one happily unaccustomed to the theological jargon of the day, it is closely reasoned and ingeniously conceived. Throughout this chapter Disraeli shows a genuine pride in his race, and exults, like the aristocrat that he was, in his ancient lineage. Having declared that the dispersion of the Jewish people was not a penalty incurred for the commission of a great crime, that such an allegation is 'neither historically true nor dogmatically sound,' he applauds the courage and persistence which have survived the worst trials ever put upon a wandering race. 'The Hebrew,' he says, 'is sustained by a sublime religion.' 'The trumpet of Sinai still sounds in his ear, and a Jew is never seen upon the scaffold, unless it be at an *auto-da-fé*.' Strengthened, moreover, by an inherited virtue and energy, and justly proud of his blood, the Hebrew despises the doctrine of human equality. 'Thus it will be seen,' says Disraeli, 'that all the tendencies of the Jewish race are conservative. Their bias is to religion, property, and natural aristocracy: and it should be the interest of statesmen that this bias of a great race should be encouraged, and their energies and creative powers enlisted in the cause of existing society.'

In these days of violent anti-Semitism, it is pleasant to

read so splendid a defence of a once down-trodden people. While the prejudice against the Jews is not altogether unnatural—for has not Disraeli himself told us 'that all is race'?—the most bigoted partisan must still be grateful for the genius that Jewry has sent us. And if it be true that every nation harbours the Jews, which it deserves, England may justly be proud of her forbearance. Nowhere else have they been received with a better welcome, and nowhere else have they rewarded the hospitality shown to them with a finer sense of statesmanship and a more grateful patriotism. But, having established the conservatism of the Jewish race on a basis of pride and wealth, Disraeli goes a step further, and attempts to prove that Christianity is but perfected Judaism. To profess the whole Jewish faith is, in his eyes, to 'believe in Calvary as well as in Sinai.' If some millions of Hebrews believe only in a part of their religion, that is an accident which he deplores, and which he attributes to the Romans. And thus we arrive at the religious position of Disraeli himself. In his own phrase, he was 'on the side of the Angels.' He was a loyal and devout Jew, who held that the religion of his race was not petrified by Moses. 'Christians may continue to persecute Jews,' said he in his famous peroration, 'and Jews may persist in disbelieving Christians, but who can deny that Jesus of Nazareth, the Incarnate Son of the Most High God, is the eternal glory of the Jewish race?' This, however, is a digression. The real purpose of the book is to set forth the part which Lord George Bentinck played in the drama of the Corn Laws, and Disraeli has performed the delicate and difficult task of writing contemporary history with the quick humour and shrewd observation one expects of him.

II

In 1845 Sir Robert Peel, the leader of the Protectionist Party in the House of Commons, suddenly changed his opinions. Cobden's prophecy that 'three weeks of showery weather when the wheat is in bloom or ripening would repeal the Corn Laws' was amply fulfilled. The autumn rain, which destroyed so much, rained away whatever scruples Peel may still have cherished. The failure of the potato crop in Ireland drove him into a panic, and he saw in that panic an excuse for legislation. The symptoms of his change instantly showed themselves in his letters. 'The accounts of the state of the potato crop in Ireland are becoming very alarming,' he wrote to Sir James Graham in October 1845, and the correspondence which followed proves that Sir James Graham was less master of himself even than the Prime Minister. As to Peel's excitement there is no lack of evidence. The Duke of Wellington told Sir Edward Knatchbull that 'he never saw a man in such a state of alarm. He was hardly himself—the potato disease seemed to occupy his whole mind.' But, whatever alarm he may have felt, the illogicality of his ultimate action would have appealed to any one whose sense of humour was keener than Peel's. 'The Irish potato crop,' said he in effect, 'has failed in 1845. Therefore in 1849 I will admit corn free of duty into the ports of Great Britain.' The evil and its remedy had no sort of relation one to the other, except that, as the evil inspired the panic, so by the remedy the panic was allayed.

But there were other influences working upon the plastic mind of Peel. The Anti-Corn Law League, which had long been 'hiring theatres,' and making its 'tawdry speeches in tawdry places,' was not likely to lose its opportunity. As has been said, there was nothing better than a bad harvest for the success of its schemes. 'The Anti-Corn Law pressure,' wrote Sir James Graham, 'is about to commence, and it will be the most formidable movement in modern times.' Cobden, in truth, knew precisely what was his strength, and how to apply it. With perfect cynicism he acknowledged, six months later, that there were 'not a hundred men in the Commons, or twenty in the Lords, who at heart are anxious for total repeal,' and in October 1845 there were still fewer. But Peel was coerced by out-of-doors opinion. Like Sir James Graham, he feared the League, and bowed his head in horror before its 'forty-shilling bludgeons.' And what makes his position the stranger is that he and the League were pursuing opposite aims. If Peel may be said to have had any clear object, it was to help the people. He asked the Irish to tighten their belts until 1849, and then he promised them the boon of cheap corn. Cobden and Villiers, on the other hand, had little interest in the masses. They were the champions of the employers, and their end and aim was to reduce the wages of the workmen.

Mr. Gladstone has told us that Villiers' argument was as follows: 'Under the present Corn Laws, the trade on which we depend is doomed, for our manufacturers cannot possibly contend with the manufacturers of the Continent, if they have to pay wages regulated by the protection price of food, while their rivals pay according to the natural or free trade price.' And Cobden, frank as his colleague, does not hide the truth. He confesses that the working-men have neither attended his meetings nor signed his petitions, that his agitation, in fact, has been 'eminently middle-class.' 'We have carried it on by those means,' says he, 'by which the middle-class usually carries on its movements. We have had our meetings of dissenting ministers; we have obtained the co-operation of the ladies; we have resorted to tea-parties, and taken these pacific means for carrying out our views, which mark us rather as a middle-class set of agitators.' This confession is candid enough, and it increases our wonder that Sir Robert Peel, once the leader of 'the gentlemen of England,' should have adopted the policy of Cobden on a false ground, and have ensured its triumph in a hostile House of Commons.

However, so strong was Peel's panic, that he could no longer endure the responsibility of office, and he resigned with a patient and loyal majority behind him. The many meetings of the Cabinet held in November 1845 arrived at no certain conclusion, and Lord John Russell, whose letter addressed from Edinburgh to his constituents had hastened the unnecessary crisis, was asked to form a Government. Having failed in this enterprise, he could do nothing else than 'hand back the poisoned chalice to Sir Robert,' who thus became Prime Minister for the third time. Bound by all the ties of custom and honour to protect the Corn Laws and to defend the agricultural interest, Peel re-assumed the duties of government with the firm purpose of opposing those who had sent him to Westminster. Yet so complete was his ascendency, so easy was his management of the ministers, that in the shuffle of opinions he lost but a single colleague—Lord Stanley. One other minister—Lord Lincoln—had a glimmering whither the path of duty led him. In his eyes the 'manly and honourable course' would be that 'in the session preceding the dissolution Peel should propound to the country his intention to propose to the new Parliament either a modification of the Corn Law, expressly framed with a view to its abolition within a given time, or a total repeal of the law.'

But Sir Robert was far too clever to expose his policy to the hazard of a dissolution. Though he knew as well as Cobden that the country and the House of Commons were both against him, he had made up his mind to carry through the measures of his opponents, and the sound advice of Lord Lincoln fell upon a deaf ear. Indeed, so accurately did Peel gauge the temper of the country that after an ominous defeat in Westminster and a pitiful collapse in North Notts, he resolved not to risk another bye-election, and two Cabinet Ministers — Mr. Gladstone and Lord Lincoln — remained during his last Parliament without seats in the House of Commons.

Now Peel's position is perfectly intelligible: he was an expert at the quick change. It is not so easy to explain the conduct of the Duke of Wellington and the rest. The Duke did not pretend that he had been converted to the doctrine of Free Trade; he claimed it as a sort of virtue in himself that in not deserting Peel he was helping to govern the country. As Lord Stanley said, the Duke 'talked of supporting the Queen's Government in measures of which he disapproves, as if he were not a member of the Government to be supported.' 'The principle laid down,' to cite Disraeli's words, 'may be an excellent principle, but it is not a principle of the English Constitution.' But the Duke with some reason believed his presence in the Cabinet essential to the public welfare, and by staying in he hoped that he was keeping Cobden out. Disraeli's attitude was more honest. 'For my part,' said he, 'if we are to have Free Trade, I, who honour genius, prefer that such measures should be proposed by the member for Stockport, rather than by one who by skilful parliamentary manœuvres has tampered with the generous confidence of a great people and a great party.' Peel, being an egoist, took another view, and, while he adopted Cobden's opinions, he suppressed Cobden's name until the hour of his doubtful victory. 'The Manchester Confederates,' wrote Disraeli, 'seemed to be least in favour with Parliament and the country on the very eve of their triumph.' The Front

Bench might have sung with one accord, 'Oh no, we never mention him, His name is never heard'; and so sincere was it at first in its suppression of the League and all its works that it wore an air of martyrdom, as who should say, 'We sacrifice our opinions to save the country from Mr. Cobden.' But resignation was soon changed to pride. That which Peel and his friends at first defended as merely expedient, they presently boasted to be virtuous.

III

Thus the contest was engaged, and the champions on either side fought with a courage and pertinacity worthy the occasion. First and foremost, in the attack upon the Corn Laws, was Sir Robert Peel, whose position alone made a sudden and complete change of opinion possible. He had sat in the House of Commons for five-and-thirty years. He had served the Crown in many offices and under many administrations. A long experience, added to a natural faculty for affairs, had given him a unique place, a unique influence. 'In the Senate,' says Disraeli, 'he was the readiest, easiest, most flexible and adroit of men. He played upon the House of Commons as on an old fiddle.' And he played upon it because his method of speech was perfectly adapted to its purpose. He was neither eloquent nor impassioned. His was not the art of oratory, which aroused sudden enthusiasms, or swayed vast multitudes. 'His flights,' in Disraeli's words, 'were ponderous; he soared with the wing of the vulture rather than the plume of the eagle; and his perorations, when most elaborate, were most unwieldy. In pathos he was quite deficient; when he attempted to touch the tender passions, it was painful. His face became distorted, like that of a woman who wants to cry but cannot succeed. Orators certainly should not shed tears, but there are moments when, as the Italians say, the voice should weep.' Peel's voice never wept; there was no taint of the histrion in his nature,—that taint which in later years made his pupil and successor, Mr. Gladstone, a danger to the State.

On the other hand, his style was always clear, logical, and persuasive. His command of facts was as rare as his industry, and years of practice had made his talent for speaking 'the most available that has ever been brought to bear upon the House of Commons.' Thus by the exercise of useful rather than brilliant gifts, he had become by far the greatest political force of his time. It had been his good fortune to rally, even to recreate, the Tory Party, and for many years he led the English aristocracy with a success which was never repeated save by Disraeli. One would not have thought that there was a strong bond of sympathy between the aristocracy and Sir Robert Peel, yet Disraeli tells us it was complete. 'An aristocracy,' he says, with a marvellous prescience of his own career, 'hesitates before it yields its confidence, but it never does so grudgingly'; and Peel could not complain that his parliamentary followers lacked either troth or cordiality. They followed him wherever he led them in blind obedience, and he accepted their allegiance without question, as a tribute justly paid to his masterful intelligence. In Westminster, then, his supremacy was undisputed. He managed the assembly, which registered his decrees, with perfect tact and dignity, and he deserved the compliment paid him by the fiercest of his opponents, that he was 'the greatest member of Parliament that ever lived.'

But Peel's ascendency was bounded by the walls of the House of Commons. A frigid and unsympathetic manner destroyed whatever influence he might have exercised in the world outside. If we may believe Greville, he had 'no popular

and ingratiating qualities, and few intimate friends.' It was
not his business to argue with his colleagues or convince his
party, but to impose his views upon the House, and through
the House upon the country. 'The right honourable
Baronet's horror of slavery,' exclaimed Disraeli in an immortal passage, ' extends to every place, except to the benches
behind him. There the gang is still assembled, and there
the thong of the whip still sounds.' And it was not only his
avowed opponents who condemned his autocratic temper.
He strained the forbearance of his loyal supporters to
breaking-point. Sir Edward Knatchbull,[1] a leader of the
Country Party and the staunchest of Tories, has left a
character of Peel, which in every point is an undesigned
confirmation of Disraeli. The character was sketched in his
Political Journal some three years before the repeal of the
Corn Laws, and was thus unbiassed by the violent passions
aroused by the defection of 1846.

' I never in my time,' wrote Sir Edward, 'saw a minister
who possessed more absolute power in the House of Commons
than Peel. His influence and power are most extraordinary
In the House he is everything—but there his power ceases
If he was the same in Council, and in all his intercourse
with mankind, he would exceed anything this country, or
perhaps any other, ever saw, but I fear he is not equal to the
situation he fills, and to the times in which he lives. By
his power in the House of Commons alone does he keep
his party together. Out of the House his conduct is well
calculated to destroy it. Cold and uncourteous to every one
—even to his colleagues in office, who appear to me to be
afraid to differ from him—at times in manner he is almost

---

[1] The extracts here given from Sir Edward Knatchbull's Political Journal
are printed for the first time, and my thanks are due to the Hon. C. M.
Knatchbull-Hugessen, who has permitted me to make use of a document as
valuable as it is sincere.

insolent. It will be found when he dies that no minister ever possessed fewer friends, or would be personally less lamented. In his policy he is deficient in vigour and in courage. He rather looks too much to popularity, and if any great emergency were to arise . . . I feel that Peel would be found wanting.' Sir Edward's sketch of Peel does not merely justify his own distrust and consequent retirement from politics; it explains Peel's sudden success in the conversion of his Cabinet, and his equally sudden defeat in what seemed the moment of victory.

But Peel's influence gained in intensity from its very narrowness. He exacted obedience, and he got it. So stern a tyrant was he that he thought it a patent disloyalty if his party did not follow him in all the tortuous twists and turns of a changing policy. To-day it was treachery to support Free Trade; to-morrow none but a traitor dare say a word in favour of Protection. In truth, Peel deemed himself far superior to the principles of his party. He demanded allegiance for himself alone, and he would, if he could, have forbidden his supporters the right of private judgment. So convinced was he of his supremacy, that he believed he would encounter no other than a fat-cattle opposition, and when a solid phalanx of Tories resolved to secede, he regarded their secession as a perfidy. 'I am fighting a desperate battle here,' he wrote to Hardinge in 1846; 'shall probably drive my opponents over the Sutlej; but what is to come afterwards I know not.' Hardinge was fighting his country's foes; Peel was fighting against his friends of yesterday; so that his Sutlej was a very different river from that which Hardinge had recently crossed. But Peel was implacable. He put an end to a friendship with Croker, which had lasted for more than thirty years, because Croker did not change his views on the same day and in the same direction as himself, and it is not difficult to say which of the two men behaved with the truer faithfulness and the finer courtesy.[1] And as he treated Croker, so most unreasonably he treated all those who dared to preserve their ancient opinions. If Croker and his friends were 'convinced that the Corn Laws were essential,' as Greville said, 'not merely to the prosperity, but to the existence of the landed interest,' Peel had been mainly instrumental in confirming this conviction, and it was not for him to regard a conviction, which he had confirmed, as a rock of offence.

Moreover, Peel had already sacrificed his party once, and it was a monstrous indiscretion to repeat the manœuvre. What is done once may be an accident; done twice, it wears the sad appearance of a habit. Sir Robert was long an energetic and consistent enemy to Catholic Emancipation. He resisted the arguments of colleagues and opponents alike. Not even the persuasive eloquence of Canning availed to move him. Nor had he formed his judgment hastily and without experience. He had been Chief Secretary in Ireland; he was familiar with the facts and prejudices of either side. And then, having remained upright for some seventeen years, he threw a political somersault, turned his head in the air, and landed on his feet a staunch supporter of the Catholic claims. What argument and reason could not achieve, was achieved in a moment by Canning's death and the Clare Election. For Peel, being first minister of the Crown, might now claim the glory of all his actions, and O'Connell's majority spoke with an eloquence denied to Canning. But the minister cannot be extricated from both horns of the dilemma. Either his sincerity or his prudence was at fault. It was he who had changed, not the situation; and, leaving out of the question

---

[1] The last letters exchanged between Peel and Croker, printed in the *Croker Correspondence* (vol. iii. 96-97), leave no doubt as to Croker's loyal conduct and Peel's unjust resentment.

the justice of the case, his party had a perfect right to resent what seemed a betrayal.

Sir Edward Knatchbull declared that Sir Robert Peel was 'deficient in vigour and courage.' Disraeli, with a keener subtlety, noted that he was without imagination and without the creative faculty. In effect the two critics agree. To want imagination is, as Disraeli said, to want prescience; to want prescience, is to want vigour. So Peel, not knowing what was to come, supinely accepted the views of his opponents, and made of necessity an ostentatious virtue. To a more energetic statesman there would have been no necessity. He would have fought for his own cause to the last ditch. Peel surrendered at the lightest hint of panic, and accused of treachery all those who did not throw down their arms with him.

But while he lacked the creative faculty, he had, as Disraeli pointed out, 'a dangerous sympathy with the creations of others.' He was always learning, absorbing, appropriating, and so fierce was his egoism that whatever he appropriated he deemed his own exclusive possession. He followed many leaders; he picked up his policies in many corners. 'In his sallet days,' says Disraeli, 'it was Mr. Horner or Sir Samuel Romilly; in later and more important periods it was the Duke of Wellington, the King of the French, Mr. Jones Loyd—some others—and finally, Mr. Cobden.' How, then, could he lead his party with courage, when he knew not what lesson he would learn on the morrow, or what new influence was destined to turn his mind or shape his opinion?

Yet after his defeat in 1846 he made a bold attempt to prove that he had been a consistent Free Trader since 1841. And it is not surprising that this attempt to throw the responsibility of defection upon his Cabinet should have failed. If ever a statesman were pledged to a policy, Peel

was pledged to the protection of the agricultural interest.
'I believe that the abolition of the Corn Laws,' said Peel in
1844, 'would produce great confusion and distress'; and
again, 'I can say with truth I have not contemplated and
do not contemplate an alteration in the present Corn Laws.'
Politicians have short memories; and not merely did Peel
contemplate in 1845 the change that he had never contemplated in 1844, but in 1848, after the episode was closed,
he asserted in a certain letter that the measures taken by
his Cabinet in 1842 were preparatory to and intended to lead
up to the Repeal of the Corn Laws.

To this statement Sir Edward Knatchbull, in the Journal
from which I have already quoted, gives a plain denial.
'I cannot hesitate to say,' he writes, 'that as far as my
recollection goes, it is entirely inconsistent with the truth.
Whether my opinions have been right or wrong, wise or
unwise, they have been deliberately formed, and acted upon
with no other view than the public good. But I have
always been in favour of the Corn Laws, in favour of protection to native industry, and opposed to what is called Free
Trade. I never could then, in Cabinet in 1842, have consented to the measures, on which every member of the
Cabinet, except that poor, silly, vain, and now ruined man,
the Duke of Buckingham, entirely agreed, if they had been
proposed with a view to the later measures of 1845. On
this point my recollection is quite at variance with the
assertion of Sir Robert Peel; and I am quite certain that
I am correct. To satisfy my mind, I have personally communicated with Lord Stanley, who admits at once that my
statement of the case is correct; with Lord Lyndhurst, whose
recollection agrees with mine; with the Duke of Wellington,
who agrees. I had a long conversation with him. We felt
it to be a very awkward question. The Duke said, that
possibly we might both of us be called upon publicly to

express our opinion on the matter. "You and I both know how the case is. All I shall say is that my recollection does not quite enable me to agree in the accuracy of the statement contained in that letter, and I advise you to say the same and no more." I have also seen Lord Hardinge since his return from India. He declared to me, that no such measures as those which were proposed in 1845, were spoken of or contemplated by the Cabinet in 1842. . . . If in 1842 Peel had hinted at any measures similar to those proposed in 1846, or if he had been suspected of entertaining any such opinions, his Cabinet I know would have fallen to pieces.'

Thus the evidence against Peel is overwhelming and irrefutable. Sir Edward Knatchbull is a sufficient witness, and his colleagues are unanimous in support. 'Either in 1842, and previously, Sir Robert was acting a deceitful part, or his mind was of that unstable, vacillating cast, as altogether to disqualify him for the position he held, as first minister of his country.' That is the conclusion, which cannot be evaded, and it is not very creditable to 'the greatest member of Parliament that ever lived.'

IV

And all the while behind Peel there loomed the figure of Richard Cobden. Peel was indeed no more than the shadow thrown by the impassioned Free Trader. Yet the two men were united by no bond of sympathy or friendship. Hitherto nothing had passed between them save hard words and bitter recriminations. If Cobden distrusted Peel, the dry, cold mind of Peel was never stirred by Cobden's hot-gospelling. On the one hand was a minister eager to come under a new influence. On the other was an agitator, willing for the moment to suppress himself, if only his measures were carried. What manner of man was it, then, whose influence in the theatre and lecture-hall equalled that which Sir Robert wielded within the walls of the House of Commons?

Sincere, indefatigable, and narrow-minded, a man of limited and pertinacious brain, who knew what he wanted, and meant to get it, though he did not realise its results— such was Richard Cobden. He was, moreover, an optimist, who believed devoutly in the perfectibility of man, and who was sanguine enough to be quite certain that he was himself incapable of error. So sure was he of his own position that in his eyes his opponents were either fools or knaves. He had a faith in the finality of his scheme which was almost touching, and since the future held as few secrets for him as the present, he professed to know, not only the cause of all existing evil, but its infallible remedy. Therefore he did not hesitate to convert what should have been a mere matter of expediency into a sort of religious belief. Protesting all the while that he was a business man, he declared that Free Trade was a panacea for all the evils to which humankind is subject. 'Free Trade! what is it?' he asked. 'Why, breaking down the barriers that separate nations; those barriers, behind which nestle the feelings of pride, revenge, hatred, and jealousy, which every now and then burst their bounds, and deluge whole countries with blood.'

Now, of course, there is no policy which could gratify these loose, if noble, sentiments, and the frequent recurrence in his speeches of such passages as this is proof enough that Cobden did not take a sternly practical view of his duties. Yet in one respect he was sternly practical: he had a very shrewd notion of what would profit him and his class. He entered upon the struggle, not to benefit the whole community, but to enrich the manufacturers, of whom none was more zealous than himself. If he could he would have replaced the domination of the great landowners, which in his eyes was an infamy, by the far more disastrous domination of the capitalist. In other words, he was supporting that new power without responsibility which came into being in the early years of the nineteenth century. As Enoch Craggs says in *Endymion*: 'Master Thornberry is the most inveterate capitalist of the whole lot, and I always say, though they keep aloof from him at present, they will all be sticking to his skirts before long. Master Thornberry is against the capitalist in land; but there are other capitalists nearer home, and I know more about them.' And Enoch Craggs proceeded to declare that he would 'sooner be ruled by gentlemen of estate, who have been long among us, than by persons who build big mills, who come from God knows where, and when they have worked their millions out of our flesh and bone, go God knows where.'

Cobden, who sat for Job Thornberry's portrait, did not share the scruples of Enoch Craggs. He believed that there was something sacred in profitable industry, that a mill-lord was invariably a nobler person than a landlord, that the dukes of England were criminals when they were not fools. And he had no fear of them. 'If the Duke of Richmond,' said he in a passage which clearly reveals his prejudice, 'sets up the Noodles and Doodles of the aristocracy, why, before we have done with them, they shall be as insignificant and more contemptible than the round-frocked peasantry upon his Grace's estate.' In spite of rhetoric, then, Cobden's agitation was conducted in the interests of a class. To buy in the cheapest market and sell in the dearest—this was his maxim: a maxim, said he, agreeable to the highest behests of Christianity, a mere paraphrase of the Christian doctrine, 'Do to all men as ye would they should do unto you.'

But it is when we consider the prophecies of Cobden that we discover most clearly the recklessness of his argument.

He was certain that if England adopted the principles of
Free Trade, the rest of the world would instantly follow
her example. On this point he had no doubt whatever.
He reiterates his prophecy with a confident assurance,
which to-day appears ridiculous. 'We have a principle
established now,' said he in 1846, 'which is eternal in its
truth, and universal in its application, and must be applied
in all nations, and throughout all times, and applied not
simply to commerce, but to every item in the tariffs of the
world; and if we are not mistaken in thinking that our
principles are true, be assured that those results will follow,
and at no very distant date.' No politician ever delivered
himself more tightly bound hand and foot than did Cobden
in this astounding pronouncement. Nearly sixty years have
passed, and 'those results' have not followed. The inference,
therefore, is clear: Cobden and his fellows were very much
mistaken in thinking that their principles were true; and
we are still asked to put our faith in Free Trade on the
mere word of an agitator.

Again and again did Cobden repeat this vain boast. 'I
believe,' he exclaimed on another occasion, 'that if you
abolish the Corn Law honestly and adopt Free Trade in its
simplicity, there will not be a tariff in Europe that will not
be changed in less than five years to follow your example.'
And, vainest hope of all, it was to America that he looked
for the speediest adoption of his opinions. 'Well,' he
declared after his cheerful fashion in 1846, 'there is one
other quarter in which we have seen the progress of sound
principles—I allude to America'; and the America to which
he alluded with so reckless a certainty is to-day supplying
us with corn, and excluding our manufactures by means of
the M'Kinley tariff.

Confident as he was that his example would be followed,
he was yet more confident that repeal would not throw

the land out of cultivation. 'Throw the land out of cultivation by removing the Corn Law! Who say that? The
worst farmers in the country—the landlords, rather, of the
worst-farmed land.' Those prophets who dared to hint
that the repeal of the Corn Laws would restrict agriculture
were denounced by Cobden as 'selfish, ignorant beings.' In
the same spirit he boldly asserted that, while the landowners
'had nothing pecuniarily, had nothing ultimately to fear
from Free Trade in corn,' if the principles of Free Trade
were fairly carried out, 'they would give just as much
stimulus to the demand for labour in the agricultural as in
the manufacturing districts.' In brief, the bagman's mil-
lenium was to be an age of gold for everybody; wages would
rise, the landowners would increase their wealth, and, above
all, the tenant-farmers of England would reap an enormous
benefit. 'I believe,' said Cobden, 'when the future historian
comes to write the history of agriculture, he will have to
state in such a year there was a stringent corn law passed
for the protection of agriculture. From that time agriculture slumbered in England, and it was not until, by the
aid of the Anti-Corn Law League, the Corn Law was utterly
abolished, that agriculture sprang up to the full vigour of
existence in England to become what it now is, like our
manufactures, unrivalled in the world.'

So vain a pronouncement as this would be ludicrous
if it were not tragic. But in Cobden's eyes repeal had no
drawback. The importation of foreign corn would not,
he was sure, lessen the sale of home-grown corn by a
single bushel. With free commerce the energies of the
people would be so vast that they would consume corn
and provisions brought from abroad faster than the quantity imported could increase. And while we were to profit
by throwing open our ports to the food of all the world,
we should still preserve our independence intact. 'Depen-

dence on foreigners!' he exclaimed in the House of Commons; 'who in the world could have supposed that that long-buried ghost would come again to light.' In fact, the mere notion that Free Trade could inflict a hardship upon any single Englishman was met by Cobden with contemptuous derision. Even though Russia and America deluged our country with corn, the value of land could not possibly diminish. The value of silks, of cottons, or of woollens might be affected by competition; but Cobden was perfectly assured that the taste for land, inherent in humankind, would never let its value decrease a shilling an acre. And while the value of our English acres would, in his fond imagination, never diminish, America would be diverted by the prospect of supplying us with corn from the development of her own manufactures. She would be content to dig and delve; she would devote her energies to a beneficent agriculture, and yet, by some miraculous process, would not prevent the sale of a single quarter grown in England.

So the Corn Laws were repealed, and, as every one knows, all Cobden's predictions were falsified. But he was not one to be daunted by the failure of his hopes. Like most Radicals, he lived in a fool's paradise where facts are of no account, and where, if principles prove fallacious, it is not the fault of the optimist who frames them, but of some vile conspirator against the common good. For many years Cobden had declared that repeal would increase the wages of the labouring class; nor was he abashed when he witnessed their speedy fall. It was enough for him to point out that the cost of living had decreased a little more than wages, and he was wholly indifferent to the fact that this argumentative jugglery was what he had been denouncing in his speeches for ten years. And he had a remedy ready. He told the landlords that they must abolish battue-shooting, and, to confront the depression of agriculture, which he had said would never be depressed, he urged the labourers ' to set gins and snares upon their allotments and in their gardens to catch all the hares and rabbits they could, and when they caught them, to be sure to put them in their own pots and eat them themselves.' This is a sad descent from the dreams of eternal peace, the visions of disbanded armies and of swords beaten into ploughshares, which were wont to decorate the agitator's harangues. The demagogue who once saw in the principle of Free Trade ' that which will act on the moral world as the principle of gravitation in the universe' was three years later forced to substitute for his multi-coloured visions a humble policy of gins, snares, and boiled rabbits.

Now, if politics be anything better than a gamble, the failure of Cobden's predictions should have shaken his own opinion, and given a sharp warning to his countrymen. But no disaster could dim the Free Trader's self-satisfaction. He had formulated a doctrine which in his eye was wholly independent of fact, a principle of moral gravitation, immovable by events. And the perfect trust, which he professed in his own creed, has been reflected for sixty years in the trust of others, to whom Cobden is but a name, and who have never been at the trouble to test his statements. Nor did Cobden limit his programme to repeal—he held firm and definite opinions on all matters of high politics; and it is well that those, who cherish a blind faith in him, should realise whither his leadership would have carried them. In the first place, he was a stalwart opponent of the army and navy. He held that the motto, *si vis pacem, bellum para*, was a monstrous perversion of the truth; and, if he did not see an immediate return for money spent, he was convinced that the enterprise was bad. ' Buy in the cheapest market, sell in the dearest'—this Christian maxim was sufficient for him, and it made no allowance for national dignity or a

policy of empire.   The brain which refused to look beyond
a monthly balance-sheet could not take a large view, and
assuredly Cobden saw no empire beyond Manchester, no
policy beyond a 'full breeches pocket.'

Though by his own action England became dependent upon
foreign countries for her supply of food, he saw no reason why
a navy should be built to keep open the seas.   When he first
travelled abroad he was struck with what he thought the
extravagance of the navy.   'The cost of the Mediterranean
Squadron,' said he, with a thought of his own commerce, 'in
proportion to the amount of trade it was employed to protect,
was as though a merchant should find that his traveller's expenses for escort were to amount to 6s. 8d. in the pound on his
sales.'   This might be true enough if hostile countries stood
to one another merely in the relation of buyers and sellers;
but, if Cobden had had his way, we should long ago have lost
any trade of our own that was worth protecting.   Nevertheless, so candidly alien were his sympathies that he believed
disarmament the natural corollary of Free Trade.   When Sir
Robert Peel had at last passed his famous measure, Bastiat,
a French economist and Cobden's friend, was gravely disappointed.   It was not enough that the markets of England
were thrown wide open to French commerce.   'What you
have to show France above all else,' said Bastiat in an astounding letter, 'is that freedom of exchange will cause the disappearance of those military perils which France apprehends.
England ought seriously to disarm.'   It would be hard indeed
to surpass the pedant naïveté of this French Free Trader.   It
was not enough that England should surrender her markets
—she must surrender herself as well, or France would not
believe in her sincerity!

And, while the policy which we should have pursued towards foreign countries demanded our disarmament, so also
did our colonial policy.   Cobden denied that our depen-

dencies over-sea needed any protection. Doubtless he would
have let our colonies go, in the same spirit in which he
would have renounced India, or 'thanked his stars that
America had broke loose.' He indignantly repudiated the
argument that ships of war were necessary to protect our
colonial trade, and he had so little knowledge of mankind
as to believe that wealth and commerce were the real tests
of a nation's power in the eyes of its enemies. Which is to say
that a traveller is safest from a highwayman when he carries
most money in his pocket. The disarmament which he
advocated was, of course, one-sided, like his free trade; but
happily the country which followed him innocently in quest
of that costliest commodity, cheap food, was not prepared
to disband its army and break up its ships at the bidding
of a rival.

In truth, it was not his business to reason or to doubt.
His sanguine mind pictured the whole world one vast
Manchester, in which 'the stream of commodities was
allowed to flow freely,' and in which the manufacturers, the
true salt of the earth, might collect mountains of gold, high
beyond the dreams of avarice. Had this famous ideal of
ledger and balance-sheet been realised, the working-man
would have had as short a shrift as the landowner. Now,
when Cobden wished to create a prejudice against the great
landlords of England, he declared that high rents and
uncertain tenure were driving the farmers to emigrate,
and thus depriving the country of its noblest citizens. But
what was sauce for the goose was not sauce for the gander.
While he thought that the farmer needed a practical
sympathy, he held that the millowner and his workmen
should be left to fight it out. He hated Factory Acts
as bitterly as he hated trades unions. He would have
permitted nothing to come between the manufacturer and
his profit. If it were necessary to restrict the hours of

labour, the workmen should rely, not upon Parliament, but upon their own efforts. Combination being manifestly intolerable, the remedy of each man was plain: he should save £20 and emigrate to America. In other words, what was tyranny in a landowner was enterprise in a manufacturer. And those eager Radicals who believe that the teaching of Cobden is infallible would do well to remember his famous pronouncement upon workmen's combinations. 'Depend upon it,' said he, in the true accent of Manchester, 'nothing can be got by fraternising with trades unions. They are founded upon principles of brutal tyranny and monopoly. I would rather live under a Dey of Algiers than a Trade Committee.'

V

But in the war of wits, which was waged in the early months of 1846, Peel and Cobden met more than their match, and the opposition which they encountered was at once unexpected and well-deserved. If Cobden's sincerity was less doubtful than his wisdom, Peel showed himself a politician rather than a statesman, and his devious past exposed him nakedly to the piercing shafts of his adversaries. His opponents, moreover, were marshalled by two leaders whose zeal was equal to their discretion, and whose honesty of purpose was as conspicuous as their prowess in debate. And of these one was the English worthy, whose life was afterwards written by Disraeli, 'the self-denying spirit, scorning rest,' who lived for a cause, and wore himself out in the service of his country.

When Lord George Bentinck rose to address the House on the 27th of February 1846, he began a career unparalleled in the history of our Parliament. Though in his youth he had served his kinsman, George Canning, in the post of

secretary, though for eighteen years he had sat at Westminster as the representative of King's Lynn, he had
hitherto taken little interest, and no part, in the debates of
the Commons. Nor was the hour of his speech less remarkable than the fact that he should have spoken at all. He
stood up at twelve o'clock to face a House already jaded by
some days of debate, and he spared his hearers no detail of
an elaborately studied case. With an unsuspected mastery
he discussed the commerce of the country, the trade in silk
and wool, the price of corn and cattle, and the many
questions, whose solution establishes a policy, if they fatigue
an audience of tired legislators. But Lord George did not
hesitate. 'Diffident but determined,' he pursued his argument to the bitter end. With that facility of managing
figures which always distinguished him, he showed, at two
o'clock in the morning, how many hundredweight of guano
would produce an extra quarter of wheat, and nicely calculated into how many pounds of mutton a ton of swedes might
be converted. Never, until his peroration, did he leave the
arid field of reality, and stately as his peroration was, there
was only one phrase in which he pictures the aristocracy of
England 'proud in the chastity of its honour,' that lingers
in our memory. Yet, by this single speech, Lord George
Bentinck was changed from 'the Lord Paramount of the
Turf' to a serious politician; by this single speech he proved
that there was one man left to rally the broken forces of the
Tories, and to lead at least a single campaign against the
minister who had betrayed them.

His aspect and antecedents, moreover, alike afforded a
contrast to the high seriousness wherewith he pleaded the
cause of Protection. A dandy after the manner of D'Orsay,
he displayed in his attire and bearing something of the
'majestic frivolity' which distinguished his class. His vest
was rolled back with as magnificent a sweep as that affected

by his great exemplar; his cravats, the envy of his contemporaries, rivalled those works of art which conferred
imperishable fame upon George Brummell, and though, as
we are told by an admirer, they cost a guinea apiece, he
never wore the same twice. Such a fashion was perfectly
adapted to the passion of his early life; for until 1846
politics had been but an interlude in his pursuit of sport. He
had attended the House as though by accident, and more
than once he had gone into the lobby with the pink of the
hunting-field concealed by a greatcoat of sombre hue.

But, if he was little known at Westminster, his sway
upon the turf was undisputed. For twenty years he had bred
horses and backed them. He easily outstripped the most
reckless of his contemporaries both in the magnificence of
his stables and the splendour of his wagers. On more than
one occasion he had stood to win £150,000, and yet he was
always something better than a mere gambler. It pleased
him to prove his confidence in the horses he bred, and
he was a sportsman fine enough to subordinate his gain
to his pride. He liked to win, not that he valued the
money, but because money was 'the test and trophy of
success.' As Greville says, 'he counted the thousands he
won after a great race as a general would count his prisoners
and his cannon after a great victory.'[1] And his courage
was equal to his generosity. No disaster availed to turn
his purpose, and however vast was the hazard, he never
betrayed the smallest flutter of excitement.

Moreover, with the pertinacity and grasp of facts which

[1] On this point Greville and Disraeli are in perfect agreement, and,
strangely enough, they use the same phrase. To whom the phrase belongs it
is difficult to say. Greville's character of Lord George Bentinck purports to
have been written before Disraeli's, and Greville declares that he read a
part of his sketch to Disraeli. But, of course, Disraeli's biography was
published many years before Greville's death, and it is not easy to award
the credit of an admirable judgment.

he presently turned to excellent account in another field, he permitted no detail of the racecourse to escape him. He watched over his stables at Goodwood with a tireless and intelligent zeal. Everything which concerned the diet and care of his horses was of the highest interest to him. The letters, which he addressed to his trainer, are so long and serious that they are comparable only to state-papers, and they are a complete explanation of the eager policy, which he pursued upon the turf. Indeed, Lord George proved himself a statesman as well as a gambler so long as his colours were carried to victory, and, when at last he threw himself into the cock-pit of politics, he began the new fight strengthened by a vast experience gained in the old. On the turf his triumphs had been great. In 1845, for instance, he had won eighty-two races, and his profit in stakes alone amounted to £31,502; but he had gained a keen knowledge of the world in addition to the money. 'I don't pretend to know much,' said he, 'but I can judge men and horses'; and it was this judgment, combined with unwearied industry and a keen sense of honour, which enabled him after a few months' trial to lead a party in the House of Commons.

None knew better than he that politics were not his natural vocation, and nothing less than a crisis would have dragged him from his retirement; but he could not look on with equanimity while his principles were sacrificed and his party betrayed. For a second time, as has been said, Peel had surrendered his friends to his ambition; and he had made the surrender with so fine an adroitness, he had hoodwinked Parliament with so masterful a skill, that it seemed as if he would repeal the Corn Laws without opposition. It was then that Lord George Bentinck, goaded by a sense of duty, 'came out like a lion forced from his lair.' His opposition to the Manchester School was sincere and well-grounded. Peel's sudden desertion of the party which had placed him in power was repugnant alike to Bentinck's sense of honour and feeling of sport. On the one hand, he held that it would have been easier 'to contend against Free Trade when completely and openly avowed, than when brought forward by one who had obtained power by professing his hostility to it.' On the other hand, he resented with all his sportsman's soul the suspicion of foul play. When Rogers, his jockey, lost a race for his own profit, Lord George was not happy until he proved the rider's guilt to the Jockey Club and got him disqualified. And he looked upon Peel as he looked upon Rogers. 'I keep horses in three counties,' said Lord George once to a Cobdenite, 'and they tell me that I shall save fifteen hundred a year by Free Trade. I don't care for that. What I cannot bear is being sold.'

But he was inspired also by a deeper feeling than sportsmanship and the dislike of being sold. He honourably and devoutly believed that Free Trade would be the ruin not only of his class but of his country. His opinions were as strong and as wise as Disraeli's own. He was strenuously opposed to the Manchester School because he knew that, when once its tenets were accepted, our territorial constitution would be subverted, our freedom impaired, an irreparable injury done to Ireland, and our colonial empire weakened to dissolution. Unlike his opponents, he possessed the real gift of prophecy which comes of a knowing imagination. He foresaw at the very outset the danger incurred by our colonies; he realised that one of the inevitable results of Free Trade would be to alienate the affection of Canada; and, resolved to protect British capital wherever it might be invested, he fought against the measures of Peel, which should have been called the measures of Cobden, with all the energy and force of an indomitable temper.

Henceforth unto the day of his death he was Peel's

bitterest opponent. He was at the House early and late. He worked harder than a slave, and lived like an anchorite. He ate no lunch, and dined at two in the morning. He overcame his natural defects of speech and gesture with a determined consciousness of his own shortcomings, and he atoned for a belated education by a superhuman industry. 'Virtually an uneducated man,' he wrote to Croker in 1847; ' never intended or attracted by taste for political life ... I am well aware of my own incapacity properly to fill the station I have been thrust into.' But a knowledge of incapacity is the first step towards its removal, and Lord George was presently pushed by sheer capacity into the leadership of a broken party.

When he exposed the fraud of Running Rein, the attorney who conducted the case declared that there was 'no sum he would not give to secure the professional assistance of such a coadjutor.' And Bentinck treated the sophistries of Peel with the same perseverance and ingenuity wherewith he baffled the supporters of Running Rein. He got up his case with a skill and energy that are beyond admiration. His speeches were incomparably superior in depth and compass to any others delivered during the campaign. He spared no trouble in amassing information. He was, so to say, a whole commission in himself. In his speeches he continually mentions a mysterious gentleman ' who had waited on him that morning,' and that gentleman was always a specialist unrivalled in his own subject. There was no trade whose battle he did not fight, and whose grievances he did not master: the Irish graziers and butter-merchants, the Leicestershire stockingers, the silk manufacturers of Coventry, the hop-growers of Kent, were all championed by this elegant and handsome sportsman, who had sometimes seemed too lethargic to make a match or lay a wager.

Yet though he proved an astonishing faculty of acquisition, he was at first disinclined to make even his own speech. For, despite a naturally arrogant temper, he had not an atom of conceit, as friends and foes agree.[1] He would, if he could, have remained, like Latour d'Auvergne, in the rank and file. 'We have had enough of leaders,' said he; but here, as in other points of policy, he allowed himself to be overpersuaded, and with Disraeli's help he put together again the broken pieces of the Country Party. Nor could he have found a better colleague than Disraeli, who was in all respects his complement. Lord George had the command of dry hard facts. Disraeli, on the other hand, was distinguished by the dash and brilliance which Lord George candidly owned himself to lack. No sooner had Lord George shattered his opponents with the heavy artillery of argument, than Disraeli rushed in with his light cavalry of taunt and epigram to complete the rout.

When the Lords had passed the second reading of the hated measure, its opponents did not relax their efforts. One battle was lost, yet, even in the moment of victory, the triumphant general might be stripped of his army, and with it of the power to win a second. And so opposition not unworthily became vengeance. Peel was a minister, in Lord George's eyes, whom the country might not trust; he had been coerced, as Cobden confessed, by 'the out-of-doors opinion' and the dread of the League; and Lord George increased his ferocity as the chance of victory disappeared. He was always a good hand at damaging an enemy, and he now employed his gift with a marvellous

---

[1] Lord George Bentinck went so far as to take counsel with a distinguished barrister, who recommended Serjeant Byles as the proper man to plead the cause of Protection in the House of Commons. But Serjeant Byles, though a convinced Protectionist, remained loyal to his profession, and dedicated to Political Economy no more than the leisure which sufficed for the composition of his *Sophisms of Free Trade*.

energy. It has been justly said that Lord George introduced a frankness of attack into parliamentary warfare that had been unknown before his time. That he had ample justification not even a Peelite would deny. Had Peel been an open and avowed Free Trader there would have been no ground for anger; despite the certainty that the Bill would pass, the Protectionists were confident that ultimately they would triumph over their foe; and the Country Party, discomfited as it was, had something of the satisfaction which comes of satisfied revenge.

For, by a stroke of unconscious drama, the Coercion Bill was thrown out on the very night when the Corn Bill became law, and Peel closed his public career in what should have been the hour of victory. But Lord George Bentinck, though his first fight was fought, was now fascinated by politics, and had no intention of returning to his stables. If the Corn Bill was passed, there was still work for him and his party to accomplish. And let it not be supposed that he was eminent merely as a destructive critic. He was, in truth, a statesman of exceedingly wise and moderate views. He would have been satisfied with a duty of four or five shillings on corn, which, he was sure, would not sensibly raise the price in this country. He was the unfailing friend of religious liberty, and he urged that equal privileges should be given to Jews and Catholics alike. He regarded Ireland never with the eye of a partisan; he publicly proclaimed his dislike of absentee landlords; he would have voted for any measure designed to improve the relations of landlord and tenant; and that he had always the welfare of the Irish at heart is proved by his elaborate scheme of railway enterprise in Ireland, his most ambitious attempt at constructive legislation. The scheme was rejected, of course; but the speech in which it was advocated remains a masterpiece of accumulated fact and serried argument.

Meanwhile he had discovered that the breeding of horses was incompatible with a political career. He was of those who do nothing by halves, and eighteen hours devoted to hard work left him little leisure in the day to attend to his stables. He therefore determined to renounce the sport of racing for ever, and the episode of his renunciation is the most dramatic episode in a life packed with drama. It was on the evening of the third day's racing at Goodwood in 1846 that Lord George, appearing half-asleep after dinner, suddenly put the question, 'Will any one of you give me £10,000 for all my lot, beginning with old Bay Middleton and ending with little Kitchener?' The question was not more startling than the method of putting it. And to keep the drama at a high level, George Payne instantly offered to pay a forfeit of £300 if he did not accept the offer by noon the following day. He paid his forfeit, and the 'lot' presently became the property of Mr. Mostyn. This act of devotion, as Greville says, has never been sufficiently appreciated and applauded. Lord George did not put a trifling price upon his horses because he did not know their value. He was perfectly conscious that there were at that moment in his stable the best yearlings that ever he had bred. But expedition was important; he had sacrificed his pleasure to what he deemed his duty; and his only wish was to rid himself of his horses as quickly as possible.

The sale was inevitable, yet it cannot be said that he never regretted it. Two years later, Surplice, a horse that once had been his, won the Derby, to achieve which had for twenty years been the end of his ambition. The disappointment can only be described in Disraeli's magniloquent words. 'He had nothing to console him,' wrote the biographer, 'and nothing to sustain him but his pride. Even that deserted him before a heart which he knew at least could yield him sympathy. He gave a sort of superb groan : " All my life I have been trying for this, and for what have I sacrificed it !" he murmured. It was in vain to offer solace. " You do not know what the Derby is," he moaned out. " Yes, I do; it is the blue ribbon of the turf." " It is the blue ribbon of the turf," he slowly repeated to himself, and sitting down at the table, he buried himself in a folio of statistics.' The passage is superb as Lord George's groan, and nobly characteristic both of the biographer and his hero.

The distinguishing mark of Lord George Bentinck's character was a lofty seriousness. He was serious in horse-racing, serious in Parliament, serious in gathering knowledge, most serious in attacking and worsting his enemies. The truth is, this dignified debonair sportsman could do nothing lightly. He must always be at work, and the transport and diet of horses satisfied him until he found his true profession in politics. His friend and biographer says of him in an admirable passage : ' He never chattered. He never uttered a sentence in the House of Commons which did not convey a conviction or a fact.' He never chattered ! What man can hope to earn a better epitaph ? And the compliment does more than many pages to light up the doubtful corners of Lord George's character. His sincerity was too deep for idle phrases, and his sincerity won him a universal popularity, which not even his arrogance and his talent of bitter speech could diminish.

Moreover, like all sincere men, he was both simple and courageous. Though he speedily mastered the mysteries of politics, he never concealed his designs, nor permitted intrigue to obscure the simplicity of his motive and action. And he was of so high a courage that he never shrank from the performance of an unpleasant duty. A shrewd observer of men and events, he possessed (or acquired) the gift of prophecy, in which Cobden was pitifully deficient. He was wont to say that ' the first who would wish again for

Protection would be the manufacturing interest of Great Britain.' And at a time when Disraeli was either feared or disliked, even by his own side, he did not hesitate to proclaim his approaching triumph. 'His speeches this session have been first-rate,' he writes to Croker in 1848. 'His last speech, altogether burked in the *Times*, but pretty well given in the *Post*, was admirable. He cuts Cobden to ribbons, and Cobden writhes and quails under him just as Peel did in 1846. And, mark my words, spite of Lord Stanley, Major Beresford, and Mr. Phillips and the *Herald*, it will end, before two sessions are out, in Disraeli being the chosen leader of the party.' Here is a prescience founded upon judgment, which is very different from the facile predictions of uninformed optimism.

That he possessed certain faults which would have interfered with his ultimate success may be admitted. He was prolix and insistent both in speech and on paper. He could give no touch of gaiety to his orations. Being a stern realist, to whom romance was an offence, he could not and would not go an inch beyond the warrant of his facts. Perfectly decorative in himself, he had not a decorative style, and this was a complete contrast to his great colleague. Moreover, he had not the power of selection. He was a late learner, and, like all late learners, was sometimes overcome by the weight of his material. It was a passion with him to exhaust his subject, and when he took up his pen to write he was never content until he had covered many sheets of paper. Against this prolixity no constitution could battle with success, and Lord George Bentinck fell a victim to his own energy. To die of hard work is not the most picturesque of deaths; yet, in his own despite, Lord George could not escape the touch of drama, even at the end.

He died suddenly on the 21st of September, between Welbeck and Thoresby—died when his work was unaccomplished, and when his hope of the future was at its highest.

It was but for two brief years that he played the game of statesmanship with perfect gravity. Yet in those two years he made a place for himself in our history, and, though the silence of death overtook him more than fifty years ago, he seems to belong to our own decade more intimately than any of our contemporaries save one. His speeches, purged of their acerbity, are as true to-day as when they were uttered, and they might be delivered again without losing their force or impairing their argument. And at a time when anxious partisans are applauding the services of Mr. Cobden, it is well to recall the high courage and splendid achievement of Mr. Cobden's great adversary, who with tireless loyalty sacrificed his pleasure and his life to the cause, whose triumph he believed essential to his country's welfare.

VI

It has already been pointed out that, in writing the life of Lord George Bentinck, Disraeli with a rare modesty suppressed himself. Now and again he declares that 'a friend' said this, or that 'a friend' counselled that, and, though it is always evident who the 'friend' was, his exclusion from the history is a conspicuous defect. For Lord George Bentinck could not have achieved what he did without the aid of his loyal and generous supporter. Never has there appeared in the House of Commons a more brilliant debater, a severer critic of inefficient policies, than Disraeli. And as he won the attention, and aroused the enthusiasm of the House, he had the added satisfaction that the arrogant prophecies of his youth had one and all been fulfilled. He had stood upon his head, and there was no head in England better worth standing on. The time had come, indeed, when the House should listen, and when, at his rising, a dropped pin might be heard. One disappointment he had suffered in that he got no office in 1841, but they who pretend that a place in the ministry would have persuaded him to endure Peel's autocratic temper singularly misjudge him. For the rest, he had an equal confidence in his own abilities and in the justice of his opinions. Already famous as a man of letters, he did not leave his splendid talents on the threshold of the House. He carried into politics his gift of literature, and his speeches are quick with the wit and epigram which sparkle in his novels.

The years, which had brought with them assurance and respect, had but increased the vigour of his mind and put a sharper edge upon the bitterness of his tongue. In spite of his achievements, and the place he had conquered in what he called the Senate, he was still the Young Disraeli, young in hope, young in courage, young in resource. His attitude towards Protection and Free Trade was logical and consistent. In 1842 he had voted for Peel's industrial measures, because he believed that 'they were founded on sound principles of commercial policy: principles which, in abeyance during the Whig government of seventy years, were revived by that great Tory statesman, Mr. Pitt.' Moreover, he objected that the term Free Trade should ever have been usurped by Cobden and his followers. 'I am a Free trader, not a Free booter,' he said; and he pointed out again and again that the policy of honest Free Trade was the invention of the Tory Party. No man was ever less a pedant than he. 'What is Protection,' he asked, 'but an expedient?' And if it be an expedient, it must depend on circumstances, and could not therefore be condemned or approved by the abstract dogmas so dear to Mr. Cobden and his friends.[1]

---

[1] The followers of Cobden now, as then, mistake a problem for a theorem. They speak as though the interchange of commodities obeyed an inexorable

Moreover, he saw clearly enough that the alternative offered to Protection was not Free Trade, which was never possible, but Free Imports; and, when Sir Robert Peel deserted his party, Disraeli's course was clear. He was not one of the converts. He was, as he said, ' a member of a fallen party, a party which had nothing left on its side, except the constituencies it had betrayed.' He supported in Parliament the same policy which he advocated with a greater deliberation in his *Lord George Bentinck*. The views which he expressed in the one place were identical with those which he expressed in the other, and from the pages of *Hansard* it is possible to fill the gaps which a too scrupulous modesty left in his political biography. But there is a difference in style and temper between the spoken and the written word appropriate to the occasion. Disraeli wrote of his friend when time and death had lessened the bitterness of the conflict; he made his speeches in the House excited by debate, and aroused to indignation by what seemed to him the perfidy of the minister. Though he does not spare Peel in his book, he attacked him face to face with a greater contempt and a more savage irony. And yet in his angriest invective there is a spice of wit, which probably made it less galling to bear than the serious indictment of Lord George Bentinck.

The head and front of Peel's offence in Disraeli's eyes was, of course, his disloyalty to his colleagues. He had come into power on the strength of Tory votes, and he relied for the permanence of his ministry upon his political opponents.

moral law. With a similar indiscretion they detect in cheapness an inherent virtue. How far wiser was Coleridge ! ' You talk about making this article cheaper,' said he, ' by reducing its price in the market from 8d. to 6d. But suppose in so doing you have rendered your country weaker against a foreign foe ; suppose you have demoralised thousands of your fellow-countrymen, and leave some discontent between one class of society and another, your article is tolerably dear, I take it, after all. Is not its real price enhanced to every Christian and patriot a hundred-fold ? '

'The right honourable gentleman,' said Disraeli in memorable phrase, 'caught the Whigs bathing and walked away with their clothes.' He had surrendered his ancient ideals, and trampled on his ancient prejudices. 'I remember him making his Protection speeches,' said his pitiless adversary. 'They were the best speeches I ever heard. It was a great thing to hear the right honourable gentleman say, "I would rather be the leader of the gentlemen of England, than possess the confidence of sovereigns." That was a grand thing. We don't hear much of the gentlemen of England now. But what of that? They have the pleasures of memory, the charms of reminiscence.' And then, in the firm conviction that a Conservative Government is an organised hypocrisy, he poured the acid of his scorn upon Peel's egoism. He reminds the House that Peel had urged it to follow him on the ground that he had held high office under four sovereigns. 'Follow him?' asks Disraeli—'who is to follow him, or why is anybody to follow him, or where is anybody to follow him to?' He recalled the time when Peel delivered himself of the oracle, 'Register, register, register.' Why were they to register? To save the Corn Laws, the Monarchy, or the Church? For none of these things: when his supporters had registered enough, Peel 'showed them the sovereign passion—they were to register to make him a minister.'

In his biography Disraeli pictures Peel as always influenced by the opinions of others, as a man whose mind was always in process of education. In the House of Commons he made the same charge, but in more violent terms. 'For between forty and fifty years,' said he, 'from the days of Mr. Horner to those of the honourable member for Stockport, the right honourable gentleman has traded on the ideas and intelligence of others. His life has been one great appropriation clause. He is a burglar of others' intellect. Search the index of Beatson from the days of the Conqueror to the termination of the last reign, there has been no statesman who has committed petty larceny on such a scale.' Even more effective was the ridicule poured upon Popkins's plan. 'We know all about it,' said a Radical to Disraeli of Peel's plan; 'it was offered to us. It is not his plan; it's Popkins's plan.' And, asks Disraeli in scorn, 'is the England of Burleigh and Walsingham, of Bolingbroke and Walpole, of Chatham and Canning, to be governed by Popkins's plan?' Nor did he spare the watcher of the atmosphere, the man who never originated an idea, the minister who thought only of posterity—of posterity which very few people reach. And in his scorn he involved the whole of the Treasury Bench.

'Throw your eyes over the Treasury Bench,' said he, in his finest passage of contempt. 'See stamped on each ingenuous front, "The last infirmity of noble minds." They are all of them, as Spenser says, "Imps of Fame!" They are just the men in the House you would fix upon as thinking only of the future. The only thing is when one looks at them, seeing of what they are composed, one is hardly certain whether "the future" of which they are thinking is indeed posterity, or only the coming quarter-day.' How excellent is the unexpectedness of the 'coming quarter-day'! How the ingenuous fronts of the Treasury Bench must have blushed at the ridicule! And Disraeli, tireless in scorn, gave them no peace until Peel had led his ragged majority into the lobby, and had himself fallen before a hostile vote.

But Disraeli, in his opposition to Peel, was not content with ridicule. He seldom made a speech which did not lift the debate to a high plane of seriousness. For some years before the Prime Minister had divided his colleagues, Disraeli had been the leader of the Young

England Party, and though after his speech on the Maynooth Grant he ceased to act with it, the views of Young
England had a profound and lasting influence on him,
and nowhere can this influence be more clearly detected
than in the speeches which were inspired by the debates
on the Corn Law. A pride in England, a love of the
people, the championship of labour—these are the substance of his most eloquent perorations. He taught in his
speeches the same lessons of devotion and honour which he
had taught in *Sybil*. When he said that he wished to secure
a preponderance of the landed interest, he was thinking of
the welfare, not of a single class, but of the whole country.
With Lord John Manners and George Smythe he regretted
the decay of the feudal system. He pointed out that the
Conqueror did not distribute the land without exacting
responsibility. ' You shall have that estate,' said he, ' but
you shall do something for it: you shall feed the poor; you
shall endow the Church; you shall defend the land in case
of war; and you shall execute justice and maintain truth to
the poor for nothing.' This, at any rate, was a better ideal
than the ideal of Manchester, to buy in the cheapest and
sell in the dearest market, to become rich and ever richer
without the interference of industry and toil. So Disraeli's
ambition was to see not a 'spinning-Jenny machine kind of
nation,' but an England which once more possessed a free
Monarchy and a privileged and prosperous People. A
very different hope from that of Richard Cobden, who
cared as little for the people as he cared for the landed
gentry, and who was straining every nerve to transfer the
power to the middle class, to create the most dangerous of
all things—wealth without responsibility.

And already Disraeli had struck the note of Imperialism
which, familiar to-day, was then rarely heard. 'I for one,'
said he in 1843, 'am not prepared to sit under the power of

a third-class, if I can be a citizen of a first-class empire.'
Moreover, he saw clearly that Peel and his supporters were
losing the chance of binding the Colonies to the mother
country. 'You turn up your noses at East India cotton,'
said he to the House, 'as you have done at everything
Colonial or Imperial.' And it is the fashion to say that
Disraeli had no interest in our empire over-sea. The de-
tractors who bring this charge rely on a hasty phrase in a
private letter, as though a statesman were on oath if he aired
a grievance to a friend.[1] Not only in his speeches but in his
policy, he was a consistent champion of Colonial interests.
In 1863 he already prophesied that Canada would become
the Russia of the New World, and he declared that, if
we were to quit the possessions that we occupied in North
America, 'we might then prepare for the invasion of our
country and the subjection of the people.'

In 1872 he was still more definite in his opinion, still
nearer to the policy of to-day. 'The two great objects of
the Tory Party,' he declared, 'were to maintain the institutions of the country and to uphold the empire of England.'
In the same speech he advocated an imperial tariff, he
insisted that the people of England should enjoy unappro-
priated lands, which belonged to the sovereign as their
trustee, he urged that a military code should precisely define
the means by which the Colonies should be defended, and
by which the country should call for aid from the Colonies
themselves. Thus he anticipated all that a generation,
keenly alive to the importance of our Empire, has hoped
or thought, and thus he takes his place in the long line

---

[1] The sentence may be found in a letter addressed, on August 13, 1852,
to Lord Malmesbury. 'These wretched colonies,' he wrote, 'will be independent in a few years, and are a millstone round our necks.' Against this
one petulant expression, not meant to be published, may be set the constant
policy of many years.

of patriotic ministers who since the time of Bolingbroke, his master, have guided the destinies of England.

When once the Corn Laws were abolished, Disraeli took the only course that was open to him: he accepted the accomplished fact. His speeches on agricultural distress, delivered within five years after Peel's measure was passed, sufficiently prove that he had not changed his opinion; and when, having gathered together the *disjecta membra* of the old Tory Party, he assumed the leadership of the House, the question was closed. Whatever distress assailed the country, the remedy of protection had passed for the moment beyond the range of practical policy, in spite of Disraeli's opposition, and with the reiterated approval of the people. 'Under these circumstances,' as Disraeli said in 1879, 'it was impossible for a public man, whatever had been their opinions upon these great commercial questions, when these important changes were first introduced, to have had an open controversy for a quarter of a century. The government of the country could not have been carried on.' And it was Disraeli's business to carry on this government. Nor, when reciprocity was suggested as a cure for the evils which beset the State, did reciprocity seem possible. We had nothing to reciprocate. We had given up the means by which an honourable system of commercial treaties could be established. But they err who assert that Disraeli renounced in his old age the principles for which he fought so valiantly in 1846; and, though it is idle to vaticinate what course he would have followed in the present crisis, the consistent policy of his whole life is an eloquent proof that he would never have surrendered the commercial supremacy of England for the sake of a dogma.

VII

With such combatants engaged on either side, the contest could not but be dramatic, and Disraeli has described it with all the resources of a literary craftsman. And most dramatic of all was the closing scene when triumph and defeat overtook Sir Robert in the same hour. The passage in which Disraeli describes the last act of the tragedy has an epic touch. He marshalls the 'men of metal and large-acred squires, the Manners, the Somersets, the Bentincks, the Lowthers, and the Lennoxes,' in the same spirit wherewith Homer numbers the ships of the Greeks. Sir Robert was beaten by 73. 'He looked very grave, and extended his chin as was his habit when he was annoyed and cared not to speak. He began to comprehend his position, and that the emperor was without his army.' Nor did the emperor ever reassemble his shattered forces. And with his army he had lost his influence. 'Peel can never be at the head of any party,' said the Duke of Wellington to Sir Edward Knatchbull—'that is, of any considerable party. He will keep his seat in the House of Commons, and will endeavour to act as a sort of umpire between parties. He will not be disposed himself again to take office. The country will not trust him again.'

Nor did the last speech which he delivered as a minister tend to recover his lost friends. For the first time he mentioned Cobden by name, and paid an unexpected tribute to the agitator. Even Mr. Gladstone was outraged by this indiscretion. 'Mr. Cobden,' said Mr. Gladstone, 'has throughout argued the Corn Question on the principle of holding up the landlords of England to the people as plunderers and as knaves for maintaining the Corn Laws to save the rents, and as fools because it was not necessary for that purpose. This was passed by, while he was praised for sincerity, eloquence, indefatigable zeal.' Thus politics also has its ironies, and it is strange to find Mr. Gladstone in public supporting the sad, lost cause of the landlords. The reception of the Corn Bill by the country emphasised the fact that it was passed not for the people, but for the manufacturers. The news, we are told by the *Annual Register*, caused much rejoicing in the manufacturing districts of England and France. 'Bells were rung; flags and banners, bearing appropriate inscriptions, were displayed from factories or carried in procession about the streets. . . . In many places arrangements were made by employers to give their workmen a holiday and an entertainment.' To the bald eloquence of this statement no word need be added.

VIII

And now at last the history of 1846 is repeating itself. The question of Protection and Free Trade is once more supremely interesting to the country. Mr. Balfour, with a discretion which escaped Sir Robert Peel, has declared himself incompetent to deal with it before appealing to the country. But, when that appeal has been made, the situation of 1846 will be repeated with surprising exactitude. Mr. Chamberlain will play the part then played by Lord George Bentinck, with not a little of that statesman's skill and persistency. He, too, will fight the battle of the manufacturers and of the Colonial farmers. He, too, will gather his information from the 'best authorities on the subject in debate.' On either side the House the same speeches will be made, and the same arguments shall not prevail. Once again the Free Traders will rest their case not upon facts, but upon sentiments. Once again we shall hear an echo of Disraeli saying: 'Protection is not a principle, it is an expedient.' And here is one speech delivered sixty years ago, which may be repeated to-day without the change of a syllable, and with increased force: 'A scheme which admits the produce of the Colonies and Indian corn duty free, and other foreign corn at a moderate fixed duty, would place the corn trade on a basis satisfactory to the mercantile interests of the country, would bind the members of our vast Colonial Empire to us by the closest ties of interest, and would afford security to the English farmer.' Thus spoke Lord John Manners on January 27, 1846. From the views then expressed the Duke of Rutland has never wavered, and his is the unique experience, after long fidelity, to witness the approaching triumph of a cause which has been neglected for more than half a century.

LORD GEORGE BENTINCK

A POLITICAL BIOGRAPHY

CHAPTER I

THE political career of Lord George Bentinck was peculiar. He had, to use his own expression, 'sate in eight parliaments without having taken part in any great debate,' when remarkable events suddenly impelled him to advance and occupy not only a considerable but a leading position in our public affairs. During three years, under circumstances of great difficulty, he displayed some of the highest qualities of political life; courage and a lofty spirit; a mastery of details which experience usually alone confers; a quick apprehension and a clear intelligence; indomitable firmness; promptness, punctuality, and perseverance which never failed; an energy seldom surpassed, and a capacity for labour which was perhaps never equalled. At the very moment when he had overcome many contrarieties and prejudices; when he had been most successful in the house of commons, and sustained only by his own resources had considerably modified the legislation of the government which he opposed on a measure of paramount importance; when the nation, which had long watched him with interest, began to congratulate itself on the devotion of such a man to the business of the country, he was in an instant taken from us. Then it was that, the memory of the past and the hope of the future blending together, all men seemed to mourn over this untimely end, and there was that pang in the public heart which accompanies the unexpected disappearance of a strong character.

What manner of man this was, who thus on a sudden in the middle term of life relinquished all the ease and pleasure of a patrician existence to work often eighteen hours a day, not for a vain and brilliant notoriety, which was foreign alike both to his tastes and his turn of mind, but for the advancement of principles, the advocacy of which in the chief scene of his efforts was sure to obtain for him only contention and unkindly feelings; what were his motives, purposes, and opinions; how and why he laboured; and the whole scope and tendency of this original, vigorous, and self-schooled intelligence; these would appear to be subjects not unworthy of contemplation, and especially not uninteresting to a free and political community.

The difficulty of treating cotemporary characters and events has been ever acknowledged: but it may be doubted whether the difficulty is diminished when we would commemorate the men and things that have preceded us. The cloud of passion in the first instance, or in the other the mist of time, may render it equally hard and perplexing to discriminate. It should not be forgotten that the most authentic and interesting histories are those which have been composed by actors in the transactions which they record. The cotemporary writer who is personally familiar with his theme has unquestionably a great advantage; but it is assumed that his pen can scarcely escape the bias of private friendship or political connection. Yet truth after all is the sovereign passion of mankind; nor is the writer of these pages prepared to relinquish his conviction, that it is possible to combine the accuracy of the present with the impartiality of the future.

The frequent meetings of the cabinet that took place towards the end of the year 1845 excited a lively interest in the country and attracted even the attention of Europe. No doubt could exist as to the cause of these assemblings. The powerful organisation for the repeal of the corn laws, which hitherto had been more remarkable for its efficient discipline and the ability of its leaders than for the degree of popular sympathy which it commanded, had received a great and unexpected assistance, and that too when its energy and its resources were both waning, by the menaced failure of one of the crops most important for the sustenance of the people of the united kingdom. Nor, it was rumoured, was this visitation limited to her majesty's dominions. It was prevalent in many other European countries, and extended even to the native region of the potato.

The difficulty which under such circumstances must have been experienced by any ministry was aggravated, in the existing instance, by the fact that the government had been formed on principles adverse to a less restricted importation of foreign food than the law then sanctioned. What would be their course? Would they recognise in the present state of affairs a proof of the error of their system, or would they esteem it a contingency which might derange, but which would not invalidate, that system? And if so, what remedial measure would they adopt to counteract that temporary disturbance? Would they suspend the import duties on foreign corn? And if so, would they obtain their object by an order in council, or by the immediate sanction of parliament to be assembled for that purpose? These were the questions which were in everybody's mouth and mind while four cabinet councils of unusual duration were held in one week.

Nor was the excitement throughout the continent of Europe, though of course less general, less eager or less anxious. The existing policy of the great cabinets had been founded on the assumption that the administration of Sir Robert Peel would be limited only by the term of his political life, and that he might probably bequeath the government to a competent successor. They esteemed the retarded but at length signal triumph of the conservative principle in England in 1841 as the complete and natural conclusion of those events and ideas which had agitated and perplexed the various communities since the fall of the elder Bourbons in 1830. They associated their interests, therefore, with the existence of a conservative government in England. They could not bring themselves to believe, in November 1845, that such a government was in danger, though it was evidently in some difficulty. So strong was their faith in the power of the triumphant tory party, and so great their confidence in the sagacity and experience and high reputation of its eminent leader, that they were on the whole perhaps rather curious than alarmed.

In the meantime the cabinet, which had met so frequently and so hurriedly, again dispersed, apparently with no decision but one of inaction. Instead of an order in council for opening the ports, the *London Gazette* contained a further prorogation of parliament, and it was evident that her majesty's ministers had no intention to solve the difficulty, either by the exercise of the prerogative of the sovereign, or by a premature appeal to the two houses.

The determination to do nothing was accepted by the foreign cabinets as evidence that the British minister had examined his position and had found it impregnable. That, however, was not the opinion of those who from their parliamentary experience, the political habits of their lives, and their personal acquaintance with the characters of the principal actors in the impending transactions, would appear to be more competent to arrive at a sound conclusion. It is difficult for foreign cabinets, however faithfully and intelligently served, to calculate the result of a political crisis in England when the elements of our party government are violently disturbed. As long as the public contest is the ordinary struggle between recognised political connections, and much depends upon individual opinion, caprice, or conduct, the social information of the diplomatist, aiding his unimpassioned scrutiny, will often lead him to a more accurate judgment of the event than that of the partisan. But it is otherwise when the great English parties are agitated without the walls of parliament by any acknowledged or assumed repudiation of the principles of their union by those in whom they have confided as their cherished organs; and it is only a parliamentary leader of great natural sagacity, matured by a considerable experience of the assembly on which this external opinion is to act, who can successfully calculate what may be its consequences on the conduct of the members.

The minister had closed the session of 1845 with an overwhelming majority in both houses. True it is, that in the four years during which he had conducted affairs he had frequently strained the patience of his supporters; but their passive murmurs only proved how necessary he was to their interests, and how accurately he had calculated their faculty of sufferance. True it is, that towards the end of the session of '45, a solitary voice from the tory benches had presumed to prophesy that protection then was in about the same condition as protestantism was in 1828, and amid tumultuous sympathy a conservative government had been denounced as 'an organised hypocrisy'; but the cheers of mutual sensibility were in a great degree furnished by the voices opposite, and the tory gentlemen beneath the gangway who swelled the chorus did so with downcast eyes, as if they yet hesitated to give utterance to feelings too long and too painfully suppressed. Practically speaking, the conservative government, at the end of the session of '45, was far stronger than even at the commencement of the session of '42. If they had forfeited the hearts of their adherents, they had not lost their votes, while both in parliament and the country they had succeeded in appropriating a mass of loose, superficial opinion not trammelled by party ties, and which complacently recognised in their measures the gradual and moderate fulfilment of a latitudinarian policy both in church and state.

Their position was also aggrandised and confirmed by a conviction then prevalent, and which it is curious to observe is often current on the eve of great changes, that the ministry of Sir Robert Peel were the only body of men then competent to carry on affairs.

The opposite benches were thronged with gentlemen who offered no opposition. Split into sections, they agreed only in affording the ministerial system a forced and grim approbation. The most noisy and bustling section was that of the English radicals, who with provident perseverance were resolved to show that no future ministry should be formed without their claims being acknowledged. In this when the crisis arrived they partially succeeded, by the graceful if not willing abnegation of some eminent members of the whig party. But generally speaking the preferments arranged by a process so painful and so costly have not been very felicitous; nor has the English radical party ever obtained that influence in the house which from their numbers might have been expected. They still mainly depend on the multifarious information and the vast experience of Mr. Hume, who towers among them without a rival. Future parliaments will do justice to the eminent services of this remarkable man, still the most hard-working member of the house, of which he is now the father. His labours on public committees will be often referred to hereafter, and then perhaps it will be remembered that, during a career of forty years, and often under circumstances of great provocation, he never once lost his temper.

Inferior in numbers, but superior in influence from their powers of debate and their external organisation, were the members of the confederation called the Anti-Corn-Law League; but the close of the session of '45 found them nearly reduced to silence. Low prices, abundant harvests, and a thriving commerce, had rendered appeals, varied even by the persuasive ingenuity of Mr. Cobden, a wearisome iteration. The Manchester confederates seemed to be least in favour with parliament and the country on the very eve of their triumph. They lost at the same time elections and the ear of the house; and the cause of total and immediate repeal seemed in a not less hopeless position than when, under circumstances of infinite difficulty, it was first and solely upheld by the terse eloquence and vivid perception of Charles Villiers.

The condition of the whig party itself was absolutely forlorn; it was spoken of as a corpse; it was treated as a phantom. With numbers scarcely exceeding one-sixth of the house in a parliament of their own summoning, the whigs were sustained alone by the dignity of Lord John

Russell. There are few positions less inspiriting than that of the leader of a discomfited party. The labours and anxieties of a minister or of his rival on the contested threshold of office may be alleviated by the exercise or sustained by the anticipation of power; both are surrounded by eager, anxious, excited, perhaps enthusiastic, adherents. There is sympathy, appreciation, prompt counsel, profuse assistance. But he who in the parliamentary field watches over the fortunes of routed troops must be prepared to sit often alone. Few care to share the labour which is doomed to be fruitless, and none are eager to diminish the responsibility of him whose course, however adroit, must necessarily be ineffectual. Nor can a man of sensibility in such a post easily obviate these discouragements. It is ungracious to appeal to the grey-headed to toil for a harvest which they may probably never reap, and scarcely less painful to call upon glittering youth to sacrifice its rosy hours for a result as remote as the experience in which it does not believe. Adversity is necessarily not a sanguine season, and in this respect a political party is no exception to all other human combinations. Indoors and out of doors a disheartened opposition will be querulous and captious. A discouraged multitude have no future; too depressed to indulge in a large and often hopeful horizon of contemplation, they busy themselves in peevish detail, and by a natural train of sentiment associate their own conviction of ill-luck, incapacity, and failure, with the most responsible member of their confederation: while all this time inexorable duty demands, or rather that honour which is the soul of public life, that he should be as vigilant, as laborious, should exercise as complete a control over his intelligence and temper, should be as prompt to represent their principles in debate, and as patient and as easy of access in private conference, should be as active and as thoughtful, as if he were sustained by all that encourages exertion—the approbation of the good and the applause of the wise.

The position of Lord John Russell during the last administration of Sir Robert Peel was a mortifying one.

Every public man is prepared to endure defeat with the same equanimity with which he should bear more auspicious fortunes; but no one likes to be vanquished unfairly. It was the opinion of Lord John Russell that he had not been fairly treated by the triumphant opposition which had ousted him from the treasury bench. He was indeed too reserved and too justly proud a man to give any vent to these feelings in the heyday of conservative exultation. But the feelings were not less lively; he brooded over them with the pain which accompanies the sense of injustice. Session after session, while his policy was appropriated in detail by those who had often condemned or misrepresented it, the frigid manner often veiled an indignant spirit, and the cynic smile was sometimes the signal of a contempt which he was too haughty to express. But when the hour of judgment had arrived, and when he might speak of his feelings with becoming dignity, in giving the reason why at the beginning of 1846, when summoned by his sovereign, he had at first respectfully declined the commission of her majesty to form a government on account of his weakness in the house of commons, he added: 'I need not now explain why it was, that, in the house of commons, those who in general agree with me in opinion, are inferior in number to those who generally follow the right honourable baronet (Sir Robert Peel); but I must say, on this occasion, that during the whole of our administration, our motives never received a fair construction, nor did our measures ever receive an impartial consideration from those who were our political opponents.'

This is a grave charge, applying as it does to a very eventful period of nearly seven years, for such was the considerable duration of the Melbourne government. Was the charge well founded? In reluctantly admitting its authenticity, there are, however, in justice to the conservative ministry, and especially in justice to the conservative party, several important considerations to be indicated.

The unfairness with which the last Melbourne administration was treated was the consequence of the irregular and somewhat scandalous conduct of the whig party during the preceding administration, and especially during the latter months of Lord Grey's government. This conduct had created a great mass of public prejudice against them. Notwithstanding the reform of parliament and the august renown of its apparent author, the whigs had contrived in a very brief space to lose the opinion of a country which at the termination of 1830, it was supposed by many, they might have ruled for half a century. A series of strange incidents, of startling changes, and almost inexplicable intrigues, had perplexed, alarmed, and disgusted the middle class. The champions of popular opinion seemed involved in cabals, and eventually as it appeared against their own venerable chief, while the ministers upheld by national sympathies were in dark but baffled confederation with an Irish section, not viewed without distrust even by the great body of the liberal party.

Unquestionably the main cause of this strange and unexpected state of affairs was the unfitness of the respectable Lord Spencer for the leading office which he occupied. Private integrity and public honour are qualities, it is to be hoped, which will never be underrated in our free, parliamentary life; but they are qualities which are not sufficient in the revolutionary hour to control cabinets and senates. His resignation, and immediate resumption of power, followed by the retirement of Lord Grey, have never been explained, though it is charitable to suppose they were the movements of a man distracted by good intentions and difficult circumstances. The impatience of the court by hurrying the catastrophe secured to the whigs, after a brief but not inglorious interval for the tories, a lengthened renewal of that power which they had so wantonly abused, and Lord Melbourne with his new cabinet had to encounter all that prejudice which was the consequence of the misconduct of his old one.

The leader of the house of commons in Lord Melbourne's new cabinet was Lord John Russell, who had hitherto, taking into consideration his parliamentary experience, his eminent services, and his name, filled comparatively speaking only a subordinate position in the government. When the cabinet of Lord Grey was formed he was not appointed a member of it, and he even, as paymaster of the forces, brought forward the great measure of parliamentary reform, as the member of the government most competent to explain and to defend its provisions, without the responsibility of being an adviser of his majesty. The whigs could hardly have treated Mr. Burke worse, and probably, in some degree, from the same cause. Lord John Russell was a man of letters, and it is a common opinion that a man cannot at the same time be successful both in meditation and in action. But in life it is wisest to judge men individually, and not decide upon them by general rules. The common opinion in this instance may be very often correct; but where it fails to apply its influence may involve us in fatal mistakes. A literary man who is a man of action is a two-edged weapon; nor should it be forgotten that Caius Julius and Frederick the Great were both eminently literary characters, and yet were perhaps the two most distinguished men of action of ancient and modern times.

The whigs were so circumstanced after the dissolution of '34 that they could only regain power by a still more intimate alliance with that ultramontane Irish party, their previous negotiation with which had been the principal cause of their overthrow. Lord John Russell, therefore, was obliged to commence his career as a principal minister by not only reviving but aggravating the prejudice which already attached to his party in this particular. He obtained power by the assertion of a principle which as a minister he was unable to enforce, and the resumption of office by the whigs was thus secured by a process which, while it was condemned by public opinion, became an enduring evidence of the essential weakness of their administration. Thus the second government of Lord Melbourne was from the first both unpopular and feeble; and this too in the face of a very powerful opposition in parliament and the country, who could not resist the conclusion that the ministry had obtained their seats under a false pretence; means scarcely within the pale of parliamentary tactics.

Laying aside for a moment this original sin, which however tainted all their course, the measures of the Melbourne government were generally moderate, well-matured, and statesmanlike schemes. The conduct of the government until '39 was highly reputable, and well would it have been for the honour of both parties if the impending and inevitable change had not then been postponed. During all this period, however, it must be acknowledged that the whigs encountered 'an opposition which never gave a fair construction to, or an impartial consideration of, their measures'; the whigs certainly during this period did not receive fair play; but it was because both parliament and the country, from the scandalous transactions of '34 and the reckless manœuvres of '35, thought that they did not deserve it.

But the position of Lord John Russell under these circumstances was different from that of the other principal members of the whig party. Although at this period leader of the house of commons, he had not been even a member of the first reform cabinet; and though tardily preferred to that eminence, can scarcely be held in any degree responsible for that management of the lower house and that guidance of the ministerial councils which, in the space of little more than three years, had succeeded in dissipating a great parliamentary force and in scattering a powerful cabinet. Forced, for the resuscitation of the whig government, to the manœuvre of the appropriation clause, he could scarcely have refrained from deploring the infirm policy which had rendered necessary for a proud and successful party such an abasement: he could scarcely have withstood contemplating what might perhaps have been his own position and that of the great whig connection, had he been deemed worthy to fill in '31 the post which he occupied in '35.

In or out of power, therefore, the position of Lord John Russell since the reform act had been more splendid than satisfactory; and when the whig party, as was inevitable from their antecedents, but apparently to his mortification in consequence of his guidance, was again overthrown, and had lost all credit and confidence with the country, it was to be expected that a man of his thoughtful ambition would seek when the occasion offered to rebuild his power and renew the lustre of his reputation with no superstitious deference to that party of which he was the victim as much as the idol, and with no very punctilious consideration for the feelings of that conservative government which had certainly extended to him an opposition neither distinguished by its generosity nor its candour.

Such was the man; such his fortunes, such perhaps his feelings; who was watching in a distant city in the autumn of '45 'four cabinet councils held in a week.' To one so experienced in political life, and especially to one so intimately acquainted with the personal character of the chief actors, it was not difficult to form some conclusion as to the nature of these momentous deliberations. When the cabinet dispersed and parliament was again prorogued, it was evident, to use the subsequent expression of Lord John Russell, that the policy decided on was a policy of inaction. It is in the season of perplexity, of hesitation, of timidity, of doubt, that leading minds advance to decide and to direct. Now was the moment to strike. And without consulting his party, which for the first time he really led, and with no false delicacy for a conservative cabinet in convulsions, he expressed his opinions on public affairs in that celebrated Edinburgh epistle, which was addressed on the 28th of November, to his constituents, the citizens of London.

CHAPTER II

THE proceedings of those four councils in a week, which in November '45 agitated England, perplexed the sagacious Tuileries, and disturbed even the serene intelligence of the profound Metternich, are no longer a secret.

The prime minister of England, in bringing before the consideration of his colleagues the temporary measures which in his judgment a menaced exigency required, intimated to them at the same time his change of opinion as to the principles on which our commercial system ought to be established, entirely rejecting those conclusions, the maintenance of which only four years before had raised him, after an official ostracism of ten years, to the pinnacle of power by a national demonstration scarcely inferior to the triumph of Mr. Pitt in 1783. This momentous conversion had for some time been known to more than one of his principal colleagues, who sympathised with his mutability, and had perhaps been suspected by most, who however were not anxious to press for any definite disclosures, so long as his defection was limited to the domain of speculation. Sir Edward Knatchbull, however, who seceded in silence both from the cabinet and parliament in the previous year, when pressed for the cause of his retirement by an anxious friend, confidentially replied that he could not remain with satisfaction, and felt that he could not long remain with honour, and that at his time of life he shrank from again mixing in the bitter strife which attended the break-up of a great party from the defection of its leaders. It was the wish and perhaps the hope of Sir Robert Peel to have postponed the public announcement of his recantation until the opinion of the country might at a general election have been again constitutionally taken on the subject of protection. The present parliament was fast waning, and had low prices and abundant harvests continued to prevail, Sir Robert Peel was prepared until the dissolution still to occupy the ostensible post of a protectionist minister. Perhaps he was sanguine that during the interval the national judgment, which had been so unequivocally expressed in '41, might be greatly modified, and that it was not impossible he might ultimately be established as a triumphant minister to revoke the very policy which he had previously been selected to defend and confirm.

But he was 'precluded from taking a course which would have been most agreeable to his personal feelings.' The menaced occurrence of a great calamity rendered it necessary in his opinion that the government should take some steps to secure the provision of the people. 'There appeared to be a great and pressing danger.' The cabinet was summoned on the 1st of November to consider what steps should be taken for the relief of the distress in Ireland. That was the avowed object of their assembling and the announced subject for their discussion. Papers were laid before the ministers representing the failure of the potato crop and the general anxiety that consequently prevailed; and then the chief minister, after dilating much upon the perilous position of Ireland and the necessity of adopting immediate steps for her succour, entered into a lengthened detail of the result of the harvest in foreign countries, which he represented to be generally deficient. It appeared that several European governments had already taken steps to prevent the export of supplies, and to permit and encourage import; that Belgium had cleared the market of Liverpool of rice in one day, thereby occasioning a rise in the price of that article to the amount of 75 per cent. Under these circumstances there were two courses which in the opinion of the first minister were open to the cabinet, neither of which was without precedent; and that was either by an order in council or by calling parliament together within a fortnight to suspend all restrictions upon the importation of foreign corn. Sir Robert Peel stated that he preferred the first course. He was for issuing at once an order in council, because that would save time; but he did not insist upon this, although as the head of the government he was prepared to take the responsibility of such a measure: he should be content if the cabinet would agree to call parliament together immediately, and recommend from the throne the instant suspension of the import duties on foreign corn, at the same time intimating his opinion that after such a suspension, it might be neither possible nor expedient to re-enact the existing law.

This statement of the first minister was coldly received by the great majority of the cabinet, and it was evident that neither of his suggestions was deemed satisfactory. Lord Stanley, then secretary of state, familiar with the condition of Ireland and the habits of the Irish, analysed with searching criticism the statements as to that country, and the effect of the proposed remedy on the cultivation of its soil. In the first place, he denied the possibility of the government, or of any one else, forming any judgment at the end of October as to the prospect of scarcity in Ireland. Not a third of the potatoes could have at that time been dug up. He impressed upon his colleagues the wide distinction there was between famine and great local and individual distress. He admitted that a total or a partial failure of the potato crop would involve in absolute destitution the whole body of small cottiers, who were not like the English husbandmen in the receipt of wages, but who had invested their labour and all their resources in the cultivation of some small plot of ground, for which they paid a high rent. If the produce of that failed their stock of provisions was gone, and having no means of employment they could not purchase food to replace the crop which was wanting. But the repeal of a corn law could not aid them now. What they required was not reduction of price, but the absolute means of purchase. But while this was the condition of the Irish cottiers, what would be the effect of a suspension of import duties on a class not less important even in numbers, a class comprising with their families not less than between five and six millions of the population; namely, the small farmers of Ireland? Fifteen acres in Ireland was called a large farm. These cultivators of the soil grew oats and potatoes. What was their compensation for the failure of the latter crop? The success of their superior one, of which they had this year a superabundance at a very fair price. This afforded them means of sustaining themselves; and by way of relieving this class when they have lost one crop, the present proposition was to inflict a further injury by reducing the price of their other. Therefore, as far as the instance of Ireland should sway them, Lord Stanley gave it as his opinion that they should not adopt either of the recommendations of the chief minister. But Sir Robert Peel had entered into other considerations. He had referred to the state of the harvest in England also, and had specially called their attention to the apprehended deficiency of the continent; foreign countries, it appeared, were even prohibiting the export of their produce. But it appeared to Lord Stanley that this was rather an additional reason against opening their ports, because the effect of such a step is always to stimulate consumption; yet to stimulate consumption while foreign nations prohibited export seemed hardly a prudent course.

These views were strongly supported by the Duke of Wellington, 'who considered the proposition of the first minister was a measure which was not necessary to be adopted,' and the great majority of the cabinet were of the same opinion, the two secretaries of state and the secretary at war being the only ministers who countenanced the project of Sir Robert Peel. It was therefore apparently abandoned; the cabinet entering into the consideration of other measures calculated to meet the emergency. They unanimously agreed to appoint a commission consisting of the heads of the departments in Ireland to take precautionary steps against a sudden occurrence of distress; and they separated on the 6th of November.

On the 22nd of that month appeared the Edinburgh letter in which Lord John Russell announced the danger of the country and condemned the inertness of the government. In the inability of the queen's ministers, it became the queen's subjects to consider how they might avert calamities of no ordinary magnitude. Two evils required their consideration: the disease in the potatoes, and the corn law of '42, 'in which the duties were so contrived that the worse the qualities of the corn the higher was the duty. Thus the corn barometer points to fair, while the ship is bending under a storm.'

Lord John confessed that on the general subject his views had in the course of twenty years undergone a great alteration. He had for several years endeavoured to obtain a compromise on the subject. In 1839 he had voted for a committee of the whole house, with the view of supporting the substitution of a moderate fixed duty for the sliding scale. Two years after, as minister, he had proposed a fixed duty of eight shillings per quarter. Even in the past session he had made another effort. These propositions were successively rejected, and thus he sketches the cause of those rejections:—

'The present first lord of the treasury met them in 1839, '40, and '41, by eloquent panegyrics on the existing system —the plenty it had caused, the rural happiness it had diffused. He met the propositions for diminished protection in the same way in which he had met the offer of securities for protestant interests in 1817 and 1825—in the same way in which he met the proposal to allow Manchester, Leeds, and Birmingham to send members to parliament in 1830. The result of resistance to qualified concessions must be the same in the present instance as in those I have mentioned. It is no longer worth while to contend for a fixed duty.'

This letter ended by an appeal to all classes to unite and to agitate in order to put an end to the system. 'The government appear to be waiting for some excuse to give up the present corn law. Let the people afford them the excuse they seek.'

A cabinet council was the consequence of this letter.

According to the view of the first minister, the letter of his rival had 'materially affected his position.' The policy which he proposed on the 1st of November, had it been adopted by his colleagues, would have appeared as the policy of a united cabinet acting under the sense of a great necessity. But an order for opening the ports on the 26th would seem but a servile adoption of the course recommended by the whig leader. Yet notwithstanding this disadvantage, Sir Robert Peel was not prepared to 'abandon the post of danger,' provided a united cabinet would support the policy which he now recommended; and that was an early summoning of parliament, for the purpose of proposing a virtual abrogation of the corn laws.

Strange to say, the same cabinet that on the 1st of the month had refused by a large majority to consent to an order in council for the suspension of a law, because they deemed that suspension might be a bar to its re-enactment, were now almost unanimously prepared to take even a stronger step, and that with a view to the virtual abrogation of the same law. Nor could this change be accounted for by any aggravation in the interval of the economic circumstances of the case. It was, confessedly by the highest authority, respecting 'the possibility of a great calamity,' and not the calamity itself, that they were deliberating; 'a calamity lighter than was at one time dreaded,' as Lord John Russell admitted on the meeting of parliament in January '46; and ultimately the expected evil never arrived in the season when it was awaited. Yet such was the inexplicable influence of the manifesto of the whig leader, that Lord Stanley, when he enforced the opinions which he had expressed at the beginning of the month, found himself with only one, and that one not a very vehement supporter.

The minister who submitted to be overruled at the beginning of the month was now dictating his measures with the menace of resignation. The situation was undoubtedly grave, and the disruption of the government at such a moment was not calculated to diminish the difficulties of the country. A united cabinet demands great efforts and deserves great sacrifices. Lord Stanley was prepared to make both. He felt deeply and painfully the prospect of separation from his colleagues; he felt more deeply and more painfully the awful responsibility which he found now was about to devolve singly on himself. The illustrious example of the Duke of Wellington was at hand. His grace had not changed his opinions. Yet for the sake of maintaining a united cabinet he was prepared to change his policy. Pressed on all hands, Lord Stanley requested eight-and-forty hours for his decision. It was therefore neither an intemperate nor a precipitate one. For two more days an anxious and impenetrable mystery involved the councils of the queen. At the end of them the ministers again met and received the decision of their scrupulous colleague. So forcibly did he feel the importance of unanimity in the cabinet, and so strongly was he convinced of the injury done by the breaking up of any government, that although entertaining serious doubts whether a suspension of the corn laws and the opening of the ports would be of avail, or might not even be injurious, he yielded his opinion, and was prepared to consent to that suspension provided suspension was alone intended. But when he was told that the temporary emergency of apprehended scarcity in Ireland was not to lead to a remedy commensurate in duration with the expected evil, but was to be made the groundwork of suspending, for the purpose of not re-enacting, the corn law, he felt that he could not take that course consistently with his own feelings as an honourable man; and that with such ulterior views, to propose to parliament to sanction the opening of the ports would be to lead those who were disposed to support the government into a snare. He said that he had tried to school himself into the belief that, under certain circumstances, the interests of the country might require even a sacrifice of personal and public character, but he had failed in bringing himself to so humiliating a conclusion. Upon this the government was broken up.

Here arises an interesting inquiry. In his subsequent
statements in parliament, Sir Robert Peel more than once
expressed his feeling that, whatever his conviction, he was
not the person who ought to propose a repeal of the corn
laws. When Sir Robert Inglis, in a tone of dignified reproach, regretted that the measure, if carried at all, was not
carried by those who for years had been its advocates, and
not by those who till the last three months had been all
along its opponents, Sir Robert Peel admitted the justice of
the comment, but vindicated himself on the ground that he
had himself so wished it, and had only failed from the
inability of the whigs to form a government. In his explanatory statement on the reassembling of parliament, Sir
Robert said that he had 'to choose between organising a
decided and interminable opposition to all change with
respect to the corn laws, and undertaking, if the noble lord
felt himself unable to undertake it, the foundation of final
legislation on the subject.' A strictly constitutional and
perfectly honourable proceeding. But if this be an accurate
description of the feelings and principles of the first minister,
how came he, a week before he gave the opportunity to
Lord John Russell, to attempt to induce his own cabinet to
carry the repeal? This inquiry was frequently urged by a
supporter of Lord George Bentinck during the important
and unexpectedly protracted debates to which the government proposition gave rise, and always occasioned great
embarrassment to the minister. Indeed, it was the only
point which he never contrived successfully to encounter,
though it was not from want of efforts. He himself more
than once recurred to it, for he was tenderly alive to the
necessity of parliamentary explanations in the long-run.
He seldom left a weak point in his public conduct without
a plausible vindication. In the present instance he once
even gave formal notice to the house that he was about to
explain this mysterious passage, though at the cost of reading a confidential minute of the cabinet. But the highly
interesting state paper left the knot unsolved, and there
appears to be only one solution left for the critical historian

—namely, that when Sir Robert Peel was of opinion that the corn laws must be repealed, he was resolved to be the repealer. Almost at the moment when he was about to be driven from office, in the middle of June '46, Sir Robert said: 'If it is asserted, that I wished to interfere in the settlement of this question by the noble lord opposite, that is the foulest calumny which the vindictive imagination of a political opponent ever dictated.' What was his wish to interfere in this manner which broke up his cabinet on the 6th of December 1845 ?

The whig leader seemed somewhat astonished at the result of his manifesto when he was sent for by the queen on the 8th of December. The summons found him still at Edinburgh, and he was not in the royal presence until the 11th. Eight days passed in somewhat hesitating attempts to form a cabinet by a chief who evidently had no confidence in the strength of his party either in parliament or in the country. A negotiation to obtain a pledge of support from Sir Robert Peel, though ingeniously managed, naturally failed. Lord John Russell felt that his position was premature. No doubt he sincerely regretted that the scruple of a solitary colleague should have deprived his rival of the glory and the odium of settling the question. Yet the country had been eight days without a government, and honour and public spirit seemed to require that the statesman should devote himself, however perilous the occasion. Lord John therefore, with becoming and characteristic resolution, determined to undertake the government without a parliamentary majority and with no enthusiasm out of doors, when suddenly he was relieved from almost overwhelming embarrassments by the scandal of an intrigue among his own friends against one of his projected secretaries of state. The intrigue was neither contrived with dexterity nor conducted with temper, but it extricated the whig leader from a false position. Availing himself with happy readiness of the distressing incident, he endured the mortification of confessing to his sovereign his inability to serve her, and handed back with courtesy the poisoned chalice to Sir Robert.

Thus was Sir Robert Peel appointed, for the third time, prime minister of England: and apparently confirmed in power with no prospect of his authority being successfully impugned. His position was so strong, that many, not without justice, deemed it impregnable. He had forced those of his colleagues who were still in favour of a protective system publicly to acknowledge that they were unable to carry on the government of the country on such principles, and, with one distinguished exception, even practically to embark in his new and contrary course, while at the same time he had committed the whigs to an absolute and unqualified adoption of the scheme of the Manchester confederation, a project odious to the great body of the parliament. All this too, while he reserved to himself the power of adopting that middle course which was ever congenial to him, and of devising some plan which, while it apparently doomed the protective principle, postponed its entire extinction, leaving a fragment for the chapter of accidents to deal with, and which, if destined ultimately to perish, might still in the interval occupy the speculation and perhaps enlist the sympathies of his former followers. Those among them, and it was supposed that they were not inconsiderable in numbers, who were anxious to maintain their allegiance to him unbroken, were furnished with a valid excuse for their fidelity by the fact ostentatiously circulated that his protesting colleagues had, when the opportunity was offered, shrunk from the responsibility of officially vindicating their opinions, while even the most deeply offended, they who at the first burst were keen and eager to strike and be avenged, were so irritated by the manifesto of the whig leader, that on reflection they were little disposed to reward Lord John Russell for his extreme movement by installing him in office on the ruins of his rival. And thus it happened that after all this tumult there was a fair prospect that the impending meeting of parliament would be a comparatively tranquil and uneventful one; if not serene, at least only sullen; the results anticipated, the conclusion foregone. This was the general conviction around all those hospitable hearths which at the season in question brighten throughout the land, where the prospects of the ensuing parliamentary campaign are freely canvassed, and form in this political country a source of diversion scarcely less interesting than the sports of the field and the festivities of the season. The resuscitated administration themselves were in high spirits: the foreign ministers wrote to their courts in a similar strain; and a witty diplomatist communicated to an illustrious personage the opinion of a member of the government, that 'it would only be a fat cattle opposition, and that the protectionists would be unable to keep up the debate for two nights.'

One man alone brooded in indignation over the unexampled scene, and he was one who from the little interest he had previously taken in political life could not have occurred to the government as a possible opponent. Lord George Bentinck had sat for eighteen years in parliament, and before he entered it had been for three years the private secretary of Mr. Canning, who had married the sister of the Duchess of Portland. Such a post would seem a happy commencement of a public career; but whether it were the untimely death of his distinguished relative or a natural indisposition, Lord George—though he retained the seat for King's Lynn, in which he had succeeded his uncle, the late governor-general of India — directed his energies to other than parliamentary pursuits. For some time he had followed his profession, which was that of arms, but of late years he had become absorbed in the pastime and fortunes of the turf, in which his whole being seemed engrossed, and which he pursued on a scale that perhaps has never been equalled.

Lord George had withdrawn his support from the government of the Duke of Wellington when the friends of Mr. Canning quitted that administration; and when in time they formed the not least considerable portion of the cabinet of Lord Grey he resumed his seat on the ministerial benches. On that occasion an administrative post was offered him and declined; and on subsequent occasions similar requests to him to take office were equally in vain. Lord George therefore was an original and hearty supporter of the reform bill, and he continued to uphold the whigs in all their policy until the secession of Lord Stanley, between whom and himself there subsisted warm personal as well as political sympathies. Although he was not only a friend to religious liberty, as we shall have occasion afterwards to remark, but always viewed with great sympathy the condition of the roman catholic portion of the Irish population, he shrank from the taint of the ultramontane intrigue. Accompanying Lord Stanley, he became in due time a member of the great conservative opposition, and as he never did anything by halves, became one of the most earnest, as he certainly was one of the most enlightened, supporters of Sir Robert Peel. His trust in that minister was indeed absolute, and he has subsequently stated in conversation that when, towards the end of the session of '45, a member of the tory party ventured to predict and denounce the impending defection of the minister, there was no member of the conservative party who more violently condemned the unfounded attack, or more readily impugned the motives of the assailant.

He was not a very frequent attendant of the house. He might be counted on for a party division, and when, towards the termination of the Melbourne ministry, the forces were very nearly balanced and the struggle became very close, he might have been observed on more than one occasion entering the house at a late hour, clad in a white greatcoat which softened, but did not conceal, the scarlet hunting-coat.

Although he took no part in debate, and attended the house rather as a club than a senate, he possessed a great and peculiar influence in it. He was viewed with interest and often with extraordinary regard by every sporting man in the house. With almost all of these he was acquainted; some of them, on either side, were his intimate companions and confederates.

His eager and energetic disposition; his quick perception, clear judgment, and prompt decision; the tenacity with which he clung to his opinions; his frankness and love of truth; his daring and speculative spirit; his lofty bearing, blended as it was with a simplicity of manner very remarkable; the ardour of his friendships, even the fierceness of his hates and prejudices; all combined to form one of those strong characters who, whatever may be their pursuit, must always direct and lead.

Nature had clothed this vehement spirit with a material form which was in perfect harmony with its noble and commanding character. He was tall, and remarkable for his presence; his countenance almost a model of manly beauty; the face oval, the complexion clear and mantling; the forehead lofty and white; the nose aquiline and delicately moulded; the upper lip short. But it was in the dark-brown eye that flashed with piercing scrutiny that all the character of the man came forth: a brilliant glance, not soft, but ardent, acute, imperious, incapable of deception or of being deceived.

Although he had not much sustained his literary culture, and of late years at any rate had not given his mind to political study, he had in the course of his life seen and heard a great deal, and with profit. Nothing escaped his observation; he forgot nothing and always thought. So it was that on all the great political questions of the day he had arrived at conclusions which guided him. He always took large views and had no prejudices about things, whatever he might indulge in as to persons. He was always singularly anxious to acquire the truth, and would spare no pains for that purpose; but when once his mind was made up, it was impossible to influence him.

In politics he was a whig of 1688, which became him, modified, however, by all the experience of the present age. He wished to see our society founded on a broad basis of civil and religious liberty. He retained much of the old jealousy of the court, but had none of popular franchises. He was for the established church, but for nothing more, and very repugnant to priestly domination. As for the industrial question, he was sincerely opposed to the Manchester scheme, because he thought that its full development would impair and might subvert our territorial constitution, which he held to be the real security of our freedom, and because he believed that it would greatly injure Ireland, and certainly dissolve our colonial empire.

He had a great respect for merchants, though he looked with some degree of jealousy on the development of our merely foreign trade. His knowledge of character qualified him in a great degree to govern men, and if some drawbacks from this influence might be experienced in his too rigid tenacity of opinion, and in some quickness of temper, which however always sprang from a too sensitive heart, great compensation might be found in the fact that there probably never was a human being so entirely devoid of conceit and so completely exempt from selfishness. Nothing delighted him more than to assist and advance others. All the fruits of his laborious investigations were always at the service of his friends without reserve or self-consideration. He encouraged them by making occasions for their exertions, and would relinquish his own opportunity without a moment's hesitation, if he thought the abandonment might aid a better man.

CHAPTER III

PARLIAMENT met on the 22nd January 1846. The session was opened by her majesty in person. The pivot of the royal speech was Ireland; its frequent assassinations, and the deficiency of its principal crop. Remedial measures in both respects were intimated, and in both respects these suggestions exercised the greatest influence on the proceedings of the session. A general eulogy of recent commercial legislation was followed by a vague recommendation to consider whether the advantageous principles on which it had been founded might not be more extensively applied.

The debate on the address in the upper house was extremely bald. Instead of receiving those explanations which are usual on the change or the reconstruction of a ministry, and which the frankness of our parliamentary government not only justifies but requires, the Duke of Richmond was met by a strange declaration from the Duke of Wellington, administered, to the astonishment of both sides of the house, by way of reproof, which, if it meant anything, meant that the government represented by the illustrious warrior had not received the accustomed permission of the sovereign to reveal circumstances which their oaths as privy councillors bound them without such sanction to keep secret. What made this more strange was that the prime minister in the lower house, followed by Lord John Russell, was at the very time entering into all the desired details, while Lord Lansdowne on the part of the whigs, and Lord Stanley on the part of his own 'personal consistency and honour,' felt bound to state, in the presence of the noble duke, that they had respectively solicited and received the permission of her majesty to make the accustomed statements, though in consequence of the singular and unexpected declaration of the Duke of Wellington, they of course felt it more decorous for the moment to be silent. No explanation was subsequently given of this remarkable incident, and the personal vindication of Lord Stanley which the whole country wished to receive was actually never made until the bill for the repeal of the corn laws reached the house of lords, four months afterwards.

In the lower house the scene was different. It was crowded, and a night of animated and protracted discussion was expected. Before the address was moved, notice was given by Sir Robert Peel of the intention of the government on the earliest possible day to submit to the consideration of the house measures connected with the commercial and financial affairs of the country. The address was to be moved by Lord Francis Egerton, the member for South Lancashire, and to be seconded by Mr. Beckett Denison, the member for the West Riding. This was well arranged. It was originally projected that this latter post should have been occupied by Mr. Stuart Wortley, the eldest son of the lord president, but the death of that nobleman, precipitated, if not occasioned, by the agitation of the crisis, had deprived his heir of the fulfilment of a duty which would have been still more significant in his hands than in those of his colleague. Mr. Beckett Denison was only the victorious champion of protection in the West Riding over the accomplished Lord Morpeth; but for Mr. Stuart Wortley had been reserved the high distinction of proposing in the newly elected parliament of 1841 the declaration of want of confidence in a government which presumed to mitigate a tariff.

Twenty years had elapsed since Lord Francis Egerton had moved the address in answer to the speech under the auspices of Mr. Canning. He may be said to have concluded his career in the house of commons by the same ceremony with which it had commenced. Yet for him the interval had not been without distinction, and in the present instance he brought to the performance of a difficult duty a character and a position which sustained each other, and unquestionably gave aid and authority to the government. Lord Francis was never a commonplace speaker, and on this occasion he travelled out of the routine with judgment and taste. Disdaining the usual but legitimate plea, that, in responding to the invitation of the crown to consider particular laws, he was not bound to approve the measures which might subsequently be proposed by the minister, he at once entered into the whole question and candidly announced to the house his conversion to the principles of the Manchester confederation. 'Accident,' he said, 'had cast his lot in the midst of a dense population, with respect to a large portion of which the same accident had made him a distributor of work and wages; and he had seen the operation of what he believed to be the connection between the prices of provisions and the happiness and employment of the people in various conditions.' But the same 'accident,' we believe, had placed the noble lord in a similar position previous to the attempt to reform the tariff by the whigs in 1841, and he had possessed the mournful opportunity of witnessing the same phenomena when the industrious districts which he represented and in which he resided were paralysed by the commercial derangements of the United States. Lord Francis, however, made a graceful apology for a somewhat graceless line of conduct. It was evident that he was cognisant of the government scheme. Mr. Beckett Denison, however, professed his absolute ignorance of it; a declaration which was received with some derision at the time, but the truth of which was demonstrated by the ingenuous indignation with which he subsequently denounced the project when the house became aware of its nature. The government, however, gained on this important night the apparent authority of the West Riding.

Great speculation was afloat as to the course of debate when on the conclusion of the speech of the seconder the

question should be put by Mr. Speaker. Would the Manchester confederation advance to seal their triumph or
demand more specific details of the ministerial policy?
Would the whigs at once, by the mouth of their leader,
give to the house the reasons why they had not succeeded
in forming a government when summoned by their
sovereign, or would some eminent and 'large-acred' member of their connection publicly announce the adhesion
of their party to the spontaneous and startling manifesto
of Lord John Russell? What would the tory country
gentlemen do? What the great bulk of the still huge
conservative party—the shipping members, the sugar members, the home-trade town members? Would the converts
be silent? Would they prudently rest content with the
elegant excuses of Lord Francis, or come forward like men,
and bear their share of the awful brunt?

A practised observer of debate would have anticipated
the first move from the country party, for the silence of
Manchester rather assisted the minister who was playing
their game, and reserve seemed the natural course of the
whigs until ministerial explanations required an opposition
revelation as a rejoinder. But the country party, although
they possessed in the members for Somersetshire, and
Dorsetshire, and Lincolnshire, and several others, gentlemen of high standing in the house, and fully capable to
represent the opinions of their friends, were entirely without concert and discipline. The great portion indeed had
only just arrived from their counties, where they had
remained to the last moment, reluctantly rejoining a scene
which, after what had occurred during the recess, could only
bring to them mortification; where they could only witness
the triumph of bitter antagonists and be placed in painful
collision with men whom they personally regarded; who in
private life were their companions, and whose establishment
in power and public authority had been the labour and
pride of their lives.

Many of these gentlemen were members of the protection
society over which presided the Duke of Richmond, a

society doubtless favourable to counsel and combination. But the ministerial crisis having occurred at a season of the year when its members were dispersed, no effective gathering of this association had been possible, and most of its parliamentary members met for the first time since those remarkable events on the floor of the house of commons. The name of Lord George Bentinck was not even enrolled in this society: with the exception of some of his intimates at a country-house, he had communicated to no one his intention of resisting the government schemes. He too had only just arrived in town, and sat below the gangway at the head of the third bench, with a stern look and a glittering eye, watching the treasury bench as an eagle would his quarry.

Mr. Speaker read the address, which was an echo of the speech, amid the buzz of general conversation. This ceremony occupied some minutes. Suddenly, as he closed it, there was a dead silence, followed by the rustling of attention. Every one ceased in the midst of the sentence he was uttering: the first minister had risen.

The speech was not distinguished by that clear conception, that lucid arrangement, and that prudential management, which were characteristic of the general style of Sir Robert Peel. On the contrary, although the occasion was critical and long awaited, the statement, though elaborate, was confused, and in some parts even contradictory. He acknowledged at once he was taking an unusual course in availing himself of the very earliest opportunity of giving that explanation which at no remote period the house would require of him. He would fain hope that it would not obstruct the course of the discussion on the address. But if no consideration of public advantage could justify him in taking this course, he was sure that the generous feelings of the house would deem his desire natural. He did not conceal that he felt much hurt at having been accused on vague surmise and having been condemned without a hearing: strange expressions, which for a moment imparted a ray of hope to some credulous bosoms among his former

supporters. But when he proceeded to a promised detail of
the circumstances which had led to the resignation of the
government, and acknowledged that, although the failure of
the potato crop was the immediate and proximate cause of
that event, it would be unfair and uncandid in him to attach
undue importance to that particular cause, for, in homage to
the progress of reason and of truth, he would not deny that
his opinions on the subject of protection had changed—they
began to ask themselves what vague surmise could be more
horrible than the reality, and why he should wish to be
heard previous to condemnation, when his vindication was
an aggravated avowal of the offence of which he was
accused.

He said, having given on the earliest day on which it was
possible notice of his intention to submit to the consideration
of the house measures connected with the commercial and
financial affairs of the country, his firm determination on
this occasion was not to anticipate discussion; his desire
was to disconnect a great political question from a mere
personal and party one; to keep the personal matters
distinct from the great question itself.   Yet with this desire,
and this 'firm determination,' he entered into a lengthened,
not to say wearisome, discussion, replete with figures, of the
effect of the tariff alterations of the last four years.   Not
content with this, soaring in a manner very unusual with
him to the highest region of abstraction, he speculated
whether the *a priori* presumption were in favour of the
principle of protection or of unrestricted import.   He
gravely demonstrated to his still astonished followers that
'the natural presumption is in favour of unrestricted importation.'   He even discussed whether the rate of wages varied
with the price of food, and whether a large debt and heavy
taxation are best encountered by abundance and cheapness
of provisions.   With a 'firm determination not to anticipate
discussion,' he proceeded to an inquiry whether employment,
low prices, and abundance contribute to the diminution of
crime.   He could no longer resist the inference that they
did.   As if any human being ever resisted the inference, or

ever drew an opposite conclusion. Finally, this eulogium of the effect of low prices was consistently closed by a variety of details, proving that the consequence of all preceding reductions of the tariff had been very greatly to increase the prices of all articles thereby affected.

All this time the house was on the tenters for the promised detail of the circumstances which had led to the resignation of the government; they wanted the 'personal matters' to which they had been informed this night was to be devoted by one who was 'desirous to keep the party question distinct from the great political question itself,' for which the earliest possible day was reserved. Instead of that, the bewildered house was listening once more to lucid narratives of the price of flax and wool, previous and subsequent to recent changes in the customs, some dissertation on domestic lard, the contract price for salt beef for the navy, and the importation of foreign cattle. It was, after all, 'a fat cattle debate' again, and the audience almost began to believe, seeing Sir Robert once more at his red box and Lord John looking as disconsolate as usual opposite to him, that the huge vagaries of December were but a hideous dream, and that instead of defection and perfidy, the great conservative party were only going through that gradual process of decomposition and destruction to which, for the last four or five years, they had been accustomed, and which, judging from their demeanour, it would seem they rather liked.

Some fine judges have recognised in all this only the artifice of a consummate master of the house of commons, lowering the tone of an excited assembly by habitual details, and almost proving by his accustomed manner of addressing them that after all he could have done nothing very extraordinary. When a senate after a long interval and the occurrence of startling transactions assembles, if not to impeach, at least to denounce, a minister, and then are gravely anointed with domestic lard, and invited to a speculation on the price of salt pork, an air of littleness is irresistibly infused into the affair from which it seems hopeless to extricate the occasion.

But now the great speaker again approached the promised explanations, and there was a renewed rustling of renovated attention. He commenced by stating that there were two important periods, in giving this explanation, to which he must draw attention : first, the period which elapsed between the 1st of November 1845 and the 6th of that month; secondly, the period which elapsed between the 25th of November and the 6th of December. And then, professing to adduce the evidence on which the conduct of the government was founded, he commenced a series of extracts of correspondence, from ambassadors and lords-lieutenant, from consuls and chairmen of excise, from anonymous salesmen in London, unknown chaplains to houses of correction, and secretaries of Irish agricultural societies; all read without the slightest discrimination between the two periods so specifically separated, and which, as bearing on the contrary opinion of the cabinet at the different periods, was of vital importance, yet all so mixed up together, so minute in detail, and so various in the sources, ranging from Alexandria to Riga and from Riga to Dublin, that it was quite impossible for those who followed him most attentively in the debate to ascertain what were the materials of judgment from the 1st to the 6th November, and what the new revelations which awaited the reassembling of the 26th.

Just at the moment when the house seemed most exhausted, after a long extract from the report of Professor Lindley and Doctor Playfair, the minister slid into an avowed narrative of the cabinet councils of November and all their consequences ; yet still the two periods of November were so blended together, that no one could clearly discriminate between the occurrences of the 6th and the transactions of the later period ; whether, for example, his protesting colleagues had offered conditionally to consent to the opening of the ports on the first occasion, and whether, that condition being the due revival of the corn law, the first minister had declined to engage himself to that extent. Nevertheless, the statement being full of personal details, the house, though perplexed, listened with interest, which heightened to excitement as the minister approached with evident emotion the concluding part of his observations.

Having stated at the commencement of his speech that 'the recollection of great indulgence and great confidence had effaced his temporary feelings of irritation at being unjustly condemned,' he recurred to the imputations to which he had before referred, but no longer with that air of mournfulness, almost humility, which had characterised his opening. Although he had then declared that he should make no allusions to particular expressions or particular accusations, he suddenly broke into a fierce reply to the statement of the Duke of Richmond, still ringing in the ears of the country, that the party which had elevated him to his present position was powerful enough also to displace him. Turning round with great scorn to his former supporters and with an expression of almost malignant haughtiness, he exclaimed, 'I see constantly put forth allusions to the power of those men to remove me from office.' He should therefore define the relation in which he conceived himself to stand with respect to party and to his sovereign. But dilating on the latter point with considerable feeling, and full perhaps of an important subject which he was fast approaching, he entirely forgot the former and on this occasion far more interesting topic. He concluded by a vindication of what he held to be true conservative policy in his best style; earnest without being solemn, and masculine without turgidity. Yet the well-considered conclusion contained a somewhat portentous confession for a conservative minister of England—that 'it was no easy task to ensure the united action of an ancient monarchy, a proud aristocracy, and a reformed house of commons.'

The first minister was naturally followed by his rival with the authentic statement of whig disasters. We have already referred to some of its remarkable passages, and much of its interest had been necessarily anticipated by the narrative of the first lord of the treasury. The statement was not brief, and the exposition of failures is never very animating. It necessarily comprised the reading of several documents. When the noble lord concluded, the house, which during the evening had rarely been excited, was tame and dispirited. There had been a general understanding that the great question was not to be entered into on this occasion, and men are not disposed to embark in discussion under such circumstances unless supported by a disciplined following. It seemed that the curtain was about to fall, and certainly not to the disadvantage of the government. In their position the first night of the session passed in serenity was comparatively a triumph. With the elements of opposition, however considerable, so inert and desponding, the first night might give the cue to the country. Perceiving this, a member, who, though on the tory benches, had been for two sessions in opposition to the ministry, ventured to rise and attack the minister. The opportune in a popular assembly has sometimes more success than the weightiest efforts of research and reason. The minister, perhaps too contemptuous of his opponents, had not guarded all his approaches. His depreciation of those party ties by which he had risen, in an assembly too in which they are wisely reverenced ; his somewhat ostentatious gratitude for the favour of successive sovereigns ; his incautious boast that his conservative government had discouraged sedition and extinguished agitation, when it was universally felt that he was about to legislate on the most important of subjects in deference to agitation ; and, above all, his significant intimation that an ancient monarchy and a proud aristocracy might not be compatible with a reformed house of commons —at least, unless he were minister—offered some materials in the handling of which the least adroit could scarcely fail. But it was the long-constrained passion of the house that now found a vent far more than the sallies of the speaker that changed the frigid silence of this senate into excitement and tumult.

CHAPTER IV

THE houses presented their addresses to her majesty on Saturday (24th of January), and on that day a rumour was afloat, or rather it might be said a statement was circulated, of so remarkable a character and so high an authority, that it at once arrested some efforts that were then in contemplation among the principal country gentlemen to organise an opposition or to test the possibility, to use the language of that day, of forming a third party, an achievement hitherto deemed by those learned in parliamentary life as essentially impossible. No less a personage than the Duke of Wellington had stated to one of the most distinguished tory members, that though the proposition of the minister to be made on the 27th certainly involved some material alteration in the corn laws, yet that at the same time it would confer such great advantages on the landed interest, that his grace felt convinced that it would prove perfectly satisfactory to all the former followers of the government; and that, when once it was made known, no one would again talk of his having betrayed his friends. This statement, made with much emphasis and scrupulously repeated, produced a considerable sensation, and the next two or three days were spent in speculations on the possible character of these mysterious and compensatory arrangements. The effect of this statement was as we have mentioned, to suspend any attempt to organise an opposition against the government. All agreed to wait until Tuesday before they decided, and many, one might say most, hoped that the exposition of the first minister would save them from a painful and mortifying struggle.

These hopes were confirmed by an extraordinary scene

which occurred in the house of lords on the following Monday (January 26), when the Duke of Richmond inquired of the Duke of Wellington, whether his grace had yet received her majesty's permission to state the reasons which induced the government to resign, and afterwards to resume, office. The Duke of Wellington answered in the affirmative with great promptness, and proceeded at once with a narrative of the transactions and opinions in question, characterised by all that condensed and idiomatic phraseology which often confers a peculiar interest to his public statements. According to his grace, he was one of those who gave a very decided resistance to the proposal of the first minister to open the ports at the beginning of November. 'I was one of those who considered that it was a measure which was not necessary to be adopted at that time.' He thought the means heretofore adopted to meet similar evils amply sufficient; and that if, under the existing corn law, it was desirable that the ports should be opened, the law itself had provided for such an emergency. In the first week of November there was an 'insinuation' that the suspension of the corn law might render the renewal of it at a future period very difficult; 'undoubtedly it was intimated that it might be necessary to make an essential alteration in the law.' But when the cabinet met at the end of November, the possible necessity of the first minister had become, in the opinion of that personage, an absolute necessity—'an absolute necessity of making an essential alteration in the corn laws.' This led to a strong difference of opinion on the subject: 'As for my part,' continued his grace, amid the sympathising glances of the surrounding peers, 'I certainly was of opinion that it was not desirable to make any essential alteration in the present corn law.'

Having arrived at this point, his grace proceeded to express the views which he entertained of his duty to the crown; and it would have seemed, that because 'he had served the crown for above fifty years in high public situations,' he considered himself exempt from the ordinary rules which regulate political life in this country, and that his fulfilment of duty was to be different from that of any other member of parliament. His grace appeared to be of opinion that neither fidelity to party nor even a conviction of right ought to be permitted to stand for a moment in his way when the assumed convenience of the crown was concerned: sentiments that have certainly never been sanctioned by the present sovereign of England, and which would appear to be more becoming in the mouth of some professional courtier than of one who had been the keen leader of a great parliamentary party, and who by their confidence and co-operation had achieved the long-contrived object of his ambition, the premiership of England. On a subsequent and even more memorable occasion in these debates his grace spoke on this head in language still less equivocal, and we will reserve until then any remarks on the propriety and policy of such a tone.

It would seem that, notwithstanding the strong opinions of his grace, the duke was prepared to adopt the propositions of Sir Robert Peel at the end of November which he had successfully resisted at the commencement of that month, and used his influence with his colleagues for that purpose. He 'considered it his duty to make every effort to maintain union in the cabinet, as the best service he could render his sovereign.' He was, nevertheless, 'unfortunate in these efforts'; and when it became a question whether Sir Robert Peel should come down to parliament, and make a proposition for the alteration of the corn laws, 'with a divided cabinet, of which the majority were against the proposition,' or resign, his grace counselled resignation.

His grace was in the country when he received a letter from Sir Robert Peel announcing that the queen had again sent for his late colleague, that her majesty had desired him to resume his post, and that Sir Robert had determined, happen what might, even if he stood alone as minister of the crown, that he would enable her majesty to meet her parliament. 'This being the resolution of my right honourable friend,' continued his grace, 'I highly applauded his decision, and I determined that I for one would stand by him.

I felt it my duty. I was of opinion that the formation of a government in which her majesty would have confidence was of much greater importance than the opinions of any individual on the corn law, or any other law.' For the sake of clearness, we may here state that his grace concluded his speech this evening by the following words: 'Upon that ground, my lords, I present myself to your lordships, and I claim from you an acquiescence in the principle I have laid down, that I positively could not refuse to serve my sovereign when thus called upon.' The principle laid down by his grace may be an excellent principle, but it is not a principle of the English constitution. To be prepared to serve a sovereign without any reference to the policy to be pursued, or even in violation of the convictions of the servant, is not the duty of the subject of a monarchy modified in its operation by the co-ordinate authority of estates of the realm. It is a direct violation of the parliamentary constitution of England, and is a principle which can only be practically carried into effect in the cabinets of absolute monarchs.

The friends of the Duke of Wellington explained these strange passages by the circumstance that it was distinctly made known by Sir Robert Peel to his grace, that if they did not undertake the conduct of the government, her majesty would be under the necessity of sending for Mr. Cobden and his friends. It was to prevent this inexpiable degradation that the Duke of Wellington was prepared to carry on the government, without any regard to the character of the measures of the cabinet. Yet it is difficult to comprehend what constitutional or what moral objection could be urged against the ministerial capacity of a member of the house of commons whom the chief minister himself, a few months later, in terms of unusual and unparliamentary panegyric, hailed, by name, as the superior to himself and his noble rival, both in political prescience and oratorical accomplishment.

Before, however, the duke terminated his speech by this singular declaration, he had entered into all that encouraging intimation of the nature of the impending scheme which had already by his conversation out of the house imparted some solace to the disheartened protectionists. The nation learnt to-night from the highest authority that the proposition would be one satisfactory not only to the public in general, but to the former followers of Sir Robert Peel in particular: 'It contemplated for the landed interest such advantages as the landed interest had a right to expect. When laid on the table, no one would then assert that the first minister had betrayed his duty.' These weighty declarations from a leading minister who frankly avowed his disapprobation of any essential change in the corn laws, followed by an unequivocal announcement from no less a personage than Lord Lansdowne, that his opinion in favour of a fixed duty was unchanged, and that he himself only consented to entire abolition of all interference with the corn trade 'on condition that it should be accompanied with the removal or alteration of every burden bearing on the landed interest,' began to make even the free-traders believe that after all Sir Robert was about to propose some marvellous combination, which, while it removed every restriction from the trade in corn, at the same time would place the English producer in an equivalent position with that favoured one which he was about to forfeit. After all the agitation, denunciation, and despair, there were yet hope and lingering faith in the ranks of the country party on Monday night.

The proceedings of the next day in the house of commons were ushered in by a startling occurrence. His royal highness the prince consort, attended by the master of the horse, appeared and took his seat in the body of the house, to listen to the statement of the first minister. Many moderate men on both sides were disquieted by this incident, which seemed unconstitutionally to control the cherished freedom of parliament. Although no minister can introduce a measure into either house without the consent of the crown, such consent is only given in the first instance in the executive capacity of the sovereign. It implies no absolute approbation of the measure, but merely signifies the royal pleasure that the two other branches of the legislature should consult upon the merits of the case. As a branch of the legislature whose decision is final, and therefore last solicited, the opinion of the sovereign remains unshackled and uncompromised until the assent of both houses has been received. Nor is this veto of the English monarch an empty form. It is not difficult to conceive the occasion, when, supported by the sympathies of a loyal people, its exercise might defeat an unconstitutional ministry and a corrupt parliament.

Lord George Bentinck was greatly disturbed by what he conceived to be the unfair and the unwise manœuvre of the minister, to give the semblance of the personal sanction of her majesty to a measure which, whatever its result, a large portion, perhaps a majority, of her subjects deemed fraught with ruin to their interests; and at one moment he was about to appeal to the speaker on the subject. But he was dissuaded from a course which would have been extremely painful by a temperate suggestion from a friend that there might be precedents for the unusual proceeding. With those precedents, however, he was never furnished, and with that tenacity of purpose which characterised him, he seized a subsequent opportunity, when he delivered his opinions on the ministerial project, to animadvert on this step, but in a tone of high-bred dignity and noble freedom.

The speech of the minister was eminently characteristic. While the agitated agriculture of the united kingdom awaited with breathless suspense the formal notification of its doom, wondering by what cunning arguments the policy of its betrayer could be palliated and by what dexterous devices its inevitable consequences might be softened, the minister addressed and pursued at considerable length to the wondering assembly an elaborate and argumentative statement, the object of which was to reconcile the manufacturers to the deprival of protection. Reminding them how much had of late been done for them, how the duty had been taken off all the raw materials which constituted the immediate fabric of their productions; how the opulent classes had subjected themselves to the imposition of an income-tax out of consideration for the permanent prosperity of our manufactures, and principally that it might take off the duty on cotton-wool; he had resolved to call upon the manufacturers of the three great articles which enter into consumption as the clothing of the great body of the community, to consent to relax the protection at present enjoyed. Considering that this protection of 10 per cent. was notoriously and confessedly merely nominal, the sacrifice did not appear to be too severe, yet the orator seemed scarcely sanguine of inducing his audience to consent to it, and to mitigate the loss retained a considerable protection to the smaller interests with which they were connected. With imperturbable gravity the minister read to the house the passage of Adam Smith in which that eminent writer acknowledges that 'country gentlemen and farmers are, to their great honour, of all people the least subject to the wretched spirit of monopoly,' and fixing, with a sort of mournful reprobation, the manufacturers as the originators of the protective system in this country, the speaker declared, amid the titter of the free-traders, which, however, was solemnly reproved, 'that it was but justice that they should set the example of relinquishing it.'

A considerable time elapsed, however, before the minister seemed to be satisfied that he had persuaded the house that Manchester, Leeds, and Belfast might contrive successfully to compete with foreigners in the manufacture of their coarser fabrics. He then approached the consideration of their finer articles with undisguised anxiety, and left them a not contemptible protection. He was still more tender of the interests of the silk manufacturer, though severer on the native industry of the paperhanger and the coachmaker, against whose high charges he delivered himself of an invective with which even the country gentlemen appeared to sympathise. Still the great subject did not even loom in the distance; and when, after a slight pause, the minister, in a tone of some solemnity, said, ' I now approach——' there was a murmur of hushed attention, followed when he concluded the sentence, 'the manufactures connected with metals,' by a laugh of indignant derision, which, with that thorough knowledge of his auditory that no one has yet equalled, he took care to mistake for impatience at his business-like details, on the absolute necessity of which he deferentially dilated, and obtained an assenting cheer from the opposite benches.

But no inability to endure the dread suspense on the part of his former adherents effected the slightest alteration in the tactics which the consummate master had arranged. He had resolved that a considerable time should elapse before they learnt their doom, and that a due impression should be conveyed to the house and the country, not the less effective because from the minuteness of the details it was somewhat perplexing, that on this night of sacrifices the agricultural classes were not the only victims. And in this he succeeded so well, that even to this day controversies are continually arising as to the nature and degree of protection still retained and enjoyed by the staple manufactures of the country.

This remarkable man, who in private life was constrained and often awkward, who could never address a public meeting or make an after-dinner speech without being ill at ease, and generally saying something stilted or even a little ridiculous, in the senate was the readiest, easiest, most flexible and adroit of men. He played upon the house of commons as on an old fiddle. And to-night, the manner in which he proceeded to deal with the duties on candles and soap, while all were thinking of the duties on something else; the bland and conciliatory air with which he announced a reduction of the impost on boot-fronts and shoe leather; the intrepid plausibility with which he entered into a dissertation on the duties of foreign brandy and foreign sugar; while visions of deserted villages and reduced rentals were torturing his neighbours, were all characteristic of his command over himself and those whom he addressed.

At length the agricultural interest, having been apprised how much they would gain by the reduction of the duties on seeds, especially clover seed, and how advantageously they might fatten cattle by the introduction of Indian corn, duty free—'I believe it is impossible to overestimate the importance of promoting the fattening of cattle'—were deemed to be prepared to listen to their fate—to hear that all foreign cattle were in future to be admitted duty free, though of course very few were expected to arrive, that there was to be a partial remission of the duties on butter, cheese, and hops, and a total and immediate repeal of the duties on fresh and salted beef. And then solemnly adjuring his former followers to remember that he had already proposed the removal of protection from those great and important articles of manufacture that are closely connected with the land; trusting that they would bear in mind that he had called upon the manufacturing interest first to set the example of relinquishing protective duties; that farm-servants, and those over whom they presided, would thus be enabled to command a greater supply of clothing at a lower rate than heretofore; though it was notorious that there was no foreign competition with the British manufacturer, and therefore these results were impossible; he announced to them his project of a total repeal of the corn laws. But then, though total, it was not to be immediate. Three years were to elapse before the ports were to be really open. 'The next question to be considered is this, what shall be the intermediate state of the law during the continuance of these duties?' Certainly the next question, and after a statement which had already lasted more than two hours, it was hardly unreasonable to expect that the information should be promptly given.

The house was anxious and restless, even the free-traders looked grave, for there had been some expressions during the last few minutes of an equivocal, not to say alarming, character. But the speaker himself showed no anxiety to approach the catastrophe. He seemed hardly yet to have made up his own mind on the subject. He looked at the opposition with respectful deference, and then to his former adherents almost with a glance of lingering kindness. After a number of ingenious and desultory comments he recurred to the theme: ' What, then, I repeat, shall be the nature of the law which is to endure for a limited period? My colleagues and myself have approached this question wholly unprejudiced, and with no other object in view than the general advancement and prosperity of the country.' But a quarter of an hour elapsed before the house learnt that, even in this last agony of agricultural protection, there was still to be a sliding-scale which at the average price of 53s. per quarter was to yield a 4s. duty.

Before the murmur which immediately sounded at this announcement could spread, the house was again chained with an attentive ear to the measures, ' not of compensation, but calculated materially to advance the interests of the land,' with which it was proposed to accompany ' this great present reduction and ultimate extinction of protection.' The mysterious promises of the Duke of Wellington were now about to be fulfilled. To be brief, the absolute remission of taxation promised by the scheme amounted exactly to that which the agricultural members had only during the preceding session, while in the enjoyment of protection, claimed as a right from a minister who had to distribute relief from the surplus of the exchequer, viz. that the government, already liable to one-half the expense of the maintenance of prisoners under sentence of felony and misdemeanour, and of the cost of prosecutions—an expenditure incurred for the general advantage of the community—should now relieve the counties of their peculiar burthen of the other moiety, and allow them merely to pay their due share of it proportionately with the other contributors to the consolidated fund. The whole of this remission, under any circumstances just, including some items too insignificant to dwell upon, did not amount to two hundred and fifty thousand pounds per annum. As far as Ireland was concerned, and ' if there were to be any part of the united kingdom which was to suffer by the withdrawal of protection,' the minister ' had always felt that it would be Ireland,' a remission of local taxation similar in amount and character was proffered by the payment on the part of the consolidated fund of the remaining moiety of the police rate, an arrangement which, from placing the police force directly and completely under their control, was admitted by the minister to be an 'immense advantage' to the government of the day, and which had already been recommended by the commission over which Lord Devon presided.

But if some disappointment might be experienced from the nature and amount of the mere fiscal relief proposed, there were other measures on which the minister dwelt with far more parade, and which he introduced as 'calculated, in his firm belief, materially to advance the interests of the classes connected with the land'—and these important measures were in number three. The first was a compulsory consolidation of the highway trusts, but not a transfer of the burthen to the general revenue of the country; the second was an alteration in the law of settlement, which subsequently appeared only in the shape of an alteration of the law of removal; the third was an advance of public money to persons applying for assistance to drain their estates. These advances were to be made, provided the security were unimpeachable; provided the expense of the preliminary survey were at the cost of the applicant; provided the loan were a prior charge on the land; and provided arrangements were made not only for payment of the interest, but of the principal by small annual instalments. The policy of the state advancing money at all for such purposes is very questionable, but on the terms quoted the favour to the borrower would seem scarcely less doubtful. It is hardly to be believed that on such conditions lenders would ever be wanting. So much for one of the great remedial measures. The alteration in the law of settlement was so ill-conceived, that it aggravated the sufferings which it aimed to alleviate, and was virtually repealed in the following session. The projected consolidation of the highways never took place.

No degree of rhetorical skill could invest with any semblance of substance these shadowy schemes of compensation. A feeling of blank disappointment or renewed indignation seemed to pervade the whole conservative benches. Men whose habits made them familiar with the subjects of projected legislation felt that the limited relief from local taxation was only the fulfilment of an arrangement which had long ago commenced, the completion of a principle already conceded, and at any rate the grant of a boon which under any circumstances could not have been long delayed; while, when they reflected on the more ostentatious proposals, they perceived that they were not the well-digested schemes of one familiar with the details of rural life and legislation, and that they must prove either impracticable or insignificant.

It was agreed that a fortnight should elapse before the introduction of the government measures, in order that the country might become acquainted with their whole scope and bearing. Although therefore several gentlemen indulged in desultory observations until a late hour, any formal discussion was avoided. The only remarkable circumstance was the first rising of Lord George Bentinck. It was to make a brief but pregnant inquiry, and he was observed with great interest. He said that the minister was well aware that the average price of wheat, for the last seven years, was 58s. 8d., and presuming that the measures of the government would reduce the price of wheat to 45s. per quarter, it would require fully seven years, for the averages on which tithe was to be paid, to work it down to the 45s.: therefore, for a period of seven years, the agricultural interests of the country would be paying tithes on the 58s. 8d. He wished to know, therefore, whether the minister was prepared to propose any measure which would effectuate an equitable payment of tithes, in the event of 45s. being the price of the quarter of wheat, instead of 58s. 8d.

Sir Robert Peel replied that he did not propose to make any alteration in the law as to tithes, as he did not believe there would be any material alteration in the price of wheat.

CHAPTER V

THE rising desire to organise some opposition to the government measures which had been arrested by the speech of the Duke of Wellington revived among the country party with increased force after the mortifying miscarriage of their expectations. But an opposition without leaders, without organisation, without any party discipline, presented no very terrible appearance, and promised no very considerable consequences. Men who feel, however, will act. The greater their disadvantages, the more lively was their sense of the injury which they had experienced in being thus suddenly deserted by those who had been the cherished champions of their cause, and the more resolute became their determination to struggle with their difficult fortunes.

There was at that time a metropolitan society for the protection of agriculture of which the Duke of Richmond was chairman, and which had been established to counteract the proceedings of the Manchester confederation. It was in communication with the local protection societies throughout the country; and although the adhesion to its service by the parliamentary members of the old conservative party had been more limited than might have been expected, nevertheless many county members were enrolled in its ranks, and a few of the most eminent were actively engaged in its management. In this they were assisted by an equal number of the most considerable tenant-farmers. In the present state of affairs, the council of the protection society afforded the earliest and readiest means to collect opinion and methodise action, and it was therefore resolved among its managers to invite all members of parliament who sympathised with their purpose, though they might not be members of their society, to attend their meeting and aid them at the present crisis with their counsel.

A compliance with this request occasioned the first public appearance of Lord George Bentinck as one of the organisers of a political party; for he aspired to no more. The question was, whether a third political party could be created and sustained; a result at all times and under any circumstances difficult to achieve, and which had failed even under the auspices of accomplished and experienced statesmen. In the present emergency, was there that degree of outraged public feeling in the country which would over-come all obstacles and submit to any inconveniences in order to ensure its representation in the house of commons? It was the opinion of Lord George Bentinck that such was the case; that if for the moment that feeling was inert and latent, it was an apathy which arose from the sudden shock of public confidence, and the despair which under such circumstances takes possession of men; that if it could be shown to the country that the great bulk of the conservative party were true to their faith, and were not afraid, even against the fearful odds which they would have to encounter, to proclaim it, the confidence and the courage of the country would rally, and the party in the house of commons would find external sympathy and support.

With these views it became of paramount importance that the discussion on the government measure should be sustained on the part of the protectionists with their utmost powers. They must prove to the country that they could represent their cause in debate, and to this end all their energies must be directed. It would be fatal to them if the discussion were confined to one or two nights, and they overborne by the leading and habitual speakers. They must bring forward new men; they must encourage the efforts of those now unrecognised and comparatively unknown; they must overcome all reserve and false shame, and act as became men called upon to a critical and leading part, not by their arrogance or ambition, but by the desertion and treachery of those to whose abilities they had bowed without impatience and reluctance.   There was a probability of several vacancies immediately taking place in counties where the seats were filled by converts, but men of too scrupulous an honour to retain the charge which they had sought and accepted as the professors of opinions contrary to those which now received their mournful adhesion.   The result of these elections would greatly depend upon the spirit and figure of the party in the house of commons in their first encounter with the enemy.

These views, so just and so spirited, advanced with high-bred earnestness by one rarely met in political turmoils, and enforced with a freshness and an affable simplicity which were very winning, wonderfully encouraged those to whom they were addressed.   All seemed touched by the flame which burnt in the breast of that man, so lofty in his thoughts but so humble in his ambition, who counselled ever the highest deeds and was himself ever prepared to undertake the humblest duties.

The business of this day was notable.   Calculations were made of those who might be fairly counted on to take a part in debate; some discussion even ensued as to who' should venture to reply late at night to the minister; a committee was appointed to communicate with all members on either side supposed to be favourable to the principle of protection to the labour of the country; a parliamentary staff was organised, not only to secure the attendance of members but to guard over the elections; finally, the form of the amendment to the government measure was discussed and settled, and it was agreed that if possible it should be moved by Mr. Philip Miles, the member for the city of Bristol, and who had the ear of the house not merely from the importance of his constituency, and seconded by Sir William Heathcote, the member for the county of Hampshire, a country gentleman of great accomplishments, and so highly considered by both sides that he was very generally spoken of as a probable successor to the chair.

All was furnished by this lately forlorn party except a

leader, and even then many eyes were turned and some hopeful murmurs addressed towards Lord George Bentinck, who in the course of this morning had given such various proofs of his fitness and such evidence of his resource. But he shook his head with a sort of suppressed smile, a faint blush, and an air of proud humility that was natural to him: 'I think,' he said, 'we have had enough of leaders; it is not in my way; I shall remain the last of the rank and file.'

During the interval between the statement of the minister and the commencement of the great engagement, Lord Ashley and his colleague, Mr. Strutt, vacated their seats for the county of Dorset; Mr. Charteris, the member for Gloucestershire, in deference to the remonstrance of his constituents, accepted the Chiltern hundreds; while the county of Nottingham, the native county of the Bentincks, was vacated by Lord Lincoln, a member of the cabinet, who had been promoted from the woods and forests to the chief secretaryship of the lord-lieutenant, and who, while accepting this superior office, had expressed his determination again to solicit the confidence of his late constituents.

The importance of carrying all these seats, and especially at this juncture of defeating a cabinet minister, in whose instance, however, success was supposed to be most problematical, was deeply felt by Lord George, and there was no effort that he spared to achieve his end. It was calculated that if the debate could be kept up for a week, that is, in parliamentary time, four days, the new members for Dorsetshire, where a contest was not anticipated, might take their seats in time to record their votes.

The 9th of February at last arrived. The house was very full. The order of the day for the house going into committee on the 'customs—corn laws' was read, and Mr. Philip Miles rose to move as an amendment, that the house should go into committee that day six months. He delivered a well-digested speech, in which he considered the whole question of the new commercial policy proposed by the government with the information and the authority which the representative of a great commercial city would command. He stated, amid assenting cheers from both sides, that he 'deemed the question to be of far greater magnitude than the reform bill.' He was seconded, to the manifest surprise and disturbance of the government, by Sir William Heathcote in a speech of admirable ability, alike remarkable for its just, temperate, and ingenious views, and its graceful rhetoric and flowing elocution. While one listened to him it was impossible not to feel, that as long as such men remained a country party need not be without a natural leader, and that of such stuff were made the Sir William Wyndhams, and the Sir John Hinde Cottons, and the other distinguished men of the earlier parliaments of the eighteenth century.

The amendment of the forlorn protectionist party, therefore, was well launched. It sailed along, gracefully and steadily, amid general applause. The succeeding speeches were on the whole interesting and animated: the most remarkable, that of Lord Sandon, who made an able and even strongly expressed speech against the government measure, which he intended to support. It was indeed upon this peculiar ground that he solicited the attention of the house. 'He rose to explain and vindicate. He was in a position different from that of any member who had yet spoken. He disapproved of the measure proposed, and yet he intended to support it by his vote. He could not honestly say that he was convinced by the arguments and facts which had convinced the prime minister and induced him to give up his former opinions. The basis of induction seemed to him too narrow for so broad a superstructure. The facts themselves were not very conclusive; they were, many of them, to be explained by special causes peculiar to themselves, independent of general principles; and whatever they were, he could not think that if all the *a priori* arguments of political economists and all the inductions from previous observations had for thirty years failed to make an impression on the mind of the prime minister, the narrow experience of the last three years, on a few small experiments, was a very intelligible or satisfactory ground for so sudden or so great a change of opinion.'

Lord John Russell, who followed in a speech which was not one of his happy efforts, agreed with Lord Sandon, 'that the minister had not laid his grounds broadly and extensively enough in point of time.' Lord John was not very felicitous in point of time himself. Embarrassed by his engagement to support the measure of his rival, little anticipating the importance and duration of the debate then taking place, and anxious to free himself as soon as possible from the fulfilment of an awkward duty, he wasted his ammunition much too soon in the engagement, spoke inopportunely and ineffectively, and the future first minister of the country was not heard of in the house of commons for three weeks.

The secretary at war closed the debate for the government; but the protectionists went home well pleased, and the general opinion of the house was, that, this night at least, they had carried away the prize.

The debate on the second night was opened by Mr. Stafford, who replied to the secretary at war in a speech of uncommon spirit and success; nor was this the only advantage which accrued to the protectionists on this occasion. The Marquess of Granby, who had resigned a high post in the household of the prince consort in consequence of his disapprobation of the ministerial scheme, proved to the house that he had carefully and deeply studied the question under discussion, and gave an earnest of that prominence in debate which he has subsequently achieved and sustained. But not the least fortunate effusion of the night was the maiden speech of Lord Brooke, delivered with energy and with a voice the tone of which at once gained the ear. He said 'that the only excuse he could himself find for the followers of the chief minister was, that the present parliament was near its dissolution. They all knew, that when a man arrived at a great age, he often lost his faculties, that his memory generally failed him. Here they had a sad example of this deficiency of that principal sense, and of the present parliament forgetting the pledges of its youth and manhood amid the decrepitude of old age. Individuals, under such unhappy circumstances, were generally taken advantage of, and thus members were called upon by the minister to make their wills, to assign away their property and possessions, to give them to aliens and foreigners, and so to defraud their rightful heirs.' This novel and happy illustration, pursued with so much ingenuity, called down the plaudits of a very full house.

A vehement personal attack of Lord Worsley called up the secretary of state, who closed the debate for the government.

It was now conceded even by the government that the debate could not terminate until Friday, and it would then have lasted four nights. The principal ammunition of the protectionists was by no means exhausted, and it was felt that the speech of the minister must naturally be of no ordinary length; nor was it supposed that the 'stubborn silence,' as it was designated by Mr. Wakley, of the Manchester school, could be successfully maintained. What made this great discussion peculiarly interesting was, that the breaking up of parties had swept away the routine of debate, which under ordinary circumstances necessarily and naturally confines discussion to a limited number of speakers, of whom the principal, for the convenience of public business, rise almost at conventional periods. But so keen was the feeling of the protectionists, and so spurring the point of honour that a flock deserted by their shepherds should not be led, as was intended, to the slaughter-house without a struggle, that a stimulus to exertion was given which has perhaps been rarely equalled in the house of commons, and members now advanced who had shown no disposition previously to partake in the principal affairs of the house. And in the present instance, while all parties were discussing the probable conduct of the third night, and speculating on the orators who might respectively solicit their critical observation, the occasion was seized by one not anticipated, and who rarely, if ever, had challenged the attention which he this night entirely captivated. The member for Huntingdon brought the great name of Baring, and all the authority of his pre-eminent position in the commercial world, to support the principle of regulated competition. His mastery of the subject would under any circumstances have commanded attention. The house liked to receive the latest and most authentic information as to the state of the markets from the greatest merchant in the country. The first minister had frightened them a fortnight before by informing them that Belgium had cleared the Liverpool market of rice, with a consequent rise of seventy-five per cent. in that article. Mr. Baring thought the house might perhaps be reassured by learning, that that rise had already been diminished one-half. But what made his speech doubly effective was its animated manner, which, while it never passed that line of restraint which good taste requires, was remarkable for a freshness of handling which is rare, and a sort of winning naturalness that often broke spontaneously into very telling points. Few things indeed happier or more successful than when, after reviewing the various grounds of the alarm of scarcity which had been so rife before the meeting of parliament, Mr. Baring said, that ‘for his part, on reviewing what had taken place, he must think the great want of the country had been the want of a ministry, and that the most appalling scarcity had been the scarcity of statesmen.’

The effect of Mr. Baring’s speech was a general feeling among the protectionists that the debate could now be carried over Friday. It was evident that Lord George Bentinck even at that time anticipated a much more prolonged duration of the discussion. The pains which he took to encourage the interposition of members, devoting his whole mornings to stimulate and to assist them, and the keen interest with which he watched in the house every word and incident from his seat, which he never quitted even for a meal, indicated the importance which he attached to the maintenance of the struggle. Three nights had passed, and it may be fairly stated that the deserted party had carried away the prize; the fourth night passed without bringing a conclusion, and the parliamentary week closed. On Monday, the fifth night, two cabinet ministers having already spoken in the debate—the secretary of state and the secretary at war, the latter as representative of a great agricultural county—it was thought, by the chief minister rising at the end of the evening, that the division must be called for. The speech of Sir Robert Peel was one of his best; indignant and vigorous, free from the affectation of fairness and that too obvious plausibility in which of late years he had somewhat luxuriantly indulged, he threw off the apologetical tone and was uncompromising both in his principles and demeanour. The peroration was in the high league style, though of course adapted to the more refined taste of the house of commons. It was a speech to divide on. Yet the intended division did not take place. And this great debate was sustained for another fortnight, extending altogether over three parliamentary weeks, with crowded and interested benches, until, on the 27th of February, it was generally understood—though Lord George Bentinck would not even then pledge himself to the understanding—that the division should take place. He was himself to speak that night, and it was generally felt that he would enter into the subject completely.

So little desirous originally was Lord George Bentinck to interfere actively in that great controversy in which ultimately he took so leading a part, that before the meeting of parliament in 1846 he begged a gentleman whom he greatly esteemed, a member of the legal profession and since raised to its highest honours, to call upon him at Harcourt House, when he said that he had taken great pains to master the case of the protective system, that he was convinced its abrogation would ultimately be very injurious to this country, but although both in point of argument and materials he feared no opponent, he felt constitutionally so incapable of ever making a speech that he wished to induce some eminent lawyer to enter the house of commons, and avail himself of his views and materials, which he had with that object reduced to writing. He begged therefore that his friend, although a free-trader, would assist him by suggesting a fitting person for this office.

Accordingly, the name of a distinguished member of the bar, who had already published a work of merit impugning the principles of the new commercial system, was mentioned, and this learned gentleman was applied to and was not indisposed to accept the task. A mere accident prevented this arrangement being accomplished. Lord George then requested his friend to make some other selection; but his adviser very sensibly replied that although the house of commons would have listened with respect to a gentleman who had given evidence of the sincerity of his convictions by the publication of a work which had no reference to parliament, they would not endure the instance of a lawyer brought into the house merely to speak from his brief, and that the attempt would be utterly fruitless. He earnestly counselled Lord George himself to make the effort; but Lord George with characteristic tenacity clung for some time to his project, though his efforts to accomplish it were fortunately not successful.

Some of the friends of Lord George Bentinck, remembering his inexperience in debate, aware of the great length at which he must necessarily treat the theme, and mindful that he was not physically well qualified for controlling popular assemblies, not having a strong voice or naturally a very fluent manner, were anxious that he should not postpone his speech until an hour so late, that an audience jaded by twelve nights' discussion would be ill-attuned to statistical arguments and economical details. But still clinging to the hope that some accident might yet again postpone the division, so that the protectionists might gain the vote of Mr. Hildyard, who had been returned that day for South Notts, having defeated a cabinet minister, Lord George remained motionless until long past midnight. Mr. Cobden having spoken on the part of the confederation, the closing of the debate was felt to be inevitable. Even then, by inducing a protectionist to solicit the speaker's eye, Lord

George attempted to avert the division, but no supporter of the government measure of any colour advancing to reply to this volunteer, Bentinck was obliged to rise. He came out like a lion forced from his lair. And so it happened that after all his labours of body and mind, after all his research and unwearied application and singular vigilance, after having been at his post for a month, never leaving the house even for refreshment, he had to undertake the most difficult enterprise in which a man can well embark, with a concurrence of every disadvantage which could ensure failure and defeat. It would seem that the audience, the subject, and the orator must be equally exhausted, for the assembly had listened for twelve nights to the controversy, and he who was about to address them had, according to his strange habit, taken no sustenance the whole day; it being his custom to dine after the house was up, which was very often long after midnight, and this, with the exception of a slender breakfast, rigidly restricted to dry toast, was his only meal in the four-and-twenty hours.

He had been forced to this regimen from food exercising a lethargic influence over him; so that, in addition to some constitutional weakness in his organ, he usually laboured when he addressed the house under the disadvantage of general exhaustion. And this was no doubt a principal cause of that over-excitement and apparently unnecessary energy in his manner of speaking, of which he was himself perfectly and even painfully conscious. He was wont to say, that before he could speak he had to make a voice, and as it were to pump it up from the very core of his frame. One who took a great interest in his success once impressed on him the expediency of trusting entirely to his natural voice and the interest and gravity of his matter, which, combined with his position as the recognised leader of a great party, would be adequate to command the attention of his audience; and he subsequently endeavoured very often to comply with this suggestion. He endeavoured also very much to control his redundancy of action and gesture, when that peculiarity was pointed out to him with the delicacy, but the sincerity, of friendship. He entirely freed himself from a very awkward feature of his first style of speaking, namely, the frequent repetition of a sentence, which seemed at first a habit inveterate with him; but such was his force of will, that when the necessity of ridding himself of this drawback was properly pointed out to him, he achieved the desired result. No one bore criticism more gently and kindly, so long as it was confined to his personal and intellectual characteristics, for he was a man absolutely without vanity or conceit, who thought very humbly of himself in respect of abilities, and deemed no labour too great to achieve even a slight improvement. But though in these respects the very child of simplicity, he was a man of almost unexampled pride, and chafed under criticism when his convictions or his conduct were questioned. He was very tenacious of his opinion, almost inexorable; and it required a courage nearly equal to his own, combined with a serene temper, successfully to impugn his conclusions.

Not therefore excited by vanity but sustained by self-respect, by an overpowering feeling that he owed it to himself and the opinions he held to show to the world that they had not been lightly adopted and should not be lightly laid aside, Bentinck rose, long past the noon of night, at the end of this memorable debate, to undertake an office from which the most successful and most experienced rhetoricians of parliament would have shrank with intuitive discretion. But duty scorns prudence, and criticism has few terrors for a man with a great purpose. Unshaken by the adverse hour and circumstances, he proceeded to accomplish the object which he had long meditated and for which he was fully prepared.

Reminding the house, while he appealed to their indulgence, that though he had had the honour of a seat for eight parliaments, he had never once ventured to trespass on its time on any subject of great debate, he at once took a clear and comprehensive ground of objection to the government scheme. He opposed it not only because he objected to the great change contemplated with respect to the agricultural interest, but on principle to the entire measure, 'a great commercial revolution, which we are of opinion that the circumstances of the country do not by any means require.'

Noticing the observation of the secretary at war, that the agricultural interest, in submitting to this great change, might now accept it with honour, instead of its being eventually extorted by force, he happily retorted that vicious as he thought the measure, he should feel it deprived of half its vice if it could be carried without loss of honour, damage to reputation, and forfeiture of public character to a vast number of gentlemen now present. And he proceeded to show among other testimonies, by an appeal to the distinct language of the speech from the throne on the dissolution of 1841, that 'every member who occupied a seat in this house was returned pledged either to oppose or maintain the principle of protection to national industry.'

Adverting to the new position that the experience of the last three years justified the reversal of the system which the existing administration had been summoned to office to uphold, he wisely remarked that, 'the country will not be satisfied with three years' experience of any system. Three years' experience is not sufficiently extensive to afford a proper criterion by which we may decide the failure or success of any description of policy whatsoever.'

Noticing that the minister had more especially founded 'his present belief in doctrines contrary to those which he had heretofore uniformly maintained,' by the assumption that the price of corn would not be more reduced than the price of cattle and other commodities affected by the tariff of 1842, and also by the results of previous experiments in the instances of silk and wool, Lord George 'accepted his challenge' on these grounds, and proceeded in great detail to investigate these examples.

The house listened with great attention for full two hours, during which he treated these subjects. This attention, no doubt, was generally accorded because it was felt due to the occasion and, under the circumstances, to the speaker; but those who, however contrary might be the results at which they had arrived, had themselves deeply entered into these investigations, recognised very soon that Bentinck was master of his subject. Sir Robert Peel looked round very often with that expression of appreciation which it was impossible for his nature to refuse to parliamentary success, even when the ability displayed was hostile to his projects. The minister, with reference to the wool trade, had dwelt on the year 1842, when prices were much depressed, while they had greatly rallied in 1844, when the importation of foreign wool had risen from forty-five to sixty-five millions of pounds; and he had drawn a triumphant inference that the increase of importation and the increase of price were in consequence of the reduction of the duty. This instance had produced a great effect; but Lord George showed the house, by a reference to the tables of 1836, that the importation of foreign wool had then risen to sixty-five millions of pounds, and that large foreign importation was consistent with high prices to the domestic grower. Nor was he less successful about the foreign cattle. He reminded his friends on the treasury bench how strenuously, previously to the introduction of the tariff of 1842, they had urged upon their agricultural friends that no foreign cattle could enter under their regulations, and that the whole object of the change was to strengthen the hands of the agricultural interest, as regarded more essential protection, by removing the odium of a nominal protection: 'Convinced by my right honourable friends, in 1842, that their tariff would be as inoperative as it has proved, I gave my cordial support to the measure.'

Perceiving that the house began to be wearied with the details of the silk trade, which he had investigated with extraordinary zeal, he postponed until the specific vote in committee his objections to the reduction of the timber duties. The fact is, he had so thoroughly mastered all these topics, that his observations on each of them would have themselves formed a speech of sufficient length and interest. But he successfully checked any interruption by what may be fairly styled his dignified diffidence.

'I trust the house will recollect that I am fighting the battle of a party whose leaders have deserted them; and though I cannot wield my weapons with the skill of the right honourable gentleman on the treasury bench, I trust the house will remember the emergency which has dragged me out to intrude upon their indulgence.'

And again, when he announced that he was now about to investigate the pretext of 'famine in the land,' and some impatience was exhibited, he drew up and said, 'I think, having sat eighteen years in this house and never once having trespassed on its time before in any one single great debate, I may appeal to the past as a proof that I duly weigh the measure of my abilities, and that I am painfully conscious of my proper place in this house.'

It was impossible to resist such appeals from such a person, even at three o'clock in the morning; and diffident but determined, he then entered into what was, perhaps, the most remarkable portion of his speech—an investigation of what was the real position of the country with respect to the supply of food in the past autumn and at the present moment. Having shown from the trade circulars that far from there being at present 'a wheat famine,' the stocks in the granaries in bond were more than double in amount to what they were in the year 1845, 'a year admitted by all to be a year of extraordinary abundance,' he proceeded to the Irish part of the question: 'I beg leave to say, that though this debate has now continued for three weeks, I am the first gentleman who has at all entered into the real state of the case as regards the allegation of a potato famine in Ireland, upon which, be it remembered, is founded the sole case of her majesty's ministers for a repeal of the corn laws.'

And this was very true. The fact is, though the protectionist party had made a most unexpected and gallant defence, no one was really prepared for the contest except Bentinck. Between the end of November and the meeting of parliament he had thrown all the energies of his passionate mind into this question. He had sought information on all points and always at the fountain-head. He had placed himself in immediate communication with the ablest representatives of every considerable interest attacked, and being ardent and indefatigable, gifted with a tenacious memory and a very clear and searching spirit, there was scarcely a detail or an argument connected with his subject which was not immediately at his command. No speeches in favour of the protective system have ever been made in the house of commons compared with his in depth and range of knowledge; and had there been any member, not connected with the government, who had been able to vindicate the merits of British agriculture as he did when the final struggle occurred, the impression which was made by the too-often unanswered speeches of the Manchester confederation would never have been effected. But the great conservative party, exhausted by the labours of ten years of opposition, thought that after the triumph of '41 it might claim a furlough. The defence of their cause was left entirely to the ministers of their choice, and ministers, distracted with detail and wearied with official labour, are not always the most willing or the most efficient champions of the organic principles of a party.

Sir Robert Peel, with respect to the disease in the Irish potato, had largely referred to the statements of the inspectors of police. Lord George wanted to know why the reports of the lieutenants of the Irish counties were not given. Being well informed upon this head, he asked the government to produce the report of Lord Duncannon, the lord-lieutenant of Carlow; especially that of his noble father, the Earl of Besborough, lord-lieutenant of Kilkenny. 'Is there any man in England or in Ireland whose opinion, from his business-like habits, his great practical knowledge, and the warm and affectionate interest which for a long period of years he has taken in everything which concerns the interests of Ireland, especially of the Irish peasantry—is there any man whose opinion would have greater weight? The opinion of Lord Besborough on an Irish subject, the lieutenant of an Irish county, and himself long a cabinet minister? Well, sir, I am assured that, having taken the utmost pains to investigate this matter, Lord Besborough has made an elaborate report to the Irish government. Well then, I desire to know why Lord Besborough's report to the Irish government is suppressed ? Is it because that report would not assist the present policy of her majesty's government ? '

He alleged the names of many other individuals of high station, who had officially reported on the subject to the government: of Lord Castlereagh, the lieutenant of Down, a member of the house; of Lord de Vesci, whose son was sitting for the Queen's County, over which his father presided in the name of the queen. A murmur ran round the house, that it would have been as well if these reports had been produced.

The last portion of this argumentative harangue referred to the most important division of the subject. Bentinck met it boldly, without evasion; nor was there any portion of his address more interesting, more satisfactory, and more successful. 'I now come,' he said, ' to the great challenge, which is ever and anon put forth by the anti-corn law league, and now by their disciples, her majesty's ministers. How are we, they ask, with our limited extent of territory, to feed a population annually and rapidly increasing at the rate of three hundred thousand a year, as generally stated by the member for Stockport—a rate increased by my noble friend, the member for the West Riding, to a thousand a day, or three hundred and sixty-five thousand a year ?'

He first proved in a complete manner that, from the year 1821 to the year 1844, the population of the country had increased at the rate of less than thirty-two per cent., while the growth of wheat during the same period had increased no less than sixty-four per cent. He then proceeded to inquire why, with such an increased produce, we were still, as regards bread corn, to a certain extent an importing nation ? This he accounted for by the universally improved condition of the people, and the enlarged command of food by the working classes. He drew an animated picture, founded entirely on the representations of writers and public men adverse to the protective system, of the superior condition of the people of 'England, happy England,' to that of other countries: how they consumed much more of the best food, and lived much longer. This was under protection, which Lord John Russell had stigmatised in his letter, 'the bane of agriculture.' 'In the history of my noble friend's illustrious family,' he continued, 'I should have thought that he would have found a remarkable refutation of such a notion.' And then he drew a lively sketch of the colossal and patriotic works of the earls and dukes of Bedford 'whereby they had drained and reclaimed three hundred thousand acres of land drowned in water, and brought them into cultivation, and thus converted into fertile fields a vast morass extending over seven counties in England.' Could the system which had inspired such enterprise be justly denounced as baneful?

To show the means of the country to sustain even a much increasing population, and that those means were in operation, he entered into one of the most original and interesting calculations that was perhaps ever offered to the house of commons. Reminding the house that in the preceding year (1845) the farmers of England, at a cost of two millions sterling, had imported two hundred and eighty thousand tons of guano, he proceeded to estimate what would be the effect on the productive powers of the land of that novel application. Two hundred thousand tons, or in other words, four million cwt., were expended on the land in 1845. Half of these, he assumed, would be applied to the growth of wheat, and the other half to the growth of turnips preparatory to the wheat crop of the ensuing year. According to the experiments tried and recorded in the royal agricultural journal, it would seem that by the application of two hundred cwt. of guano to an acre of wheat land, the produce would be increased by one quarter per acre. At this rate one hundred thousand tons, or two million cwt. of guano, would add one million quarters of wheat to the crop, or bread for one year for one million of people. But as he was very careful never to overstate a case, Lord George assumed, that it would require three hundred cwt. of guano to an acre to produce an extra quarter of wheat. According to this estimate, one hundred thousand tons of guano applied to the land in 1845 must have added six hundred and sixty-six thousand six hundred and sixty-six quarters of grain to the wheat crop, or in other words, bread for six hundred and sixty-six thousand six hundred and sixty-six additional mouths. 'And now for turnips,' he continued. The Norfolk authorities, whom he quoted, have in like manner proved that two cwt. of guano will add ten tons per acre to the turnip crop. But again, for fear of exaggeration, he supposed that three cwt. would be requisite to create such increased fertility. In this case, two million cwt. of guano would add six million six hundred and sixty-six thousand six hundred and sixty tons to the natural unmanured produce of the crop. Now it is generally considered that one ton of Swedes would last twenty sheep three weeks, and that each sheep should gain half a pound of meat per week, or one pound and a half in three weeks; thus twenty sheep feeding on one ton of turnips in three weeks should in the aggregate make, as the graziers say, thirty pounds of mutton. But to be safe in his estimate, he would assume that one ton of turnips makes only half this quantity. 'Multiply then,' exclaimed Bentinck with the earnest air of a crusader, 'six million six hundred and sixty-six thousand six hundred and sixty by fifteen, and you have no less than ninety-nine million nine hundred and ninety-nine thousand and nine hundred pounds of mutton as the fruits of one hundred thousand tons of guano; which, at ninety-two pounds per man—the average Englishman's allowance—affords meat for one million eight hundred and sixty thousand nine hundred and fifty-five—nearly two millions of her majesty's subjects.'

This is a specimen of those original and startling calculations to which the house was soon to become accustomed from his lips. They were received at first with astonishment and incredulity, but they were never impugned. The fact is, he was extremely cautious in his data, and no man was more accustomed ever to impress upon his friends the extreme expediency of not overstating a case. It should also be remarked of Lord George Bentinck that in his most complicated calculations he never sought aid from notes.

We have necessarily only noticed a few of the traits of this remarkable performance. Its termination was impressive.

'We have heard in the course of these discussions a good deal about an ancient monarchy, a reformed house of commons, and a proud aristocracy. Sir, with regard to our ancient monarchy, I have no observation to make; but, if so humble an individual as myself might be permitted to whisper a word in the ear of that illustrious and royal personage, who, as he stands nearest, so is he justly dearest, to her who sits upon the throne, I would take leave to say, that I cannot but think he listened to ill advice, when, on the first night of this great discussion, he allowed himself to be seduced by the first minister of the crown, to come down to this house to usher in, to give *éclat*, and as it were by reflection from the queen, to give the semblance of the personal sanction of her majesty to a measure which, be it for good or for evil, a great majority at least of the landed aristocracy of England, of Scotland, and of Ireland imagine fraught with deep injury, if not ruin, to them—a measure which, not confined in its operation to this great class, is calculated to grind down countless smaller interests engaged in the domestic trades and interests of the empire, transferring the profits of all these interests—English, Scotch, Irish, and Colonial—great and small alike, from Englishmen, from Scotchmen, and from Irishmen, to Americans, to Frenchmen, to Russians, to Poles, to Prussians, and to Germans. Sir, I come now to the reformed house of commons; and as one who was a party to that great measure, I cannot but feel a deep interest in its success, and more especially in that portion of it which extended the franchise to the largest and the most respectable body in the kingdom—I mean the landed tenantry of England; and deeply should I regret should any large proportion of those members, who have been sent to parliament to represent them in this house, prove to be the men to bring lasting dishonour upon themselves, their constituencies, and this house, by an act of tergiversation so gross as to be altogether unprecedented in the annals of any reformed or unreformed house of commons. Sir, lastly, I come to the "proud aristocracy." We are a proud aristocracy, but if we are proud, it is that we are proud in the chastity of our honour. If we assisted in '41 in turning the whigs out of office, because we did not consider a fixed duty of eight shillings a quarter on foreign corn a sufficient protection, it was with honesty of purpose and in single-mindedness we did so; and as we were not before the fact, we will not be accomplices after the fact, in the fraud by which the whig ministers were expelled from power. If we are a proud aristocracy, we are proud of our honour, inasmuch as we never have been guilty, and never can be guilty, of double-dealing with the farmers of England —of swindling our opponents, deceiving our friends, or betraying our constituents.'

The division was called. The West India interest, notwithstanding the amendment was moved by the member for Bristol, deserted the protectionists. Deaf to the appeals and the remonstrances and the warnings of Lord George, one of their leading members replied, with a smile of triumphant content, that 'they had made a satisfactory arrangement for themselves.' How satisfactory did the West Indians find it four months subsequently? All the shipping interest deserted the land. They were for everything free, except navigation; there was no danger of that being interfered with; 'it rested on quite distinct grounds—national grounds.' They were warned, but they smiled in derisive self-complacency. Lord George Bentinck lived to have the West India interest, and the shipping interest, on their knees to him to defend their perilled or to restore their ruined fortunes; and with characteristic generosity and proud consistency, he undertook the task and sacrificed his life in the attempt.

Notwithstanding these terrible defalcations, when the numbers were announced, at nearly four o'clock in the morning, the majority had not reached those three magical figures supposed necessary under the circumstances to success. In a house of five hundred and eighty-one members present, the amendment of the protectionists was defeated only by ninety-seven; and two hundred and forty-two gentlemen, in spite of desertion, difficulty, and defeat, still maintained the 'chastity of their honour.'

CHAPTER VI

THE great object which Lord George now proposed to himself was to delay the progress of the government measures, that they should not reach the house of lords before Easter. He believed that time might still ensure their discomfiture. The majority of the 27th of February was only in favour of going into committee of the whole house to consider the existing customs and corn acts, when the minister was to propose resolutions, which if carried were to be the foundations of bills which he would then proceed to introduce. Before therefore any bill for the repeal of the existing corn laws could be brought forward, the principle of every projected alteration in the tariff must individually be sanctioned by a particular vote. The opportunities for resistance, therefore, were considerable and encouraging. Nor was the majority itself, considering the coalition of parties and the vagueness of the course to which it committed the house, looked upon as excessive, but the reverse. All the elections too went against the minister; a member of the cabinet was rejected by two important constituencies, and a near relative of Lord George returned in his stead. But what most influenced Bentinck to adopt the tactics of delay was the conviction, which turned out to be just, that the failure of the potato crop had been greatly exaggerated. With these views he availed himself of the motion of Mr. Villiers, brought forward on the 2nd of March, for the total and immediate repeal of the corn laws, to secure an adjourned debate. He himself made a brief and animated speech on the second and last night, though it had not been his intention to address the house. An influential member of the protectionist party, Mr. Miles of Somerset, had stated on an early night of the session the preference by the landed interest of the immediate repeal to the government measure; and Sir Robert Peel, on the motion of Mr. Villiers, had adroitly availed himself of this admission of an opponent, and announced that though the minority were of opinion that their own course was the more prudent, still if the landed party chose to unite with Mr. Villiers on the present occasion, it might carry his proposition and the government could accept it. Upon this Lord George Bentinck rejoined: ' It has been alleged that an honourable friend of mine, who is absent to-night, stated, on behalf of the agricultural interest, that the farmers of England would prefer to have immediate repeal to a repeal hanging over them for three years, and in that I believe my honourable friend was correct. But the reason of my preference of the government proposition to immediate repeal is, that we do not consider it quite certain that at the end of three years the corn laws will be repealed'; and again, ' We prefer to postpone the day, because we know that in the interval we must be returned to the people, and then we hope to be able to restore things to what they were before.'

A fortnight elapsed ere the resolutions in committee of the whole house, on which the government bills were to be introduced, were passed. The efforts of Lord George Bentinck during this period, from the 6th to the 20th of March, were unceasing. He fought the battle of the Irish graziers and butter-merchants, ' butter rightly described by the vice-president of the board of trade as one of the principal staple manufactures of Ireland, that suffering country to which we are going to subscribe by a vote of this house the sum of £230,000, and on which by a vote of this house we are at the same time entailing a loss, by the reduction of the duties on butter, of half a million sterling. If the object of reducing duties is to relieve the consumer, I beg ministers to tell us, whether they do not think a reduction of the duty on tea would not be as advantageous to the consumer as a reduction of the duty upon butter? And why have they not made such a proposition? For no reason that I can see, except that tea does not come into competition with the produce of Great Britain.'

He fought the battle of 'the Leicestershire stockingers,' one hundred thousand persons engaged in the stocking business. If protection were that bane to the stockingers, how came it that the Saxon, under protection the most stringent, was able to enter into competition with the stockingers of England, so as to be able almost to drive them out of the market? Stockings were made in Saxony, as appeared by reports on the table of the house, at 3d. per pair; but the member for Nottingham had just told the house that here the charge was 8s. per dozen. He wanted to know how the stockinger of Nottingham and Leicester could compete with the Saxon who sold his stockings at 3s. per dozen?

He fought in great detail the battle of the silk manufacturers; he had very minutely investigated the circumstances of the trade, and when a member interrupted him by saying that the silk manufacturers themselves were in favour of the change, he retorted: 'Sir, the honourable gentleman seems to express an opinion, that it is no business of this house to interfere in matters where the parties immediately concerned do not ask for such an interference. I thought the constitution of this country required, that we should consider what is best for the general good of the country; and that it was not for us to be taught by the constituencies, what is best for the interest of the country. We have well considered this question. It is one which has been before parliament for five-and-twenty years, and we think ourselves as well qualified to judge of this matter as any manufacturers that may live at Goole or elsewhere. But, if any honourable gentleman thinks that the silk manufacturers of this country are in favour of this measure, I can tell him a different story. The honourable member knows the character of the three gentlemen who called on me yesterday morning. What did these gentlemen tell me? Why, that since there was a free trade in silk, only two mills had been erected in Coventry; that Coventry stood still while St. Etienne, its rival, flourished—that St. Etienne flourished at the expense of Coventry.'

He fought the battle of the hop-grower. 'It had been stated by the chancellor of the exchequer, that hop-growing had been a losing concern for some years past; but the chancellor of the exchequer proposed a different remedy from what he should propose. He should propose that the excise duty be taken off. He was glad to hear in the earlier part of the evening strong proofs of the advantage of the abolition of excise duties. Their abolition upon glass had brought a considerable reduction of expenditure, by the employment of less officers. One hundred excise officers might come off, and £10,000 per annum be saved by abolishing the present excise on hops. That would be a means of assisting the hop-growers. A gentleman who had waited on him that morning had shown him how in 1836 he had paid 18s. 8d. per cwt. excise upon fifteen tons and a half of hops, grown in 1836, which was a good year. He was obliged to hold his hops till 1840, when, wearied with delay, he had to sell them for 16s. per cwt., on which 18s. 8d. per cwt. had been paid as an excise duty. Would they admit foreign hops to remedy such disasters as these? And if they threw hop grounds out of cultivation, what did the government mean to do with the tithe commutation? While wheat paid 7s. per acre towards the tithes, hop land paid 29s.'

Finally, on the 20th of March, in a speech of great research and vigour, he fought the battle of the colonial timber interest. On all these questions there were considerable divisions, and whatever difference of opinion there might be as to the wisdom of the policy he recommended, there was none, and could be none in the house, as to the complete mastery which he exhibited of his subject. The reader will indeed have observed, in the slight passages which have been just given from his speeches, more than one characteristic trait of the newly adopted habits of his life, by which

he acquired, and so rapidly, such sound and extensive
information on such various and varying subjects. The
first merchants and manufacturers of the country were the
companions of his mornings; and from an early hour to the
time when it was necessary to appear in his place, he was
occupied in investigating with their assistance the questions
affecting the commerce and industry of the country then
submitted to the legislature. 'The gentleman who had
waited on him that morning,' was sure to be about the best
authority on the subject in debate. Nor must it be supposed from this, that Lord George, in his eagerness to
acquire information, was proportionably easy in accepting
the details and conclusions which were offered to him.
Quite the reverse; he was eminently scrutinous. No one
cross-examined with more acuteness or pursued a sceptical
research with more tenacity. It was impossible to evade,
and difficult to baffle, him. Although he had strong prejudices, which with him were an affair of humour, not of
bigotry and false reasoning, his mind was peculiarly judica-
tive. He collected and weighed evidence with great ability;
and though apparently immersed in details, his scheme of
thought was never petty. All fell into its right place and in
lucid order, and he ever had a clear conception of the case,
and struck the balance with a full control over the contending evidence and arguments.

The second reading of the bill for the repeal of the corn
laws was fixed for the 23rd March. This bill was introduced
in pursuance of one of the resolutions passed in the committee of the whole house, which had just closed its labours.
The first reading of a bill under such circumstances is a
matter of course, and almost of form. The standing orders
of the house of commons require that every bill affecting
the trade or religion of the country should be founded on
a preliminary resolution of the whole house in committee,
a wise precaution of our predecessors against sudden legislation on matters of such grave import.

The question, that the bill be read a second time, was
met by an amendment that it be read that day six months,

moved with graceful rhetoric by Mr. Eliot Yorke, the member for Cambridgeshire, and seconded with all the weight and authority of Sir John Yarde Buller. The debate lasted four nights; sustained on the part of the protectionists on the second night by Sir John Trollope in a very effective speech. As one of the members for the great agricultural county of Lincoln, he successfully repelled the statements of the advocates of free imports, that 'the cultivators of the soil had been unable to provide food for the people.' He could not call to mind a single acre of land lying waste in the division of the county which he represented: not an unenclosed parish. From 1828 to 1841 there had been an increase in the produce of the county of Lincoln to the extent of 70 per cent. in the article of wheat alone; and he was satisfied, from the improvements that had since taken place, from the great amount of drainage, the breaking up of pasture land, the artificial manures, and other processes applied to the land, that a much greater increase had since taken place in the county, and that the increase in the last sixteen years could not amount to less than 100 per cent. During the same period the population of the county had not increased above 20 per cent., so that there was a large available surplus for the food of the population in the manufacturing districts.

Lord George Bentinck closed the debate on the third night, which rather languished till he rose. He spoke with unusual animation, and concluded with these words:—

'I recollect that the secretary of state (Sir James Graham), in 1841, complained that the noble lord (Lord John Russell) and his late colleagues on the benches opposite had excited the people, and compared them to pirates, who rather than surrender the ship and their command had applied the torch to the magazine. I would ask my right honourable friends on the treasury bench what do they think of themselves now? Are they not pirates too? Have they not pirated the doctrines, the arguments, and the speeches of the anti-corn law league? But I cannot pay you the compliment of saying that you possess the dare-devil courage of pirates—that rather than yield, you would sink the ship. I cannot say that you have stood by your craft as long as you could keep her afloat. No; you have left your ship in the dark of the night, when you had chartered to carry her home in safety. You have brought her on a lee shore and left her among the breakers. You have placed her under the guns of the enemy's battery while your faithful crew were asleep in their hammocks. You have scuttled your ship—you, the captain and lieutenant, master and mate— you scuttled the ship, stole the compass, sneaked away in the longboat, and deserted to the enemy, hoping that the gallant crew would become an easy prey to those who would board her. But you judged of the mettle of the crew by your own craven hearts, and though for a moment we may have been thrown into confusion, we never have been dis- couraged—we have rallied from the temporary shock, and we will yet bring the good ship off the lee shore, and carry her safe home to port.'

This peroration, vivid, true, passionate and picturesque, and delivered with energy, was loudly cheered, and the government made a great effort the next night to restore the spirit of their supporters. The debate was opened by the secretary of state in a very elaborate speech, marked by a virulent retort to the recorder of Dublin, who, on the preceding night, had ventured 'to cast the horoscope of a falling government.' Later in the evening, the chief minister himself exerted his utmost powers in vindication of his policy and personal conduct. Sir Robert had seldom spoken better.

The difficult duty of following him devolved this night to Mr. Stafford. Not the least remarkable speech of the evening, though one at the time little comprehended, was that with which Lord Palmerston unexpectedly followed Mr. Stafford and closed the debate. Amid an abstract eulogium of free trade, apparently so uncompromising that it filled the free-traders with rapture while they listened to the reproduction of their own arguments in sentences so lucid and in forms so neat, his lordship with adroit audacity suddenly unfurled the standard of a moderate fixed duty, and with blended hardihood and discretion acknowledged that he had not relinquished his faith in such a policy, though he feared, and almost felt, that the opportunity had been lost for its adoption.

'I hold that there is no reason why freedom of trade in corn should not be as advantageous to the country as freedom of trade in every other commodity. But by free trade I do not mean, necessarily and in all cases, trade free from customs duties. We are obliged, as I have already said, to raise a large yearly revenue, and we must for that purpose have heavy taxes. The least inconvenient and least objectionable method of raising a large portion of that revenue is by indirect taxation, and that involves the necessity of customs duties. Therefore, when I speak of free trade, I do not mean trade free from duties laid on for the purpose of revenue, and which, in order to accomplish their purpose, must be so moderate as not to cripple or impede commercial transactions. Now, my opinion has been, and, I own, still continues to be, that there is no reason why the trade in corn should, in this respect, be an exception to the general. I am for a moderate fixed duty. My noble and honourable friends near me have also been of the same opinion; and allow me to say, that this opinion was not taken up by us, as stated last night by the noble lord, the member for King's Lynn, when the late government was, as he said, *in articulo mortis*; but as far back as in 1839, when there was no reason to expect an early termination of our official career. I say, then, that my wish would have been to have had a low fixed duty on the importation of corn. I think that a duty of four or five shillings would not sensibly raise the price of corn in this country; would be felt by nobody; would produce a revenue not undeserving of consideration; and what is of more importance, would enable us to accomplish a great transition with less violence to the feelings and prejudices of a large class of men.'

The countenances of the free-traders changed very much

while this portentous confession was taking place. The cheers suddenly stopped; and a member for a metropolitan district who had been applauding vociferously whispered to a neighbour, 'He has spoilt a capital speech; what could have induced him to bring in a fixed duty!' Penetrating member for a metropolitan district! As if the 'capital speech' had been made for any other purpose than to introduce the very declaration which you looked upon as so damaging! There is diplomacy even in debate: Lord Palmerston threw a practised and prescient eye over the disturbed elements of the house of commons, and two months afterwards, when a protectionist ministry on moderate principles (principles moderate and not fixed) was not impossible, the speech of the noble lord was quoted by many as a rallying-point.

The division was called: the majority of the government was not increased by two months' discussion since the 27th February; on the contrary, it was now only eighty-eight.

CHAPTER VII

In the meantime, besides the prolonged and unforeseen resistance of the protectionists, there were other and unexpected causes at work, which equally or perhaps even more powerfully tended to the fulfilment of the scheme of delay, which Lord George Bentinck had recommended his friends to adopt and encourage.

In the latter months of the year 1845 there broke out in some of the counties of Ireland one of those series of outrages which have hitherto periodically occurred in districts of that country. Assassination and crimes of violence were rife: men on the queen's highway were shot from behind hedges, or suddenly torn from their horses and beaten to death with clubs; houses were visited in the night by bodies of men, masked and armed—their owners dragged from their beds, and in the presence of their wives and children maimed and mutilated; the administration of unlawful oaths, with circumstances of terror, indicated the existence of secret confederations, whose fell intents, profusely and ostentatiously announced by threatening letters, were frequently and savagely perpetrated.

These barbarous distempers had their origin in the tenure of land in Ireland and in the modes of its occupation. A combination of causes, political, social, and economical, had for more than a century unduly stimulated the population of a country which had no considerable resources except in the soil. That soil had become divided into minute allotments, held by a pauper tenantry at exorbitant rents of a class of middlemen themselves necessitous, and who were mere traders in land. A fierce competition raged amid the squalid multitude for these strips of earth which were their sole means of existence. To regulate this fatal rivalry and restrain this emulation of despair, the peasantry enrolled in secret societies found refuge in an inexorable code. He who supplanted another in the occupation of the soil was doomed by an occult tribunal from which there was no appeal to a terrible retribution. His house was visited in the night by whitefeet and ribbonmen—his doom was communicated to him by the post in letters signed by Terry Alt or Molly M'Guire, or he was suddenly shot like a dog by the orders of Captain Rock. Yet even these violent inflictions rather punished than prevented the conduct against which they were directed. The Irish peasant had to choose between starving and assassination. If in deference to an anonymous mandate he relinquished his holding, he and those who depended on him were outcasts and wanderers; if he retained or accepted it, his life might be forfeit, but subsistence was secured; and in poor and lawless countries the means of living are more valued than life. Those who have treated of the agrarian crime of Ireland have remarked, that the facility with which these outrages have been committed has only been equalled by the difficulty of punishing them. A murder, perpetrated in noonday, in the sight of many persons, cannot be proved in a court of justice. The spectators are never witnesses; and it has been inferred from this, that the outrage is national and that the heart of the populace is with the criminal. But though a chief landlord or a stipendiary magistrate may occasionally be sacrificed, the great majority of victims are furnished by the humblest class. Not sympathy but terror seals the lip and clouds the eye of the bystander. And this is proved by the fact, that while those who have suffered have almost always publicly declared that they were unable to recognise their assailants, and believed them to be strangers, they have frequently in confidence furnished the police with the names of the guilty.

Thus there is this remarkable characteristic of the agrarian anarchy of Ireland which marks it out from all similar conditions of other countries : it is a war of the poor against the poor.

Before the rapid increase of population had forced governments to study political economy and to investigate the means of subsisting a people, statesmen had contented themselves by attributing to political causes these predial disturbances, and by recommending for them political remedies. The course of time that had aggravated the condition of the Irish peasantry had increased the numbers, the wealth, and the general importance of those of the middle classes of Ireland who professed the roman catholic faith. Shut out from the political privileges of the constitution, these formed a party of discontent that was a valuable ally to the modern whigs, too long excluded from that periodical share of power which is the life-blood of a parliamentary government and the safeguard of a constitutional monarchy. The misgovernment of Ireland became therefore a stock topic of the earlier opposition of the present century; and advocating the cause of their clients, who wished to become mayors, and magistrates, and members of the legislature, they argued that, in the concession of those powers and dignities, and perhaps in the discreet confiscation of the property of the church, the only cures could be found for threatening notices, robbery of arms, administering of unlawful oaths, burglary, murder, and arson.

Yet if these acts of violence were attributable to defective political institutions, why, as was usually the case, were they partial in their occurrence? Why were they limited to particular districts? If political grievances were the cause, the injustice would be as sharp in tranquil Wexford as in turbulent Tipperary. Yet out of the thirty-two counties of Ireland, the outrages prevailed usually in less than a third. These outrages were never insurrectionary: they were not directed against existing authorities; they were stimulated by no public cause or clamour; it was the private individual who was attacked, and for a private reason. This was their characteristic.

But as time elapsed, two considerable events occurred: the roman catholic restrictions were repealed, and the whigs became ministers. Notwithstanding these great changes, the condition of the Irish peasantry remained the same; the tenure of land was unchanged, the modes of its occupation were unaltered, its possession was equally necessary and equally perilous. The same circumstances produced the same consequences. Notwithstanding even that the Irish church had been remodelled and its revenues not only commuted but curtailed; notwithstanding that roman catholics had not only become members of parliament but even parliament had been reformed; Irish outrage became more flagrant and more extensive than at any previous epoch—and the whigs were ministers.

Placed in this responsible position, forced to repress the evil the causes of which they had so often explained and which with their co-operation had apparently been so effectually removed, the whig government were obliged to have recourse to the very means which they had so frequently denounced when recommended by their rivals, and that too on a scale of unusual magnitude and severity. They proposed for the adoption of parliament one of those measures which would suspend the constitution of Ireland, and which are generally known by the name of coercion acts.

The main and customary provisions of these coercion acts were of severe restraint, and scarcely less violent than the conduct they were constructed to repress. They invested the lord-lieutenant with power to proclaim a district as disturbed, and then to place its inhabitants without the pale of the established law; persons out of their dwellings between sunset and sunrise were liable to transportation; and to secure the due execution of the law, prisoners were tried before military tribunals, and not by their peers, whose verdicts from sympathy or terror were usually found to baffle justice.

These coercion acts were effectual; they invariably obtained their end, and the proclaimed districts became tranquil. But they were an affair of police, not of government; essentially temporary, their effect was almost as transient as their sway, and as they were never accompanied with any deep and sincere attempt to cope with the social circumstances which produced disorder, the recurrence of the chronic anarchy was merely an affair of time. Whether it were, that they did not sufficiently apprehend the causes, or that they shrank from a solution which must bring them in contact with the millions of a surplus population, there seems always to have been an understanding between the public men of both parties, that the Irish difficulty should be deemed a purely political or at the utmost a religious one. And even so late as 1846, no less a personage than the present chief secretary, put forward by his party to oppose an Irish coercion bill which themselves had loudly called for, declared that he could not sanction its penal enactments unless they were accompanied by the remedial measures that were necessary, to wit, an Irish franchise bill, and a bill for the amendment of municipal corporations!

When Sir Robert Peel, in 1841, after a memorable opposition of ten years acceded to office, sustained by all the sympathies of the country, his Irish policy, not sufficiently noticed amid the vast and urgent questions with which he had immediately to deal, was, however, to the political observer significant and interesting. As a mere matter of party tactics, it was not for him too much to impute Irish disturbances to political and religious causes, even if the accumulated experience of the last ten years were not developing a conviction in his mind, that the methods hitherto adopted to ensure the tranquillity of that country were superficial and fallacious. His cabinet immediately recognised a distinction between political and predial sources of disorder. The first, they resolved into a mere system of agitation, no longer justifiable by the circumstances, and this they determined to put down. The second, they sought in the conditions under which land was occupied, and these they determined to investigate. Hence, on one hand, the O'Connell prosecution: on the other, the Devon commission.

This was the bold and prudent policy of a minister who

felt he had the confidence of the country, and was sustained by great parliamentary majorities; and when the summoner of monster meetings was convicted, and the efficient though impartial manner in which the labours of the land commission were simultaneously conducted became to be bruited about, there seemed at last some prospect of the system of political quackery of which Ireland had been so long the victim being at last subverted. But there is nothing in which the power of circumstances is more evident than in politics. They baffle the forethought of statesmen, and control even the apparently inflexible laws of national development and decay.

Had the government of 1841 succeeded in its justifiable expectation of terminating the trade of political agitation in Ireland, armed with all the authority and all the information with which the labours of the land commission would have furnished them, they would in all probability have successfully grappled with the real causes of Irish misery and misrule. They might have thoroughly reformed the modes by which land is holden and occupied; have anticipated the spontaneous emigration that now rages by an administrative enterprise scarcely more costly than the barren loan of '47, and which would have wafted native energies to imperial shores; have limited under these circumstances the evil of the potato famine, even if the improved culture of the interval might not have altogether prevented that visitation; while the laws which regulated the competition between home and foreign industry in agricultural produce might have been modified with so much prudence, or, if necessary, ultimately repealed with so much precaution, that those rapid and startling vicissitudes that have so shattered the social fabric of Ireland might altogether have been avoided.

But it was decreed that it should be otherwise. Having achieved the incredible conviction of O'Connell by an Irish jury, the great culprit baffled the vengeance of the law by a quirk which a lawyer only could have devised. As regards his Irish policy, Sir Robert Peel never recovered this blow, the severity of which was proportionably increased by its occurrence at a moment of unprecedented success. Resolute not to recur to his ancient orangeism, yet desperate after his discomfiture of rallying a moderate party around his ministry, his practical mind, more clear-sighted than foreseeing, was alarmed at the absence of all influences for the government of Ireland. The tranquillity which might result from a reformed tenure of the soil must, if attainable, be a distant blessing, and at present he saw only the obstacles to its fulfilment—prejudiced landlords and the claims and necessities of pauper millions. He shrank from a theory which might be an illusion. He required a policy for the next post and the next division. There was in his view only one course to take, to outbid his predecessors as successfully in Irish politics as he was doing in taxes and tariffs. He resolved to appropriate the liberal party of Ireland, and merge it into the great conservative confederation which was destined to destroy so many things. He acted with promptitude and energy, for Sir Robert Peel never hesitated when he had made up his mind. His real character was very different from his public reputation. Far from being timid and wary, he was audacious and even headstrong. It was his cold and constrained demeanour that misled the public. There never was a man who did such rash things in so circumspect a manner. He had been fortunate in early disembarrassing himself of the orange counsellors who had conducted his Irish questions when in opposition ; vacant judgeships had opportunely satisfied the recognised and respectable claims of Mr. Serjeant Jackson and Mr. Lefroy ; and so Sir Robert Peel, without a qualm, suddenly began to govern Ireland by sending it 'messages of peace.'

They took various forms : sometimes a charitable bequests act virtually placed the roman catholic hierarchy in friendly equality with the prelates of the established church ; sometimes a 'godless college' called forth a moan from alarmed and irritated Oxford; the endowment of Maynooth struck wider and deeper, and the middle classes of England, roused from their religious lethargy, called in vain to the rescue of a protestantism betrayed. But the minister was unshaken. Successful and self-sufficient, impressed with a conviction that his government in duration would rival that of a Walpole or a Pitt, and exceed both in lustre, he treated every remonstrance with imperious disdain. He had even accustomed his mind to contemplate an ecclesiastical adjustment of Ireland which would have allied in that country the papacy with the state, and have terminated the constitutional supremacy of the anglican church, when suddenly, in the very heat of all this arrogant fortune, the mighty fabric of delusion shivered and fell to the ground.

An abused and indignant soil repudiated the ungrateful race that had exhausted and degraded its once exuberant bosom. The land refused to hold those who would not hold the land on terms of justice and of science. All the economical palliatives and political pretences of long years seemed only to aggravate the suffering and confusion. The poor-rate was levied upon a community of paupers, and the 'godless colleges' were denounced by Rome as well as Oxford.

After a wild dream of famine and fever, imperial loans, rates in aid, jobbing public works, confiscated estates, constituencies self-disfranchised, and St. Peter's bearding St. James's in a spirit becoming Christendom rather than Europe, time topped the climax of Irish misgovernment; and by the publication of the census of 1851 proved, that the millions with whose evils no statesmen would sincerely deal, but whose condition had been the pretext for so much empiricism, had disappeared, and Nature, more powerful than politicians, had settled the 'great difficulty.'

Ere the publication of that document the mortal career of Sir Robert Peel had closed, and indeed several of the circumstances to which we have just alluded did not occur in his administration; but the contrast between his policy and its results was nevertheless scarcely less striking. It was in '45 that he transmitted his most important 'message of peace' to Ireland, to be followed by an autumnal visit of her majesty to that kingdom, painted in complacent and prophetic colours by her prime minister. The visit was not made. In the course of that autumn, ten counties of Ireland were in a state of anarchy; and, mainly in that period, there were one hundred and thirty-six homicides committed, one hundred and thirty-eight houses burned, four hundred and eighty-three houses attacked, and one hundred and thirty-eight fired into; there were five hundred and forty-four cases of aggravated assault, and five hundred and fifty-one of robbery of arms; there were eighty-nine cases of bands appearing in arms; there were more than two hundred cases of administering unlawful oaths; and there were nineteen hundred and forty-four cases of sending threatening letters. By the end of the year, the general crime of Ireland had doubled in amount and enormity compared with the preceding year.

Instead of a visit to her Irish subjects, Queen Victoria had thus to address her parliament on its meeting in 1846 :—

'My lords and gentlemen,—

'I have observed, with deep regret, the very frequent instances in which the crime of deliberate assassination has been of late committed in Ireland. It will be your duty to consider, whether any measures can be devised calculated to give increased protection to life.'

In accordance with this important declaration from the throne, the Earl of St. Germans, then chief secretary to the lord-lieutenant, called the attention of the house of lords, on the 24th of February, to the new 'message of peace' of the government of Sir Robert Peel, which took the shape of a COERCION BILL.

CHAPTER VIII

LORD GEORGE BENTINCK had large but defined views as to the policy which should be pursued with respect to Ireland. He was a firm supporter of the constitutional preponderance allotted to the land in our scheme of government, not from any jealousy or depreciation of the other great sources of public wealth, for his sympathy with the trading classes was genuine, but because he believed that constitutional preponderance, while not inconsistent with great commercial prosperity, to be the best security for public liberty and the surest foundation of enduring power. But as reality was the characteristic of his vigorous and sagacious nature, he felt that a merely formal preponderance, one not sustained and authorised by an equivalent material superiority, was a position not calculated to endure in the present age, and one especially difficult to maintain with our rapidly increasing population. For this reason, he was always very anxious to identify the policy of Great Britain with that of Ireland, the latter being a country essentially agricultural; and he always shrank from any proposition which admitted a difference in the interests of the two kingdoms.

Liberal politicians who some years ago were very loud for justice to Ireland, and would maintain at all hazards the identity of the interests of the two countries, have of late frequently found it convenient to omit that kingdom from their statistical bulletins of national prosperity. Lord George Bentinck, on the contrary, would impress on his friends, that if they wished to maintain the territorial constitution of their country, they must allow no sectarian considerations to narrow the basis of sympathy on which it should rest; and in the acres and millions of Ireland, in its soil and its people, equally neglected, he would have sought the natural auxiliaries of our institutions. To secure for our Irish fellow-subjects a regular market for their produce; to develop the resources of their country by public works on a great scale; and to obtain a decent provision for the roman catholic priesthood from the land and not from the consolidated fund, were three measures which he looked upon as in the highest degree conservative.

When the project of the cabinet of 1846 had transpired, Lord George at once declared, and was in the habit of reiterating his opinion, that 'it would ruin the 500,000 small farmers of Ireland,' and he watched with great interest and anxiety the conduct of their representatives in the house of commons. It was with great difficulty that he could bring himself to believe, that political liberalism would induce the members for the south and west of Ireland to support a policy in his opinion so fatal to their countrymen as the unconditional repeal of the corn laws; and indeed before they took that step, which almost all of them have since publicly regretted and attempted to compensate for by their subsequent votes in the house of commons, the prospect of their conduct frequently and considerably varied.

The Earl of St. Germans, the chief secretary of the lord-lieutenant, introduced the coercion bill to the house of lords on the 24th February, and, considering the exigency, and the important reference to it in the speech from the throne, this step on the part of the government was certainly not precipitate. It was observed that the strongest supporters of the measure in the house of lords on this occasion were the leaders of the whig party. Lord Lansdowne, 'so far from complaining of the government for bringing forward the measure at so early a period of the session, was ready to admit, that after the declaration of her majesty, a declaration unhappily warranted by facts known to many of their lordships, every day was lost in which an effectual remedy was not at least attempted to put an end to a state of society so horrible.' Lord Clanricarde 'gave his ready assent to the bill'; and even Lord Grey, 'though he regretted the necessity for this measure, was of opinion that the chief secretary had established a sufficient case for arming the executive government with some additional powers.' When, therefore, at the end of the month of March, Lord George Bentinck was invited to attend a meeting of his friends, held at the house of Mr. Bankes, to consider the course which should be adopted by the protectionist party with respect to the coercion bill, it was assumed as a matter of course that the coalition of the government and the whigs must secure the passing of the measure, even if the protectionists were disposed, for the chance of embarrassing the ministry, to resist it; and of course there was no great tendency in that direction. Men are apt to believe that crime and coercion are inevitably associated. There was abundance of precedents for the course, which seemed also a natural one.

In less than a century there had been seventeen coercive acts for Ireland, a circumstance which might make some ponder whether such legislation were as efficacious as it was violent. However, assassination rife, Captain Rock and Molly M'Guire out at night, whigs and tories all agreed, it was easy to catch at a glance the foregone conclusion of the meeting. One advantage of having a recognised organ of a political party is that its members do not decide too precipitately. They listen before they determine, and if they have a doubt, they will grant the benefit of it to him whose general ability they have acknowledged, and to whom they willingly give credit for having viewed the question at issue in a more laborious and painful manner than themselves. Without a leader they commit themselves to opinions carelessly and hastily adopted. This is fatal to a party in debate; but it often entails very serious consequences when the mistakes have been committed in a less public and responsible scene than the house of commons.

In the present case, there was only one individual who took any considerable lead in the management of the party who ventured to suggest the expediency of pausing before they pledged themselves to support an unconstitutional measure, proposed by a government against which they were

arrayed under circumstances of urgent and unusual opposition. The support of an unconstitutional measure may
be expedient, but it cannot be denied that it is the most
indubitable evidence of confidence. This suggestion, though
received with kindness, elicited little sympathy, and Lord
George Bentinck, who had not yet spoken, and who always
refrained at these meetings from taking that directing part
which he never wished to assume, marking the general
feeling of those present, and wishing to guide it to a practical
result advantageous to their policy, observed that the support
of the coercion bill by the protectionists ought to be made
conditional on the government proving the sincerity of their
policy by immediately proceeding with their measure; that
if life were in such danger in Ireland as was officially stated,
and as he was bound to believe, no corn or customs bill
could compete in urgency with the necessity of pressing
forward a bill the object of which was to arrest wholesale
assassination. He was therefore for giving the government
a hearty support, provided they proved they were in earnest
in their determination to put down murder and outrage in
Ireland by giving a priority in the conduct of public business
to the measure in question.

This view of the situation, which was certainly adroit, for
it combined the vindication of order with an indefinite delay
of the measures for the repeal of the protective system,
seemed to please every one; there was a murmur of approbation, and when one of the most considerable of the country
gentlemen expressed the prevalent feeling, and added that
all that was now to be desired was, that Lord George Bentinck
would kindly consent to be the organ of the party on the
occasion, and state their view to the house, the cheering was
very hearty. It came from the hearts of more than two
hundred gentlemen, scarcely one of whom had a personal
object in this almost hopeless struggle beyond the maintenance of a system which he deemed advantageous to his
country; but they wished to show their generous admiration
of the man who in the dark hour of difficulty and desertion
had proved his courage and resource, had saved them from

public contempt, and taught them to have confidence in themselves. And after all, there are few rewards in life which equal such sympathy from such men. The favour of courts and the applause of senates may have their moments of excitement and delight, but the incident of deepest and most enduring gratification in public life is to possess the cordial confidence of a high-spirited party, for it touches the heart as well as the intellect, and combines all the softer feelings of private life with the ennobling consciousness of public duty.

Lord George Bentinck, deeply moved, consented to become the organ of the protectionists in this matter, but he repeated in a marked manner his previous declaration, that his duty must be limited to the occasion; he would serve with them, but he could not pretend to be the leader of a party. In that capacity, however, the government chose to recognise him, and there occurred in consequence, very shortly after this meeting, a scene in the house of commons which occasioned at the time a great deal of surprise and scandal. The secretary of the treasury, in pursuance of one of his principal duties, which is to facilitate by mutual understanding the conduct of public business in the house of commons, applied to Lord George Bentinck, confessedly at the request of Sir Robert Peel, to 'enter into some arrangement' as to the conduct of public business before Easter. The arrangement suggested was, that if the protectionists supported the coercion bill, which it was the wish of Sir Robert Peel should be read a first time before Easter, the third reading of the bill for the repeal of the corn laws should be postponed until after Easter. The interview by appointment took place in the vote office, where the secretary of the treasury 'called Lord George aside' and made this proposition. Lord George stated in reply, 'what he believed to be the views of the party with whom he served,' and they were those we have already intimated. The 'arrangement' was concluded, and it was at the same time agreed that certain questions, of which notice had been given by Lord John Russell, relative to the progress of these very measures, should be allowed by the protectionists to pass *sub silentio*. This 'pledge,' made by the noble lord for himself and his friends, was 'scrupulously observed.' Nevertheless after all this, a letter arrived from the secretary of the treasury, addressed to the noble lord, stating that the secretary 'had not been authorised in saying as much as he had said,' and requesting that the conversation which had taken place might be considered private. Upon this Lord George Bentinck drew up a statement, 'setting forth all that had passed,' and forwarded it to the secretary as his reply. Subsequently he met that gentleman, who admitted that 'every word in that statement, as respected the conversation which had passed, was perfectly correct.'

This being the state of the case, on the second night of the debate on Mr. Eliot Yorke's amendment which we have noticed, and after the adjournment had been moved and carried, the government proceeded with some motions of form, which indicated their intention to secure, if possible, the third reading of the corn bill before Easter. Upon this Lord George Bentinck, after a hurried and apparently agitated conversation with the secretary of the treasury and others connected with the government, rose to move the adjournment of the house. He then gave as his reason the circumstances which we have briefly conveyed. A scene of considerable confusion occurred: the secretary of the treasury admitted the correctness of the statement; the first lord of the treasury rejected the alleged authority of the secretary. Mr. Tuffnell, on the part of the whigs, intimated that public business could not be carried on if the recognised organs were repudiated by their chief. The feeling of all parties coincided with Mr. Tuffnell; finally, an Irish repealer rose and announced that the government were bartering their corn bill to secure coercion to Ireland. Lord George Bentinck said the coercion bill was 'a second curfew act,' that nothing but necessity could justify it, and if it were necessary it must be immediate. Sir Robert remained irritated and obstinate. He would not give up a stage either of the corn bill or the coercion bill; he wanted to advance both before Easter. The mere division of the house between free-traders and protectionists had already ceased; there were breakers ahead, and it was not difficult from this night to perceive that the course of the government would not be so summary as they had once expected.

This strange interlude occurred after midnight on the 26th of March. On Friday, the 27th, the house divided on the amendment of Mr. Eliot Yorke, and the corn bill was read for the second time. On the reassembling of the house on Monday, the 30th, an extraordinary scene took place.

It appears that the cabinet after painful deliberation had arrived at the conclusion that, notwithstanding the importance of sending up the corn bill to the house of lords before Easter, it was absolutely necessary to proceed at once with the coercion bill; and it was resolved that the secretary of state should on this evening lay before the house the facts and reasons which 'induce the government to believe in the necessity of the measure.' Mr. O'Connell and his followers had already announced their intention of opposing the first reading of the bill, an allowable but very unusual course. It is competent to the house of commons to refuse a first reading to any bill sent down to it; but the journals afford few examples of the exercise of such a privilege. A member of the house of lords may lay on the table as a matter of pure right any bill which he thinks proper to introduce, and it is read a first time as a matter of course; the orders of the house of commons are different, and a member must obtain permission before he introduces a bill. This permission is occasionally refused; but when a bill comes from the house of lords, the almost invariable custom is to read it for the first time without discussion. There are, however, as we have observed, instances to the contrary, and the Irish coercion bill of '33 was one of them. So pregnant a precedent could not be forgotten on the present occasion. The government therefore were prepared for an opposition to the first reading of their bill; but trusting to the strength of their case and the assumed support of the whig party, they believed that this opposition would not be stubborn, more especially as there were numerous stages of the measure on which the views of its opponents might be subsequently expressed, and as they themselves were prepared to engage that they would not proceed further than this first reading until the corn bill had passed the house of commons. The consternation therefore of the government could scarcely be concealed when they found on Monday night that they had to encounter a well-organised party opposition headed by Sir William Somerville and sanctioned and supported in debate by Lord John Russell and Sir George Grey.

It would seem indeed a difficult and somewhat graceless office for the whigs to oppose the first reading of a government bill, concerning too the highest duties of administration, which had received such unqualified approval from all the leading members of their party in the house of lords, who had competed in declarations of its necessity and acknowledgments of its moderation, while they only regretted the too tardy progress of a measure so indispensable to the safety of the country and the security of her majesty's subjects. A curious circumstance, however, saved them from this dilemma, which yet in the strange history of faction they had nevertheless in due time to encounter.

As the coercion bill, coming from the lords, appeared on the paper of the day in the form of a notice of motion, the secretary of state, this being a day on which orders have precedence, had to move that such orders of the day should be postponed, so that he might proceed with the motion on the state of Ireland of which notice had been given. The strict rule of the house is, that on Mondays and Fridays orders of the day should have precedence of notices of motion, so that it was impossible for the secretary of state to make his motion, that a certain bill (the protection of life (Ireland) bill) should be read a first time without permission of the house, a permission always granted as a matter of course on such nights to the government, since the business which can be brought forward, whether in the shape of orders or motions, is purely government business, and thus the interests and privilege of no independent member of parliament can be affected by a relaxation of the rules which the convenience of a ministry and the conduct of public business occasionally require. However, on this night, no sooner had the secretary of state made in a few formal words this formal request, than up sprang Sir William Somerville to move an amendment that the orders of the day should not be postponed, which he supported in a spirited address, mainly on the ground of the great inconvenience that must be suffered from the postponement of the corn bill. The motion of the secretary of state would produce a long, exciting, and exasperating debate. Time would be lost—for what? To advance one stage of a measure which it was avowedly not the intention of the government to press at the present moment. Sir William concluded with a very earnest appeal to Lord George Bentinck and his friends, 'who might at no very distant period have the government of Ireland intrusted to them,' not for the sake of a momentary postponement of the corn bill, to place themselves, by voting for this measure of coercion, in collision with the Irish nation. He called upon Lord George Bentinck to weigh the position in which he was placed.

This amendment was seconded by Mr. Smith O'Brien, the member for the county of Limerick, who warned the government that they 'were entering on a contest which would continue for months.' He taunted the minister with governing the country without a party. What chance was there of reconciliation with his estranged friends? After the treatment of that 'disavowed plenipotentiary,' the secretary of the treasury, who would be again found willing to undertake the mission of patching up a truce? He was not present when the terms of the treaty were exposed: but he understood, that if the government introduced this coercion bill before Easter, then that Lord George Bentinck would deem it wise, proper, and expedient; but if after Easter, then the complexion and character of the bill were in the noble lord's judgment utterly transformed, and it was

declared to be quite untenable and unconstitutional. Was
that the kind of support on which the government calculated
for passing this measure?

The secretary of state made a dexterous, conciliatory,
almost humble address in reply to the taunts of Mr. Smith
O'Brien. He said that he was well aware of the fact of
which he had been just reminded, that in the present state
of parties, the declared adherents of the government were
a small minority; he even, while excusing the delay in the
progress of the Irish measure, reminded the house of the
curious fact, that since the meeting of parliament two successive Irish secretaries had lost their seats in the house of
commons in consequence of supporting the administration
of which they were members.

The case of the government was really so good and clear,
that for a moment it seemed the opposition could hardly
persist in their unusual proceeding: but this was a night of
misfortunes.

There had been for some time a smouldering feud between
the secretary and the recorder of Dublin. The learned
gentleman had seized the occasion which the present state
of parties afforded, and in the course of the recent debate
on the second reading of the corn bill had declared that the
asserted famine in Ireland was on the part of the government 'a great exaggeration.' The secretary had addressed
himself particularly to this observation in his speech on
the 27th, the night of the division; and had noticed it in
a tone of acerbity. He had even intimated that it might
have been used by one who was a disappointed solicitor for
high office, and whom the government had declined to assist
in an unwarrantable arrangement of the duties and salary
of the judicial post he at present occupied. The learned
recorder, justly indignant at this depreciating innuendo, resolved to make an opportunity on the following Monday
for his vindication and retort. He rose, therefore, immediately after the skilful and winning appeal of the secretary
and pronounced an invective against the right honourable
gentleman which was neither ill-conceived nor ill-delivered.

It revived the passions that for a moment seemed inclined to lull, and the protectionists, who on this occasion were going to support the government, forgot the common point of union while the secretary was described as 'the evil genius of the cabinet.'

After this, it was impossible to arrest the course of debate. Mr. O'Connell, who appeared to be in a state of great debility, made one of those acute points for which he was distinguished. He said the government complained of the threat held out by those who opposed the bill, that they would avail themselves of the forms of the house to give it every opposition in their power. But what did the government do themselves? Why, they were trying to trample upon one of the sessional orders and to abrogate the forms of the house in order to coerce the Irish people. Lord George Bentinck said, that 'the chief minister had told them, that this was a bill to put down murder and assassination; in that case, if this bill were delayed, the blood of every man murdered in Ireland was on the head of her majesty's ministers.' Sir George Grey followed, and avoiding any discussion of the state of Ireland in which Lord George had entered, supported the amendment of Sir William Somerville on the broad ground that the bill for the repeal of the corn laws ought not to be for a moment delayed. 'The debates on that measure had continued several weeks; and all who had any lengthened parliamentary experience must be convinced, that if the further progress of the corn bill was postponed until after Easter, they would have much longer and protracted debates in its future stages than if the bill were pushed *de die in diem*. As he had understood, the government had intended that this bill should have gone up to the house of lords before Easter, when it would have been printed, and the second reading could have taken place at an early day after the holidays; but if it were put off until after Easter, he would defy any man to show any reasonable expectation of its getting to a second reading in the other house before June, or July, or even August.'

This was encouraging, and the plot seemed to thicken.

The secretary at war was put up by the government to neutralise the effect of the speech of Sir George Grey, and he said: 'I speak not only as a cabinet minister, but also as a considerable Irish proprietor.' He said, 'that anything so horrible as the state of demoralisation and crime in which many parts of Ireland were plunged, anything so perfect as the suspension of the law in those parts of that country, anything, in short, so complete as the abrogation of liberty that obtained there, was, perhaps, never known.' He thought that 'no man and no minister could, under these circumstances, decline to admit that every and any measure ought to be postponed until a division had been taken, at least upon the principle of a measure which had for its object the suppression of these horrors.' After such a declaration it was clear the government were in a false position when by the same organ it had to state, 'that in asking to read this bill to-night, they only intended to postpone the corn bill for one night.'

Lord John Russell following, admitted that, 'in voting for the motion of Sir William Somerville it was not to be supposed, that if the secretary of state made out a case, he would not support the government bill'; yet how the secretary was ever to find an opportunity of making out his case if the amendment of Sir William Somerville was carried, was not very apparent. Sir Robert Peel, who was disquieted by the whole proceedings connected with the coercion bill, irritated by the episode of 'the disavowed plenipotentiary,' from which he did not for some time recover, and really alarmed at the indefinite prospect of delay in passing his all-important measures which now began to open, could not conceal his vexation in the remarks which he offered; and speaking of the amendment as one 'of a frivolous character,' indignant cries of 'No, no,' from his usual admirers, obliged him to withdraw the expression. His feelings were not soothed when, later in the evening, even Mr. Cobden rose to deplore the conduct of that minister whom he otherwise so much admired. 'He certainly regarded it as a great calamity. Something had actuated the government which he could not understand. He had a perfect belief in the sincerity of the prime minister, but in all human probability the corn bill would not now enter the house of lords before the beginning or middle of May; and when it would come out again, heaven only knew!'

The house now divided, and being supported by all the protectionists present, the government had a majority of 39, so the standing order was for that night rescinded, and, although the hour was late for such a statement, the secretary proceeded with the official exposition. Notwithstanding the depressing circumstances of the previous debate, the speech of Sir James Graham was distinguished by all that lucid arrangement of details and that comprehensive management of his subject which distinguish him. The statement made a great impression upon the house and the country, but unfortunately for the government, the more necessary they made the measure appear, the more unjustifiable was their conduct in not immediately and vehemently pursuing it. They had indeed in the speech from the throne, at the commencement of this memorable session, taken up a false position for their campaign, and we shall see, as we pursue this narrative of these interesting events, that the fall of Sir Robert Peel was perhaps occasioned not so much by his repeal of the corn laws as by the mistake in tactics which this adroit and experienced parliamentary commander so strangely committed.

On this night of the 30th the government made no advance: immediately that the secretary had finished, the followers of Mr. O'Connell moved the adjournment of the house, and persisted in this line notwithstanding the almost querulous appeal of the first minister.

CHAPTER IX

LORD GEORGE wrote the next morning (Tuesday, March 31st) to a friend, who had not been able to attend the debate: 'I look upon last night as the most awkward night the government have had yet; I believe they would have given their ears to have been beaten. We have now fairly set them and the tail at loggerheads, and I cannot see how they are to get another stage of either the tariff or corn bill, before next Tuesday at any rate. I doubt if they will do anything before Easter.'

It was understood that the house would adjourn for the Easter recess on the 8th instant. There were therefore only two nights remaining for government business before the holidays. On the first of these (Friday, April the 3rd), Mr. O'Connell had announced that he should state his views at length on the condition of Ireland and the causes of these agrarian outrages. Accordingly, when the order of the day for resuming the adjourned debate was read, he rose at once to propose an amendment to the motion. He sat in an unusual place—in that generally occupied by the leader of the opposition—and spoke from the red box, convenient to him from the number of documents to which he had to refer. His appearance was of great debility and the tones of his voice were very still. His words indeed only reached those who were immediately around him, and the ministers sitting on the other side of the green table, and listening with that interest and respectful attention which became the occasion.

It was a strange and touching spectacle to those who remembered the form of colossal energy and the clear and thrilling tones that had once startled, disturbed, and controlled senates. Mr. O'Connell was on his legs for nearly two hours, assisted occasionally in the management of his documents by some devoted aide-de-camp. To the house generally it was a performance of dumb show, a feeble old man muttering before a table; but respect for the great parliamentary personage kept all as orderly as if the fortunes of a party hung upon his rhetoric; and though not an accent reached the gallery, means were taken that next morning the country should not lose the last and not the least interesting of the speeches of one who had so long occupied and agitated the mind of nations.

This remarkable address was an abnegation of the whole policy of Mr. O'Connell's career. It proved by a mass of authentic evidence, ranging over a long term of years, that Irish outrage was the consequence of physical misery, and that the social evils of that country could not be successfully encountered by political remedies. To complete the picture, it concluded with a panegyric of Ulster and a patriotic quotation from Lord Clare.

Lord John Russell, who as an experienced parliamentary leader had already made more than one effort to extricate the whigs from the consequences of the hearty support given to the government measures in the other house by Lords Lansdowne and Clanricarde and even by Lord Grey, ventured to-night even to say that if he should agree that the house would do well to assent to the first reading of this bill, he thought he was bound to state also, that in the future stages of it he should have 'objections to offer going to the foundations of some of its principal provisions.'

His speech was curious, as perhaps the last considerable manifesto of whig delusion respecting Ireland. Coercion bills might be occasionally necessary; no doubt of it; Lord Grey had once a coercion bill, and Lord John Russell had voted for it; but then remedial measures ought to be introduced with coercive ones: the evil should be repressed, but also cured. Thus, Lord Althorp, when the government introduced their great coercion bill, introduced also a measure which, besides making a great reform in the pro-

testant church of Ireland, exempted the whole catholic
community of Ireland from the payment of church cess,
which had previously been felt as a very great grievance.
On another day Lord Althorp declared his intention of
pressing through parliament a jury bill which had been
brought into the house the previous session, but which was
allowed to drop in the house of lords.

Again, there was another declaration which Lord Althorp
had made which, somehow or other, seemed to have been
forgotten. It was a declaration with respect to the municipal corporations of Ireland. Lord Althorp said it was
exceedingly desirable that the institutions of the two
countries should be assimilated as much as possible; and
that as a general rule the corporate bodies of Ireland should
be the same as England. Mr. O'Connell had said on that
occasion that there was no greater grievance in Ireland than
the existence of corporations in their then shape. Lord
John contrasted this language of Lord Althorp, 'simple,
plain, emphatic, and decided,' with the language of the
government of Sir Robert Peel; and held up to admiration
the whig policy of 1833, certainly coercive, but with remedial
measures, a measure for the abolition of church cess introduced ten days before the coercion bill and a promise of
municipal reform made simultaneously with the proclamation of martial law. This was real statesmanship and
touching the root of the evil. Whereas 'Sir Robert Peel
had only consented to passing the municipal bill in a
crippled state, and only now (in 1846) promised, that the
corporations of Ireland should be placed on the same footing as the corporations of England.' Who could be surprised
that such a policy should end in famine and pestilence?

The followers of Mr. O'Connell again succeeded in
adjourning the debate until Monday the 6th. On that
day Sir Robert Peel made 'an earnest appeal' to extricate
himself from the almost perilous position in which he found
his administration suddenly involved. In case the division
on the first reading of the Irish bill should not take place
that night, he endeavoured to prevail on those members

who had notices on the paper for the following night (Tuesday the 7th), the last night before the holidays, to relinquish their right and to permit the Irish debate to proceed and conclude. 'He had no wish to interfere with the due discussion of the measure; but he believed that the Irish members, if they permitted the house to proceed with the corn bill, by concluding the discussion on the Irish bill, would be rendering an essential service to their country.'

But this earnest appeal only influenced still more the fiery resolves of Mr. Smith O'Brien and his friends. They threw the responsibility for delay of the corn bill on the government. The inconvenience which the country suffered was occasioned by the minister, not by the Irish members. He ought on Friday last to have adjourned the discussion on the coercion bill until after Easter. He and other members who were on the paper for to-morrow would willingly relinquish their right of priority in favour of the corn bill, or of any measure of a remedial kind, but not in favour of a coercion bill. He did not wish to have any concealment with the minister as to the course which the Irish members would pursue. It was their bounden duty to take care that *pari passu* with the discussion of the coercion bill there should be discussions as to the mis-government of Ireland; and that in the absence of any remedial measures of the government, they should have an opportunity of suggesting such as they thought advisable for removing those evils which they utterly denied that the measure now before the house would remove.

In vain Sir Robert, in his blandest tones, and with that remarkable command of a temper, not naturally serene, which distinguished him, acknowledged to a certain degree the propriety of the course intimated by Mr. Smith O'Brien; but suggested at the same time that it was compatible with allowing the Irish bill to be now read for a first time, since on its subsequent stages Mr. O'Brien and his friends would have the full opportunity which they desired of laying before the house the whole condition of the country. All was useless. No less a personage than Mr. John O'Connell treated the appeal with contempt, and lectured the first minister on the 'great mistake' which he had made. Little traits like these revealed the true parliamentary position of the once omnipotent leader of the great conservative party. With the legions of the protectionists watching their prey in grim silence, while the liberal sections were united in hostile manœuvres against the government, it was recognised at once that the great minister had a staff without an army; not a reconnoitring could take place without the whole cabinet being under orders, and scarcely a sharpshooter sallied from the opposite ranks without the prime minister returning his fire in person.

Sir Robert Peel mournfully observed that he 'did not wish to provoke a recriminatory discussion,' and he resigned himself to his fate. Immediately the third night of the adjourned debate on the Irish bill commenced, and was sustained, principally by the Irish members, until a late hour. It had not been the intention of Lord George Bentinck to have spoken on this occasion, though he had never been absent for a moment from his seat, and watched all that occurred with that keen relish which was usual with him when he thought things were going right; but having been personally and not very courteously appealed to by the late Mr. Dillon Browne, and deeming also the occasion, just before the holidays, a not unhappy one, he rose and concluded the debate. His speech was not long, it was not prepared, and it was very animated.

Recapitulating himself the main features of the disturbed district, he said: 'It is because of these things, sir, that I am prepared to support at least the first reading of a bill, which I freely admit to be most unconstitutional in itself.'

Noticing a speech made in the course of the evening by Lord Morpeth, who had himself once been chief secretary of the lord-lieutenant, Lord George thought it discreet to remind the house of the unequivocal support given to this bill by the whig leaders in another place: 'Sir, I think when we see all the great leaders of the whig party supporting the measure elsewhere, we cannot be justly impugned for doing as they do.' Lord Morpeth had referred to 'remedial measures which he thinks should be introduced for Ireland: to measures for the extension of the municipal, and also of the parliamentary franchise of that country; and he expressed his desire to see those franchises put on the same footing as the franchises of England.' 'For the life of me,' exclaimed Lord George, 'I confess, I cannot see in what way the extension of political franchises of any description in Ireland would afford a remedy for the evils which this measure aims to suppress. I think, sir, it is impossible not to perceive that there is a connection between agrarian outrage and the poverty of the people.'

After noticing the inadequate poor law which then existed in Ireland, he added: 'There is also another point immediately connected with this subject to which I must refer. I allude, sir, to the system of absenteeism. I cannot disguise from myself the conviction, that many of the evils of Ireland arise from the system of receiving rents by absentee landlords who spend them in other countries. I am well aware that, in holding this doctrine, I am not subscribing to the creed of political economists. I am well aware that Messrs. Senior and M'Culloch hold, that it makes no difference whether the Irish landlord spends his rents in Dublin, on his Irish estates, in London, in Bath, or elsewhere. I profess, sir, I cannot understand that theory. I believe that the first ingredient in the happiness of a people is, that the gentry should reside on their native soil, and spend their rents among those from whom they receive them. I cannot help expressing a wish that some arrangement may be made connected with the levying of the poor rate in Ireland, by which absentee landlords may be made to contribute in something like a fair proportion to the wants of the poor in the district in which they ought to reside. There is an arrangement in the hop-growing districts in England in respect to tithe, which might, I think, afford a very useful suggestion. There are two tithes: the one, the ordinary tithe, the other, extraordinary, which is levied only so long as the land is cultivated in hops. I think if there were two poor rates introduced into Ireland, the one applying to all occupiers of land, and the other to all those who did not spend a certain portion of the year on some portion of their estates in Ireland, it would prove useful. I think that by thus appealing to their interests, it might induce absentee landlords to reside much more in Ireland than is now unfortunately the case.

'But, sir, I think there are other remedial measures. Some days ago, the secretary of state told the member for Stroud (Mr. Poulett Scrope), when he suggested some such measure, that he was treading on dangerous ground, and that the doctrines he was advocating might be written in letters of blood in Ireland; but, notwithstanding all this, I still say that I think measures might be introduced for improving the relations between landlord and tenant in Ireland. I do think that some guarantee might, and ought to be, given to the tenantry of Ireland for the improvements they make upon their farms.

'Sir, the secretary of state in introducing this measure, maintained a doctrine which, I think, much more likely to be written in letters of blood, for he bound up the question of the corn laws with the present one. He said, that unless he could have prevailed on his colleagues to accede to his free trade measures as regards corn, he would not have introduced this bill. Why, sir, far from giving food to the people of Ireland, in my opinion the measures of her majesty's ministers will take away from the people of Ireland their food, by destroying the profits of their only manufacture—the manufacture of corn—and injuring their agriculture; depriving them of employment; in fact, by taking away from them the very means of procuring subsistence. Sir, I cannot see how the repeal of those laws affecting corn can be in any way connected with the suppression of outrage and the protection of life. What is this but to say that, unless we have a free trade in corn, we must be prepared to concede a free trade in agrarian outrage—a free trade in maiming and houghing cattle—a free trade in incendiarism—a free trade in the burning and sacking of houses—a free trade in midnight murder and in noon-day assassination? What is this but telling the people of Ireland, that assassination, murder, incendiarism, are of such light consideration in the eyes of the secretary of state, that their sanction or suppression by the minister of the crown hinges upon the condition of the corn market and the difference in the price of potatoes?

'Sir, what has the potato disease to do with the outrages in Ireland? Some think a great deal. I have taken the trouble of looking into the matter. I have examined into the state of crime in at least five counties: Tipperary, Roscommon, Limerick, Leitrim, and Clare; and I find, that during the three months prior to the first appearance of the potato disease, and when in fact food was as cheap in Ireland as at almost any former period—when plenty abounded in all quarters of the empire—that the amount of crime exceeded that in the three months immediately following. Now, those who doubt this statement will have an opportunity of ascertaining the correctness of my figures, for I will not deal in general assertions. Well then, sir, I find in the three months, May, June, and July last, that the number of crimes committed in the five counties I have mentioned amounted to no less than 1180, while in the three months immediately after the potato disease, or famine, as it is called, the amount of crime committed in the same three months was not 1180, but 870. I should like to know therefore what this agrarian outrage has to do with the potato famine; and where is the justification for a minister coming down to this house, and declaring that unless we pass a free trade measure we are not to obey her majesty's commands by passing a measure for the protection of life in Ireland. Why, sir, I think when this language reaches the people of Ireland, coming too, as it does, from the treasury, above all from the secretary of state for the home department, there is indeed danger to be apprehended that such a doctrine may be written in letters of blood in that country. Why, sir, if we are to hear such language as this from that minister of the crown charged with the peace of the country, we may just as well have Captain Rock established as lord-lieutenant in the castle of Dublin, a whiteboy for chief secretary, and Molly Maguire installed at Whitehall with the seals of the home department.'

And afterwards he remarked: 'I have been taunted that when I may be entrusted with the government of Ireland, I should perhaps then learn, that Tyrone was an orange county. Sir, in answer to that taunt, I must take leave to ask what expression of mine, either in this house or out of it, justifies any such remark? When or where can it be said, that I have ever permitted myself to know any distinction between an orangeman and a catholic; when, in the whole course of my parliamentary career, have I ever given a vote or uttered a sentiment hostile or unfriendly to the roman catholics, either of England or Ireland?'

This speech, though delivered generally in favour of the Irish bill, attracted very much the attention and, as it appeared afterwards, the approbation of those Irish members, who, although sitting on the liberal benches, did not acknowledge the infallible authority of Mr. O'Connell, and was the origin of a political connection between them and Lord George Bentinck which on more than one subsequent occasion promised to bring important results.

Two successive motions were now made for the adjournment of the debate, and Sir Robert Peel at length said, that he 'saw it was useless to persist.' He agreed to the adjournment until the next day, with the understanding that if it did not come on he would name the time to which it should be postponed after the holidays.

Upon this, Sir William Somerville made one more appeal to the minister to postpone the further discussion of the Irish bill altogether until the corn bill had passed the commons. He intimated that unless the government at once adopted this resolution they would find themselves after Easter in the same perplexity which now paralysed them. They would not be permitted to bring on this measure except upon government nights, and the discussion might then last weeks.

The minister, exceedingly embarrassed, would not however relent. On the following day, when he moved the adjournment of the house for the holidays, he reduced the vacation three days, in order to obtain Friday, a government night, which otherwise would have been absorbed in the holidays, and he announced the determination of the government again to proceed on that night with the Irish bill in preference to the corn bill. The Irish members glanced defiance, and the protectionists could scarcely conceal their satisfaction. The reputation of Sir Robert Peel for parliamentary management seemed to be vanishing; never was a government in a more tottering state; and the whigs especially began to renew their laments that the Edinburgh letter and its consequences had prevented the settlement of the corn question from devolving to the natural arbitrator in the great controversy, their somewhat rash but still unrivalled leader, Lord John Russell.

CHAPTER X

THE members of the protectionist opposition returned to their constituents with the sanguine feelings which success naturally inspires. Their efforts had surprised, not displeased, the country; the elections were in their favour; the government business halted; the delay in the calculated arrival of the famine had taken the edge off the necessity which it was supposed would have already carried the corn bill through the commons, while the twin measure which the throes of Ireland had engendered had developed elements of opposition which even the calmest observer thought might possibly end in overthrow. Above all, that seemed to have happened which the most experienced in parliamentary life had always deemed to be impracticable; namely the formation of a third party in the house of commons.

How completely this latter and difficult result was owing to the abilities and energies of one man, and how anomalous was the position which he chose to occupy in not taking the formal lead of a party which was entirely guided by his example, were convictions and considerations that at this juncture much occupied men's minds. And it was resolved among the most considerable of the country gentlemen to make some earnest and well-combined effort during the recess to induce Lord George Bentinck to waive the unwillingness he had so often expressed of becoming their avowed and responsible leader.

When Lord George Bentinck first threw himself into the breach, he was influenced only by a feeling of indignation at the manner in which he thought the conservative party had been trifled with by the government and Lord Stanley, his personal friend and political leader, deserted by a majority of the cabinet. As affairs developed, and it became evident that the bulk of the conservative party throughout the country had rallied round his standard, Lord George could not conceal from himself the consequences of such an event, or believe that it was possible that the party in the house of commons, although Lord Stanley might eventually think fit to guide it by his counsels and become if necessary personally responsible for its policy, could be long held together unless it were conducted by a leader present in the same assembly, and competent under all circumstances to represent its opinions in debate. Lord George, although a very proud man, had no vanity or self-conceit. He took a very humble view of his own powers, and he had at the same time a very exalted one of those necessary to a leader of the house of commons. His illustrious connection, Mr. Canning, was his standard. He had been the private secretary of that minister in his youth, and the dazzling qualities of that eminent personage had influenced the most susceptible time of life of one who was very tenacious of his impressions. What Lord George Bentinck appreciated most in a parliamentary speaker was brilliancy: quickness of perception, promptness of repartee, clear and concise argument, a fresh and felicitous quotation, wit and picture, and if necessary a passionate appeal that should never pass the line of high-bred sentiment. Believing himself not to be distinguished by these rhetorical qualities, he would listen with no complacency to those who would urge in private that the present period of parliamentary life was different from the days of Mr. Canning, and that accumulated facts and well-digested reasoning on their bearing, a command of all the materials of commercial controversy, and a mastery of the laws that regulate the production and distribution of public wealth, combined with habits of great diligence and application, would ensure the attention of a popular assembly, especially when united to a high character and great social position. This might be urged; but he would only shake his head, with a ray of humour twinkling in his piercing eyes, and say in a half-drawling tone: 'If Mr. Canning were alive, he could do all this better than any of them, and be not a whit less brilliant.'

There was also another reason why Lord George Bentinck was unwilling to assume the post of leader of the conservative party, and this very much influenced him. Sprung from a great whig house, and inheriting all the principles and prejudices of that renowned political connection which had expelled the Stuarts, he had accepted in an unqualified sense the dogma of religious liberty. This principle was first introduced into active politics in order to preserve the possessions of that portion of the aristocracy which had established itself on the plunder of the church. It was to form the basis of a party which should prevent reaction and restitution of church lands. Whether the principle be a true one, and whether its unqualified application by any party in the state be possible, are questions yet unsettled. It is not probable, for example, that the worship of Juggernaut, which Lord Dalhousie permits in Orissa, would be permitted even by Lord John Russell at Westminster. Even a papist procession is forbidden, and wisely. The application of the principle, however, in Lord George Bentinck's mind was among other things associated with the public recognition of the roman catholic hierarchy by the state, and a provision for its maintenance in Ireland in accordance with the plan of Mr. Pitt. What had happened with respect to the vote on the endowment of Maynooth in 1845 had convinced him that his opinions on this subject presented an insuperable barrier to his ever becoming the leader of a party which had contributed three-fourths of the memorable minority on that occasion. It was in vain that it was impressed upon him by those most renowned for their protestant principles, and who were at the same time most anxious to see Lord George Bentinck in his right position, that the question of Maynooth was settled, and there was now no prospect of future measures of a similar character. This was not the opinion of Lord George Bentinck. He nursed in his secret soul a great scheme for the regeneration and settlement of Ireland, which he thought ought to be one of the mainstays of a conservative party; and it was his opinion that the condition of the roman catholic priesthood must be considered.

It was in vain, in order to assist in removing these scruples, that it was represented to him by others that endowment of a priesthood by the state was a notion somewhat old-fashioned, and opposed to the spirit of the age which associated true religious freedom with the full development of the voluntary principle. He listened to these suggestions with distrust, and even with a little contempt. Mr. Canning had been in favour of the endowment of the Irish priesthood, that was sufficient for that particular; and as for the voluntary principle, he looked upon it as priestcraft in disguise; his idea of religious liberty was, that all religions should be controlled by the state.

Besides these two prominent objections to accepting the offered post, namely, his unaffected distrust in his parliamentary abilities and his assumed want of concordance with his followers on a great principle of modern politics, we must also remember that his compliance with the request involved no ordinary sacrifice of much which renders life delightful. He was to relinquish pursuits of noble excitement to which he was passionately attached, and to withdraw in a great degree from a circle of high-spirited friends, many of them of different political connection from himself, by whom he was adored. With all his unrivalled powers of application when under the influence of a great impulse, he was constitutionally indolent and even lethargic. There was nothing therefore in his position or his temperament to prick him on in '46; it was nothing but his strong will acting upon his indignation which sustained him. It is not therefore marvellous that he exhibited great reluctance to commit irretrievably his future life. At a subsequent period, indignation had become ambition, and circumstances of various kinds had made him resolve to succeed or die.

On the adjournment, Lord George had gone down to Newmarket, which he greatly enjoyed after his exhausting

campaign. Here some letters on the subject of the leadership passed, but nothing was definitively arranged till some
time after the reassembling of parliament. For convenience
we mention here the result. The wish of the party was
repeatedly and personally urged by the popular and much-
esteemed member for Dorsetshire, and at last Lord George
consented to their wishes, on these conditions: that he
should relinquish his post the moment the right man was
discovered, who, according to his theory, would ultimately
turn up; and secondly, that his responsible post was not
to restrict or embarrass him on any questions in which a
religious principle was involved.

Before, however, this negotiation was concluded, and while
yet at Newmarket, he wrote to a friend, the day before the
house met (April 16th):—

'I think there is no doubt, but that the Irish will take
care of Friday (to-morrow) night. I have not much hope of
their keeping up the debate beyond Friday.

'It is quite clear from O'Connell's language at Dublin that
we have no hope from the Irish tail.

'I still think myself, that delay affords a great chance of
something turning up in our favour; already the rejection
of any reciprocity by M. Guizot has provided us with a grand
weapon, which, I trust, you will drive well home into ——'s
vitals; a very short delay would probably bring over similar
intelligence from the United States and their congress. I
trust we shall have an important deputation over from
Canada, representing that the inevitable results of these
free trade measures in corn and timber will be to alienate
the feelings of our Canadian colonists, and to induce them
to follow their sordid interests, which will now, undoubtedly,
be best consulted and most promoted by annexation to the
United States.

'Lord ——'s intended tergiversation has been, I believe,
some time known; he admits, that all farmers without
capital, in short all little men, must be sacrificed. What a
barbarous and odious policy, that goes upon the principle,
that none but capitalists are henceforth to be allowed to

live, as farmers at least. We must turn the tables upon Lord —— and all such heartless doctrinaires!

'I fear the majority in the lords will be greater than was expected; I am told that we must endeavour to put ministers in a minority two or three times before the bill gets to its second reading in the lords, no matter upon what question. I hear there are many peers whose votes depend entirely upon their notions whether or not Peel can, by hook or by crook, carry on.'

CHAPTER XI

IT seems that Lord George Bentinck took a too desponding view of the resources and intentions of the Irish members. They returned not merely resolved to continue their opposition to the coercion bill, but with a determination among several of them not only to defeat the particular measure but to overthrow, if possible, the minister altogether.

Notwithstanding the efforts of Mr. O'Connell, who was anxious to hasten the passing of the corn bill in order to facilitate the return of his old allies to power, the repeal of the corn laws was a measure which a great many of the Irish members found it very difficult to digest, and which they could not help suspecting was a somewhat heavy price to pay for the benefit of restoring the whigs to office. The declining energies of Mr. O'Connell and the complete failure of his policy, every day becoming more evident, had of late combined to develop in Ireland the first germs of a party, now prevalent, which, while still avowing what are styled liberal opinions, sought the regeneration of that country in social rather than political remedies, and aimed to unite men for that object without reference to their religious opinions. Country, and not creed, was held out as the foremost consideration by these persons, national rather than ecclesiastical objects, material more than spiritual aims, and, at the bottom, the superintendence of the landlord rather than the supremacy of the priest. Like everything else, this tendency was a reaction, occasioned by the abuse and disaster of the system for which it desired to be substituted.

It is due to an unfortunate gentleman who had many generous qualities, to state that Mr. Smith O'Brien, the member for the county of Limerick, was one of the first who perceived the necessity of this course, and if his judgment had been equal to his abilities, which were far from inconsiderable, there is little doubt he might have filled a very useful and gratifying position. The speech of Lord George Bentinck on the state of Ireland, which was noticed in our ninth chapter, had attracted the attention of Mr. O'Brien and his friends, who thought they perceived in that address an outline of measures much more calculated to alleviate and ultimately remove the evils of their country than the effete programme of the whig leader, or the precipitate and violent scheme of the minister which, while introduced on the plea of encountering the emergency of Ireland, was well known to have been framed only to meet the exigency of Manchester, and which, while it affected to consider above all things the condition of the Irish people, warned the house at the same time not to trench on the sacred subject of tenure, or to attempt to cure the chronic evil of national pauperism.

The attempt of Mr. O'Connell, made at Dublin during the recess, to secure at all hazards the passing of the corn bill, and which was noticed in the letter of Lord George Bentinck, determined those who had freed themselves from the ancient thraldom of the delegate of the Irish priesthood, to take some decisive step on their return to England, which might open in impending changes some better prospect for their country than a mere transfer of office from Sir Robert Peel to his accustomed rival.

Accordingly when the house met on the 17th of April, and the secretary of state moved the order of the day for the adjourned debate (the fourth night) on the coercion bill, Mr. Smith O'Brien, with characteristic impetuosity, interposed to 'make an appeal to the government with respect to that part of Ireland with which he was connected.' The people were starving, 'but the circumstance which appeared most aggravating was, that the people were starving in the midst of plenty.' Every tide carried from the Irish ports corn sufficient for the maintenance of thousands of the Irish people. He then criticised in considerable detail the ineffective measures of the government to meet this state of affairs. He was for increased assessments for the poor and additional assessments from absentees. He distinctly announced that he was one of those who differed from the great majority at his own side of the house with respect to measures to alter the corn laws. No doubt such alteration might be of service to England, but it must be for some time injurious to Ireland. It was unfair and ungenerous on the part of the government with respect to members who differed from them, to mix up the question of the corn laws with the coercion bill.

This address, well digested, full of detail, and evincing an acquaintance with the subject, forced a vindication of the government at some length from the secretary of state. Mr. Roche, the member for the county of Cork, and a gentleman who has always taken a very independent part in the house of commons, supported the views of Mr. Smith O'Brien so earnestly and effectively, that Sir Robert Peel himself felt obliged to rise and defend the administration. This interesting discussion threw back the adjourned debate, which was continued later in the evening in a languid spirit, when a further adjournment was again moved, on the ground that, 'though the debate had continued for four nights, only two members of the government had spoken, while not a single Irish member had yet come forward to advocate the measure.'

Mr. Ellice, the member for Coventry, whose practised eye began to perceive that the embroilment was becoming serious, and that unless some arrangement were brought about, it was quite possible that the government might break up without passing the corn bill, appealed to the Irish members with specious sympathy not to persist in their course. He felt very strongly with them; for nearly thirty years he had voted for a liberal policy to Ireland; this appeal came from a warm friend to their country, but there were measures for which both England, Scotland, and even Ireland were waiting with anxiety. He entreated them to reflect on the course they were pursuing, and on the effect it would have on the country, suffering from one end to the other from the little progress yet made in the business of the session.   But those persuasive tones and all that faculty of affectionate expostulation, which had so often soothed and stifled the mutiny of faction, were now employed in vain. Mr. Dillon Browne 'could come to no other conclusion, than that the Irish members were treated with contempt,' so they divided on the adjournment, and being defeated, moved a fresh adjournment; on which the minister surrendered, and postponed the debate until the next Monday, when to complete the vexation of the government they did not succeed in making a house.

Thus after the recess a whole week passed without the government advancing a single step, either with their corn or their coercion bill.   So feeble and barren a behaviour, when above all things progress and even a little audacity were required, confirmed the suspicion in the public mind that had been for some time rising, that the minister had undertaken a measure beyond his powers and one of a character unnecessarily extreme.   The lovers of compromise, always the strongest party in this country, were now active.   Why did not the whigs step in and settle the question in a spirit consistent with all their previous declarations, which even the protectionists would now willingly accept ?   A moderate fixed duty was the whig policy ; it would save the honour of the landed party ; it would meet the scientific objections of those economical authorities, who, however favourable to interchange, were of opinion that it was injurious to encounter hostile tariffs by free imports; it might prove a fruitful source of revenue ; finally, it would permit the formation of a strong government, and the whigs would only be in their natural position as the leaders of the aristocracy of the country.

Nor were the objections and obstacles to a course so temperate and conciliatory very apparent.   There was no excitement in England in favour of the government scheme ; on the contrary, the only excitement then was that of the farmers, and that was against the measure ; all the important elections had invariably been decided against the ministry; Ireland, for whose advantage it was especially introduced, viewed it with distrust and even dislike. There was the clamour of Manchester to encounter; but the manufacturing districts were by no means unanimous in favour of total repeal, and the proud confederation which now demanded that abrogation had, only a few months previously to the meeting of parliament, been on the point, with empty coffers, of withdrawing from a struggle which they then considered hopeless.

What then prevented the overthrow of Sir Robert Peel's government after the Easter recess of 1846 ? The whigs were sufficiently patriotic not to shrink from office; they were as a party both from feeling and conviction unanimous in favour of a fixed duty; Lord Palmerston's speech was still ringing in the ears of the house of commons, and not to run the risk of its being forgotten his lordship had properly taken care to have it printed; they were sure under the circumstances of the unanimous support of the Irish members, who would have got rid at the same time of the corn and the coercion bills; they would have received from the landed interest a permanent support; and if Lord George Bentinck had entered the new cabinet, which many among the whigs talked of and desired, he would have only reverted to that ancient political connection of which his house for generations had been one of the main props.

What then prevented this important and desirable consequence ? The Edinburgh letter.

Some time, however, elapsed before the insurmountable nature of this barrier transpired; and during this period of suspense, intrigue was active and prolific. Young Ireland was not sluggish. It was important to remove the prejudice which might be raised against the protectionist party, on the ground that in opposing the repeal of the corn laws they were preventing the necessary supplies from being poured into famished Ireland; and it was therefore resolved that some public declaration of the disposition of the protectionists on this head should be immediately elicited. It was, therefore, on Tuesday, the 19th of April, at Harcourt House, and while in conversation with Mr. Baron Martin, that Lord George Bentinck received a letter from Mr. Smith O'Brien, preparatory to the anticipated meeting of the house on the morrow, in which he inquired, ' whether in the event of the government bringing in a bill to suspend the existing corn laws as regards Ireland, so as to admit grain duty free, the noble lord and the party with which he was connected would support such a measure ? ' Lord George Bentinck had no personal acquaintance with Mr. Smith O'Brien, and this was the first letter he had received from him. He opened it, and read it aloud without first reading it to himself, so that Mr. Martin became aware of its purport as soon as Lord George. The answer to the inquiry of Mr. Smith O'Brien was immediate and straightforward. Lord George said he would give no reply to such an inquiry without consulting his friends; that he would confer with them; and that if the question were addressed to him in his place in the house of commons, he would state the resolution at which they might arrive. These slight circumstances are noticed, because this inquiry led to no inconsiderable results; the government became much alarmed, and a cabinet minister, who some days after was seeking the suffrages of the electors of a Scotch borough, declared that a ' compact ' had been entered into between the protectionists and the Irish members to defeat the repeal of the corn laws.

Mr. Smith O'Brien did not obtain his opportunity until Friday, the 24th of April, when the order of the day was again moved for the fifth night of the adjourned debate on the coercion bill. Then he rose and put the question at once in the language we have quoted; but without waiting for an immediate answer, he proceeded to illustrate his inquiry by a speech of some length, and very skilfully prepared.

Since he had called the attention of the house to the condition of his countrymen a week ago, the government had laid documents on the table which were now in everybody's hands. They proved that famine was rapidly approaching in Ireland, nay that it actually existed.   Quoting from these documents in great detail, he said that such a state of things could not continue without some resort to violence by the people.   With these documents before them he could hardly believe that government would persevere in a measure which took away from the people the right of being out of doors half an hour after sunset.   Ministers declared they had foreseen famine.   Why then had they not taken due precautions ?   If the minister saw so clearly in November what has since occurred, was it not his business to have made arrangements to prevent starvation ?   And now the Irish members were taunted with preventing an influx of food into Ireland, because the government will not proceed with the corn bill until the house has sanctioned their coercion bill.

The Irish members had attended in their place for the purpose of supporting those measures of free trade which the English liberals considered so essential to the welfare of the country.   They might therefore have reasonably expected, that the English liberals would have concurred with them in offering such resistance to the coercion bill as would render it impossible for the minister to pass it.   It was not so difficult to control a government which had only one hundred and twelve supporters.

The Irish members were denounced for doing their duty to their country ; but they were not the only persons who received this welcome vituperation.   Lord George Bentinck and his friends came in for a share of it.   They were present to answer for themselves.   He did not know what answer he should receive to the question that he had put to the noble lord, but as far as he could observe, the course of the protectionists up to the present moment had been this : ' You have no right,' they said to the government, ' to couple the question of Irish famine with the question of free trade ; and if you had come down to this house and told us the people of Ireland were starving, we would have assented to placing a greater abundance of food at the disposal of the Irish government.'

Mr. O'Brien felt the same; he felt there was a want of candour in mixing up the famine of Ireland with the repeal of the corn laws. 'The repeal of the corn laws was evidently an English measure; it was not an Irish measure.' Although hitherto silent on that subject, he would speak on it now without reserve. He was now, as he had been in '42, an advocate for a fixed duty. Lord John Russell, whom he followed on that occasion, had left him in the rear; but he had seen no reason to change his views, which he considered best for Ireland and England too.

The house was very full when this declaratory inquiry was made, and great interest was felt when Lord George Bentinck rose to reply to it.

There had been a very numerous meeting held at Mr. Bankes's house in Palace Yard, to take the proposition of the Irish members into consideration, and which had scarcely concluded in time for Lord George to take his seat at five o'clock. It was the first occasion on which Lord George had met his friends as their avowed leader. It might be thought, he said, that under ordinary circumstances it was not fair to ask an independent and isolated member what might be his intentions; but then the circumstances in which they found themselves were not ordinary. There was a ministry endeavouring to govern the country in which only a sixth of the members of the house of commons placed confidence, while those with whom Lord George Bentinck acted and agreed 'numbered two hundred and forty, constituting with the Irish members a clear majority of the house.' He thought these were circumstances which entitled Mr. O'Brien to put to him the question which had been asked, and he would give to it a frank and honest answer.

If, through a cry excited by the ministry, a feeling had been created in Ireland that the protectionist party, or the opponents of the coercion bill, were standing between the starving people of Ireland and their food, the protectionist party were willing to remove that delusion by passing, instantly, any measures which for a period should open the ports of Ireland. But in so doing they solemnly protested against the assumption that they believed such a measure would afford any relief to the people of Ireland. Into London and Glasgow alone, within the three months subsequent to the 1st of January '46, 260,000 quarters of oats had been imported from Ireland. How was it possible by suspending the corn laws in Ireland to supply oats for the people when the price of oats in the London market, exclusive of duty, was now one shilling a quarter higher than in Cork, the dearest market in Ireland? So as to wheat, it was 49s. 6d. per quarter at Cork, while foreign wheat in bond averaged 54s. Cork was the most distressed part of Ireland, yet in this year ('46), this year of scarcity, Cork had sent us more than 386,000 barrels of grain. If then the people of Cork were starving, it was not for the want of food, but for the want of money to purchase food, and the want of employment. Money must be afforded, or the employment which may be the means of obtaining money, in order to enable the people to purchase food.

The Devon commission had reported, that one year with another, there were always 2,300,000 destitute poor in Ireland, and deducting the establishment expenses (£90,000), there was raised by the poor law £166,000 to provide for their sustenance. That amounted to something less than one farthing and a half per head per week. There were at that moment 37,000 persons in the workhouses. £166,000 would give these persons one shilling per head per week, and there were 2,263,000 paupers totally unprovided for. 'And you wonder that riots and agrarian outrages occur with such a state of things!'

There was but one remedy: to make a sufficient provision for the poor of Ireland. Was it to be endured that £10,000,000 in food should come from Ireland, and that no more than £166,000 should be given to the poor of that country. But a poor law could not be carried in haste: immediate relief was wanted. In '33 we could give £1,000,000 to the tithe owners of Ireland: were the rigid rules of political economy not to be broken through when the people were starving? We must supply the immediate wants of the Irish people from the funds of this country, and then we must seriously endeavour to make a permanent provision for them.

'These are not new opinions,' continued Lord George; 'they were the opinions of one who possessed the full confidence of this house. Mr. Huskisson said, that in a poor law for Ireland would be found the introduction of a feeling of security which would invite and retain the employment of English capital in that country. It was that feeling of security which had occasioned the greatness and wealth of this country, and which alone would produce similar results in Ireland. Mr. Huskisson even said, that unless such a measure were quickly brought in, all the hopes which he entertained of the benefit to Ireland from the passing of the emancipation act would be dissipated.

'I look to that period,' concluded Lord George, with considerable emotion, 'with the greatest satisfaction. In my humble office of private secretary to Mr. Canning, nearly a quarter of a century past, I had the satisfaction of possessing the confidence of that illustrious statesman. I have often heard Mr. Canning say, that it was to the poor laws of this country that England owed her successful struggles with Europe and America; that they reconciled the people to their burthens, and had saved England from revolution. These are the measures to which my friends around me look for the salvation of Ireland; for quieting disturbance and for promoting peace.'

There was considerable cheering when he concluded an address which the house generally felt was not unworthy of the leader of a great party. His friends were extremely gratified, and the expressions of confidence in him on the part of several of the Irish members who sat on the liberal benches marked and uncompromising. An interesting debate took place, and this again arrested the progress of the coercion bill. Late in the evening, Mr. Cobden, who had studiously kept in the background during the session, watching his game played by less notorious hands, alarmed at the appearance of affairs, thought it expedient to sound the note of danger, and rated the protectionist party in that clear and saucy style which he knows how to manage.

He said, that the house had rather lost sight of the origin of this discussion. Irregular and unexpected, it had originated in a question from Mr. Smith O'Brien to Lord George Bentinck, 'which it seems had arisen out of a private communication between them.' That question was, whether Lord George Bentinck and his party would be willing to vote for a suspension of the corn law for three months, limited to Ireland only. But the house had another proposition before them, one not to suspend, but to abolish, the corn law; and therefore the object of Mr. O'Brien was, instead of abolishing the corn law for the united kingdom, to substitute a three months' suspension, applicable to Ireland only. Now he begged, in the first place, to tell Mr. O'Brien, and Lord George Bentinck, and the two hundred and forty gentlemen who sat behind him and cheered his speech, that there were other parties to be consulted with regard to such a proposition—the people of England—'not the country party, but the people who live in towns, and will govern this country.'

The question of the corn laws, he said, could no longer be made matter for manœuvring and compacts within the walls of the house of commons. It was disposed of, settled, out of doors; and although their artifices here might delay the measure and cause anxiety out of doors, still they could only delay it; and, in fact, the only thing that could be substituted for the deferred measure, was total and immediate repeal. There was a delusion in the minds of the opposition as to the state of public opinion on this question, and he wished that circumstances would permit the minister to appeal to the country, and make an example of honourable gentlemen below the gangway which they little anticipated.

He then argued, with great acuteness, that it was impossible to limit the suspension of the corn laws to Ireland, and added, 'I have intruded but seldom in this debate. I am anxious to be a party to nothing, which, in reference to the coercion bill, stands in the way of the corn bill. I deeply regret that those two measures should have got into a deadlock. The people of England are utterly perplexed and puzzled at the state of things here. I am almost perplexed myself. During the recess I was repeatedly asked to attend meetings at Manchester and elsewhere, to censure the delay. Upon my honour, I know not whom to blame. I cannot blame the government, for, though I were disposed to do so, I see them so much blamed by other gentlemen, that I may well abstain.'

Mr. Cobden was repeatedly cheered as he spoke by the treasury bench, and particularly by Sir Robert Peel. The protectionists murmured among themselves, that the first minister had cheered the declaration, that this country should be governed by the towns, and that such a demonstration in a minister was unconstitutional, and in him, considering his antecedents, indecent. Several gentlemen having privately stated that they had personally observed the minister cheer the obnoxious sentiment, a member of the protectionist party deemed it right to rise and charge the minister with what, if it had occurred, was undoubtedly an offensive indiscretion.

This member said, that Mr. Cobden had threatened the country party with the indignation of the people, and had followed up his threat by a terse definition of what the people was—namely, the people who lived in towns. This sentiment had been cheered and this definition accepted by one gentleman, the expression of whose opinion or of whose feelings must always make a great impression on the house and the country. It was the more curious, because the cheer came from the same right honourable individual, who was once so proud of being the head of the gentlemen of England.

Sir Robert Peel sprang from his seat, and emphatically denied the cheer. A scene of great excitement and confusion occurred. Various members favoured the house with their impressions as to the conduct of the minister. Of that, however, there could be no doubt after his declaration. The minister had cheered Mr. Cobden generally, but not that particular definition, 'the validity of which,' as he stated subsequently in the evening, 'he did not recognise. He totally dissented from the principle stated by Mr. Cobden.' At length all was tranquil, but the fifth night of the adjourned debate only produced one speech, and that from Mr. John O'Connell.

As the house broke up at half-past one o'clock, members, as they put on their greatcoats and lit their cigars, said, 'It is impossible that this can last.'

It was about this time that a strange incident occurred at the adjournment of the house. The minister, plunged in profound and perhaps painful reverie, was unconscious of the termination of the proceedings of the night, and remained in his seat unmoved. At that period, although with his accustomed and admirable self-control he rarely evinced any irritability in the conduct of parliamentary business, it is understood, that under less public circumstances, he was anxious and much disquieted. His colleagues, lingering for a while, followed the other members and left the house, and those on whom, from the intimacy of their official relations with Sir Robert, the office of rousing him would have devolved, hesitated from some sympathy with his unusual susceptibility to perform that duty, though they remained watching their chief behind the speaker's chair. The benches had become empty, the lights were about to be extinguished ; it is a duty of a clerk of the house to examine the chamber before the doors are closed, and to-night it was also the strange lot of this gentleman to disturb the reverie of a statesman.

CHAPTER XII

WHEN political affairs are critical, Sunday is always a great day for rumours. There was a rumour on the Sunday following the last adjournment; namely, that the government had resolved at all events to terminate 'the deadlock,' as Mr. Cobden called it; and that next day the minister was not only himself to speak on the coercion bill, but to make a declaration of the danger in which cheap food for the people was placed by a factious opposition, and to intimate that if the obstacles were not removed he would counsel the queen to dissolve parliament.

This piece of news reached Lord George Bentinck from such a quarter that, though very scrupulous, he credited it, and not at all alarmed at the consequences, devoted all his energies to the maintenance of 'the deadlock.' He liked the phrase, and, as was his custom under such circumstances, it was often in his mouth.

On Monday the house was very full. 'Sir Robert will be up early,' was the word of order. The debate was opened by a dashing speech from Mr. M'Carthy, worthy of the historical society in the most fervent hour of its Rhodian eloquence. This coloured the atmosphere, but though it gained a deserved compliment from the first minister, the feeling was not sustained. The understanding that Sir Robert was to rise early checked debate. The promise was fulfilled. The minister rose about half-past nine o'clock, and with that abstracted air which generally announced an important statement or a great effort.

After having vindicated the conduct of the government in their resolution of persisting in asking the house to read the Irish bill for a first time, and stating that 'it was from

no mere punctilious deference for the house of lords that
they took that course, but because they were deeply convinced, that if they permitted that bill, so recommended
from the throne and so passed by the house of lords, to lie
on the table without notice, the representatives of Ireland
might accuse them, and justly accuse them, of offering an
insult to their country': he thus proceeded:—

'Sir, I think I need hardly refer to the injurious surmises
which I have heard thrown out, that her majesty's government had become indifferent to the progress of the corn bill,
and that they had interposed this discussion, or rather this
first reading of another measure, with a view to the defeat
of that bill. I know that honourable gentlemen have not
said so for themselves, but they have said in the course of
discussion that such an impression exists on the part of the
public. Sir, I shall be prepared to give whatever proof may
be required of the sincerity of my convictions on the subject
of the corn bill. It is sufficient for me now to state, that the
progress of the discussion, the lapse of time, and intervening
events, have more strongly confirmed me in the feeling which
I expressed when I proposed the permanent and final adjustment of this measure. Sir, I will not deny, that even during
these debates, my opinions on that subject have undergone
a change; but it is this change—that restrictions which I
at first believed to be impolitic, I now believe to be unjust,
and consequently a sense of their injustice precludes any
compromise on my part. That which I have proposed, both
with respect to the amount and the continuance of duty,
is all that I am enabled to offer; and in answer to injurious
suspicions, I think it enough to say, that I shall be perfectly
ready to testify, by any public act, the sincerity of my
intentions.'

There was a dead silence in the house. Lord George
Bentinck whispered to the member who sat next to him,
'He has taken new ground; that which he believed to be
impolitic, he now believes to be unjust. Note that.'

'Any public act to testify sincerity' was generally accepted
by both sides as dissolution. The protectionists as a body

desired that result and were prepared for it; the whigs shrank from the settlement of the corn question devolving on them or disappearing as a party in the storm of a general election, a still more probable catastrophe. Lord George Bentinck never would believe that Sir Robert Peel would dissolve parliament, because whatever might be the national decision as to the principle of policy which was to be adopted, he was convinced that the whole body of the present men in office, at least with rare exceptions, must lose their seats. What he wanted was to force the ministry to resign, and secure the dissolution for their successors, whoever they might be.

After this pointed declaration of the minister, he addressed himself to the bill before the house in detail, and spoke at great length and in his best manner. Nevertheless he did not succeed, as was anticipated, in securing the division. Although from the line which they had adopted, it was not in the power of the protectionists to protract the debate, and although it was understood that the whigs began to be apprehensive of the possible consequences of further delay, and although Mr. Smith O'Brien had been withdrawn in the interval from the scene and was imprisoned by the house for refusing to attend on a railway committee, the Irish members contrived, not only to adjourn the debate until the next Friday, the 1st of May, but to sustain it, though somewhat languidly, the whole of that night, or rather till two o'clock on the morning of Saturday the 2nd, when the division on the first reading of the coercion bill took place, and the government carried it by a majority of 274 to 125.

Lord John Russell voted for the bill; Lord George Bentinck voted for the bill; followed by his brother, the Lord Henry, Mr. Bankes, Mr. Baring, the Marquess of Granby, Mr. Christopher, Sir John Trollope, Mr. Miles, and the great majority of the most influential members of the protectionist party. The individual who had ventured to oppose this step in council, on the ground that the support of an unconstitutional measure was equivalent to a vote of confidence in the government which introduced it, and might eventually embarrass an opposition, left the house, as he would not be told from a different lobby from that in which his friends were counted.

The great obstacle which for five weeks had arrested the progress of business at so critical a period was at length removed. The members felt like men in a great thoroughfare when some desperate stoppage has been broken up. The wheels of the state chariot were unlocked again, and the minister expected on Monday, the 4th of May, to go into committee on his corn bill as a matter of course. But this was not the intention of Lord George Bentinck. He was resolved to have an explanation from Sir Robert Peel of the strange announcement on the previous Friday of his present feelings with respect to the corn laws. Lord George had been brooding over it ever since it was made, and was armed to the teeth for the combat for which he panted. At the meeting of the house, therefore, Lord George opposed the speaker leaving 'the chair,' as a new feature and a new character had arisen in the discussion of this question since it came under the consideration of the house. The first minister had allowed it to go forth to the country, that those laws which he desired to have repealed, and which, at the time he first intimated his intention to that effect, he deemed to be impolitic, he now considered unjust; that he, who had a hand in the construction of every corn law that had been devised for the last thirty years, had now been induced, by the debate of the last three months, so far to change his opinion, that those laws, which at the early part of last autumn he had deemed injudicious for the first time, he now deemed to be unjust. Lord George thought the house ought not to allow the measure to proceed until the minister had stated the views which had induced one to come to this extraordinary and sudden conclusion, who had for so many years exerted himself to maintain those laws.

Lord George then proceeded to consider the subject under all the heads on which new facts might have occurred since the opening of the session to authorise the statement of the minister. Was there anything in the state of the markets, either as to the existing prices, or the quantity that was to be consumed, which should induce us to forget the interest of the farmer for the sake of the consumer? The average price of wheat, on that day, was beneath that which, four years ago, this very minister stated was the price which was the object of the law he then as a minister introduced.

They had heard much of stagnation of trade; not they who resist a change in the laws of commerce, but those who would create that change, are responsible for that stagnation. But Lord George showed by elaborate tables, with which he was prepared, that there had been 116,000 quarters more of grain sold in the 288 markets of England in this year of stagnation, than were sold in the four corresponding weeks of the previous year. Well, then, the stagnation of trade had not interfered with the supply and consumption of corn.

Was it the anxiety of foreign countries to establish an interchange with us, that made the minister so suddenly sensible of the injustice of the regulations that might prevent that intercourse? Lord George reviewed the latest information received from foreign countries on this important object. He quoted a recent declaration of M. Guizot not favourable to the English policy, he appealed to the latest intelligence from the United States extremely hostile to a mitigated tariff, he proved that Prussia was not yet 'shaken.'

Had anything occurred then in Ireland to operate this change in the convictions of the right honourable gentleman? Hardly that. And here he quoted a variety of documents from individuals of all ranks and journals of all opinions in Ireland, to prove that there was no sympathy with the measures of the government in that country, and a denial of the justness of the representations of its condition. 'I think, therefore,' said Lord George, 'that we are entitled to know before we go into committee on this question, what are the new circumstances which have come to the knowledge of the minister and which have caused him for the last time to change anew his opinions?'

The reply of the minister was very remarkable. The appeal to him was unexpected; but when master of his case, he never spoke with more vigour and facility than when taken unawares. Preparation was apt to make him cumbrous. In the present instance, disposing at first of the Irish part of the case, and acknowledging 'that he knew very well that scarcity was not universal in that country,' he addressed himself to the particular inquiry of the protectionist leader. What had induced him to change his opinions, even in the course of this session, and now to believe that those restrictions, which, at the commencement of the session, he only thought impolitic, were also unjust.

In the first place the minister 'adopted and deliberately repeated that statement.' And he then proceeded to assign the grounds on which he had arrived at the opinion after listening to the discussions of the last three months and after mature consideration. He informed the house that there was an abstract presumption against restrictions on food, which he endeavoured to establish; that he did not believe that a free trade in corn involved any dependence on foreign nations for the necessaries of life; that he did not believe that the rate of wages varied with the price of food; that he did not believe that protection was necessary to farmers of adequate intelligence and means; that he did not believe that heavy taxation was a reason for the continuance of the duties on corn, but quite the reverse. On these heads he dilated, and stated that, because of his belief in these opinions, he had come to the conclusion, that it was unjust to continue legislative restrictions upon food.

Both sides of the house listened with no little astonishment while the minister, with an apparent interest in the subject which it would have been supposed novelty could have alone inspired, recapitulated all those arguments which for years the anti-corn law league had presented to the consideration, not only of the community, but even of the house of commons, in every form which ingenuity could devise and a versatile and experienced rhetoric illustrate and enforce. But when, with an air of discovery, he availed himself of one of the most subtle but certainly not least hackneyed tactics of Mr. Cobden, and, in order to depreciate the importance of wheat-growing, called upon the house to take the map of Great Britain, and divide the island by a line from Inverness and Southampton, and observe that, generally speaking, to the westward of the line, the country had no interest in the restrictions on the importation of wheat, the gentlemen who had left their agricultural constituents in the lurch because they had been told that unless Sir Robert Peel were permitted to repeal the corn laws, Mr. Cobden might actually become a minister, began to ask themselves whether, after all, such an event would not have been the honestest arrangement of the two. Unlike the corn laws, the exclusion of Mr. Cobden might have been politic, but, 'after the discussion of the last three months,' it certainly seemed unjust.

This general feeling was expressed later in the evening by one of the protectionist party, who, noticing the observation of the minister that the debate was unexpected, observed ' that not being prepared for debate was certainly not an excuse for not being prepared to answer the speech of the right honourable gentleman. It was not a speech that was heard for the first time. It had been heard in other places, in different localities, and he might be permitted to add, from a master-hand. That speech had sounded in Stockport; it had echoed in Durham. There had been on the stage of the classical theatre a representation of it on the finest scale, and, as is usual in such cases, the popular performance was now repeated by an inferior company. Especially, when he heard the line drawn, which marks on the map the corn-growing districts of Great Britain, he thought he might say, as he heard sometimes said on railway committees upon rival lines, " That is surely the line of the honourable member for Stockport " ' (Mr. Cobden).

This remarkable declaration of the minister that he had changed his opinions as to the character of the corn laws even during the present session, was noticed also on a subsequent night by Mr. Ker Seymer, the member for

Dorset, in a very happy passage of a maiden speech, which was also generally distinguished by its vivacity and acuteness.

'The minister,' he said, 'had admitted that changes had taken place in his opinion since his first introduction of the question, and in that respect he illustrated a well-known principle in human nature, according to which, persons became attached to that for which they had made sacrifices; and he believed that the sacrifices which the minister had made, with respect to this question, had been greater than was anticipated. He brought forward the measure on the ground of *policy*; but he found himself opposed by two hundred and forty members of that house, and then he raised it to a question of *justice*; and if he found hereafter, that the opposition to it in another place should be still more determined than that which it had met with in this house, he might raise it, as some reverend orators at Covent Garden theatre had done, into a *religious* question. But whatever might be the changes in the views of the minister, the question itself remained the same. It was no more a question of religion or justice now than it was last year. It was a question involving great commercial and social considerations, but was no more a question of justice or religion than the duties on hair powder.'

What was the cause of this remarkable declaration of the minister, made with so much form and repeated with so much emphasis? It was not an ebullition. It was a preconcerted statement, at a very important crisis in the condition of his government (April 27th), every word of which had been weighed, though apparently not calculated to please those who, at great sacrifice, had remained attached to him. This declaration denoted a change in the parliamentary position of Sir Robert Peel, and an approachment to the Manchester confederation.

When Lord John Russell failed to form a government in Christmas '45, and Sir Robert Peel was again sent for by her majesty, in resuming the reins of government and in appealing to his colleagues to co-operate with him in the

subversion of the protective system, he justified his course
by the assurances, that there was no other mode of preventing a third party from being called into the management of
public affairs, and that too a democratic party: that the
incompetency of the whigs to take charge of the administration when their turn and time had constitutionally arrived,
rendered it necessary for the tories to fulfil those liberal
functions which, according to the practice, if not the theory,
of our political scheme, the whigs ought to have been
prepared to fulfil. In a word, the Manchester confederation
was held up as the alternative to a conservative government. What a catastrophe for the territorial constitution!

The position, therefore, which Sir Robert Peel assumed
and intended to preserve at the meeting of parliament was
that of the patriotic individual who by great sacrifices had
succeeded in preventing Mr. Cobden from becoming a
minister. It was in this spirit that the appeal was made to
the Duke of Wellington, and it was in this spirit that it
received a sympathetic response. Not only was Mr. Cobden
not to be a minister, but Sir Robert was to remain one.
And in one of the last of those strange, unconstitutional
speeches, full of naïveté and secret history, which the Duke
of Wellington was in the habit of addressing to the peers
when his grace led the house of lords, he said: 'That, whatever may be the result of this bill (the corn bill, May 28,
1846) in this house, it appears very clear, that the object
I had in view in resuming my seat in her majesty's councils
will not be attained. I conclude that another government
will be formed.'

After the alleged refusal of Lord Stanley to attempt to
form a protectionist ministry in 1845, and the avowed
failure of Lord John Russell to form a free trade one, it
was not perhaps unjustifiable for a minister, elate with long
success, haughty with court favour, continental influence,
and parliamentary sway, to believe that his position was
impregnable. The private tone of the treasury bench,
therefore, when parliament met, was martyrdom. They
were sacrificing their opinions to save the country from

Mr. Cobden, and several gentlemen of great weight were so touched by the interesting position of these statesmen, that although they entirely disapproved of the policy of the minister, they permitted their names to be seen in every division list with that of Mr. Cobden, in order to save the country from the pernicious influence of his councils. Not very fine in their observation of the phases of political life, they remained, notwithstanding some awkward incidents like the 'injustice' speech, in the same fool's paradise, until having, as they supposed, repealed the corn laws in order to prevent the triumph of Mr. Cobden, they heard the member for Stockport hailed by their prime minister as the saviour of the country and the ornament of the senate.

When the first minister discovered that his original calculations were erroneous, and that the conservative party was lost to him, a remarkable change took place in his tone, and especially towards the Manchester league.

The union of simplicity and sagacity which was the characteristic of Lord George Bentinck, shrank with indignation and a little disgust from what appeared to him to be jesuitical. He sincerely believed that the system of the Manchester confederation was hostile to the greatness and permanent prosperity of this country, and that for the sake of a temporary expansion of our commerce, it was sacrificing the durable sources of power and public wealth. But he respected Mr. Cobden; for his talents, his position, the clear manner in which he had obtained it, and the considerable public sympathy which supported him. He thought Mr. Cobden a dangerous foe, but he was at least an open one; and if the Manchester principles were to predominate, he could not comprehend why they should not be administered by Manchester men. Nay, more; believing their principles were injurious, Lord George thought that he had a better chance of defeating them, when they were openly and completely avowed, than when they were carried into operation in detail by one who had obtained power by professing his hostility to them.

The 'injustice debate' took up the whole of the night.

The protectionists, at a certain hour, adjourned the committee on the corn bill, as the Irish members had adjourned the first reading of the coercion bill. The minister resisted the adjournment, and divided twice on it. He then gave up. 'I have not strength to go through with this contest,' he exclaimed; 'I do not wish to subject others to it.' The opposers of the Irish bill, however, had a great advantage over the opposers of the corn bill. Liberal members always gave up their motions to ensure precedence to the corn bill. The government therefore obtained the next night, otherwise devoted to private members, for the committee to sit again. Nevertheless they were again invited to battle.

On the first item in committee, the chairman reading the words, that 'upon all wheat, barley, oats,' Lord George Bentinck rose and said : 'I rise, sir, to move the omission of the word "oats."' And on this text, he delivered a most able speech on the agriculture of Ireland.

'Our former discussions,' he said, 'have almost entirely turned upon the species of grain with which mainly the people of England are concerned, and scarcely at all upon that species of grain in which the people of Ireland, Scotland, and Wales are more particularly interested. When we come to consider that there are 558,000 occupiers of land in Ireland, almost every one of whom is a grower of oats, we cannot but admit how important it is to Ireland that we should not hastily alter the law which protects their grain in the English market.'

After entering into very protracted calculations upon the effect of free importation on the oat producers of Ireland, he observed: 'The minister last night referred to a statement of mine, that there were 558,000 farmers in Ireland, with no other capital than their industry and their honesty, and he said that if it could be asserted generally of the farmers of Ireland, that they are without capital, can we contend that protection has been for their interests; but the minister omitted the very important portion of my statement, that these farmers held but fifteen acres of land. How can it be possible that a farmer of fifteen acres should

have much capital? Can he have threshing and winnowing
machines? We must deal with the state of things we find.
We did not make that state of things; but we find 558,000
occupiers of land in Ireland who hold but fifteen acres, and
we are to say, if we agree with my Lord Essex, with whom
the right honourable gentleman seems very much to sympathise, that they ought never to have been farmers, and
consequently, that they ought at once to be sacrificed; that
558,000 farmers, employing or sustaining three millions and
a half of human beings, are to be sacrificed because they
do not possess a sufficient amount of capital. It might
certainly be better that there should not be these small
tenures in Ireland—but they exist; we must deal with
things as we find them. I cannot cut up human beings like
a log of wood.

'The minister asks what has protection done for these
holders of land in Ireland? I rather think the question to
be answered is, whether the five or six hundred thousand
small farmers of that country are worse off than they were
at the time of the union, when free trade prevailed? Why,
Ireland previously imported grain, while now she is an
exporting country to the amount of nearly five millions
sterling, and of other agricultural produce, which will be
affected by the measures now in agitation, to the extent
probably of ten millions per annum. But the secretary of
the savings' banks of Cork tells us that in the past year
£200,000 were paid into that bank by small farmers of the
class I speak of, in sums not exceeding £30. Was not that
ground for believing that Ireland was making progress
under a protective policy? These sums of £30 would
certainly not constitute the capital necessary to a system of
farming on a greater scale, or perhaps even to save the class
of people possessing such a small amount of capital from
being sacrificed by the minister at the shrine of free trade.
Still, this indicated a state of independence much to be
rejoiced at, and showed the existence of a race of men, who,
though they might not perhaps "cultivate their land to the
best advantage," or know how " to make five quarters grow

where three did before," are yet a class of men whom it would be worse than unwise to sacrifice for the sake of a system.'

He contrasted this conduct with the policy towards Ireland so earnestly supported by Mr. Burke and Mr. Pitt. 'But our measures now, it seems, are to be of such a description that you must drive her agricultural produce out of the market. It may be true that you are not about to divorce her; but you are going to admit into the arms of England concubines from every part of the world.'

Noticing the often repeated declaration of the minister, and which had been elaborately made on the previous night, that he felt no humiliation in confessing his errors and acknowledging that he had hitherto been wrong with respect to the commercial policy of the country, Lord George said, that he did not wish to say much on that head. 'It may not be humiliating in a private gentleman to acknowledge that for thirty years of parliamentary life he has been entirely in error in his opinions on a great branch of public policy. But I cannot agree that it is not humiliating to a great minister, to one who aspires to be a great statesman, to be obliged to confess, that the whole course of his public career has been one continued series of errors. Why, what advantage is there in having men at the helm of public affairs, if not to direct the public judgment? And if he direct it entirely in a wrong course, surely it is humiliating, and surely it cannot be otherwise than a humiliating avowal, that he has governed the country erroneously for a long series of years. Sir, it is the privilege of girls to change their opinions; but even they cannot do so without risk of a damaged reputation.'

But notwithstanding the dauntless energy and inexhaustible resources of the protectionist leader, who watched every opportunity to resist the progress of the enemy, and was prepared always for every point; notwithstanding all his researches, his vast correspondence, his multifarious information, his conferences, interviews, deputations, his indefatigable life; notwithstanding he was never absent from his seat, retired the last and rose the earliest to a day of constant toil and never of sufficient sustenance, the inevitable hour arrived, and, on the 11th of May, the bill for the repeal of the corn laws was to be read a third, and last time.

Lord George Bentinck was extremely anxious that the protectionist party should sustain their reputation on this occasion, and also that the bill should not go up to the lords with a majority of three figures, which, it was boasted by the government and their new friends, would be the case. The amendment was moved at this instance by the Marquess of Granby, who, by his careful study of the question then under discussion, the earnestness of his disposition, and the firmness of his character, had attracted the attention and gained the confidence of his leader. Lord Granby more than fulfilled all that was hoped from him. He placed the whole question before the house in a style, comprehensive, masculine, and sincere. He was seconded by Mr. Milnes Gaskell, who had retired from the treasury from his unwillingness to support the policy of the administration of which he had been recently a member. He brought to official experience the accessories of a cultivated mind and a classic elocution. The debate, after having occupied the 11th and 12th of May, was adjourned to Friday the 15th of that month, when, after a discussion of perhaps unexampled excitement in the house of commons, the division was called at four o'clock in the morning of Saturday, and in a house of 560 members, the third reading of the bill for the repeal of the corn laws was carried by a majority of 98.

CHAPTER XIII

On the 13th of May in the heart of the adjourned debate on the third reading of the corn bill, news arrived of the rejection by the legislative assembly of Canada of the new commercial policy of her majesty's government, and Lord George Bentinck seized the following night, the 14th, which did not belong to the government, to bring forward, though at a late hour, the whole question of the effect of our new commercial policy on our relations with Canada.

This is mentioned as illustrative of his energy and vigilance; certainly throughout his remarkable and too brief career he never lost an opportunity. Even after the passing of the corn bill in the commons, which took place as we have stated on Friday the 15th, on the Monday following, on the ministerial motion that the amendments made by the committee be read a second time, Lord George rose, and moving an amendment that the resolutions be read that day six months, made an elaborate and able statement in which he laid down two principles, the effects of which he developed in detail: 1stly, that it was our duty to remit excise duties in preference to customs duties; and 2ndly, that the principle of reciprocity in our commercial intercourse, as laid down by Mr. Huskisson, should never be abandoned.

He urged also, that if we were to reduce customs duties in preference to excise, we ought to reduce the duties on the produce of those countries which take most of our produce, and should give the preference to duties on articles which do not come into competition with the industry of this country. When excise duties were reduced, independently of the relief to the subject, the expenses of collection were got rid of. The salaries of four hundred and fifty officers were saved by the mere reduction of the duties on auctions and glass. But when customs duties are reduced, the services of not a single officer are dispensed with. Also, when you reduce customs duties, the foreigner shares with the consumer in this country the benefit of the reduction. But if you reduce the duties on excise articles, the whole benefit is derived by the subjects of the queen. 'I cannot understand,' observed Lord George, 'on what principle, so long as there are any excise duties to be reduced, the legislature should prefer to levy these duties and to reduce the duties of customs.'

Lord George said that Mr. Huskisson never contemplated free trade without reciprocity. The government appeared to have a pleasure in reducing the duties on the products of those countries which have hostile tariffs. The wiser policy would be to reduce the duties upon the products of those countries which take our manufactures at a low duty— China especially.

Lord George repeated and enforced the opinion of one of his supporters, that hostile tariffs could not be encountered by free imports. A very long debate ensued upon this interesting subject which terminated at a late hour.

The question whether hostile tariffs can be successfully combated by free imports has not yet received a satisfactory solution. Those who suppose they answer it when they point to the fact that under such circumstances our trade with a restrictive country has increased, have mistaken its bearing. The question refers not to the increase of trade, but to the terms of interchange. A trade may increase with diminished profits. Diminished profits must ultimately lead to diminished wages. If a trade be increased, or even sustained, by our exchanging more of our productions for a less quantity of a foreign article, it can scarcely be esteemed in a flourishing condition. The action of a hostile tariff seems to be equivalent to an increase in the cost of production in the country against whose industry it is directed, and to alter the terms of exchange accordingly. So a reduction in the duties laid upon British goods in foreign countries would be as beneficial to England as an equivalent diminution in the cost of producing goods for foreign markets. If this be true, an increase of the duties imposed upon British goods in foreign countries, or a decrease of the duties imposed by England upon foreign goods, would be as injurious as the other movement would be beneficial.

It has been frequently urged that a hostile tariff exacts from a country whose ports are free what is equivalent to paying a tribute, and it has been replied that this can hardly be the case, as the Manchester manufacturer, for example, sells his goods at the same price at Cincinnati as at Aylesbury. How then, it is asked, can the Manchester manufacturer pay a tribute to the American when he receives from him the same price as he receives from his fellow-subjects? But hostile tariffs diminish the demand for British goods in the foreign market; this diminished demand lowers their value in the Manchester market; and the fall of prices in the Manchester market causes a corresponding and a general fall in the prices of British goods throughout all the markets, domestic or foreign, in which those goods are sold.

It is also urged that countervailing duties on the raw materials of the manufacturer would be a very questionable mode of sustaining him against the taxes of the foreigner on his manufactured goods, but eminent men who have scientifically treated the important question of reciprocity have never sanctioned a tax upon a raw material. The object of the reciprocal system is to maintain the efficacy of native industry, and therefore it is opposed to any tax on a material which enters into native fabrics.

If the effect of this country combating hostile tariffs with free imports be, that its labour exchanges for a less quantity of foreign productions than heretofore, that result would of course equally apply to the precious metals which are foreign productions, and important considerations respecting our currency arising from our diminished command over the standard of value have naturally occurred to economical writers and have engaged much of their attention. But all those questions which are dependent on the distribution and command of the precious metals have assumed a new aspect since the vast metallic discoveries that have taken place since the debates and discussions of 1846.

Irrespective of this last consideration the principle of reciprocity appears to rest on scientific grounds, and it is probable that experience may teach us that it has been recklessly disregarded by our legislators.

CHAPTER XIV

AFTER a discussion of three nights, closed by the Duke of Wellington in a speech in which he informed the house of lords, that 'the bill for the repeal of the corn laws had already been agreed to by the other two branches of the legislature,' and that, under these circumstances, 'there was an end of the functions of the house of lords,' and that they had only to comply with the projects sent up to them; a sentiment the bearing of which seems not easy to distinguish from the vote of the long parliament which openly abrogated those functions; the lords passed the second reading of the measure on the 28th of May, by the large majority of 47.

On the day following in the commons the minister moved the adjournment of the house for one week, for the Whitsun recess; and gave notice that, on Monday the 8th, the day of reassembling being necessarily devoted to supply, the government would proceed with their coercion bill, and continue to do so in preference to all other business.

The time had now arrived when it became necessary for those who were responsible for the conduct of the protectionist party very gravely to consider the state of affairs, which had become critical, and to decide upon the future course. The large majority in the house of lords had extinguished the lingering hope that the ministerial scheme might ultimately be defeated. Vengeance therefore had succeeded in most breasts to the more sanguine sentiment. The field was lost, but at any rate there should be retribution for those who had betrayed it. Proud in their numbers, confident in their discipline, and elate with their memorable resistance, the protectionist party as a body had always assumed, that when the occasion was ripe, the career of the minister might be terminated: it was not until the period had arrived when the means to secure the catastrophe were to be decided on, that the difficulty of discovering them was generally acknowledged.

How was Sir Robert Peel to be turned out?

Here was a question which might well occupy the musing hours of a Whitsun recess.

The impetuous demanded a formal vote of want of confidence in the government, but the objection to this suggestion was, that in all probability the vote would not have been carried. The whigs might have joined in it, and perhaps would have done so, on the ground subsequently taken by Lord John Russell, that, although they supported the government measures, the very introduction of those measures was a practical testimony that in former years the members of that government had been mistaken, and the whigs had been right. But although the whigs might have joined in the vote of condemnation, there was reason to believe that the great body of the liberal party would not have followed Lord John Russell, and, personally, the mere whig connection in the second parliament of the queen was extremely weak. The pure free-traders could not with any grace censure the administration; and it was very questionable whether Mr. Hume and the English radicals generally would have co-operated in such a proceeding. Add to all this, an element of calculation, which, though an unknown quantity, could not be omitted by a sagacious leader—viz. the defalcation which would occur in the protectionist ranks themselves, if such a line were adopted. There were many who were not prepared to add to the mortification, which they had already experienced, the re-establishment in power, and by their own means, of that party to which they had ever been opposed.

If indeed the whigs had been prepared to form a government on the economical principles of their own budget of 1842, the whole of the protectionist party would have arrayed itself under their banners, and the landed interest, whose honour they would have then saved, would have been theirs for ever. This was a result which the whigs as a party were desirous to accomplish; and a nobleman, whose services have been since prematurely lost to the country, and whose excellent sense, imperturbable temper, and knowledge of mankind, had for many years exercised a leading influence in the councils of the whigs, and always to their advantage, was extremely anxious, that by a reconstruction in this spirit an end should be put to that balanced state of parties, which, if permitted to continue, frustrated the practicability and even the prospect of a strong government. What he wished particularly to accomplish was, to see Lord George Bentinck in the new whig cabinet. But though this eminent individual conducted his negotiations under the happiest auspices, for Lord George Bentinck entertained for him great personal regard, and was united to his son by ties of very warm and intimate friendship, his object was not attained. Lord John Russell could not recede from the Edinburgh letter, and he was more valuable to his party than a fixed duty on corn. Lord George Bentinck offered, and promised, to support the whig government, but would not become a member of any administration which was not prepared to do justice to the land.

When all hope of reconstructing the Whig party on a broad basis was reluctantly given up, and the future ministers reconciled themselves to that prospect of a weak government which was so clearly foreseen by their sagacious friend and has been subsequently so unfortunately realised, those active spirits who busy themselves with the measures of parties fixed upon the sugar duties as the inevitable question on which the government might be expelled from office. The existing government, it was understood, had pledged itself to the colonial interest to maintain their old policy of excluding slave-grown sugar; and, in fact, it was only by such an engagement that the votes of those members of the house of commons connected with the two Indies had been lost to the protectionists in the division. It was supposed that the agricultural interest, having lost the

protection which the land enjoyed, would not be indisposed
to console themselves for this deprivation by the enjoyment
of cheap sugar, especially when the representatives of dear
sugar had exhibited so decided a predilection for cheap
bread. But when Lord George Bentinck was sounded on
this scheme he shook his head, with that peculiar expression
which always conveyed to those who were appealing to him
the utter hopelessness of their enterprise. 'No,' he said,
'we have nothing to sustain us but our principles. We are
not privy-councillors, but we may be honest men. True to
the principle of protection, we must support East and West
India interests. We think it the wisest policy, at once, to
give protection to colonial interests and thereby to our
manufacturing interests at home. We are resolved to
support British capital wherever it may be invested.'

Slave-grown sugar would have united the whole of the
liberal party under the auspices of Lord John Russell and
Lord Palmerston, but then unfortunately it was just the
question which would have brought the entire protectionist
body back to the standard of the treasury, and instead
of turning out the administration there would have been
a painful resuscitation of the old conservative majority
of 96.

Thus it happened, that, although for several weeks the
persons most adroit in such affairs had been planning the
overthrow of a government which was only supported by
one-sixth of the members of the house of commons, the
Whitsun recess had closed and parliament had again re-
opened without apparently any approximation to the means
which were to accomplish their purpose. The bill for the
repeal of the corn laws could not be carried through the
house of lords until the end of June; and until that
measure was secured the whigs and their liberal allies were
not prepared to strike. What opportunity would they have
of dealing the blow after June? There was no reason why
the government, having carried their measure, might not
rapidly wind up the session and prorogue parliament. Was
it probable that at the end of another month, the govern-

ment having achieved their great object, those who were conspiring their overthrow would be richer in their resources or more felicitous in their expedients than at the present moment, when vengeance, ambition, the love of office, and the love of change, all combined to advance and assist their wishes. Notwithstanding the frank confession of the Duke of Wellington, which we have noticed, that he was disappointed in the object for which he had consented to the repeal of the corn laws and that a change of government was impending, the house of commons, better judges of such a contingency, began to suspect that his grace was a little misinformed, and that he only represented, which was the fact, the opinion of his colleagues after the Easter recess, and not after the Whitsun. If there were any doubt in the mind of Lord George Bentinck, that the government were convinced on the reassembling of parliament that they had weathered the storm, this doubt was removed by an interesting occurrence.

About this time, Louis Philippe of Orleans, king of the French, exercised a great influence over public affairs. This prince had entirely identified himself with the Peel administration. There existed between his majesty and the English minister not only a sentiment of sympathy but one of reciprocal admiration. Each believed the other the ablest man in their respective countries: their system of government was the same, to divert the public mind from political change by the seduction of physical enjoyment,[1] and to neutralise opinion in the pursuit of material prosperity: finally, they agreed in another point, that their tenure of power was as interminable as the nature of things admitted, and that it was ensured by mutual co-operation.

No one was more amazed and more alarmed by the breaking up of the conservative government in November '45 than the king of the French. With the quickness of

[1] 'I have thought it consistent with true conservative policy, that thoughts of the dissolution of our institutions should be forgotten in the midst of physical enjoyment.'—*Speech of Sir Robert Peel on the opening of Parliament, January* 22, 1846.

perception, which with him always seemed rather instinct than thought, he instantly trembled before a long vista of war and revolution. His fears of Lord Palmerston were fed by all the diplomacy of Europe, and especially by the connections of the late conservative cabinet, who still hoped that the repugnance of the European courts to the appointment of that minister might, in conjunction with the domestic weakness of the whig party, yet bring back the game to Sir Robert.

One, to whom the king had disburthened his mind in an hour of intolerable anxiety and from whom his majesty asked that counsel which circumstances permitted to be given, tried to relieve him from these bugbears of state, in a truer appreciation of the position than those around him cared to encourage. It was represented to the king, that a cordial understanding between the two countries had become a necessity for every English administration; that the parliament and the people of England would never support a minister whom they believed to be inclined to treat the French connection with levity or disregard; and that it was especially the interest of the whigs in their present feeble condition to prove to the country that they took office with no prejudice against their neighbours. With these views, and in order at once to relieve his mind, it was suggested to the king that through the medium of some private friend, it might be wise to make an effort to disembarrass this question of the personal complications with which it had been the interest of certain individuals too long to invest it; and that he should seek for some frank explanation of the feelings with respect to France with which the new English minister returned to office.

The king, who was a man of great impulse, grasped at the suggestion and acted upon it immediately. The appeal was promptly attended with the most satisfactory results, and the king of the French, with a countenance radiant with smiles, was assuring the whole diplomatic circle that he was never less uneasy as to the prospects of Europe, and that Lord Palmerston had resumed office with a determination to act cordially with France, when to the astonishment of his majesty, he learnt that Lord John Russell had resigned his mission, in consequence of an absurd and really discreditable intrigue against Lord Palmerston by a portion of his own party, on the plea that his appointment to the foreign office would endanger our friendly relations with the Tuileries.

The excitement of the king was very great on the return of Sir Robert Peel to power. His majesty looked upon all the intervening incidents which had occasioned him so much disquiet and perplexity merely as dexterous tactics preliminary to a crowning triumph. He thought that the sovereign, the parliament, and the nation had combined to give the minister *carte blanche*. A member of the British parliament who was then at Paris presumed, with great humility, to question the justness of the royal conclusions.

'Do you not think then,' said the king, 'that Sir Robert Peel will carry his measures?'

'Yes, sir.'

'And what then?'

'And then, sir, he will be turned out.'

'Who is to turn him out? Lord John Russell has had the offer, and has refused. I can tell you the Duke of Wellington says the government is established. I remember,' the king added with a smile of confidence, 'when they said that Mr. Pitt would not remain in for six weeks, and he was minister for twenty years.'

The confidence of his majesty in the star of Sir Robert Peel remained unfaltering until at Easter he was apprised, from a quarter that could not be deceived, that the administration tottered. For more than a month the king was in the habit of assuring the royal circle, that in case there was a change of ministry in England, Lord Palmerston would be found inspired with the most cordial feelings towards France, which were reciprocated. It was at the very moment, when his majesty had reconciled himself to the worst, that the news of the large majority in the house of lords reached him, and he was assured at the same time that all danger was over, and that there were no existing means, and that none would certainly be afforded, of disturbing the government.

It was on the 6th of June, that the contents of this communication to the king of the French were placed before Lord George Bentinck, whose own experience at that moment proved how much foundation there was for the statement. It was clear that the blow must be dealt immediately. Even with that determination, the difficulty of proceeding seemed almost insurmountable. It might be three weeks before the corn bill was returned from the lords, and it was evident that the commons would not place the government in a minority until that measure was secured. A notice of a vote of want of confidence in the ministry was the only motion from which it was certain that the government would not shrink and would not attempt to avoid by prorogation; but then that was a motion which it was sufficiently clear must end in failure. It seemed that they had escaped, and that the king of the French, as usual, was right.

In this state of affairs it was submitted to the consideration of Lord George Bentinck, that there appeared only one course to be taken, and which, though beset with difficulties, was with boldness and dexterity at least susceptible of success. The government had announced their intention of moving the second reading of the Irish coercion bill on Monday the 8th of June. If this second reading were opposed both by Lord John Russell and Lord George Bentinck, the defeat of the administration seemed more than probable.

The first great difficulty to be considered in this project was that presented by the fact, that both Lord John Russell and Lord George Bentinck had hitherto supported that measure.

To support a government in an unconstitutional measure is tantamount to a vote of confidence in them; and the step therefore taken by Lord John Russell and Lord George Bentinck, in the first instance, was unskilful and unwise. But Lord John had been embarrassed and entrapped by the precipitate acts and indiscreet admissions of his colleagues in the house of lords; and Lord George, though warned against taking a course which was in itself foreign to his policy with respect to Ireland, had been seduced into the proceeding by the irresistible temptation of securing delay in the progress of the corn bill.

Yet both of these leaders had been provident even in their errors. Lord John Russell had, very early in the discussion, prepared, if necessary, a retreat. When the bill was brought in, notwithstanding the unqualified approbation of it by his friends in the other house, he had ventured to hint that there were some clauses to which he had objections; advancing with circumstances, he had, on a subsequent occasion, expressed his disapproval of the curfew clause, supposed to be a vital part of the measure; and just before the house was adjourned for the Whitsun holidays, he said, 'he thought it would be the fairer and more direct course to oppose the second reading of the bill, rather than so to mutilate it as to leave none of its important clauses.' Thus, about the 25th of May, when these expressions were used, though at the time they did not attract all the attention they deserved, Lord John Russell had contrived to extricate himself pretty completely from the engagements of Lord Lansdowne, Lord Clanricarde, and Lord Grey.

The position of Lord George Bentinck in this respect was even stronger than that of Lord John Russell. When the coercion bill was first brought forward in the commons, he had described it as an unconstitutional measure and had even christened the curfew clause; but had stated, that he and his friends were prepared to support the measure, provided the government evinced an earnestness to press it forward and suffer no unnecessary delay or obstruction to interpose which they could reasonably avoid. But if on the contrary it should appear from the conduct of the government that they were lukewarm or indifferent, and that permitting other measures of less necessity to be carried through the house in preference they gave the house cause to believe that in their own minds no such emergency as

they spoke of existed, then under such circumstances the
protectionist party should not feel themselves bound to
continue their support of such a measure.

Nor could there be any misconception in the mind of the
government as to the intentions of Lord George Bentinck
in this respect. They were not to be collected merely from
his speech. The reader will recollect that after the Easter
recess a communication on the conduct of public business
was opened with Lord George by the secretary of the
treasury on the part of Sir Robert Peel, and will recall the
circumstances under which that gentleman, the present Sir
John Young, M.P. for Cavan, figured as the 'disavowed
plenipotentiary.' That conference had led to a correspondence which the noble lord at the time had expressed his
wish should be read to the house; but no member of the
government had responded to that proposition, and the
correspondence therefore had remained in obscurity. The
following passage, afterwards quoted by Mr. Stafford in the
course of the debate on the second reading of the coercion
bill, indicated with precision the views of the protectionist
party on the 21st of March '46.

*Extract of a letter from Lord George Bentinck to John
Young, Esq., Secretary of the Treasury.*

' I then frankly told you, with respect to the anti-murder
bill, that I believed the whole party with whom I served
were but of one opinion, that it was a most unconstitutional
measure, and only to be justified by some dire exigency. I
believe I termed it another curfew act, and said, that nothing
but the most imminent danger could excuse it; but that if
the government were prepared to state that the emergency
did exist, and were ready to have their honesty and sincerity
tested by pressing the measure with all possible speed
through the house, we should be disposed to give them
credit for the existence of so dire an emergency, and support
them. But if, on the contrary, it should appear from their
conduct, that in their hearts they did not believe such

dire necessity did exist, if the danger to life was so little imminent that they could afford to postpone the measure on which the security of life was said to depend, then the complexion of the case would be very much altered, and I conceive we should feel ourselves bound to take a different course, presuming, as we must under such circumstances, that no true or lasting ground did in fact exist for the adoption of so unconstitutional a measure.'

Well, then, 'was the complexion of the case' very much altered by the subsequent behaviour of the government, and might it be inferred 'from their conduct, that, in their hearts, they did not believe in the "dire necessity,"' which was the alleged cause of their proposition?

It could not be denied that this coercion bill came down from the house of lords on the 13th of March and was not read for the first time until the 1st of May; and that since that period nearly six weeks had elapsed without her majesty's ministers attempting to take any steps to forward the measure. It might be replied, that these six weeks had been devoted to the discussion and passing of the corn and the customs bills; and that although Lord George Bentinck might not credit the urgent necessity of such measures, that, at any rate, was not the predominant opinion of the house of commons. But this plea would not bear analysis. It appeared that, irrespectively of the government night on which no house had been made, four other of their nights had been occupied with government business other than the corn and the customs bills; that these nights too were only partially occupied; that they were wasted; that on three of these occasions the house rose before eight o'clock, and on the fourth before nine o'clock.

Lord George Bentinck was of opinion that the case of the protectionists, as against the government, was a good one; he was also definitively of opinion that opposition to the coercion bill afforded the only opportunity of overthrowing the administration; but he doubted whether the protectionist party, after having voted once for the measure, would be generally, or in a sufficient degree, induced to strike the blow. One section of his most zealous supporters, and a body of gentlemen too among whom he counted many warm personal friends, namely the Irish protectionist members, could certainly not be expected to vote against the bill; all those members, who from the strong feeling of their constituents might be counted on in any division against the government where the protective principle was involved, but who in their hearts had no wish to disturb the administration, would certainly avail themselves of the opportunity of voting with a minister whom they had been obliged too frequently to oppose; strong measures also with respect to Irish outrage, it could not be denied, were popular with many most respectable persons, who, not having very deeply investigated the condition of our sister isle, held that violence could only be successfully encountered by restraint.

On Saturday therefore nothing was decided; on the following day Lord George Bentinck took the opportunity of breaking the situation to several of the leading country gentlemen who were in the habit of acting with him; the reception of his suggestion was not favourable. They were embarrassed by their previous vote, and were astonished to learn that if they repeated it, the 'government was in for ever.'

On Monday, before the meeting of the house, Lord George held a rapid council with such of his friends as he could immediately collect. Only one voice supported him on the ground that the step was not only wise but indispensable. The rest, while they declared they would not desert him in any course which he pursued, gave it as their opinion that the movement would fail and might then become unpopular in the country.

Nothing was decided when Lord George had taken his seat, and while Sir William Somerville was moving the amendment that the coercion bill should be read that day six months. His solitary supporter in the council was sitting by his side. They had agreed their course should be decided by the report which they should receive from a gentleman who had the best acquaintance with the individual feelings of the members of the party, and who, through absence from town, had not, unfortunately, been present at the previous consultations. While Sir William Somerville was closing his speech with an appeal to Lord George Bentinck, this much expected individual appeared at the bar.

'I call on all who prize liberty,' said Sir William, 'and value the constitutional rights of the subject, to support this amendment; and, above all, I call upon the noble lord, the member for King's Lynn, to be true to his own words, and to carry out his engagement by withholding his advocacy from a measure which the government had by their delays proved to be unnecessary, and into which they had introduced such changes as showed that they did not know their own will, nor clearly understand what measure of power they required.'

When Sir William Somerville sat down, Lord George exchanged signals with the member who had just arrived to join him in the library, and then requesting his companion to watch the debate, he repaired to that spot which has been the scene of so many important and interesting conferences.

While he was absent, the house was nearly counted out.

He came back in about a quarter of an hour, and remarked, 'There are no means of calculating at this moment how our men will go, but he agrees with us. It may be perilous, but if we lose this chance the traitor will escape. I will make the plunge, and as soon as I can. There is a rumour that Lord John is hardly up to the mark. I suppose he has heard that our men will not vote against the bill. Now, if I speak early and strongly, it will encourage him to be decided.'

When the seconder of the amendment sat down, no one rose, and the division was called for. How strange, that a debate, which lasted nearly three weeks, led to such memorable consequences, and was distinguished by so many remarkable incidents, should twice, within an hour of its commencement, have been on the verge of an untimely end.

However, on the present occasion Mr. Osborne interposed with some of those sprightly taunts which often revive the fight, and drew forth the new Irish secretary, the Earl of Lincoln, who of course had never seriously intended to avoid speaking, as was proved by his address, which, though at first it did not escape the depreciating interruptions of some of the Irish members, was soon recognised by the house as a statement, both for argument and detail, quite worthy of the occasion and the office.

Lord Lincoln, now sitting for a Scotch borough, had originally been member for the native county of Lord George Bentinck, and had been driven from that honourable post mainly by the exertions of the leader of the protectionists and his energetic appeals to the indignant farmers of Nottinghamshire. There was therefore something of a public feud between the two noble lords, who rarely spared each other. Hitherto, the attacks of Lord Lincoln had been confined to the hustings, though that limitation scarcely deprived him of opportunities, for he had enjoyed the singular fortune of appearing on the hustings of three different places since the meeting of parliament. Lord George naturally delivered his rejoinders and criticism in the house, and they were certainly always prompt and in general tolerably plain. To-night, towards the close of an apparently temperate speech, Lord Lincoln, reminding the house of the difficulties which the government had to encounter in Ireland, said 'that they had to adopt measures to meet a great emergency in the teeth of taunts and opprobrium from many of their former friends. They had received insults and reproaches that, out of the house, would not have been cast on them—taunts and reproaches that they had fabricated returns for party purposes, and which, though uttered by honourable gentlemen sitting there, they would not have dared to pronounce out of the house.'

The house being now full, for Lord Lincoln had spoken at considerable length, Lord George Bentinck rose, not encouraged to make a less decided declaration than he was prepared to do by the somewhat defying comments of one between whom and himself there perhaps existed local emulation as well as political difference.

Lord George touched lightly on the provisions of the bill, though he corrected one important statement of the chief secretary with great effect. 'The noble lord, the chief secretary for Ireland, who announced on the hustings of Falkirk, that he was to be returned to this house in order to rescue ministers from that defeat which otherwise, he said, was hanging over them, says it is a notorious fact, that crime in Ireland invariably diminishes in proportion as the days grow long. Well, sir, if that be the case, I think it was reason enough for passing this measure whilst the days were short and the nights long. This statement surely furnishes no grounds for postponing the second reading until the middle of the month of June. But, sir, the very reverse of what the noble lord tells us is the fact. So far from this being the case, I find, that looking at the return of crimes committed last year, that the month of June, which it is perhaps known to the noble lord has the longest day, is precisely the very month when the greatest number of offences of this kind occurred.'

Then dwelling on the conduct of the government, who, 'at the expiration of five months, call upon the house to proceed with a measure to meet an emergency which occurred five months ago,' he added, 'But, sir, there are much stronger and heavier reasons for my opposing the government on the present occasion. I and the gentlemen around me refuse to trust her majesty's ministers. We have for good reasons ceased to place any confidence in them. We are of opinion that we cannot with safety entrust them with the charge of so unconstitutional a power as this bill contains.

'I will not stay to discuss this measure. Is there any one who thinks the government mean to carry it through? After such postponements, such obstructions, such delays, with five months suffered to elapse between the first and the second reading, we know the session must be over before this bill is dragged through the house of commons.'

He said this, he continued, 'because some of my Irish friends may be disposed to support this measure from an honest conviction that some measure of coercion is required.

'We have been told that the government were as much in earnest about carrying this measure as in carrying the corn law. But how different has been their conduct in the one measure and the other. They devoted every day, order and motion days, to the discussion of the corn bill, to repeal that law which they had so often pledged themselves to support. They acted with the zeal of converts; they forced on the measure, they were willing to sacrifice the holidays, they were to be worked up to Good Friday eve, in short, no toil too great, no question so important, no delay so fatal, as those which occurred on the corn bill. But how different the case with the coercion bill—delay, obstruction, months' intermission, short sittings. Why, bad and unkind as the government is, I cannot believe they are yet so far lost to a sense of propriety as to consent to a waste of so much valuable time if they really considered that the bill was necessary. No sooner does it become a question of the coercion bill instead of the corn law, than the house is indulged with long holidays; and on Monday night, Tuesday, and Thursday nights, permitted to adjourn at half-past seven. Does this look like earnestness, like sincerity?

'I should certainly have preferred an amendment which took the shape of a direct vote of want of confidence in her majesty's ministers; but if we can believe any pledges which are given from the treasury bench, we may, I suppose, conclude that when they find they are no longer able to carry their measures, they will think it time to retire. We used, sir, I recollect, to be told by the right honourable baronet, that he would not consent to be a minister on sufferance; but I think he must be blinded indeed by the flattery of those around him if he has not learnt that he is now a minister on sufferance, tossed from one side to the other, sometimes depending on honourable gentlemen opposite, sometimes on my friends around me, supported by none but his forty paid janissaries, and some seventy other renegades, one-half of whom, while they support him, express their shame of doing so.

' We are told now—we hear it from the minister himself —that he thinks there is nothing humiliating in the course which he has pursued—that it would have been base and dishonest in him, and inconsistent with his duty to his sovereign, if he had concealed his opinions after he had changed them; but I have lived long enough, I am sorry to say, to remember, and to remember with sorrow—with deep and heartfelt sorrow—the time when the right honourable baronet chased and hunted an illustrious relative of mine to death; and when he stated that he could not support his ministry, because, as leading member of it, though he had changed no opinion, yet from his position he was likely to forward the question of catholic emancipation. That was the conduct of the right honourable baronet in 1827; but in 1829 he told the house that he had changed his opinions on that subject in 1825, and had communicated that change of opinion to the Earl of Liverpool.

' If, therefore, the right honourable baronet says it is base and dishonest, and inconsistent with the duty of a minister to his sovereign, to continue to maintain opinions after he has changed them, does not he stand convicted, by his own verdict, of base and dishonest conduct, and conduct inconsistent with the duty of a minister to his sovereign? When I recollect his conduct in 1827 and in 1829, after his change of opinion in 1825, though he has been sitting long on the stool of repentance, I am satisfied that the country will not forgive twice the same crime in the same man. A second time has the right honourable baronet insulted the honour of parliament and of the country, and it is now time that atonement should be made to the betrayed constituencies of the empire.'

The speaker sat down in a tumult of applause, amid which the secretary at war rose, with great indignation, to notice ' charges against her majesty's government couched in language seldom heard in that house, language which, for the sake of the character of that house, it would be better should not be heard.

'The noble lord,' continued the secretary, after having spoken for some time amid much interruption, ' says we are not in earnest in passing this bill. He quotes, with that unfortunate love of arithmetic which leads him to calculations in human blood now, just as it led him to in grain, tallow, and timber before—a calculation to show that, though three weeks back it might be worth the while of the government to interfere, it is not worth while to interfere now, because he finds only 552 homicides in the returns. Only 552 homicides! The whole tone of his mind in fact is changed in consequence of some prospects he entertains from the combination of parties in this house, but totally irrespective of the opinions he himself advanced.'

After denouncing the conduct of Lord George Bentinck in changing his course upon this measure at some length and with no inconsiderable acrimony, and saying that the country would judge between him and the government, the secretary at war added, that under a paramount sense of duty, the government would persevere with the coercion bill, 'notwithstanding all his vituperation, and all his factious combinations.

' I make no charge against honourable gentlemen opposite,' continued the secretary at war. 'It is those who alter their course without any alteration in the circumstances I denounce. Sir, if I may be allowed to allude to the rumours circulated for the last few days, I may repeat, that I have heard it stated, that proposals have been made to the noble lord opposite (Lord John Russell) to bring to his assistance the services of a number of gentlemen, who are more anxious to divide with him than to consider the merits of the question—a proposal in reference to which the noble lord has acted as I should have expected him to act—he treated it with that silence which I suppose it is hardly parliamentary to designate as the silence of contempt.'

At these strange expressions, unwise even if they had had some foundation, singularly unfortunate in the actual circumstances, there was a burst of exclamations from below the gangway, where the protectionist host were encamped, and loud cries of 'Name, name.' The secretary at war declined to name those who had 'preferred to make a combination to unseat a government, rather than to support a policy to which they were pledged,' and said their names would be found in the division list; then, pursuing his speech, and reiterating his declaration that to 'this measure the government was determined to adhere,' resumed his seat. Whereupon the Marquess of Granby, with promptness and spirit, said that the secretary at war had complained that Lord George Bentinck had used language in that house which was most unusual; but Lord Granby complained that the government had taken a course which was most unusual. The conduct of the government had been such as had not before been witnessed in that house. Unusual conduct required unusual expressions. They had been told that they had entered into a compact with those opposite. Lord Granby was not aware of this compact. He believed the only agreement between the protectionists and the opposition was, that they had no confidence whatever in her majesty's government.

An Irish member then moving the adjournment of the house, Mr. Stafford rose, and said he would take advantage of the question of adjournment to ask the secretary at war for an explanation of his remarkable statement, that a proposition for a compact had been made between the protectionists and Lord John Russell and had been treated with silent contempt. If said only in the heat of debate, an explanation might be offered, but if said 'decidedly, believing it, and intending to adhere to it,' the house had a right to require a reiteration of that statement in detail,

and the names of the members of the protectionist party
who had endeavoured to make this compact. The secretary
at war, thus pointedly appealed to, rose and stated, that
'he had not asserted of his own knowledge any fact, nor
had he quoted any authority. But rumours had flown
about town that Lord George Bentinck had made an offer
to Lord John Russell of the kind described, "Rumour had
no name."' Upon this, Mr. Eliot Yorke said, that it had
been most distinctly stated that a negotiation had been
carried on. No other construction could be put upon the
words of the secretary at war but that some application
had been made to Lord John Russell. If so, by whom
made? Let Lord John Russell inform the house, and let
the individual who made the application have an opportunity of stating his authority to do so.

Lord John Russell upon this rose and said, that 'no
application or proposition had been made to him on the
part of Lord George Bentinck, or of any other member.
Some of his own friends indeed had asked what he intended
to do with regard to the coercion bill, and far from using
any contemptuous silence, he had replied, that it was his
intention to oppose its second reading, and that they might
tell that to any person who required information on the
subject. Lord George Bentinck had come to his conclusion
on grounds satisfactory to himself; and he, Lord John
Russell, had come to the same conclusion with regard to
the bill on grounds which were satisfactory to himself.
Those grounds were entirely public; he should be prepared
to state them in debate; but they mainly rested on this,
that he thought it would be injurious to Ireland and to
the protection of life to allow the government measure
to pass.'

Thus closed this eventful night. The field on which the
fate of the administration depended was fixed. The leaders
of the three parties were pledged. The government would
stand or fall by their measure: Lord John Russell and Lord
George Bentinck had come 'to the same conclusion' on
different grounds, but 'satisfactory to themselves.' But

what would the house do? At present it adjourned at two o'clock in the morning, in great agitation. Rage rather than despair was conveyed by the countenances of the 'janissaries' and the 'renegades.' The 'moderate men,' who wished to be at the same time on the best terms with their constituents and the treasury bench, keep in the government and yet keep their seats, murmured their disapprobation of 'strong language,' and said, that a vote of non-confidence would have been the proper course, knowing very well that they would not have supported it. Many trimmers were observed to walk home with 'janissaries,' or lighting their cigars with 'renegades,' declare, with a glance of secret sympathy, that they being thorough protectionists should certainly vote for protection of life.

CHAPTER XV

EVERY influence that existed or that could be created was now used and devised to break up the protectionist party on the impending question. The estimate of those whose authority on such matters with the first minister was deservedly great was, that two-thirds of the two hundred and forty gentlemen, who had 'maintained the chastity of their honour' on the famous division of February, would be found on the critical night in their old conservative ranks.

Three days had to elapse before the struggle could be continued, and they were days teeming with intrigue; with calculations, combinations, and canvassing. At least a fortnight must pass before the decision could be arrived at. The debate must be maintained until the third reading of the corn bill had been agreed to by the house of lords. What a situation! And what might not be managed in such a fortnight, for such a stake? The assailant and the assailed were not fighting on equal terms: they were not rivals. Power, place, patronage might reward those who upheld the minister; they might even at this conjuncture become 'janissaries' without ever having been 'renegades.' On the contrary, if Lord George were victorious, he handed over the prize to another, and the fulfilment of retribution was the only return that he could afford his supporters. Besides, there was a very lively recollection among the tory party generally of the evil effects which had accrued in 1830 from their former punishment of Sir Robert Peel. Old gentlemen at clubs shook their heads, remembering the family boroughs that they had lost by avenging the betrayed protestantism of '29. It was felt that if the conservative

party were broken up again a period of terrible indefinite-
ness must elapse before its reappearance on the political
stage. And why should Lord John be brought in? Was
he not as bad as Sir Robert Peel? Rather worse, because
had it not been for that mischievous Edinburgh letter there
might have been a politic solution of the affair in a respectable, moderate, fixed duty, which might have benefited no
one and satisfied everybody.

On Friday, June 12th, the minister concluded a tame
discussion by a spirited speech. He spoke with an alacrity
which of late had somewhat deserted him. His manner
was confident, his voice merry, and his eye sparkled with
that rich humour of which he had a store, but of which
he had favoured the house with no ebullitions in this sad,
fierce session. He threw off that martyr aspect which
hitherto he had very ostentatiously worn. It was thought
that his manner was auspicious of the impending event.
He fastened at first upon the recorder of Dublin, who, on a
previous occasion, 'in order to prove the ignorance in England, from highest to lowest, on the condition of Ireland,'
appeared to have stated that a housemaid in his establishment had very inconveniently declined to accompany the
right honourable gentleman to the seat of his judicial duties.
Sir Robert stated the circumstances with great gravity but
with playful misrepresentation, in tones of sympathy but
with a twinkling eye. The recorder, impatient of the
malicious narrative and anxious for the cause of truth,
interrupted the orator and indignantly exclaimed, 'No, no,'
which was exactly what Sir Robert was angling for, who,
turning round with respectful gravity, and saying, 'Well,
then, at this stage of the discussion, I must really ask the
right honourable gentleman to explain to the house what
he did say respecting his housemaid,' amid the roars of his
audience, provisionally resumed his seat.

This made good sport, and it was continued, for the
learned judge had on his legs to repeat what the minister
had already described as 'the housemaid argument'; and
Sir Robert had a further opportunity of stating 'with perfect

sincerity, that nothing could be further from his mind than to cast any reflection whatever on the conduct or motives of the right honourable and learned gentleman, *ne sit ancillæ tibi amor pudori!*' There was much merriment in the house; it was even general. It was thought that every protectionist who laughed must be going to vote for the government.

After discussing the bill in detail and with much animation for more than an hour, the minister, suddenly assuming a solemn tone, said that he should here have stopped, but he felt it incumbent on him not to sit down without noticing the speech made on the last night by Lord George Bentinck. There was a general rustling in the house and a momentary pause of the speaker.

When his voice again sounded, it was in tones of sorrowful indignation, not for his own sake but for the sake of the character of the house he deeply regretted: 'Yes, I do deeply regret, that during this session there has been, for the first time, a licence assumed which is, I think, injurious to the cause of legitimate debate.' He descanted much upon this; at least his parliamentary life for five-and-thirty years could afford no example for such licence. There were bounds which ought to be respected by every one who respects the usages of parliament. 'Janissaries and renegades!' He had heard Lord George Bentinck absolutely speak of those with whom 'he was connected by official ties,' as paid janissaries and renegades, 'gentlemen engaged in the public service, acting from as pure and conscientious a sense of public duty as ever influenced any member of this house. Unless a restraint was placed upon the exercise of such language, however right party feeling may prevail, it was calculated to create unmitigated disgust.'

He now came to the personal attack upon himself; he rejoiced that he did not attempt to answer those personal imputations until he had had an opportunity of ascertaining how far they were well founded. The reply of the minister was therefore made with ample research and the advantage of four days for reflection, but it consisted mainly of inferences. Would the friends of Mr. Canning have joined Mr. Peel in '28 when the Duke of Wellington formed a cabinet, if he had so conducted himself towards Mr. Canning in '25 and '27 ? Amongst Mr. Canning's most intimate friends were Mr. Huskisson, Lord Dudley, Mr. Grant, and Lord Melbourne. Not one of them made any objection to join him on account of any preceding transaction. They one and all consented to serve with him in the government and cabinet. Is it likely that, if such an impression respecting him prevailed in their minds, as would appear now for the first time to rankle in the heart of Lord George Bentinck, they would, in five months after the death of Mr. Canning, join with him in the cabinet and admit him as the leader of the house of commons ? Was it likely that Lord Angle- sea, 'the personation of a gallant and chivalrous spirit, the embodiment of every generous and manly emotion, the intimate friend of Mr. Canning,' would have gone as lord- lieutenant to Ireland when Mr. Peel was secretary of state if he had thought that Mr. Peel 'had chased and hunted Mr. Canning to death' ?

How came it that the minister heard of these feelings on the part of Lord George Bentinck for the first time on Monday last? Lord George had been in parliament since '26. 'There may have been intermissions,' observed Sir Robert, 'but since 1835 I have been honoured with the noble lord's cordial, and, I must say, his pure and disin- terested support. He called me his right honourable friend; he permitted me to be the leader of the party to which he belonged; he saw me united to his own immediate con- nections and followers; never, and until Monday last, in June 1846, did I harbour the suspicion that the noble lord entertained such feelings in respect to me and believed me to be a man who had hunted and chased his relation to death.'

But the minister was not satisfied with inferences. He gave the whole statement an unequivocal denial: he declared, that the charge that in 1829 he had avowed a change of opinion in 1825, which change of opinion he concealed in

1827, was utterly and entirely destitute of foundation. To confirm his statement, Sir Robert read a long extract from his speech of 1827, which he made in the presence of Mr. Canning, but it was observed that he did not refer to the speech in question, the speech of 1829, and prove to the house that no such passage as described could be found in it. Finally, dwelling strongly on the possible error but the positive purity of his conduct in his present measures, he concluded by this extraordinary statement: 'I may have been mistaken in my views respecting the corn laws, and the mistake, if it be one, may and ought, perhaps, to involve the forfeiture of political confidence; but that I have been influenced in this course by any desire to rob others of the credit which is their due, by any desire to interfere with the noble lord (Lord John Russell) whom I should have been glad to have seen in office—this imputation to me of motives so base, I declare to be as foul a calumny as a vindictive spirit ever directed against a public man.'

It being fresh in the recollection of the house, the statement indeed emanating from his own lips, that Sir Robert Peel, in the previous November, had proposed to his cabinet the repeal of the corn laws, and was prepared, if they had assented to his proposition, to attempt to carry that repeal, without any effort or inclination whatever to yield the measure to Lord John Russell, or any one else, this emphatic declaration was listened to by all with an air of perplexity and astonishment, so that the applause when the minister sat down was not such as might have been expected from so able and interesting an address, but was feeble and partial.

The house adjourned till Monday the 15th.

Lord George Bentinck had made the charge against Sir Robert Peel, that he had admitted in 1829 that, four years previously, he had expressed to Lord Liverpool an opinion that the catholic question ought to be settled, while, in the interval (1827), he had declined acting with Mr. Canning inasmuch as he was a minister favourable to such settlement, because Lord George Bentinck believed that he had himself heard such a declaration at the time from the lips of Mr. Peel. He did not refer to the circumstance as a matter of controversy, but as a fact acknowledged by all those who sat in the parliament of that day, or who were familiar with the political transactions of those times. The charge was a statement from his personal experience and memory, the tradition of the circle in which he lived, and the conviction of his hearth. He was prepared for an explanation from Sir Robert Peel, but he was not prepared for his denial of the fact. But since Sir Robert had denied the fact unequivocally, and had referred to authoritative reports of parliamentary proceedings in support of such denial, it became necessary for Lord George Bentinck in the interval occurring until the next night of debate to examine the evidence on which the minister rested his vindication and generally to investigate the subject.

Of course the admission in question did not occur in the report of the speech of 1829 in Hansard, since that was a republication of the pamphlet in which the speech had authoritatively been published, as avowedly corrected and revised by Sir Robert Peel.

The alleged admission was, however, found in the *Mirror of Parliament*, a publication which had ceased, but which according to its prospectus was edited by a Mr. Barrow with the assistance of the ablest parliamentary reporters. Mr. Barrow was a well-known and accomplished parliamentary reporter, a writer of shorthand, and a gentleman of character and education.

The alleged admission appeared also in the parliamentary report of the *Times* newspaper of that day.

There appeared also in the *Mirror of Parliament* a very full version of a somewhat celebrated speech, ending with ' *nusquam tuta fides,*' made by Sir Edward Knatchbull in answer to the speech of Mr. Peel, in which was the alleged admission, and in which speech Sir Edward Knatchbull attacked the admission with bitterness and in a spirit of great reproach. 'If, as he now says, he had discovered in 1825 the necessity of passing this question, I ask why he did not say so in 1827, and give his support to Mr. Canning then, when the supposed difference between him and Mr. Canning obtained for him the support of many honourable gentlemen, who differed with him only on that, which I confess was the case with me.'

Here were the materials of a good reply. Indeed the case seemed conclusive, especially to one whose memory and personal experience only required these documents as confirmation. Unfortunately, as he had already spoken in the debate, it was not open to Lord George Bentinck to avail himself of the fruits of his researches, which he gave therefore on Monday morning to a friend who had not yet interfered in the discussion.

Late at night, therefore, on Monday this reply was made on his behalf. The extraordinary declaration with which the minister had concluded his speech on the preceding Friday was noticed and contrasted with his own official statements in the course of this very session; Lord George Bentinck was vindicated from the use of unparliamentary language, and quotations from celebrated speeches of Mr. Fox and of Mr. Grenville were read, not only far exceeding any observations of Lord George in vituperative expression, but absolutely using, in both instances, that particular phrase of 'janissary,' the unprecedented use of which in debate had been denounced by the minister in tones of such solemn indignation. The documentary evidence was then clearly put before the house and enforced, and the speaker sat down.

The minister rose confused and suffering. He said he had no right to reply, but continued to make deprecatory and feeble observations. Finally, he called upon the house to 'suspend their judgment' until an opportunity for reply came.

The house adjourned until Thursday. The general opinion was that the minister was greatly damaged, and that had the division then taken place the government would certainly have been in a minority. On Thursday the debate was very vapid: it was supposed that Sir Robert

Peel would have made his explanation on that night, but he was silent. There were rumours from the treasury bench that certain papers that were expected from Drayton had not arrived; the delay made the protectionists confident. When the house broke up, it was bruited about that the 'explanation' would certainly be made on the next day.

Consequently on Friday, at five o'clock, the house was crowded; the gallery of the peers was full and the diplomatic body were present; the minister entered the house with an air of injured innocence, with his eyes cast upon the floor, and as if he felt that, until his character was cleared, it was not becoming in him to assume the deportment befitting his high office.

When the statement was made on the 15th by the friend of Lord George Bentinck in vindication of the charge and in rejoinder to the reply of the minister, a member of the liberal party had sent across the house a number of the *Edinburgh Review*, of April 1829, in which was an article on the state of parties, written, it was understood, by an individual, who had subsequently become a member of the whig government, and in which article it was stated, 'that at the very time Sir Robert Peel told Mr. Canning, in the house of commons, that his unlooked-for opposition to that statesman was grounded on a difference of opinion on the catholic question, he had in his desk a letter, in which, two years before, he had told Lord Liverpool that, in his opinion, the catholic claims ought to be granted, and proposing that he should retire from office in the meantime.'

This document, thus casually turning up and inadvertently introduced, was used by the speaker after he had concluded that portion of this statement which depended upon evidence; 'after this, I think, it is unnecessary to produce any more evidence,' were his words. 'I have accomplished the vindication of my noble friend who had not the power of speaking again in this debate'; and then, with reference to an observation of the minister in his reply that the charge made by Lord George Bentinck was heard by him for the first time, it was observed that that was remarkable, since, although an anonymous publication was no authority, there were publications of that kind of such high character, as the *Edinburgh* and *Quarterly* Reviews for example, to which many cabinet ministers of both sides had been contributors, that they might fairly be adduced not as evidence of any fact, but certainly as evidence of the belief of well-informed circles on particular circumstances; and in one of them this charge had been made without reserve, and with the allegation of circumstances, which Lord George Bentinck on an anonymous authority did not for a moment adduce, and then the authority was read.

It is necessary to record this insignificant circumstance, because it illustrates the admirable art with which Sir Robert Peel managed a case in the house of commons. In the present instance, after a prelude in which he ran over the long series of great political events that had occurred since the period in controversy: 'There have been great political conflicts and great political excitement since that period. Since 1825 there has been the severance from Mr. Canning; the formation of his government; the formation of the government of Lord Goderich; the union of the friends of Mr. Canning with the Duke of Wellington and myself in 1828; the separation from us of those friends of Mr. Canning in the same year, on matters totally unconnected with the reputation or character of Mr. Canning. Then followed the fierce conflicts of 1829, when I felt it my duty to propose the adjustment of the catholic question. In 1830, the government of the Duke of Wellington, the combination of parties against that government, and the loss of power by the Duke of Wellington, and those who held office under him. Then followed the government of Lord Grey, and the severe conflicts of reform; the dissolution of the government of Lord Melbourne in 1834; and the formation of that government over which I presided in 1835, attempting to conduct the affairs of this country by a minority of this house for about three months, when I yielded to the right honourable gentlemen opposite, and the formation of their government in 1835 ensued.'

Surely after such a series of party contentions he was justified in presuming that, so far as they could be the subject of crimination against him, they were buried in oblivion. Every document connected with these events had been sent, many years ago, to a distance from London, in the full confidence that future reference to them would not possibly be required. Occupied by urgent public duties, he had been unable himself to repair to their place of deposit. The private secretaries by whose aid the correspondence of that period was conducted had passed away; the whole of the correspondence had been sent to his country residence in Staffordshire. He was obliged to have it examined by those who were no parties to the conduct of it; they had brought to London a confused and complicated mass of documents, from which, for the last three days, he had been attempting to collect the materials for his vindication from charges directed against his veracity and honour.

This picture quite carried away the feelings of the house. A minister, at such a moment of public duty, forced to investigate such a mass of documents for the vindication of his private character, 'a confused and complicated mass.' And why was all this, and what was all this about?

Now came the skilful disposition of the case. Because a charge had been made against him by a member of parliament, that there was a letter of his to Lord Liverpool in existence, which proved that he had intimated to Lord Liverpool that there had been not only a wish to relinquish office, but that there was a change of opinion on his part on the roman catholic question. 'And he cited, as a proof of that, an article in the *Edinburgh Review*, in which it was stated that I had a copy of that letter in my desk.'

No such charge had ever been made and no such proof ever been adduced. Admitting that his communications with Lord Liverpool, 'whom he saw every day,' were verbal ones, and that he was 'not in the habit of making formal written communications' to that minister; that he 'had not the slightest doubt,' that on the subject in question 'no written communication took place between them,' he informed the house that the whole of his correspondence, for seven years, under the letter L, had been brought to London, and, as he had anticipated, the written communications with Lord Liverpool were very few. Nothing should be concealed; he would read every one of these letters to the house. And he did read, amid profound silence, three gossiping notes, marked *private* and *most confidential*, under date of 1825. This was not much fruit from a 'confused and complicated mass of documents,' which yet too seemed sufficiently digested and in order, in well-arranged pigeon-holes, with appropriate initial letters. Such an investigation would hardly seem to have required three days. But the audience was not critical. It was full of sympathy, admiration of such public devotion, and gratitude for such confidential revelations. The vindication which did not even meet the imaginary charge was held complete, and the house only checked its cheers that it might not lose a syllable of this great historic and personal 'explanation.'

The answer to the 'letter in the desk' took about an hour, though the time passed so quickly that all were unconscious of its lapse, except one individual who carefully watched the dial, and that was the orator himself. Hitherto all had gone off to his perfect satisfaction. Scarlett himself in the days of his *nisi prius* glory had never shown more adroitness or more intimate acquaintance with the tribunal to which he appealed. But this was nothing to his next position.

He now addressed himself to the report of his speech contained in the *Mirror of Parliament*, which comprised the admission in controversy. He denied that there was any report in the *Mirror of Parliament* at all. He said the alleged reports of that publication were compilations from the newspapers; he denied that Mr. Barrow wrote shorthand; he denied that he was even a parliamentary reporter; finally, he denied that there was such a man as Mr. Barrow, for he was dead, or otherwise he should have referred to him. As it was, he had referred to those who from their pursuits were acquainted with this subject; gentlemen connected with the public press, beyond his influence, beyond his control, who had given him this information, who, actuated by no other feelings than those which are suggested by a love of justice, had generously come forward to supply him with the information necessary to vindicate himself, and to prove that the equivocal expressions appeared only in one organ, the *Times*, and that the report in the *Times* was adopted and engrafted into the *Mirror of Parliament*.

All this was very victorious; but when the minister, feeling the wind was in all his sails, described himself as ' oppressed with public business, yet having to devote three days to the collating and contrasting of newspaper reports and speeches delivered seventeen years ago,' some might have remembered that only one space of three days had elapsed, and that that had already been occupied by the ' confused and complicated mass of documents,' sent up from his country residence in Staffordshire, from which he had ' to attempt to collect the materials for his vindication from charges directed against his veracity and honour.'

The awkward speech of Sir Edward Knatchbull was treated gingerly. It still remains a very singular circumstance. Sir Edward was then alive and had been the colleague, and the recent colleague, of Sir Robert Peel. A line from the county of Kent might have thrown some light upon this perplexed affair, and have saved Sir Robert a very elaborate statement; but no application was made to Sir Edward Knatchbull. Sir Robert indeed suggested that Sir Edward was not present in the house when he made his speech in 1829, but unfortunately a division happened to take place on that evening, and in the list of names that of Sir Edward Knatchbull appears. Glancing only at this, the minister recurred to some personal considerations, attacked, though cautiously, his principal assailant in this affair, declared that nothing would have tempted him to condescend to a defence, but for ' the plausibility of the charge and the concatenation of circumstances which had been brought together as evidence '; and then with the air and tone of a man who thus assailed might have become a victim, had he not been saved by the generous interposition of the press and the spirit of justice in the house of commons, almost overcome by his emotions, and observing that it was exactly half-past seven o'clock, he sent the peers, the diplomatic body, and two-thirds of the house of commons to dinner, knowing very well that Demosthenes himself under such circumstances and at such an hour could not have revived the fight and turned the tables against him.

There never was a more successful 'explanation': and nobody, except perhaps Lord George Bentinck, would have had the courage to have risen amid the noise and disregard of a dissolving assembly to reiterate his charges, and to declare that they either were not met or that they were evaded. And thus he ended: 'I will maintain, as long as I have a seat in this house, my right to denounce the men, whether they are ministers or private individuals, who shall have betrayed the trust confided to them by their constituents.'

Mr. Bickham Escott, interrupting him—'Who has betrayed them?'

'You ask me,' replied Lord George, 'who has betrayed them! Why you! On high constitutional grounds I say we ought not to wrap up in deceitful language the crime of tergiversation of which so many have been guilty. And I use the sentiments of Lord Chatham, when I say that "if the country cannot place confidence in the promises and pledges of their representatives, the power and authority of this house will fall," and it is because for the second time the right honourable baronet has attempted to lower the character of English gentlemen who are representatives in this house and to drag them through the mire, that I denounced such conduct so strongly as I did on a former occasion. Sure I am of this, that the tendency—I will not say the object—but the tendency of the measures of the minister is to lower the character and to sap and undermine the confidence reposed in the characters of English gentlemen, and so to destroy them. He has subverted that feeling of placing political trust in the representatives of the people which is essential to maintain the power and dominion of the house of commons. He has brought things to this pass, that by his example he has taught the representatives of the English people, that if it is not their duty, it is their privilege, to betray their constituents. And I venture to say, without fear of contradiction, that there was not when parliament met—though I hope things are different now—a great constituency in the country, that did not apprehend more danger from those whom they had themselves sent to parliament to protect their property and to defend their rights, than from their most open and daring enemies.'

Later in the evening, a very interesting criticism on the career of Sir Robert Peel was given in his presence by Lord John Russell. Lord John noticed in detail the points of the evidence that had been laid before the house. He acknowledged that, some time before, 'in the course of this very year,' the report in the *Mirror of Parliament* had been pointed out to him by a friend, and had 'made some impression on him,' and that there were other passages in the speeches of Sir Robert Peel on this subject at the time, as his answer to Lord Uxbridge and others, which without careful comparison with other statements, were liable to misconstruction, but recapitulating all the heads of the case, he expressed his opinion, after hearing the statement of the minister, that the charges were in his opinion unfounded.

'Sir, having said thus much,' continued Lord John, 'I must add that I think these questions are entirely different from any which my noble friend or others can raise as to the political conduct of the right honourable gentleman. As to his opposition to Mr. Canning in 1827, I have myself a strong opinion, but my opinion is not now in question. As to the general political conduct of the right honourable gentleman, I think he has rendered great service to his country, in taking the post he has taken on the present occasion; but, at the same time, I cannot express surprise or wonder at any warmth or vindictive feeling being directed against him, because in his political career he has done that which, perhaps, has never happened to so eminent a man before. He has twice changed his opinion on the greatest political questions of his day. Once, when the protestant church was to be defended, and the protestant constitution rescued from the assaults of the roman catholics, which, it was said, would ruin it, the right honourable gentleman undertook to lead the defence. Again, the corn laws were powerfully attacked in this house, and out of it. He took the lead of his party to resist a change, and to defend protection. I think, on both occasions, he came to a wise conclusion, and to a decision beneficial to his country; first, when he repealed the roman catholic disabilities; and secondly, when he abolished protection. But that those who had followed him—men who had committed themselves to these questions on the faith of his political wisdom, on the faith of his sagacity, led by the great eloquence and ability he displayed in debate—that when they found he had changed his opinions, and proposed measures different from those on the faith of which they had followed him, that they should exhibit warmth and resentment was not only natural, but I should have been surprised if they had not displayed it.'

Not the least curious circumstance connected with this episode is that, six months after it had occurred, and when it was already forgotten in the important result which had immediately followed, Mr. Barrow, whose existence even was denied by Sir Robert Peel, called at Harcourt House on Lord George Bentinck. He had just returned from India, where he had been on an important mission from a London newspaper, as 'our own correspondent,' and not a little indignant that he was described by the highest authority as being dead, unable to write shorthand, and never a member of that distinguished body, the parliamentary reporters of England, in whose brotherhood, although a barrister-at-law, he was justly proud of having been once enrolled and as one of its ablest members, Mr. Barrow wished his case to be brought before the house, and the honour and accuracy of the *Mirror of Parliament* vindicated on certain representations which he was prepared to make, and Lord George Bentinck was very inclined to undertake the office, but he was persuaded that, on the whole and under the existing circumstances, it were better not to revive the controversy; and if the writer of these pages had any influence in that resolution, and thus deprived Mr. Barrow of his opportunity, he has tried to compensate a very respectable and intelligent gentleman for this deprivation by recording his name and merits in a volume which perhaps may live as long as a personal debate.

The truth about the question which so conveniently occasioned this interesting episode in the debates on the coercion bill appears to be this: that Sir Robert Peel, in 1829, having to make a complicated and very embarrassing statement respecting his change of opinion and policy with regard to the roman catholics, and to refer by dates to several periods, both as to his positive and his contingent conduct upon that subject, conveyed by some expressions a meaning to the house of a very perplexing character and quite different from that which he intended; that the reporter of the *Times* caught the sentence, and although it was inconsistent with the reputation of Sir Robert Peel, perhaps imperfectly preserved it; that the reporters of the other journals, not comprehending the remark, and deeming it quite incongruous and contrary to received impressions, omitted it, as under such circumstances is not unusual; that Sir Robert Peel, when he corrected the version of his speech, which he did from the report of the *Times*, finding a sentence which conveyed a false meaning, and which was authorised by no analogous expressions in the other papers, very properly struck it out; that the reporter of the *Times*, who, after due comparison and consultation with the reporters of some other principal journals, prepared with them the matured version for the *Mirror of Parliament*, adhered to his text with the general concurrence of his colleagues, and thus embalmed the error. Perplexing as it is, we have no doubt that the speech of Sir Edward Knatchbull can be explained to the entire vindication of Sir Robert Peel; the solution of this, however, as far as we are concerned, must be left to Œdipus, with a full admission that though Lord George Bentinck was perfectly justified in making the particular charge which he advanced, it was without real foundation. For the rest, those who are well informed of the political history of this country know that between Mr. Canning and Mr. Peel there existed an antipathy. They disliked each other: Mr. Canning was jealous of Mr. Peel, and Mr. Peel was a little envious of Mr. Canning.

CHAPTER XVI

THERE are few circumstances more remarkable in parliamentary history than the suspense which attended the fate of the Peel government. The opposing hosts were drawn up in array for three weeks without the possibility of a general engagement. The return of the corn bill from the house of lords was to be the signal for a general battle, and a bill of such vast importance could not be hurriedly passed by either house of parliament. Had it not been for the Canning episode, it is difficult to see how the evenings devoted to the adjourned debate on the coercion bill could have been filled up.

But that episode was now concluded, and it was said that another week must inevitably elapse before the corn bill could come down. The friends of the government, elate with the last rally of their chief, and encouraged by several circumstances which then occurred, redoubled their efforts to detach the protectionist party from Lord George Bentinck. The colonial and shipping interests were very active in this endeavour. They had deserted the land on the great division, and were now very busy through their representatives in the house of commons, canvassing the votes of protectionist members and trying, as they styled it, to reconstruct the conservative party. Sugar yet remained to be conserved, and the wooden walls of old England, as with Kyan's patent. The colonial and shipping interests therefore were very stirring; denounced unprincipled coalitions with revolutionists and radicals, and were decided in their reprobation of 'strong language.'

There were, however, deeper heads working at this crisis than those gentlemen, whose efforts, though not without effect, were rather on the surface. Sir Robert had always been well served in the unseen management of his party. The great conservative party that destroyed everything was the creation of individuals who did not figure in senates or cabinet councils; above all, of one gentleman who by his knowledge of human nature, fine observation of opinion, indefatigable activity, universal correspondence, and fertility of resource, mainly contributed to the triumph of '42, though he was spoken of only in a whisper and moved only behind the scenes.

Such scheming spirits, at such a crisis, did not desert the chief whom they had so laboriously placed upon so mighty a pedestal. It was thought that some signal demonstration from an unsuspicious quarter, made before the division, appealing to the conservative sympathies of the party, and disapproving of the spirit in which the opposition to the minister had been conducted, might have a very great effect, and in the present wavering disposition of members turn the scale of the division. But where was the personage to perform the evolution? No small man would do. Several petty squires, who had of course voted against the ministerial measure to save their seats, had already been egged on to take what was called a temperate tone, that is to say, cheapen Lord George Bentinck and keep out the whigs; but these efforts had been quite uninfluential, indeed unnoticed; the house would not listen to and the reporters would not record these prim philippics, elaborately prepared and precisely delivered, with all the solemn conceit of a quarter-sessions pedant.

But if small men would not do, where were great ones to be found? The Francis Egertons, the Sandons, the Wilson Pattens, and men of that stamp, from whom a selection is generally made when an influential diversion is desired to extricate a minister from embarrassment, were all 'renegades,' and had consequently forfeited all authority.

In this state of affairs some judicious and faithful friends of the minister had the happy hardihood to address themselves to the Duke of Buckingham, a nobleman who from his long and faithful services as a county member, and from the undeviating consistency of his political life, justly possessed the confidence and the regard of the agricultural interest. There were few public men on whom the ministry had less claims than the Duke of Buckingham. His grace had quitted the cabinet of Sir Robert Peel almost immediately after its formation, deeming its policy inconsistent with the professions by which its members had obtained power. After his secession, there was an ungracious and unwarrantable delay in conferring upon him the garter, which conveyed an impression that this great distinction was the consequence of some disreputable compact, whereas it had been arranged that the duke should have the garter long before he had felt the necessity of resigning his office as lord privy seal. No one also had given a more earnest opposition to the present measure of the minister than his grace, which he had proved by very decided conduct.

It would seem, therefore, at the first blush that the application for assistance to such a quarter was not likely to prove favourable. But the Duke of Buckingham had had a long and very active experience of party life; he had witnessed the overthrow of the tory party by the Duke of Wellington, and had felt all its dangerous, not to say fatal, consequences. No one was more conscious of the difficulties of reconstructing a great party than the Duke of Buckingham, for no one had made greater exertions for such an object or greater sacrifices. He shrank from a repetition of ten years of balanced parties and weak governments. Indignant and irritated by the conduct of those with whom he was associated, he was still unprepared to assist in handing over the government to the whigs, who offered by their accession to office nothing to the tories but the gratification of vengeance. The Duke of Buckingham, therefore, was not willing to see the government overthrown, and he listened with sympathy, if not with cordiality, to their overtures.

The plan was most ingenious: a combination of the highest class, and worthy of the only political brain capable of devising it.

A member of the ministry, high in office and returned to

parliament on strong protection principles, had been called upon by his constituents at the commencement of the session to oppose the government measure or to resign his seat to one more faithful to their cause. The right honourable gentleman after reflection felt it his duty to quit the house of commons, and the son of the Duke of Buckingham, the Marquess of Chandos, was elected in his stead. Entering parliament as a true protectionist, on the very corpse of a convert and a victim, having voted in every division against the government measure, pure from all antecedents, and the son of the Duke of Buckingham— what an authoritative organ to rally round the minister the distracted and scattered sympathies of the conservative party! But Lord Chandos was a youth who had not long completed his majority, little known and extremely reserved, and had never opened his mouth in the house of commons. Tender shoulders whereon to place so weighty a charge! A party manifesto and a maiden speech; the rescue of a powerful ministry by an inexperienced stripling!

On the 22nd the debate proceeded: at the end of the night the secretary of state relieved the dulness; it was observed that his tone was more cheerful; he particularly impressed on those who were satisfied of the necessity of the measure to give the government a manly and cordial support, apart from all questions of confidence or want of confidence in the existing administration. That question could be raised at any time and upon other issues. 'I may be wrong,' concluded the secretary, 'but I have a deep conviction, that if all those who are conscientiously satisfied that in the present circumstances of Ireland this bill is necessary shall support the present reading, the result of the division will not be doubtful.'

The debate was adjourned till the next government night, Thursday, the 25th of June. Fine calculators thought it possible that the corn laws might come down from the lords that night; but at all events it must come down early on the following day, Friday, so the decision was inevitable that week. All were wearied and exhausted with suspense.

On Thursday morning Lord George Bentinck was informed in confidence, but with circumstances of some exaggeration, of the intended movement of Lord Chandos, and of the great defalcation in the protectionist ranks which would certainly take place. It reached him also that an application of the greatest urgency was made late at night, on Wednesday, to a member of the cabinet whose seat was in the house of lords, on a subject which might considerably affect the division; that the secretary of the treasury had stated to this personage, that 'things never looked better,' and that, at the worst, the majority against the government could not exceed eleven. It was added, that the government would not feel it necessary to retire if the majority were so light under the circumstances of coalition.

Thursday came at last. The debate was languid until Mr. Charles Buller rose, who spoke with his usual vivacity and clear argument. While he was speaking, Mr. Buller was interrupted by messengers from the lords. Two masters in chancery were here introduced, bringing several bills from the upper house, among which were the corn importation and customs duties bills. Mr. Speaker, amid profound silence, announced that the house of lords had agreed to the corn importation bill, and the customs duties bills, without any amendment. This announcement was followed by loud cheering.

Seated on the highest bench, hid by a column, with his back against the wall, in a position from which no person ever yet did, or apparently ever could, address the house, a young man whom nobody knew now sprang up, very pale, and solicited Mr. Speaker's eye, who called Mr. Bankes. 'Chandos,' whispered a member to Lord George, who looked round and threw at him a scrutinising glance.

Mr. Bankes was down, and Lord Chandos rose again, but the speaker called Mr. Spooner. When Mr. Spooner had finished it was about ten o'clock, and the speaker retired to his coffee and his only relaxation of ten minutes, preliminary to the great speech of the night, which, on this occasion, was to be offered by an orator no less accomplished than Mr.

Shiel, whose name had of course been called before the chair was vacated. The house broke into groups, members talked together on the floor with their hats on, some lounged in the lobby, some sauntered to the galleries. 'Well, we shall divide at last,' was the general observation, 'and how will it be?' At that hour, neither Sir Robert Peel nor perhaps even Lord George Bentinck could exactly tell. The result depended on what number of protectionists would stay away. If all those members of the protectionist party who did not follow their leader in the present instance voted with the government, it was concluded that the majority in favour of the ministry might not be contemptible. The managers for the government were certain of the support of a very large portion of the protectionist party. They were induced to believe that many of that party would avoid the division, but that very few indeed would bring themselves to vote against a bill which they had already stoutly supported. The ministerial managers felt quite assured that all the tory members for Ireland would be found in the government lobby. The protectionists were very discreet and their tactics extremely close; the party was never better managed than on this division. As late as midnight Lord George Bentinck received bulletins of the varying circumstances of the impending event.

The house listened with glowing attention to the last great Irish harangue of the most brilliant of modern rhetoricians. It was so eager for division that none but he could have commanded and charmed it. When Mr. Shiel sat down, Lord Chandos and a member of the government, the solicitor-general, rose at the same time. The speaker of course called the minister, but the restlessness and impatience of the house were so uncontrollable that the learned gentleman was quite inaudible during his address. When he concluded, the calls for a division were overpowering; nevertheless Lord Chandos rose again, and this time, as he rose alone, he was necessarily named. The cries for Lord Chandos from the treasury bench were vehement, and the voices of more than one of the leading members of the administration were easily to be distinguished. The position of the speaker, the novelty of the example, for surely a maiden speech was seldom made under such difficult circumstances, the influence of the treasury bench in their neighbourhood, and the conciliatory circumstance that he was a 'new member,' combined suddenly to produce in this disturbed scene a complete stillness.

Very pale, looking like the early portraits of Lord Grenville, determined but impassive and coldly earnest, Lord Chandos, without any affectation of rhetorical prelude, said in a clear and natural tone that he wished to state his intention of recording his vote for the measure of the government. And he gave succinctly his main reasons for so doing. Those reasons convinced him of its necessity. He had felt it his duty since his return to parliament to oppose the measures of her majesty's ministers, voting with a portion of the party sitting on the same side as himself; but he wished to take this opportunity of saying, that he should be sorry it should be thought he concurred in the language which had been directed by that party against the government, and especially against the right honourable baronet who was at the head of it. They were told that the question to-night involved a vote of confidence in the minister. He did not acknowledge the justness of that conclusion. He gave his vote on this bill solely with reference to the condition of Ireland, but if he could bring his mind to understand that the question of general confidence in the administration was the principal question on which they were going to decide to-night, and the proper government of Ireland only a secondary one, then he thought it fair to say that he for one was not prepared to vote a want of confidence in the present conservative government. He supported them as an administration founded on conservative principles, and he for one did not agree, that conservative principles depended on tariff regulations, or that the existence of the institutions of the country relied upon the maintenance of a fiscal principle. Whatever the result of the division, he should have the satisfaction of knowing that his vote would be registered freely and fairly on the merits of the question, and that he was not actuated by personal prejudice or factious opposition.

There is unfortunately no report of these observations. Sir Robert Peel, turning his face to Lord Chandos, listened to him with great attention and watched him with approving interest. When he sat down, the cheering from the treasury bench and its quarter was vociferous. The observations of Lord Chandos prolonged a little the debate, which was concluded by Mr. Cobden offering the reasons why he voted against a minister in whom he had the utmost confidence, and on whom he delivered a fervent panegyric, tendering him 'his heart-felt thanks for the unwearied perseverance, the unswerving firmness, and the great ability, with which he had, during the last six months, conducted through the house of commons one of the most magnificent reforms ever carried through any country.'

At length, about half-past one o'clock, the galleries were cleared, the division called, and the question put. In almost all previous divisions where the fate of a government had been depending, the vote of every member with scarcely an exception had been anticipated: that was not the case in the present instance, and the direction which members took as they left their seats was anxiously watched. More than one hundred protectionist members followed the minister; more than eighty avoided the division, a few of these, however, had paired; nearly the same number followed Lord George Bentinck. But it was not merely their numbers that attracted the anxious observation of the treasury bench as the protectionists passed in defile before the minister to the hostile lobby. It was impossible that he could have marked them without emotion: the flower of that great party which had been so proud to follow one who had been so proud to lead them. They were men to gain whose hearts and the hearts of their fathers had been the aim and exultation of his life. They had extended to him an unlimited confidence and an admiration without stint. They had stood by him in the darkest hour, and had borne him from the depths of political despair to the proudest of living positions. Right or wrong, they were men of honour, breeding, and refinement, high and generous character, great weight and station in the country, which they had ever placed at his disposal. They had been not only his followers but his friends; had joined in the same pastimes, drank from the same cup, and in the pleasantness of private life had often forgotten together the cares and strife of politics.

He must have felt something of this, while the Manners, the Somersets, the Bentincks, the Lowthers, and the Lennoxes passed before him. And those country gentlemen, 'those gentlemen of England,' of whom, but five years ago, the very same building was ringing with his pride of being the leader—if his heart were hardened to Sir Charles Burrell, Sir William Jolliffe, Sir Charles Knightly, Sir John Trollope, Sir Edward Kerrison, Sir John Tyrrell, he surely must have had a pang when his eye rested on Sir John Yarde Buller, his choice and pattern country gentleman, whom he had himself selected and invited but six years back to move a vote of want of confidence in the whig government, in order, against the feeling of the court, to install Sir Robert Peel in their stead.

They trooped on: all the men of metal and large-acred squires, whose spirit he had so often quickened and whose counsel he had so often solicited in his fine conservative speeches in Whitehall Gardens: Mr. Bankes, with a parliamentary name of two centuries, and Mr. Christopher from that broad Lincolnshire which protection had created; and the Mileses and the Henleys were there; and the Duncombes, the Liddells, and the Yorkes; and Devon had sent there the stout heart of Mr. Buck—and Wiltshire, the pleasant presence of Walter Long. Mr. Newdegate was there, whom Sir Robert had himself recommended to the confidence of the electors of Warwickshire, as one of whom he had the highest hopes; and Mr. Alderman Thompson was there, who, also through Sir Robert's selection, had seconded the assault upon the whigs, led on by Sir John Buller. But the list is too long; or good names remain behind.

When Prince Metternich was informed at Dresden, with great ostentation, that the emperor had arrived—'Yes; but without his army,' was the reply. Sir Robert Peel was still first minister of England, as Napoleon remained emperor for a while after Moscow. Each perhaps for a moment had indulged in hope. It is so difficult for those who are on the pinnacle of life to realise disaster. They sometimes contemplate it in their deep and far-seeing calculations, but it is only to imagine a contingency which their resources must surely baffle; they sometimes talk of it to their friends, and oftener of it to their enemies, but it is only as an insurance of their prosperity and as an offering to propitiate their Nemesis. They never believe in it.

The news that the government were not only beaten, but by a majority so large as 73, began to circulate. An incredulous murmur passed it along the treasury bench.

'They say we are beaten by 73!' whispered the most important member of the cabinet in a tone of surprise to Sir Robert Peel.

Sir Robert did not reply or even turn his head. He looked very grave, and extended his chin as was his habit when he was annoyed and cared not to speak. He began to comprehend his position, and that the emperor was without his army.

CHAPTER XVII

THE house met the next day (Friday), but the first minister was not in his place, and it having been privately notified that in consequence of the vote of the previous evening the government was at an end, all business was postponed, and the house adjourned.

On Monday, at five o'clock, the public notification of the resignation of the ministry was made by Sir Robert Peel, to a crowded house, and in a remarkable speech. He said that the ministers had advised her majesty to accept their resignations without adopting the alternative of dissolving the parliament, though had they failed in carrying in all their integrity the main measures of their commercial policy, they would have recommended an appeal to the country. Sir Robert then passed in review the principal acts of his administration in every department. He did not forget to touch on the bank charter act of 1844, as 'giving stability to the monetary system of the country without interfering with legitimate speculation, without paralysing or at all deranging the credit of the state.' The speech was considered one of glorification and pique. It included an unparliamentary eulogium of Mr. Cobden, whom it mentioned to the surprise of the house by name; and it terminated with a panegyric of himself, elaborate, but rather clumsily expressed, in which he talked of his leaving a name which would be execrated by monopolists, but sometimes remembered perhaps with good-will by those who recruited their exhausted strength with abundant and untaxed food, the sweeter because it was no longer leavened by a sense of injustice.

Little was said: Lord John was absent, having repaired, by command, to her majesty 'for the purpose of rendering his assistance in the formation of a government.' Lord Palmerston very properly said something, that 'the silence of himself and his friends should not be construed into an acquiescence in the general commendation which Sir Robert Peel had passed on the measures of his own government.' After this protest, the house adjourned.

Nature had combined in Sir Robert Peel many admirable parts. In him a physical frame incapable of fatigue was united with an understanding equally vigorous and flexible. He was gifted with the faculty of method in the highest degree; and with great powers of application which were sustained by a prodigious memory; while he could communicate his acquisitions with clear and fluent elocution.

Such a man, under any circumstances and in any sphere of life, would probably have become remarkable. Ordained from his youth to be busied with the affairs of a great empire, such a man, after long years of observation, practice, and perpetual discipline would have become what Sir Robert Peel was in the latter portion of his life, a transcendent administrator of public business and a matchless master of debate in a popular assembly. In the course of time the method which was natural to Sir Robert Peel had matured into a habit of such expertness that no one in the despatch of affairs ever adapted the means more fitly to the end; his original flexibility had ripened into consummate tact; his memory had accumulated such stores of political information that he could bring luminously together all that was necessary to establish or to illustrate a subject; while in the house of commons he was equally eminent in exposition and in reply: in the first, distinguished by his arrangement, his clearness, and his completeness; in the second, ready, ingenious, and adroit, prompt in detecting the weak points of his adversary, and dexterous in extricating himself from an embarrassing position.

Thus gifted and thus accomplished, Sir Robert Peel had a great deficiency; he was without imagination. Wanting imagination, he wanted prescience. No one was more sagacious when dealing with the circumstances before him;

no one penetrated the present with more acuteness and accuracy. His judgment was faultless provided he had not to deal with the future. Thus it happened through his long career, that while he always was looked upon as the most prudent and safest of leaders, he ever, after a protracted display of admirable tactics, concluded his campaigns by surrendering at discretion. He was so adroit that he could prolong resistance even beyond its term, but so little foreseeing that often in the very triumph of his manœuvres he found himself in an untenable position. And so it came to pass that roman catholic emancipation, parliamentary reform, and the abrogation of our commercial system, were all carried in haste or in passion and without conditions or mitigatory arrangements.

Sir Robert Peel had a peculiarity which is perhaps natural with men of very great talents who have not the creative faculty; he had a dangerous sympathy with the creations of others. Instead of being cold and wary, as was commonly supposed, he was impulsive and even inclined to rashness. When he was ambiguous, unsatisfactory, reserved, tortuous, it was that he was perplexed, that he did not see his way, that the routine which he had admirably administered failed him, and that his own mind was not constructed to create a substitute for the custom which was crumbling away. Then he was ever on the look-out for new ideas, and when he embraced them he did so with eagerness and often with precipitancy; he always carried these novel plans to an extent which even their projectors or chief promoters had usually not anticipated; as was seen, for example, in the settlement of the currency. Although apparently wrapped up in himself and supposed to be egotistical, except in seasons of rare exaltedness, as in the years 1844-5, when he reeled under the favour of the court, the homage of the continent, and the servility of parliament, he was really deficient in self-confidence. There was always some person representing some theory or system exercising an influence over his mind. In his 'sallet-days' it was Mr. Horner or Sir Samuel Romilly; in later and more important periods, it was the Duke of Wellington, the king of the French, Mr. Jones Lloyd—some others—and finally, Mr. Cobden.

Let us now see how this peculiar temperament influenced his career and the history of this country.

There never was such an opportunity of forming a strong and enlightened administration, and rendering the tory party famous and popular in the country, as on the junction of the friends of Mr. Canning after his decease with the followers of the Duke of Wellington. All personal jealousies had ceased, and men like Mr. Huskisson, Mr. Lambe (Lord Melbourne), and Lord Palmerston, had without reluctance or reserve recognised the leadership of Mr. Peel, then only in the perfection of his manhood, and were acting with him with deference and cordiality. The times were ripe for a calm, prudent, and statesmanlike settlement of two great questions: the admission of roman catholics into the house of commons, and some reconstruction of that assembly itself. Very moderate measures would have sufficed. The enfranchisement of half a dozen of the great manufacturing towns would have been hailed with general satisfaction. The Duke of Wellington was against all change. Sir Robert Peel was then under the influence of the Duke of Wellington. He believed that the Duke of Wellington was indicated as the man who would govern the country for the next quarter of a century. He joined the duke, therefore, in resistance to those who would have transferred the forfeited franchise of a corrupt Cornish borough to some great town of the north. The followers of Mr. Canning who would not agree in so short-sighted a policy were rudely expelled from the cabinet, and Sir Robert Peel, remaining the leader of a parliamentary party destitute, with his own exception, of parliamentary renown, was forced in a short space of time hurriedly to concede to the violence of external agitation so unconditional a satisfaction of the claims of the roman catholics that he broke up the tory party, and the reform of the house of commons was consequently carried and in the midst of a revolution.

After a great disaster it was observable of Sir Robert Peel

that his mind seemed always to expand. His life was one of perpetual education. No one more clearly detected the mistakes which he had made, or changed his course under such circumstances with more promptness; but it was the past and the present that alone engrossed his mind. After the catastrophe of '30, he broke away from the Duke of Wellington, and announced to his friends with decision that henceforth he would serve under no man. There are few things more remarkable in parliamentary history than the manner in which Sir Robert Peel headed an opposition for ten years without attempting to form the opinions of his friends, or instilling into them a single guiding principle, but himself displaying all that time on every subject of debate wise counsels, administrative skill, and accomplished powers of discussion. He could give to his friends no guiding principle, for he had none, and he kept sitting on those benches till somebody should give him one. He was so blind to the future, that when the whigs, utterly prostrate, yielded him the government of the country on a colonial defeat in '39, he did everything he could to avoid taking the helm, when he might have come into office comparatively unpledged, and free at least, whatever course he had taken, from the painful and deserved reproaches that accompanied his last acts. But it so happened the finances of the country at that time were not flourishing; the great interests under such circumstances were beginning as usual to grumble; and Sir Robert Peel wanted to be brought in by the great interests. He succeeded in this object, and in the course of five years he was denouncing those great interests as monopolies, and destroying them.

The roman catholic association, the Birmingham union, the Manchester league, were all the legitimate offspring of Sir Robert Peel. No minister ever diminished the power of government in this country so much as this eminent man. No one ever strained the constitution so much. He was the unconscious parent of political agitation. He literally forced the people out of doors to become statesmen, and the whole tendency of his policy was to render our institutions mere forms. In a word, no one with all his conservative language more advanced revolution. In an ordinary period he would have been a perfect minister, but he was not a minister for stormy times: he wanted depth, and passion, and resource for such an occasion.

After destroying the tory party in '46, he fell a-thinking again over the past and the present as he did after his fall in '30, and again arrived at a great conclusion. In '30 he said he would act no longer as a subordinate; in '46 he said he would act no longer as a partisan. In '30 he visited his position on the Duke of Wellington; in '46, on the political ties of '41; but if he had been a man of genius, he would have guided the Duke of Wellington, and in '41 would have given a creed to his party, always devoted to him, instead of borrowing their worn-out ideas.

No one knew better than Sir Robert Peel that without party connection that parliamentary government which he so much admired would be intolerable; it would be at the same time the weakest and the most corrupt government in the world. In casting this slur upon party, Sir Robert Peel meant only to degrade the combinations of which he had experience, and by which he had risen. Excluded from power which he ought to have wielded for a quarter of a century, he sat on his solitary bench revolving the past. At sixty he began to comprehend his position. The star of Manchester seemed as it were to rise from the sunset of Oxford, and he felt he had sacrificed his natural career to an obsolete education and a political system for which he could not secure even an euthanasia.

Sir Robert Peel had a bad manner of which he was sensible; he was by nature very shy, but forced early in life into eminent positions, he had formed an artificial manner, haughtily stiff or exuberantly bland, of which, generally speaking, he could not divest himself. There were, however, occasions when he did succeed in this, and on these, usually when he was alone with an individual whom he wished to please, his manner was not only unaffectedly cordial, but he could even charm. When he was ridiculed by his opponents in '41, as one little adapted for a court, and especially the court of a queen, those who knew him well augured different results from his high promotion, and they were right. But generally speaking he was never at his ease, and never very content except in the house of commons. Even there he was not natural, though there the deficiency was compensated for by his unrivalled facility, which passed current with the vulgar eye for the precious quality for which it was substituted. He had obtained a complete control over his temper, which was by nature somewhat fiery. His disposition was good; there was nothing petty about him; he was very free from rancour; he was not only not vindictive, but partly by temperament and still more perhaps by discipline, he was even magnanimous.

For so very clever a man he was deficient in the knowledge of human nature. The prosperous routine of his youth was not favourable to the development of this faculty. It was never his lot to struggle; although forty years in parliament, it is remarkable that Sir Robert Peel never represented a popular constituency or stood a contested election. As he advanced in life he was always absorbed in thought, and abstraction is not friendly to a perception of character, or to a fine appreciation of the circumstances of the hour. After the general election of '34-5, a nobleman, who was his warm friend, and who had exerted himself very greatly to establish Peel in power, expressed his regret that the result of the appeal to the country had not been so favourable as they could have wished. In short, the tories on their own dissolution were in a minority. Sir Robert, however, did not share the apprehensions of his friend. ' I have confidence in my measures,' said Sir Robert, with an expression of satisfaction. Now to suppose that any measures, had they been arch-angelic, could have influenced the decision of a liberal parliament that had been rudely dissolved by a court intrigue, of which, by the bye, Sir Robert Peel was perfectly innocent, and which was panting for vengeance, displayed a confidence in the abstract justice of man which experience does not warrant. The minister of a court which had outraged a parliament, and that minister in a minority, was not exactly the personage to carry measures. As might have been expected, the house of commons refused even to put his speaker in the chair, in order that accepting the intimation his measures might not even be brought forward.

After the reform of the house of commons, Sir Robert Peel was naturally anxious to discover who was to be the rival of his life, and it is noticeable that he was not successful in his observations. He never did justice to Lord John Russell until he found Lord John not only his rival, but his successful one, and then, according to his custom and his nature, he did the present minister of England full justice. No person could be more sensible of the grave import of the events in Canada which occurred on his accession to office in '34 than Sir Robert Peel. They were the commencement of great calamities and occasioned him proportionate anxiety. It was obvious that everything depended on the character of the individual sent out by the metropolis to encounter this emergency. The highest qualities of administration were demanded. After much pondering, Sir Robert selected the amiable and popular Lord Canterbury. It was entirely his own selection, and it was perhaps the most unfit that could be made. But Sir Robert Peel associated Lord Canterbury with the awful authority of twenty years of the speaker's chair. That authority had controlled him, and of course he thought it must subdue the Canadians. It was like a grown-up man in the troubles of life going back for advice to his schoolmaster. But perhaps his want of perception of character was never more remarkably illustrated than in the appointment of his secretaries of the treasury in the government of '34. The party had been managed in opposition by two gentlemen, each distinguished by different but admirable qualities. One was remarkable for the sweetness of his temper, his conciliatory manners, and an obliging habit which gains hearts oftener than the greatest services; he knew every member by name, talked to all sides, and had a quick eye which caught every corner of the house. His colleague was of a different cast; reserved and cold and a great parliamentary student; very capable of laborious affairs and with the right information always ready for a minister. Sir Robert appointed the man of the world financial secretary of the treasury, locked him up in a room or sealed him to a bench, and entrusted to the student, under the usual title of patronage secretary of the treasury, the management of the house of commons, a position which requires consummate knowledge of human nature, the most amiable flexibility, and complete self-control. The administration did not last five months; but enough occurred in the interval to induce the minister to change on the next occasion the positions of these two gentlemen, who then served him as efficiently as they had before done with fidelity and zeal.

As an orator Sir Robert Peel had perhaps the most available talent that has ever been brought to bear in the house of commons. We have mentioned that both in exposition and in reply he was equally eminent. His statements were perspicuous, complete, and dignified; when he combated the objections or criticised the propositions of an opponent, he was adroit and acute; no speaker ever sustained a process of argumentation in a public assembly more lucidly, and none as debaters have united in so conspicuous a degree prudence with promptness. In the higher efforts of oratory he was not successful. His vocabulary was ample and never mean; but it was neither rich nor rare. His speeches will afford no sentiment of surpassing grandeur or beauty that will linger in the ears of coming generations. He embalmed no great political truth in immortal words. His flights were ponderous; he soared with the wing of the vulture rather than the plume of the eagle; and his perorations, when most elaborate, were most unwieldy. In pathos he was quite deficient; when he attempted to touch the tender passions, it was painful. His face became distorted, like that of a woman who wants to cry but cannot succeed. Orators certainly should not shed tears, but there are moments when, as the Italians say, the voice should weep. The taste of Sir

Robert Peel was highly cultivated, but it was not originally fine; he had no wit; but he had a keen sense of the ridiculous and an abundant vein of genuine humour. Notwithstanding his artificial reserve, he had a hearty and a merry laugh; and sometimes his mirth was uncontrollable. He was gifted with an admirable organ; perhaps the finest that has been heard in the house in our days, unless we except the thrilling tones of O'Connell. Sir Robert Peel also modulated his voice with great skill. His enunciation was very clear, though somewhat marred by provincialisms. His great deficiency was want of nature, which made him often appear even with a good cause more plausible than persuasive and more specious than convincing. He may be said to have gradually introduced a new style into the house of commons which was suited to the age in which he chiefly flourished and to the novel elements of the assembly which he had to guide. He had to deal with greater details than his predecessors, and he had in many instances to address those who were deficient in previous knowledge. Something of the lecture, therefore, entered into his displays. This style may be called the didactic.

After his fall, in the autumn of '46, when on a visit to one who had opposed his policy but who was his friend, sauntering with his host and sitting on a stile, Sir Robert Peel spoke very fully of the events that had just occurred. He said then, and was then in the habit of saying, though it was quite a self-illusion, that nothing should ever induce him to accept power again. And he gave among many interesting reasons for arriving at this conclusion, not only the untimely end of so many of his predecessors, significant of the fatal trust, but a consciousness on his own part that his debating powers were declining. But this would seem to have been a false judgment. Sir Robert Peel encountered in '46 an opposition which he had not anticipated and partly carried on in a vein in which he did not excel. To be bearded, sometimes worsted, in that scene where he had long reigned paramount, at the moment galled and mortified him, and he accounted for the success of his opponents by the decay of his own powers. But Sir Robert Peel made some of his most considerable efforts in the great struggle of '46; and it may be a question whether his very best speeches were not those which he made during the last three years of his life. They were more natural than his speeches either as minister or as leader of opposition. There was more earnestness and more heat about them, and much less of the affectation of plausibility.

It is often mentioned by those political writers who on such a subject communicate to their readers their theories and not their observations of facts, that there was little sympathy between Sir Robert Peel and the great aristocratic party of which he was the leader; that on the one side there was a reluctant deference, and on the other a guidance without sentiment. But this was quite a mistake. An aristocracy hesitates before it yields its confidence, but it never does so grudgingly. In political connections under such circumstances the social feeling mingles and the principle of honour which governs gentlemen. Such a following is usually cordial and faithful. An aristocracy is rather apt to exaggerate the qualities and magnify the importance of a plebeian leader. They are prompted to do this both by a natural feeling of self-love and by a sentiment of generosity. Far from any coldness subsisting between Sir Robert Peel and the great houses which had supported him through his long career, there never was a minister who was treated with such nice homage, it may be said with such affectionate devotion. The proudest in the land were prouder to be his friends, and he returned the feeling to its full extent and in all its sincerity.

Sir Robert Peel was a very good-looking man. He was tall and, though of latter years he had become portly, had to the last a comely presence. Thirty years ago, when he was young and lithe, with curling brown hair, he had a very radiant expression of countenance. His brow was very distinguished, not so much for its intellectual development, although that was of a very high order, as for its remarkably frank expression, so different from his character in life.

The expression of the brow might even be said to amount to beauty. The rest of the features did not, however, sustain this impression. The eye was not good; it was sly, and he had an awkward habit of looking askance. He had the fatal defect also of a long upper lip, and his mouth was compressed.

One cannot say of Sir Robert Peel, notwithstanding his unrivalled powers of despatching affairs, that he was the greatest minister that this country ever produced, because, twice placed at the helm, and on the second occasion with the court and the parliament equally devoted to him, he never could maintain himself in power. Nor, notwithstanding his consummate parliamentary tactics, can he be described as the greatest party leader that ever flourished among us, for he contrived to destroy the most compact, powerful, and devoted party that ever followed a British statesman. Certainly, notwithstanding his great sway in debate, we cannot recognise him as our greatest orator, for in many of the supreme requisites of oratory he was singularly deficient. But what he really was, and what posterity will acknowledge him to have been, is the greatest member of parliament that ever lived.

Peace to his ashes! His name will be often appealed to in that scene which he loved so well, and never without homage even by his opponents.

CHAPTER XVIII

THE retribution which attended the colonial interest for their vote against agricultural protection was swifter than the most prophetic vengeance could have dreamed. Within a month of his accession to power, at the end of an exhausting session, the new minister announced a sweeping measure which was at once to admit sugar the produce of slave labour, to the British market. The measure was in accordance with the views which the whigs in opposition had always maintained, but it was not thought probable that they would have involved the house and the government in the permanent settlement of so complicated a subject at so late a period in the year, especially when political vicissitudes had broken up the house and little disposed it for the prudent consideration of an important question. Lord John, however, remembered that sugar was an article of colonial produce which had been embarrassing if not fatal to many governments. Strange that a manufacture which charms infancy and soothes old age should so frequently occasion political disaster. The minister therefore was resolved to rid himself of this perpetual difficulty by precipitating a settlement while the elements of opposition on this question, though powerful, were distracted. Until the year 1846, the duties on sugar had been voted annually. It was the constitutional practice to leave a large amount of revenue dependent on an annual vote of the house of commons in order that the allegation, and if proved, the redress of grievances might be secured. The minister, and very wisely, did not think it expedient that the duties on sugar should be made a subject of annual debate. He proposed therefore a permanent settlement of these duties; and in order not to depart from a constitutional practice, promised to substitute in their stead at the same time another branch of revenue which it would be less objectionable to take as an annual vote. One advantage of settling great questions in a hurry and at the end of a session, is that a minister often obtains his main object without fulfilling the conditions on which it was to have been dependent. Thus, in the present case, the sugar duties ceased to be an annual vote and the immediate influence of the house of commons on that large branch of revenue was abolished, but the substitute which was to have secured the same amount of constitutional control was unfortunately forgotten to be appropriated.

The new minister dilated on the inconsistency of our receiving slave-grown cotton, and slave-grown coffee, and slave-grown tobacco, and rejecting slave-grown sugar; he showed that the British merchant would not be baulked of his profit by our legislation and that he purchased slave-grown sugar notwithstanding all our restrictions, but had to dispose of it in an indirect manner instead of in our own market; that we therefore did not by our laws prevent the employers of slave labour in Cuba and Brazil from selling their sugar in Europe and obtaining a profitable return, but that this was done with inconvenience and loss to English commerce, and above all with a very great loss to the English consumer. The result of our legislation was that Cuba and Brazil carried on a thriving trade, supplying the world by our means with cheap sugar while we ourselves paid a very high price for the article. The minister showed also that under the stipulations of treaties we were bound to admit the slave-grown produce of countries which were on the footing of the most favoured nation.

The case of the whigs thus stated was unanswerable, but it was a condemnation of all that this country has done for the abolition of slavery, a cause too which the whigs had especially taken up in their generation for party purposes and which they had most vehemently stimulated. Before the abolition of slavery the British colonies could successfully compete with any country in the world in the production of sugar. Having deprived our colonies of those successful means of general competition, it would seem that the metropolis was at least bound to secure them a home market. If the consequence of such a monopoly were a dear article, the increased price must be considered as an amercement for the luxury of a philanthropy not sufficiently informed of the complicated circumstances with which it had to deal.

The movement of the middle classes for the abolition of slavery was virtuous, but it was not wise. It was an ignorant movement. It showed a want of knowledge both of the laws of commerce and the stipulations of treaties; and it has alike ruined the colonies and aggravated the slave trade. But an enlightened aristocracy who placed themselves at the head of a movement which they did not originate, should have instructed, not sanctioned, the virtuous errors of a well-meaning but narrow-minded community. If, instead of quoting in the house of commons, in 1846, 'the correspondence of an ancestor of mine, John Duke of Bedford, who was employed in negotiating the treaty of 1762,' Lord John Russell and the whigs had warned the people of the West Riding, a quarter of a century before, that the policy of a nation must be directed with reference to public engagements, such as the treaty of Utrecht for example, of which the abolitionists probably had never heard, they would have fulfilled one of the offices of their position. The first duty of an aristocracy is to lead, to guide, and to enlighten; to soften vulgar prejudices and to dare to encounter popular passion. The plea of the free-traders for the admission of slave-grown sugar in 1846 on the ground of inconsistency in excluding it since we admitted other products of slave-grown labour, can be characterised only by an epithet too harsh for polite composition when we recollect that when the whole community shrunk from the abomination of consuming the slave-grown sugar of our own colonies, they had then for years, nay, in some instances almost for centuries, been in the habit of drinking slave-grown coffee, smoking slave-grown tobacco, and spinning slave-grown cotton. They therefore took their resolution with a full knowledge of these inconsistent accessories. The history of the abolition of slavery by the English and its consequences, would be a narrative of ignorance, injustice, blundering, waste, and havoc, not easily paralleled in the history of mankind.

Lord George Bentinck met the motion of the government with an amendment couched in very temperate and guarded language. It did not express so much as he himself felt, but he wished to unfurl a flag which might rally many round it. He adopted therefore the language of the famous amendment moved by Lord Sandon when member for Liverpool to the whig proposition of '41, and which, if the memory of the present writer does not deceive him, was drawn up by the late prime minister himself. With Sir Robert Peel sitting opposite Lord George Bentinck, and Lord Sandon sitting beneath him, this was rather a dainty device of the protectionist leader.

The amendment declared that in the present state of the sugar cultivation in the British East and West Indian possessions, the proposed reduction of duty upon foreign slave-grown sugar was alike unjust and impolitic, as tending to check the advance of production by British free labour, and to give a great additional stimulus to the slave trade.

Lord George spoke well to his resolution, and in an ample but well-digested address fully considered the three points of the case; the probable supply of sugar under the existing laws, the probable amount of revenue under the projected change, and finally the influence of that change, if agreed to, on the interests of the African race. Sir Robert Inglis, peculiarly entitled on such a subject to offer his opinion to the house, said 'that the speech of Lord George Bentinck was a speech so comprehensive in details and so abounding in facts—every fact too an argument in itself—that he, for his part, could have been content to have rested the decision of the question on it.'

That consequence of being obliged to take office without a parliamentary majority, which the late Lord Bessborough fervently deplored and endeavoured to prevent, now occurred.

Although the government had been in office only a month, and no party, however anxious they might be to assert their opinions, wished to dislodge them, nothing but violent sacrifices of parliamentary consistency and even of personal conviction on the part of those who had no political connection with them, could maintain them in their places. It was clear from the speech of Sir Robert Inglis, cheered by Sir Thomas Acland, that the pure abolitionists were not going to compromise their principles for the convenience of any government past or present. When Lord Sandon rose there was a dead silence. The noble lord delivered a funeral oration over the cause of abolition. 'He confessed that in his opinion every government which had been in power since the passing of the emancipation act had failed in dealing with this subject.' He had made inquiries of competent persons, who had informed him that this measure was not likely to promote or encourage the slave trade. He thought under these circumstances that the time was come when this fallacy, which had produced a great degree of irritation in Brazil, Spain, and other countries, and which threw great obstructions in the way of British commerce, should be dispelled. Shortly after this Sir Robert Peel rose, and after declaring that had he remained in office it had been his intention to have persisted in his resistance to the admission of slave-grown sugar, and offering in a very lucid manner every argument that could be urged against the resolutions of the government, concluded by saying that it was his intention to support ministers. And on this ground, that if the ministers resigned office, which they ought to do if defeated, he was not prepared to take the reins, and he wished to prevent Lord George Bentinck from taking them, he being at the head of a party which conscientiously sought the reversal of the new commercial system.

This was the reward of the sugar members for deserting their party and voting against their constituents and their convictions a month ago. It was sad to watch their countenances; they knew what was at hand from the carrying of this bill, of which before two years had passed

several of them were among the noblest victims. As for
Lord John Russell, if he had only pulled his hat a little more
over his eyes than usual, and in the magic of abstraction
called up the tumultuous scene of '41, when the Sandon
amendment sounded the knell of his government and
virtually made Sir Robert Peel prime minister of England,
he must have moralised over the strange vicissitudes of
political life.

In the course of this debate a follower of Lord George
Bentinck, lamenting the destruction of our colonial system
and expressing his belief that we should ere long have to
reconstruct it, observed that it was a characteristic of our
history that this country generally retraced its steps. He
attributed the prosperity of England in a great measure to
this cause. We did not commit less blunders than other
countries, but we were a people more sensible of our errors.
The history of England, he said, is a history of reaction.
We destroyed, for example, our church establishment and
we replaced it. We destroyed our ancient monarchy and
we restored it. We destroyed the house of lords, and yet we
were now obliged to take up our bills to them for their
sanction. We even abolished the house of commons, and
yet here we were at the end of the session debating a great
question. This gentleman pursued his illustrations, which
nevertheless were not exhausted by him.

These observations amicably nettled the new prime
minister, who being an advocate of slave-grown sugar,
naturally looked upon himself, at any rate for the nonce,
as the representative of progress. He therefore replied to
them and vindicated his cause. Lord John Russell said the
illustrations which had been adduced had been chiefly
drawn from times of violence, though what bearing that
had on the argument was not very apparent. Great changes
naturally will often take place in times of violence, and the
political characters of 1630-40 on both sides, in ability,
education, energy, and social weight, have never been surpassed by any body of public men who have influenced
opinion and events. The county gentlemen certainly never

stood so high as at that period. But then, said Lord John Russell, in happier and more modern times have we retraced our steps? Has not the triumph of reason, of liberty, and of truth, been decided and continuous? The habeas corpus act, the bill of rights, the act of toleration? Have they been repealed? In these instances have we retraced our steps? His lordship even adduced the act for the abolition of the slave trade, which, considering the subject under discussion and the consequences which it involved, seemed, notwithstanding Lord Sandon, somewhat bold. Lord John Russell may now recollect, that before two years had passed he was himself retracing his steps on this very sugar bill of '46, and mitigating its stern provisions. But this is a little matter.

What does Lord John Russell say to the county courts which he has helped to establish? To that measure which has shaken to its centre, nay, has almost swept from the face of the land, that mighty fabric of centralised jurisprudence which was the most enduring element and perhaps proudest achievement of the Norman conquest? Is that progress? Or is it reaction?

The truth is progress and reaction are but words to mystify the millions. They mean nothing, they are nothing, they are phrases and not facts. All is race. In the structure, the decay, and the development of the various families of man, the vicissitudes of history find their main solution. The Norman element in our population wanes; the influence of the Saxon population is felt everywhere, and everywhere their characteristics appear. Hence the honour to industry, the love of toil, the love of money, the love of peace, the hatred of the Pope, the aversion to capital punishments, the desire to compensate for injuries, even the loss of life, by a pecuniary mulct, the aversion to central justice, finally the disbelief of our ever being invaded by the French. The state of public opinion in this country at present more resembles that of England under Edward the Confessor than under Queen Anne.

CHAPTER XIX

IF we take a general view of the career of Lord George Bentinck during the last seven months — from the time indeed when he was trying to find a lawyer to convey his convictions to the house of commons until the moment when her majesty prorogued her parliament, the results will be found to be very remarkable. So much was never done so unexpectedly by any public man in the same space of time. He had rallied a great party which seemed hopelessly routed; he had established a parliamentary discipline in their ranks which old political connections led by experienced statesmen have seldom surpassed; he had brought forward from those ranks entirely through his discrimination and by his personal encouragement considerable talents in debate; he had himself proved a master in detail and in argument of all the great questions arising out of the reconstruction of our commercial system; he had made a vindication of the results of the protective principle as applied to agriculture which certainly, so far as the materials are concerned, is the most efficient plea that ever was urged in the house of commons in favour of the abrogated law; he had exhibited similar instances of investigation in considerable statements with respect to the silk trade and other branches of our industry; he had asserted the claims of the productive classes in Ireland and in our timber and sugar producing colonies with the effect which results from a thorough acquaintance with a subject; he had promulgated distinct principles with regard to our financial as well as to our commercial system; he had maintained the expediency of relieving the consumer by the repeal of excise in preference to customs duties, and of establishing fiscal reciprocity as a condition of mercantile exchange. On subjects of a more occasional but analogous nature he had shown promptitude and knowledge, as in the instances of the urgent condition of Mexico and of our carrying trade with the Spanish colonies, both of which he brought forward in the last hours of the session, but the importance of which motions was recognised by all parties. Finally, he had attracted the notice and in many instances obtained the confidence of large bodies of men in the country, who recognised in him a great capacity of labour combined with firmness of character and honesty of purpose.

At the close of the session (August 28), Lord George visited Norfolk, where he received an entertainment from his constituents at King's Lynn, proud of their member, and to whom he vindicated the course which he had taken, and offered his views generally as to the relations which should subsist between the legislation of the country and its industry. From Norfolk he repaired to Belvoir Castle, on a visit to the Duke of Rutland, and was present at a banquet given by the agriculturists of Leicestershire to his friend and supporter the Marquess of Granby. After this he returned to Welbeck, where he seems to have enjoyed a little repose. Thus he writes to a friend from that place on the 22nd September:—

'Thanks for your advice which I am following, having got Lord Malmesbury's Diary; but I am relapsing into my natural dawdling, lazy, and somnolent habits, and can with difficulty get through the leaders even of the *Times*.

. . . 'The vehemence of the farmers is personal against Peel; it is quite clear that the rising price of wheat has cured their alarm. The railway expenditure must keep up prices and prosperity, both of which would have been far greater without free trade, but in face of high prices, railway prosperity, and potato famine, depend upon it we shall have an uphill game to fight.

'O'Connell talks of parliament meeting in November, to mend the Irish labour rate act. Do you believe this?'

The labour rate act passed at the end of the session ('46)

was one by which the lord-lieutenant was enabled to require special barony sessions to meet in order to make presentments for public works for the employment of the people, the whole of the money requisite for their construction to be supplied by the imperial treasury, though to be afterwards repaid. The machinery of this act did not work satisfactorily, but the government ultimately made the necessary alterations on their own responsibility, and obtained an indemnity from parliament when it met in '47. The early session, therefore, talked of by Mr. O'Connell became unnecessary. As the only object of this labour rate act was to employ the people, and as it was supposed there were no public works of a reproductive nature which could be undertaken on a sufficient scale to ensure that employment, the Irish people were occupied towards the end of the autumn of '46 mainly in making roads which, as afterwards described by the first minister, 'were not wanted.' In the month of September more than thirty thousand persons were thus employed; but when the harvest was over and it was ascertained that its terrible deficiency had converted pauperism into famine, the numbers on the public works became greatly increased, so that at the end of November the amount of persons engaged was four hundred thousand, receiving wages at the rate of nearly five millions sterling per annum. These immense amounts went on increasing every week, and when parliament met in February 1847, five hundred thousand persons were employed on these public works, which could bring no possible public advantage, at an expense to the country of between £7 and 800,000 per month. No board of works could efficiently superintend such a multitude or prevent flagrant imposition, though the dimensions of that department appeared almost proportionably to have expanded. What with commissioners, chief clerks, check clerks, and pay clerks, the establishment of the board of works in Ireland, at the end of '46, consisted of more than eleven thousand persons.

Always intent upon Ireland, this condition of affairs early and earnestly attracted the attention of Lord George

Bentinck. So vast an expenditure in unproductive labour dismayed him. He would not easily assent to the conclusion that profitable enterprise under the circumstances was impossible. Such a conclusion seemed to him unnatural, and that an occasion where we commenced with despair justified a bold and venturesome course. The field is legitimately open to speculation where all agree that all is hopeless. The construction of harbours, the development of fisheries, the redemption of waste lands, were resources which had been often canvassed, and whatever their recommendations with the exception of the last they were necessarily very limited, and the last, though it might afford prompt, could hardly secure profitable employment. Prompt and profitable employment was the object which Lord George wished to accomplish. Where millions were to be expended by the state something more advantageous to the community should accrue than the temporary subsistence of the multitude.

Lord George had always been a great supporter of railway enterprise in England on the ground that, irrespective of all the peculiar advantages of those undertakings, the money was spent in the country; and that if our surplus capital were not directed to such channels it would go as it had gone before, to foreign mines and foreign loans, from which in a great degree no return would arrive. When millions were avowedly to be laid out in useless and unprofitable undertakings, it became a question whether it were not wiser even somewhat to anticipate the time when the necessities of Ireland would require railways on a considerable scale; and whether by embarking in such enterprises, we might not only find prompt and profitable employment for the people, but by giving a new character to the country and increasing its social relations and the combinations of its industry might not greatly advance the period when such modes of communication would be absolutely requisite.

Full of these views, Lord George in the course of the autumn consulted in confidence some gentlemen very competent to assist him in such an inquiry, and especially

Mr. Robert Stephenson, Mr. Hudson, and Mr. Laing. With their advice and at their suggestion two engineers of great ability, Mr. Bidder and Mr. Smith, were despatched to Ireland, personally to investigate the whole question of railroads in that country.

Meditating over the condition of Ireland, a subject very frequently in his thoughts, and of the means to combat its vast and inveterate pauperism, Lord George was frequently in the habit of reverting to the years '41—'42 in England, when there were fifteen hundred thousand persons on the parish rates; eighty-three thousand able-bodied men actually confined within the walls of the workhouse, and more than four hundred thousand able-bodied men receiving out-door relief. What changed all this and restored England in a very brief space to a condition of affluence hardly before known in her annals? Not certainly the alterations in the tariff which were made by Sir Robert Peel at the commencement of his government, prudent and salutary as they were. No one would pretend that the abolition of the slight duty (five-sixteenths of a penny) on the raw material of the cotton manufacturer, or the free introduction of some twenty-seven thousand head of foreign cattle, or even the admission of foreign timber at reduced duties, could have effected this. Unquestionably it was the railway enterprise which then began to prevail that was the cause of this national renovation. Suddenly, and for several years, an additional sum of thirteen millions of pounds sterling a year was spent in the wages of our native industry; two hundred thousand able-bodied labourers received each upon an average twenty-two shillings a week, stimulating the revenue both in excise and customs by their enormous consumption of malt and spirits, tobacco and tea. This was the main cause of the contrast between the England of '41 and the England of '45.

Was there any reason why a proportionate application of the same remedy to Ireland should not proportionately produce a similar result? Was there anything wild or unauthorised in the suggestion? On the contrary: ten years before (1836), the subject had engaged the attention of her majesty's government, and a royal commission had been issued to inquire into the expediency of establishing railway communication in Ireland. The commissioners, men of great eminence, recommended that a system of railways should be established in Ireland, and by the pecuniary assistance of government. They rested their recommendation mainly on the abundant evidence existing of the vast benefits which easy communication had accomplished in Ireland, and of the complete success which had attended every parliamentary grant for improving roads in that country.

The weakness of the government, arising from the balanced state of parties, rendered it impossible at that time for them to prosecute the measures recommended by the royal commissioners, though they made an ineffectual attempt in that direction. Could it be suspected that the recommendation of the commissioners had been biassed by any political consideration? Was it a whig commission attempting to fulfil a whig object? Another commission, more memorable, at the head of which was the Earl of Devon, was appointed by a tory government some years afterwards virtually to consider the condition of the people of Ireland, and the best means for their amelioration. The report of the Devon commission confirmed all the recommendations of the railway commissioners of '36, and pointed to these new methods of communication by the assistance of loans from the government as the best means of providing employment for the people.

When Mr. Smith of Deanston was examined by a parliamentary committee and asked what measure of all others would be the one most calculated to improve the agriculture and condition of Ireland, he did not reply, as some might have anticipated, that the most efficient measure would be to drain the bogs; but his answer was, 'advance the construction of railways, and then agricultural improvement will speedily follow.'

To illustrate the value of railways to an agricultural

population, Mr. Smith of Deanston said, 'that the improvement of the land for one mile only on each side of the railway so constructed would be so great, that it would pay the cost of the whole construction.' He added that there were few districts in Ireland in which railway communication could be introduced, where the value of the country through which the railway passed would not be raised to an extent equal to the whole cost of the railway.

Arguing on an area of six hundred and forty acres for every square mile, after deducting the land occupied by fences, roads, and buildings, Mr. Smith of Deanston entered into a calculation of the gain derivable from the mere carriage of the produce of the land, and the back carriage of manure, coals, tiles, bricks, and other materials, and estimated the saving through those means on every square mile to more than £300, or something above £600 on 1280 acres abutting each mile of railway, this being the difference of the cost of carriage under the old mode of conveyance as compared with the new. Following up this calculation, he showed that fifteen hundred miles of railway would improve the land through which it passed to the extent of nearly two million acres at the rate of a mile on each side; and taken at twenty-five years' purchase would equal twenty-four millions sterling in the permanent improvement of the land.

The ground therefore was sound on which Lord George cautiously and after due reflection ventured to place his foot.

And now, after the reports of these two royal commissions, what was the state of railway enterprise in Ireland in the autumn of '46, when a vast multitude could only subsist by being employed by the government, and when the government had avowedly no reproductive or even useful work whereon to place them; but allotted them to operations which were described by Colonel Douglas, the inspector of the government himself, 'as works which would answer no other purpose than that of obstructing the public conveyances?'

In '46, acts of parliament were in existence authorising the construction of more than fifteen hundred miles of railway in Ireland, and some of these acts had passed so long as eleven years previously, yet at the end of '46 only one hundred and twenty-three miles of railway had been completed, and only one hundred and sixty-four were in the course of completion, though arrested in their progress from want of funds. Almost in the same period, two thousand six hundred miles of railway had been completed in England, and acts of parliament had passed for constructing five thousand four hundred miles in addition : in the whole eight thousand miles.

What then was the reason of this debility in Ireland in prosecuting these undertakings ? Were they really not required ; were the elements of success wanting ? The first element of success in railway enterprise according to the highest authorities is population ; property is only the second consideration. Now, Ireland in '46 was more densely inhabited than England. A want of population could not therefore be the cause. But a population so impoverished as the Irish could not perhaps avail themselves of the means of locomotion ; and yet it appeared from research that the rate of passengers on the two Irish railways that were open greatly exceeded in number that of the passengers upon English and Scotch railways. The average number of passengers on English and Scotch railways was not twelve thousand per mile per annum, while on the Ulster railway the number was nearly twenty-two thousand, and on the Dublin and Drogheda line the number exceeded eighteen thousand.

The cause of the weakness in Ireland to prosecute these undertakings was the total want of domestic capital for the purpose and the unwillingness of English capitalists to embark their funds in a country whose social and political condition they viewed with distrust, however promising and even profitable the investment might otherwise appear. This was remarkably illustrated by the instance of the great southern and western railway of Ireland, one of the under-

takings of which the completion was arrested by want of
funds, yet partially open.   Compared with a well-known
railway in Great Britain, the Irish railway had cost in its
construction £15,000 per mile, and the British upwards of
£26,000 per mile; the weekly traffic on the two railways,
allowing for some difference in their extent, was about the
same on both, in amount varying from £1000 to £1300 per
week; yet the unfinished British railway was at £40
premium in the market, and the incomplete Irish railway
at £2 discount.   It was clear therefore that the commercial
principle, omnipotent in England, was not competent to
cope with the peculiar circumstances of Ireland.

Brooding over the suggestions afforded by the details
which we have slightly indicated, Lord George Bentinck,
taking into consideration not merely the advantage that
would accrue to the country from the establishment of a
system of railroads but also remembering the peculiar
circumstances of the times, the absolute necessity of employing the people, and the inevitable advance of public
money for that purpose, framed a scheme with reference to
all these considerations and which he believed would meet
all the conditions of the case.   He spared no thought, or
time, or labour, for his purpose.   He availed himself of
the advice of the most experienced and prosecuted his
researches ardently and thoroughly.   When he had matured
his scheme, he had it thrown into the form of a parliamentary bill by the ablest hands, and then submitted the
whole to the judgment and criticism of those who shared
his confidence and counsels.   Towards the end of November
he was at Knowsley, from whence he communicated with
the writer of these pages.   ' I am here hatching secret plans
for the next session; and now if you have not quite abjured
politics, as you threatened for the next three months to do,
devoting yourself to poetry and romance, I think I ought
to have a quiet day with you in order that we may hold
council together and talk over all our policy.   I shall be at
Harcourt House on the 30th.   I shall stay there till the 3rd
of December, for a meeting on that day of the Norfolk

estuary company of which I am chairman. Would that evening suit you? or Friday? or Wednesday? I am not well acquainted with the geography of Buckinghamshire, but presume you are accessible either by rail or road in less than twelve hours.

'The activity in the dockyard must be in preparation to interfere in Portugal to keep king Leopold upon the Portuguese throne: it cannot be for Mexico, for our friend the *Times* formally abandoned Mexico in his leader some days ago.

'—— has been entertaining Lord —— in Ireland, and writes: "How Peel must chuckle at the whig difficulties." I dare say he does, but in Ireland it seems to me Lord Bessborough is putting the late Irish government to shame, whilst the rupture of the *entente cordiale,* the conquest of California and New Mexico, and the complications in the river Plata, are complete inheritances from Lord Aberdeen.

'Eaton has come to life again: else there was a prospect of George Manners quietly succeeding him in Cambridgeshire. I fear we shall do no good in Lincolnshire, notwithstanding the industry of our dear friend the *Morning Post* in getting hold of Lord Ebrington and Lord Rich's letters to Lord Yarborough. I suppose there is no mistake in Lord Dalhousie ("the large trout") going out to Bombay with the reversion of Bengal.

'The Duchy of Lancaster is to be put in commission, Lord —— to be one of the commissioners, *but unpaid.* He has begun, I presume, to overcome the false delicacy which prevented his acceptance of office under the whigs in July. S—— thought G—— was to be another of the board, but that turns out a mistake, but Lord H—— is to be.

'The manufacturers are working short time, and reducing wages in all directions, John Bright and sons at Rochdale among the rest. The Zollverein increasing their import duties on cotton and linen yarn, and putting export duties of 25 per cent. (some of the states at least) on grain.'

We must not omit to record, that in the autumn of this

year at Goodwood races, the sporting world was astounded by hearing that Lord George Bentinck had parted with his racing stud at an almost nominal price. Lord George was present, as was his custom, at this meeting held in the demesne of one who was among his dearest friends. Lord George was not only present but apparently absorbed in the sport, and his horses were very successful. The world has hardly done justice to the great sacrifice which he made on this occasion to a high sense of duty. He not only parted with the finest racing stud in England, but he parted with it at a moment when its prospects were never so brilliant; and he knew this well. We may have hereafter to notice on this head an interesting passage in his life.

He could scarcely have quitted the turf that day without a pang. He had become the lord paramount of that strange world, so difficult to sway, and which requires for its government both a stern resolve and a courtly breeding. He had them both; and though the blackleg might quail before the awful scrutiny of his piercing eye, there never was a man so scrupulously polite to his inferiors as Lord George Bentinck. The turf too was not merely the scene of the triumphs of his stud and his betting-book. He had purified its practice and had elevated its character, and he was prouder of this achievement than of any other connected with his sporting life. Notwithstanding his mighty stakes and the keenness with which he backed his opinion, no one perhaps ever cared less for money. His habits were severely simple and he was the most generous of men. He valued the acquisition of money on the turf, because there it was the test of success. He counted his thousands after a great race as a victorious general counts his cannon and his prisoners.

CHAPTER XX

THE new year ('47) opened under circumstances of gloom. Two bad harvests had precipitated and aggravated the consequences of the reckless commercial speculations which had prevailed since '45. The state of Ireland, however, was not one merely of deficient harvest, it was one of absolute dearth. Three-fourths of the potato crop, the food of the millions, had failed, while no less than one-third of the oat crop which they exported was deficient. The estimated loss of produce on these two crops, for the year '46, was £16,000,000; that is to say, calculated by weight and measure, eight millions and a half tons of potatoes, and more than five million two hundred thousand quarters of oats. There is no population, however prosperous their ordinary circumstances, that would not have felt such a visitation acutely. But the ordinary circumstances of the Irish population were not prosperous. It appears by the report of the commissioners of poor law inquiry made in '35, that there were then between eleven and twelve hundred thousand agricultural labourers in Ireland whose average earnings did not exceed from two shillings to half a crown a week; that one-half of that number were destitute of work during thirty weeks in the year; and that these with their families made a total of nearly two millions and a half of human beings out of work and in distress thirty weeks in the year. One of the witnesses before that commission said, 'that the county of Mayo alone could furnish beggars for all England.'

It was said by the royal commission over which Lord Devon presided, that these people were the worst housed, the worst fed, and the worst clothed of any in Europe.

They live in mud cabins littered upon straw; their food consists of dry potatoes of which they are often obliged to stint themselves to one spare meal; sometimes a herring or a little milk may afford them a pleasing variety, but sometimes also they are driven to sea-weed and to wild herbs. Dwelling in hovels and feeding upon roots, they are clothed in rags.

Those were the ordinary circumstances of Ireland, and to such a state of affairs famine was now added with all its attendant horrors, pestilence and death. In the southern and western parts of the country the population was decimated: ten thousand persons at the meeting of parliament had died in the union of Skibbereen, which numbered one hundred thousand souls. Scenes were enacted worthy of the page of Josephus or Thucydides. It was truly and tersely said by Lord John Russell, that it was a famine of the thirteenth century with a population of the nineteenth.

That under such circumstances, and especially in such a country, crime should have increased is not remarkable; but it is strange, and it is interesting, that the character of that crime should have altered. The increase in offences was entirely in offences against property. Burglaries abounded, and highway robbery was almost for the first time introduced. Agrarian outrage greatly diminished: the influence of the secret societies died away; the spirit of combination ceased, and although the offences were numerous there was no difficulty in obtaining convictions or in enforcing the law. All of which shows that the difficulty of vindicating the law in cases where the tenure or occupation of land is concerned does not arise from any inherent repugnance to order and justice in the hearts of the Irish multitude.

The social machinery which was to cope with these dreadful perplexities was very feeble. Most of the great proprietors were absentees; the number of the smaller gentry resident was in no part considerable; the clergy of the various creeds had long been prevented from co-operation by sectarian animosities; generally speaking the capitalist farmer and the substantial tradesmen were two characters unknown; indeed one striking feature of Ireland was the total absence of the machinery of retail trade; the farmer paid his servants with the roots which were produced by their labour, and receiving no money wages they required no village shop to supply their wants. There were very few towns in fact of trade sufficient to create a responsible class of shopkeepers. It might almost be said that in Ireland parochial authority did not exist. Over this land patrolled an armed constabulary whose iron discipline rather avenged outrage than secured order.

The famine which was apprehended by Sir Robert Peel in '45-6 was averted by a variety of circumstances, but one of the principal causes of its not happening was the abundant crop of potatoes in '44-5, so that the quantity of food in Ireland when parliament met in '46 was much more considerable than the ministry supposed or led parliament to believe, and in the first five months of that year can scarcely be said to have been deficient. The government of Sir Robert Peel took at once two precautionary measures against the apprehended scarcity. They purchased Indian corn considerably but secretly in foreign markets, which they supplied to the people from government depôts, and they immediately carried a measure authorising advances of money from the treasury to baronies presenting for public works, so that the destitute might be employed during the spring and summer months. That act proceeded upon what was called the half-grant system, a repayment of only half the amount expended being required from the proprietors. When the government of Lord John Russell succeeded to office it was their opinion that the Irish proprietors had availed themselves of the provisions of this act to an extent far beyond what the necessity of the country required. The Irish proprietors had then made presentments exceeding in amount one million sterling, and although a sum less than three hundred thousand pounds had only been expended in wages by the 1st of September '46, that sum had already deranged the labour market of

Ireland, affected the supply of labour to England and Scotland, and even the harvest in Ireland stood uncut for want of labourers. It was on the petition of the Irish farmers themselves that the works under this act were stopped in order that they might get labourers to reap their corn.

But although the government of Lord John Russell had stopped this public employment of the people at the beginning of the autumn, they had nevertheless, in case of emergency, providently passed a new labour rate act of their own before parliament was prorogued, which was avowedly constructed with the object of checking that extravagance which had already alarmed them. To secure this result it was resolved to terminate the half-grant system as the great inducement to over-presentment, and to exact repayment of the whole of the sums advanced, charging that repayment on the poor rates of the country. Such was the origin of that famous labour rate act to which we have already referred and which produced such enormous results!

This law, which was to prevent fraud and to check extravagance, was destined immediately to encounter that famine which had been so long hovering over the Irish people. A crisis arrived that defied all prudential calculations and all economical checks. Notwithstanding their absolute liability for the whole advances from the treasury out of the three hundred and sixty baronies into which Ireland is divided, nearly three hundred when parliament met had held presentment sessions and sanctioned the expenditure of several millions. The number of persons employed under the labour rate act, principally in useless and entirely in unproductive works, which in the month of September had amounted to thirty thousand, reached when parliament met the awful sum of half a million, representing it was said, as far as the means of subsistence were concerned, two millions and a half of her majesty's subjects. A nation breaking stones upon the road! Equal to the population of Holland, a community enjoying ancient renown and present respect and prosperity; all those sources of moral satisfaction and material comfort which render a people proud and content. The payment of wages in this enormous enterprise will always form one of the most singular documents in the archives of the exchequer. It was when parliament met about £200,000 per week distributed by five hundred pay clerks; and subsequently was very much increased. These clerks, however, formed only a small portion of the staff of officers which superintended the operations. There were seventy-four chief inspectors, and thirty-six principal engineers, three hundred and eighty-five assistant surveyors and engineers, nearly three thousand check clerks, and nearly seven thousand overseers.

The government trembled before this appalling creation of an act of parliament, while their confidential agents advised them that while the system had become so extensive the destitution, certainly the demand, had proportionably increased. This was no doubt in some degree occasioned by the frauds inseparable from so vast and peculiar an undertaking. The great difficulty in its conduct was of course to obtain efficient labour from the people employed. When the works commenced, those who travelled through the country generally reported that the alleged labourers were loitering idly about the roads. In this state of affairs the lord-lieutenant ordered task work to be introduced, and at first his resolution met with great resistance. But his excellency was peremptory and successful. A new evil, however, sprang from this apparently prudent arrangement. The public labourers at task work earned wages considerably higher than any money wages which could otherwise be obtained. They earned from 1s. 4d. to 1s. 10d. per day; there was consequently a great run upon the public works, and amid the general competition to be placed upon them the farmers were left without labourers, and the cultivation of the soil, after all the most pressing necessity of a country, was neglected. It was even found that farmers themselves, men holding twenty, thirty, and even sixty acres of land, had obtained tickets from the relief committees and were placed upon the works, receiving the money intended for those who were dying by their side. In the course of one fortnight in the county of Clare five thousand persons were struck off who had been thus improperly preferred by the relief committees of the district. The chancellor of the exchequer frankly told the house of commons that the system could be carried no further, and that the labour rate act had broken down.

Notwithstanding this somewhat petulant admission of an able minister and the fierce criticism with which the conception and the conduct of the labour rate act were assailed by persons in and out of the house of commons, the future historian of our country will not ratify this condemnation. With a nation starving it was not difficult, however painful, to adduce numerous instances of fatal destitution. One might paint with terrible ease the cabin tenanted only by a corpse, or sketch the wild dogs grossly feeding on human flesh; the churchyard converted into a charnel-house, and emaciated figures staggering to the union that they might enter and die, and secure by a legal application for relief at the last moment of their flitting life the solace of a consecrated burial. But no one heard of the lives that were saved. It is perhaps impossible to overstate and exaggerate the amount of human suffering which in many parts of Ireland was then endured. Thousands perished, but hundreds of thousands were preserved. That was a period when all classes of the community were pervaded with an admirable sympathy; religious rancour and political discord alike vanished; the clergyman and the priest laboured in the same vineyard; the contributions of private charity, especially those collected and managed by a committee of London merchants, were princely in amount and distributed with skilful zeal; even distant states and foreign lands forwarded their tributes of tenderness; the sultaun of Turkey sent his purses from the Bosphorus to the desolation of Mayo and the agony of Connemara; but all these unprecedented efforts would not have sustained the people a single week. Notwithstanding the severe evils which it has undoubtedly entailed upon the country, it was the labour rate act that saved Ireland, and especially the courageous manner in which it was administered, for it was worked with a large deviation from its strict provisions. No government ever before assumed so great a responsibility. The ministers were at one moment spending a million sterling a month without the sanction of parliament; but they had a wise confidence in the disposition of the English people. It is easy to criticise disbursement under such novel circumstances and to prove waste in so vast and hurried an outlay. Against all this it would perhaps be but generous to remember as a set-off the priceless labours of those functionaries who had shaken their constitutions and shortened their days in the fulfilment of this measure. But the question must be considered in a larger manner. A country in a state of famine, and its population suddenly employed at wages by the state and so sustained for months without disturbance or confusion, will stand out from the crowd of cotemporary incidents and rank among the memorable events of history.

Lord George Bentinck shared these sentiments, although he disapproved of the policy pursued by the ministry with respect to the Irish famine. It was his opinion, in the first place, that all public works should be reproductive; and in the second, that, under the circumstances, it was the duty of a government not only to employ, but to feed, the people; but remembering that the occurrence of the famine was almost cotemporaneous with the accession of the government to office, he felt that circumstance took their conduct out of the pale of criticism, and that no time or opportunity had been afforded them to prepare for the most effectual encountering of such a visitation. 'But, sir,' he said on the first night of the session, 'at the same time we must be permitted to deal frankly with the conduct of ministers; and while we are not disposed to say that they acted wrongly in declining to call parliament together, nor to censure them for having over-ridden the law and superseded the duties of the legislature itself, we are disposed to say, that the measures to which they have had recourse are

not those in which we can altogether agree.' He expressed
his disapprobation of a mode of employing the people which
was unprofitable, which was worse than useless, since according to the inspector-general of works, it only obstructed
the public conveyances, and which was even injurious, since
it had withdrawn the people from the cultivation of the
fields. 'With respect to the supply of food to the people,
I for one cannot agree altogether with those principles of
political economy which have been advanced by the chief
secretary. This principle of non-interference with the
import and retail trade may be good in ordinary times,
but in times such as the present, when a calamity unexampled in the history of the world has suddenly fallen
upon Ireland—when there are no merchants or retailers in
the whole of the west of Ireland—when a country of which
the people has been accustomed to live upon potatoes of
their own growth, produced within a few yards of their
own doors, is suddenly deprived of this the only food of
its people, it was not reasonable to suppose that suddenly
merchants and retailers would spring up to supply the
extraordinary demands of the people for food. Therefore,
I should say this was a time when her majesty's ministers
should have broken through these severe rules of political
economy and themselves have found the means of feeding
the people. The chief secretary says, that the ministers
did wisely in this decision, but I differ from him when I
hear every day of persons being starved to death, and when
he himself admits that in many parts of the country the
population had been decimated.'

Whether under any circumstances it should be the office
of a government to supply the people with food is a very
interesting question. When famine prevails there will
always be a numerous party who will maintain the affirmative. Death and decimation are stern facts which seem to
bring conviction. Yet it is the duty of a minister to consider, whether, if the government were to interfere, the
dearth might not be increased and the rate of mortality
aggravated. In the first place, when a minister enters the

market all private merchants withdraw; they cannot compete with a rival who seeks no profit in his transactions; and though he thus appears to assume the advantageous position of a purchaser without contest, a dealer who has undertaken the responsibility of feeding a nation has in reality no option. Prices therefore rise, and considerably. But this, though a great, is not the chief evil. Commerce is not a mere affair of gross purchase; it is a pursuit of skill; of traditionary means, of local knowledge and organised connection. The employment of capital must be combined with all these incidents to render commerce not merely profitable but competent to supply a demand. The imports of the government would therefore not only be expensive but they would be scanty. The government would have to pay more for a less quantity than they require.

But if these be the evils inseparable from public imports, what might be the consequences of a government undertaking not only to obtain but to distribute food, and the retail trade of a country being carried on in Downing Street? Perhaps a host of subordinates more fatal than the famine. The colossal staff superintending the public works would be but an intimation of these legions of hucksters. No metropolitan authority could control such a multitude, or prevent an endless series of inefficiency, embezzlement, and waste.

The peculiarity of Ireland that it was without the usual class of retail dealers overweighed, according to Lord George Bentinck, clearly the last head of objections. He thought the difficulties under such circumstances of a government becoming chapmen ought to have been encountered and might have been overcome. And certainly if any minister could have satisfactorily conducted the experiment he was the man, for he combined with a fiery energy of soul and a stern determination a love and mastery of details which rarely accompany those higher qualities of the human disposition. He was alike vigilant and inflexible; nothing escaped him and nothing melted him where duty was concerned. In vain would the sluggard and the shuffler appeal to him; to such he was ever inexorable. The ministry, although they resolved not to interfere in the import of food, were nevertheless of opinion that to a certain degree it was incumbent on them to assist its distribution in the lonelier parts of Ireland, and they established some depôts west of the Shannon. They justified this course by a precedent afforded by Sir Robert Peel, but the cases were not similar. The late administration had established depôts in Ireland for the sale of Indian corn, because they wished to introduce a new species of food to the people, against which there was that prejudice which novelty in such matters generally entails. The course of trade could not have introduced this grain to the Irish people, for its import was prohibited by high duties. In establishing depôts for its distribution the government of Sir Robert Peel performed a political rather than a mercantile office. There is reason to believe that the establishment of government depôts at the end of '46, however cautiously introduced, tended in the localities to arrest the development of that retail trade which was then rapidly extending throughout Ireland.

Upon this subject, however important in itself, Lord George on the first night of the session did not much dwell. It was an affair of the past, and he had commenced by expressing his determination to view the past conduct of the government, 'placed in very difficult circumstances,' in no critical spirit. But with regard to the employment of the people, inasmuch as the ministry announced that the system established by their labour rate act must with all convenience be abrogated and other means be found for the object which it proposed to attain, he felt it his duty to speak explicitly as to the course which he thought they ought to adopt.

'With respect,' he said, 'to the other measures proposed by her majesty's ministers which have not yet been propounded, all I will say is, that I trust they will be measures of such a description as will encourage the employment of capital in Ireland. It is not by grants and by gifts, and additional taxes on the people of this country, that the permanent interests of Ireland can be promoted. Her majesty's ministers must propound some large measures by which enterprise shall be encouraged in Ireland; some great measure by which English capital may be induced to pour itself into Ireland. I hope the measures of her majesty's ministers will be such as without any interference on our part will attain that object. I know nothing as to what they may be; but if her majesty's ministers should not bring forward some comprehensive measures of this kind, I give notice to the house, that at the earliest opportunity I shall, with the advice of my friends, bring forward a large comprehensive measure for this purpose.'

During the discussions on the state of Ireland which more or less spread over the first week of the session, and in which the government at different times announced the various measures of relief which it was their intention to introduce, Lord George carefully considered whether any were proposed calculated to effect the object which he desired. The first measure of the government was to suspend the duties on corn, established for three years by the law of 1846. Mr. Ricardo, who seconded the address, had anticipated objections from the protectionists to this measure, on the ground that the law of '46 was a compact between parliament and the agricultural interest. 'I for one,' said Lord George Bentinck, 'repudiate the idea of any such compact. We do claim a compact in 1842 with the late ministry, which was broken in '46. But we have never consented to any compromise in '46, and we release altogether the government from any notion that they are bound by any compact to us, or we by any compromise to them. It is not our intention to offer any obstacle to the repeal of the 4s. duty. But when we say this, we do not admit that the repeal of that 4s. duty will confer any benefit whatever on the consumer. That it will be a loss to her majesty's exchequer, no one can doubt. But if the chancellor of the exchequer is prepared to say that the revenues of the country are in so prosperous a condition, that he can afford to spare three or four hundred thousand pounds, it is not for us to oppose him. But it is our opinion that every farthing of that £400,000—of that 4s. duty—will go into the pockets of these corn-merchants and forestallers; that it will go into the hands of men who, while they buy at New York Indian corn at 3s. a bushel, sell it in Ireland at 9s.; that it will go into the pockets of the American merchant and the American agriculturist. Better by half to retain the 4s. duty, and give the money accruing from it to Ireland to feed the people with.'

He said he did not expect to see much benefit derived from any interference with our navigation laws. It was too late in the day to assemble foreign ships to send them to America. If the government wanted ships, there were eight ships of the line, which Lord Hardwicke, 'one of the finest seamen in the British service,' would undertake to get ready in little more than four-and-twenty hours, 'would have the guns out of all of them, batten down their ports, and caulk them up, and bring eighty thousand quarters of grain in ten weeks from the American ports to the western coast of Ireland. These ships might make four voyages before harvest, and bring altogether three hundred and twenty thousand quarters. That would bring down prices at London, Liverpool, and Glasgow; that was the way to succour the people, if the government would only 'cast off their too devoted regard to the principles of political economy.' If it were proposed to make a permanent alteration in the navigation laws, 'which I do not believe is intended, I should have felt it my duty,' he added, 'to oppose any such proposition.'

In the course of the next ten days the government measures of relief distinctly transpired. One of these was a public undertaking to reclaim a portion of the waste lands of Ireland; but it was faintly proposed by the first minister, sneered at a few days after by his own chancellor of the exchequer, and finally fell prostrate before a bland admonition from Sir Robert Peel, who was skilful always in detecting when the cabinet was not confident in a measure, and by an adroit interposition often obtained the credit with the country of directing the ministry, when really he had only discovered their foregone conclusion. Then there were to be loans for the improvement of private estates, an extension of the system of drainage by the board of works, some encouragement of fisheries, and an improved poor law. Projects for ordinary times, hardly adequate to absorb the teeming millions of the public works, whose numbers increased with every telegraph, and alarmed the cabinet like a fresh invasion of some barbaric host appalling the trembling senators of Rome.

How were the ministry to cope with this awful perplexity? The confidential agents of the government had informed them that the means of employing the people on public works had reached their limit. 'Any extension of those works was impossible.' Even had those means not been exhausted a further outlay would not meet the difficulty. The famine was increasing, deaths became more frequent, the prospect was one which might appal the stoutest heart. There were many classes of persons, and those the most destitute, by whom labour could not be performed, and to whom therefore relief was not given. In many parts of the country crowds flocked to the works who were unable from weakness to perform their task, and who only reached the spot to faint and die. Many persons too, who at the commencement of the visitation could earn even large wages by task work, were now unable to earn enough to procure themselves subsistence. The pulse of the community was so depressed that it began to be incapable of employment. Labour was no longer a specific. When the labour rate act was called into full play in the autumn, the only alternative was gratuitous alms. In the sudden outbreak of a widespread calamity, wholly unparalleled in Europe in this or any other age, it had gained time. During the interval thus obtained the thoughts of the ablest men in Europe had been fixed on the subject of feeding a famished people, the extent and nature of the particular evil had been more clearly ascertained, and a terrible experience now suggested measures which were deemed more suitable to the exigency. It was desirable that the vast expenditure should afford more effectual relief, and it was hoped that the evils which were now encountered in its administration might be removed or at least greatly mitigated.

The plan of the ministry was to form relief committees in every electoral district; to empower those committees to levy rates and to receive subscriptions, and to assist them with public grants. With these means they were to purchase food and to distribute rations to the people, not requiring as the condition of relief the test of labour. The substitution of this system for that of the public works was to be made as easy in the transition as possible. There was to be no rude dismissal of the people at once, but when the arrangements of the new system were completed no new public works were to be undertaken. It was thought that the temptation to abuse would be less if relief were afforded by food instead of wages; that the expense of the staff of inspection might be greatly diminished; and that by allowing the labouring man while you secured him a certain quantity of food to work on his own account, the ordinary operations of agriculture would be less neglected.

In stating this measure to the house the minister announced that the government now looked upon the Irish famine as an imperial calamity, and therefore no longer thought it right that the whole burthen occasioned by it should remain on Irish property. They therefore proposed an arrangement by which in each succeeding year when an instalment became due, upon half that instalment being paid, the other half should be remitted. They proposed however that the whole debt should be kept up until one-half of it was discharged, but eventually one moiety of the whole charge was to fall upon the treasury of the united kingdom.

The drift of the ministerial propositions was not satisfactory to Lord George Bentinck. They were a confession according to his views that the system of employing labour on useless and unprofitable undertakings, while it had occasioned and was occasioning a prodigious outlay, had failed in its main object, namely, sustaining the people. Nor did there seem any certainty, scarcely any prospect, of the vast sum of one million sterling a month thus expended being speedily or considerably reduced. The new plan could not be immediately put in practice, and it might fail. Even if it succeeded it was by no means clear that the expenditure would be reduced. Alms-giving had in fact succeeded to fruitless employment; such projects were the desperate efforts of an emergency, but sufficient time had now elapsed for the substitution of less reckless methods. If the capital or the credit of the nation were to be thus largely called upon they should be employed if possible in a manner which, while it afforded some remedy for the immediate evil, might improve the country and ultimately raise the tone of the community. Influenced by these views he summoned his friends, and with their full approbation gave notice that on Thursday, the 4th of February, he should move for leave to bring in a bill, 'to stimulate the prompt and profitable employment of the people by the encouragement of railways in Ireland.'

Although a slight circumstance, it ought perhaps to be noticed that some change took place at the commencement of this session ('47) in the local position of parties in the house of commons. On the accession of the whigs to office in the preceding year, the protectionists had retained their seats beneath the gangway on the ministerial side. They did this on the reasonable ground, that as it was their intention to support the general policy of the new government, it was unnecessary for them to cross the house with the late cabinet which they had themselves mainly driven from power. But as time advanced considerable inconvenience was found to result from this arrangement, for the protectionists were so numerous, that the greater portion of the habitual supporters of the whigs were obliged to range themselves on the benches opposite the men whom they had always supported and with whom they were still voting. This led to some conversation between the treasury bench and Lord George Bentinck, and it was finally agreed that on the whole it would be more convenient that on the meeting of the house in '47, he should take the seat usually occupied by the leader of the opposition, and that his friends should fill the benches generally allotted to an adverse party. This was the origin of his taking a position which he assumed with great reluctance, and of his appearing as the chief opponent of a ministry which he was anxious to uphold. He was indeed so unwilling to appear in the shape of an opponent of the government, that he communicated privately with the first minister, between whom and himself there were relations of mutual regard, as to his intentions in the course he was pursuing. He referred to this interview and these feelings in his statement. 'In introducing, sir, this measure to the house, it has not been my wish to bring forward any proposition either of hostility or rivalry to the government of my noble friend. I have assured the house publicly, and privately I have pledged my honour to my noble friend the first minister, that I seek no advantage from the carrying of this measure; and that it is my anxious hope that we may come to the consideration of it as if it were a great private bill, and we were all selected members of a committee to inquire into its worth.'

The speech in which he introduced his measure was the best he ever made. Although he spoke for two hours, and had necessarily to deal greatly with details, he treated them with so much dexterity that he commanded during the whole time the unbroken attention of his audience. Confident in his subject and himself he was throughout animated and interesting, and received when he resumed his seat general applause. The subject was treated in a masterly manner. 'It is not my intention to make a very long preface,' he said, 'on the condition of Ireland. Enough that there are half a million able-bodied men in that country living upon the funds of the state, commanded by a staff of eleven thousand five hundred and eighty-seven persons, and all employed upon works, which have been variously described as "works worse than idleness"; by the yeomanry of Ulster as "public follies"; by the inspector-general of these works himself as "answering no other purpose than that of obstructing the public conveyances."' He said he would not despair of Ireland. A loss of property to the value at least of £10,000,000 sterling was a great calamity, but not enough to daunt a nation which in the time of war had expended on an average of three years more than £103,000,000 a year. We ought, he said, to have a confident hope that good would come out of evil, have the spirit to look our difficulties fairly in the face instead of 'lying down and weeping over our misfortune like children lost in a wood.'

He went over the points which we have touched on in the preceding chapter, on the influence and effects of railway enterprises in England, and of the high authorities who had recommended an extension of their beneficial consequences to our sister island; and after very clearly placing before the house what had been already effected in Ireland as to the construction of railways, what works were unfinished, and what ought to be commenced and completed, sketching with much liveliness the lines of communication and the undeveloped resources of the districts through which they ran, and showing that if his plans were supported, 'there would not be a single county in Ireland which would not be traversed by railways,' he made his proposition that the imperial government should come to the aid of these enterprises.

The proposition of Lord George Bentinck was, that for every £100 expended to the satisfaction of the imperial government in railway construction, £200 should be lent by government at the very lowest interest at which, on the credit of the government, that amount could be raised, so that if two millions were produced annually for four years by the Irish companies, the imperial government should advance an additional four millions, ensuring in Ireland for four years the expenditure of six millions a year in public works of an useful and reproductive nature. This proposition was recommended by Lord George as offering an ample security for the public loan. For this purpose he adduced evidence to show that the worst railroad ever yet constructed in this country, or Scotland, or Belgium, would afford an ample security under such circumstances. He assumed that the government would lend the money at $3\frac{1}{2}$ per cent. and take the whole railway as security. Consequently a line paying £7 upon £300 expended would afford ample security for £200 lent by the state, at £3, 10s. per cent., and he was therefore prepared to prove that a line which paid but a dividend of £2, 6s. 8d. per cent. would afford perfect security for the interest of the loan made by the government.

Establishing this point, he proceeded a step further and proved to the house that there was no line in existence which would not yield a greater dividend than this. He took the line in the empire of which the gross traffic receipts were the lowest; a Scotch railway, between Arbroath and Forfar. Previous to the formation of that railway all the traffic that was carried on between these places was carried on by one horse and a light cart, which travelled between the two towns twice a week. The population of these towns, nearly equal, was together only about eighteen thousand, and the intermediate villages not numerous, yet the number of passengers, and it was only passenger lines that were treated of in this measure, amounted to ninety thousand a year, or two hundred and forty-seven a day, yielding an average amount of receipts of £150 to £200 a week, which was a profit of 5 per cent. on the whole of the expenditure, that being £145,000. Now this railroad, 'the worst line in the empire,' cost £9,000 a mile; the gross receipts in the first year were £468 a mile, while the cost of working the line was £202 a mile, and yet upon that line, even at that low amount of traffic, the government would receive their $3\frac{1}{2}$ per cent. interest, leaving nearly 2 per cent. over for the shareholders.

The project which offered this security was in its immediate influence on labour to employ one hundred and ten thousand able-bodied men upon productive works, and in its ultimate and yet speedy results nearly to double the amount of persons thus employed. But while it secured 'prompt and profitable employment' to the people, beneficial consequences were not limited to the mere labourers; the landowners would receive large sums for their land, the farmers for their tenant right, but, above all, the state would greatly profit by sanctioning this proposition. 'The state,' said Lord George, 'will be a sleeping partner in the concern, for while the state lends really nothing but its credit and its name, it will reap from the expenditure not of £16,000,000, but of that sum lent by the government with £8,000,000 share capital added, making in the whole £24,000,000 in Ireland, an enormous amount of increased revenue.' And then he entered into one of his characteristic calculations on this head which greatly amused and interested the house.

'We have it stated by Messrs. Grissell and Peto,' said Lord George, 'who are constantly employing nine thousand labouring men on English railways, that in order to promote habits of sobriety it was thought advisable to restrict each man to one gallon of strong beer a day. Now, a gallon of strong beer brewed from malt and hops, pays 4d. duty; so that each railway labourer, setting aside what his family consumes and what he pays on other articles such as tea, tobacco, and sugar, actually pays the sum of £5, 0s. 4d. per year in excise on beer alone. Let us see then how this calculation may be worked out. On looking at and comparing the amount of excise paid by the Irish people with the amount of excise paid by the Scotch, we find that the Scotch, in the excise duty alone, pay £1, 0s. 2d. per head on the whole population, while in Ireland the amount is only 3s. 10¾d. per head. This, after excluding and deducting the soap and brick duties not paid in Ireland, shows a difference in the amount of excise duties paid as between the Irish and Scotch of 16s. 3¼d. per head. Now, I am not going to say that this calculation would be correct as regards the entire population of Ireland; it was made, however, by Mr. Stanley of the board of works about ten years ago; nor do I mean to state that the effect of making one thousand five hundred miles of railway will be to raise the entire population of Ireland to the level of the population in Scotland. But I think I may say, and not overcharge the case, that that population of five hundred and fifty thousand represented by one hundred and ten thousand labourers will be raised to the average level of all Scotland. If, then, we calculate what 16s. 3¼d. per head will come to on five hundred and fifty thousand persons, we shall find an additional yearly amount to the revenue to the extent of £447,448, and this at 3½ per cent. interest will represent a capital of £12,784,000. Well, then, there are the customs duties; and I think when we are constructing railways it will not be unfair to assume that the customs will be as much increased as the excise. I am aware there is great difficulty in getting at the exact amount of customs duties paid by Ireland and Scotland, so large a portion of those duties being received in this country; but from an official estimate made, either by Mr. Porter or Mr. M'Gregor, the gross amount of customs in Ireland shows an average of 5s. 8d. per head, Scotland 13s., making a difference between the two countries of 7s. 4d. per head. This difference would represent a sum of £202,000 a year, representing at 3½ per cent. interest a capital of nearly £6,000,000 sterling. If it were fair to calculate on this employment continuing after the railways were completed and in full vigour, it would be right for me to say there would be an increase of revenue to the state for ever of no less than £649,000, representing a capital of more than £18,000,000 sterling. But stating the amount at half, or even one-third, the sums respectively would be nine or six millions, and there are good grounds for thinking that the construction of one thousand five hundred miles of railway will employ as many people hereafter as when in the course of execution.'

After a desultory discussion, leave was given to bring in the bill 'to stimulate the prompt and profitable employment of the people by the encouragement of railways in Ireland,' although the first minister, with a full recognition of 'the ability with which Lord George Bentinck had displayed both in forming his plan and explaining it to the house,' declared that the government would feel under the necessity of opposing its progress on the next stage. The conduct of the government in acceding to the motion under such circumstances was very much arraigned by some, but generally speaking few propositions have ever been made in the house of commons which were received at the outset with so much favour as the present one, and when late in the evening Lord George Bentinck appeared at the bar with the bill, and was ordered by the speaker to bring it up, as he advanced to the table he was loudly cheered by both sides.

A week elapsed before the second reading of this bill, but as regarded its fate and fortunes, the week was a memorable one. The bill when printed confirmed the favourable impression which the exposition of its scope by Lord George Bentinck had at once created. Admitting its premises it is still agreed that this bill was one of the best legislative projects that was ever introduced into the house of commons; never were details matured in a more business-like manner; from the means for raising and applying the capital to the provisions for the benefit and advantage of the labourers employed, securing them weekly wages in coin of the realm and the construction of decent and suitable dwellings for them during their work, the machinery was acknowledged to be perfect. Also, when a great outlay of public money is inevitable, popular opinion will naturally lean to that proposition which would favour reproductive industry rather than useless labour. It was said, 'True it is that the plan of Lord George Bentinck demands a large sum, but it is the credit of the state, not the capital of the nation, that is required. There appears to be sufficient security for the advance, and the fair prospect of a good return. And even if the worst were to occur, and the four millions per annum were entirely lost, that might be a cheap expenditure were it to relieve the country from the ministerial system of useless works, which at the present moment requires in the wages of labour about a million sterling per month, with no prospect of a cessation of the cost.'

The lord-lieutenant of Ireland too, it was known, had pressed very much the construction of railways on the attention of the government, as a source not only of immediate relief but of permanent improvement to the country, and the government had more than listened to his excellency's recommendation; hence probably the want of decision with which the first minister had encountered the scheme of Lord George Bentinck, which although alarming from its dimensions was nevertheless far from discordant with the actual tendencies of the cabinet. The proposition of Lord George Bentinck likewise was avowedly not brought forward as a party question. If the second reading of the bill were carried, it did not follow that the original scheme would be entirely consummated; the principle might be successfully asserted, and its application if necessary be partially or even considerably modified. No one was pledged by voting for the second reading further than to the salutary and popular principle that the public funds should be expended in achieving the useful instead of the useless. These considerations and circumstances combined so operated that within a very few days of the speech of Lord George Bentinck it was generally felt that the second reading of his bill would be carried.

The bill had been attacked by Lord Brougham in the house of lords opportunely to a vindication of his own character from some imaginary charge the very day after the motion of Lord George Bentinck, which called up Lord Stanley, who entirely concurred in the observation of Lord Brougham that this was a time of all others when public men ought not to be subjected to misrepresentation with regard to their motives, and particularly when their motives and actions had reference to the relief of public distress, in whatever part of the empire that distress might exist. It was his entire concurrence in that observation which led him to notice a remark that fell from Lord Brougham conveying, unintentionally of course, an entire misrepresentation of the motives and intent of the measure which had been introduced by a noble friend of his into the other house of parliament. Lord Brougham had stated that the object of Lord George Bentinck was to introduce a measure the effect of which would be to raise the price of Irish railway shares, and enable railway proprietors to make large profits. Now, he was certain that Lord Brougham could not have heard the able, the eloquent, the statesmanlike speech delivered by Lord George Bentinck last night when introducing the bill; otherwise the monomania of opposition to railways, which in many cases biassed his judgment, would not have caused him to misunderstand the object of a measure which, whatever its intrinsic merits, was undoubtedly introduced with a feeling which commanded the attention and sympathy of all parties in parliament, and which he believed also commanded the admiration and approval of a great portion of the community of this country. The time might come when that measure might have to be argued in their lordship's house, unless some extraordinary exercise of the prerogative of the crown should be made to stop its progress; but he must assure Lord Brougham that its object and intent were not to raise the price of railway shares, or to facilitate their disposal by those who now held them in Ireland. The object of the measure was to interpose the credit of Great Britain without the loss of one single shilling, or the imposition of one single shilling of taxation upon the people of this country, to stimulate and facilitate employment in a country more than all others, and especially at this time, in want of employment; to carry out works of great public utility, and which, without the intervention not only of the aid but of the credit of the state, must be abandoned; to facilitate communication in Ireland, which next to the employment of labour was most necessary to the well-being of the country; to improve the condition of the agricultural labourer in that country; and to furnish the means of constant employment to a large portion of the population for the next four years at least without withdrawing them from agricultural employment by tendering too easy or too well-paid work; and to facilitate the application of capital—for the expenditure of private capital was now checked by the political position of the country. The intention of the measure was to render assistance to Ireland under securities and guarantees which would ensure that the people of this country would not by the advances which they would be called upon to make be liable to one shilling of ultimate expenditure, or to any immediate addition to their burthens, for the purpose of effecting what was proposed to be done by the interposition of the state. He had little thought to have said a word upon the subject at the present time; but with the respect and regard which he felt for Lord George Bentinck and for the opinion and weight of authority of Lord Brougham, he would not permit the statement which had been made to go forth, that the scheme propounded had for its object private benefit, when his firm conviction and belief certainly was, that it had for its object and would produce as its effect great national improvement and great public advantage, and that without entailing public loss or inconvenience upon any portion of the subjects of this empire.

This accurate and animated vindication of the measure of Lord George Bentinck elicited a characteristic declaration from Lord Brougham, that he never read the debates in the house of commons and certainly never heard them, since he had never been in the house of commons since the 20th of November 1830; but whether it were remorse or patrician pride that prompted this conduct, his lordship did not deign to add.

Let us now consider the position of the administration when they learnt that it was not improbable that the house of commons would sanction the second reading of the bill to stimulate prompt and profitable employment in Ireland. Properly to comprehend it, we must refer to the price of consols at that time. In the original draft of his bill, Lord George Bentinck had fixed the rate of interest which the government was to receive from the Irish railway companies at $3\frac{1}{4}$ per cent., which, so far as the mere money market could be a guide, he was justified in doing. When he introduced his bill in February enough had happened to induce him to alter the rate of interest to $3\frac{1}{2}$ per cent. Before the second reading could come on, the price of consols had again fallen. Assuming always in his own mind that a certain expenditure for the employment or sustenance of the Irish must be incurred, and that his plan if adopted would not increase the sum of that expenditure, but that the four millions he would require for the year '47 would only be deducted from the amount which otherwise would be necessary, the state of the money market with Lord George Bentinck was a secondary consideration. With the government resolved not to give up any of their own measures, except that for the redemption of waste lands, and who felt that if they adopted this proposition for the construction of railways it would be an addition to their inevitable expenditure, the state of the money market was a primary consideration. Under these circumstances, after due deliberation, the ministers called a meeting of their friends at the foreign office, and announced to them their resolution, that, in the event of the measure of Lord George Bentinck being sanctioned by the house of commons, they should feel it their duty to place their offices at the disposal of her majesty.

This declaration was especially directed to those Irish members, a powerful section, who were in the habit of supporting a whig administration, but who almost to a man had, either in or out of the house, expressed their approbation of the scheme of the leader of the protectionists and of their determination to support it. The consequences of a change of ministry to these gentlemen, irrespective of all private feeling, might be very momentous. 'A change of ministry might,' to use the language of one of the most active members of this confederation, 'throw into confusion legislation of the most urgent and immediate importance to the poor of Ireland, measures on which perhaps depended the existence of many thousands of their fellow-countrymen. A gathering of this section of the Irish members, forty in number, was held therefore after the general meeting of the party in Downing Street; 'they met in conclave,' as one of them assured the house, and the result of their deliberations was that Lord George Bentinck should be publicly requested in his place, on their behalf, to postpone for a fortnight the second reading of his measure. Desirous as they were of supporting the 'prompt and profitable employment' of the people of Ireland, they were also equally anxious to secure the accomplishment of the measures of the government recently announced and in progress. Mr. Roebuck told them that they wanted to get the good things offered by both sides. 'Give us,' they said to the ministers, 'as much as you can, and when we have squeezed you dry, let the noble lord bring in his plan, and give us something more.'

The threat of the government to resign, repeated with modesty but with firmness, by the first minister in the house of commons did not however influence merely a section of those members who sat habitually on the ministerial side of the house. There was not a section or an individual in the house of commons who wished to disturb the government, least of all Lord George Bentinck, who both on political and personal grounds was anxious to uphold them, but he was not a man who would ever shrink from the consequences of his acts ; and when the first minister called upon him not to listen to the proposition made to postpone his measure but to be prepared for its consequences if it were carried, or to give up his plan entirely for the present session; offering him at the same time the first night at the disposition of the government, in order that the country might know, by an immediate decision, what was the policy to be pursued, Lord George said that though he had heard with the deepest regret the announcement from the first minister, that the fate of the government must be staked on this measure, he must do his duty. As to the request of the gentlemen from Ireland, he would have been willing to have paid due attention to them, but challenged as he was by the first minister of the crown, told by him who is responsible for the situation of the country, that it is for the public advantage that this measure should be forthwith discussed and decided, he felt he should be wanting in duty to her majesty, as well as to his country, if he were to hesitate in proceeding at once. 'And, sir,' he concluded, 'whatever may be the result, however important the consequences, upon my head is not the responsibility. Should it be the pleasure of her majesty's ministers, in the present difficulties of Ireland, to desert the helm of state, great as I admit those difficulties to be—

greater than any which any previous government has ever encountered in the conduct of the affairs of Ireland—my friends are not appalled by those difficulties, and will not shrink from any responsibility which, unsought, may be forced upon us.'

There was no misconception in the position of affairs. The declaration of Lord John Russell and the rejoinder of Lord George Bentinck were alike explicit. No member now could give his vote under a false impression; if the ministry were in a minority, they were pledged to go out, and Lord George Bentinck, 'not appalled,' to take the helm. It must be confessed, however, that he was almost the only member of his party who was undaunted. A sort of panic pervaded the protectionist ranks, and they deplored the weakness of a government which never could be opposed without summoning their party to Downing Street and staking their existence on a vote. This was the second occasion on which this had happened since the whigs had acceded to the administration. At the end of the last session ('46), on the sugar duties, they had only been saved by Sir Robert Peel forfeiting his pledge to his deluded West Indian friends, and voting with all his followers against his judgment in order to preserve the ministry; and now not two months of parliamentary life had again elapsed, and here was the same critical state of affairs; and the government could only be saved by their Irish adherents acting against their acknowledged convictions, and a considerable body of the protectionists being induced to absent themselves from the house, or to divide against their party. Men complained of the unreasonable conduct of the ministers, but the fact is it was the inevitable consequence of the government being carried on by a party which had not a parliamentary majority. But this false position which has strained and injured our happy parliamentary government is not attributable to the whigs, but rather to that statesman, who, with all his great qualities, seems never to have been conscious that the first duty of an English minister is to be faithful to his party, and that good and honourable government in this country is not only consistent with that tie but in reality mainly dependent upon its sacred observance.

The debate on the second reading of the bill lasted three nights, and was sustained on both sides in a manner becoming the importance of the subject. It still may be referred to as a repertory of interesting facts and for a masterly discussion of the principles involved in the measure. Sir Robert Peel, who took a very leading part in the debate, addressed his efforts mainly to sustaining the proposition that the state should under no circumstances interfere in commercial enterprise, and in combating the position enforced by a principal supporter of Lord George Bentinck, that the commercial principle came into contact with circumstances in Ireland with which it was not strong enough to cope. This moot point was very fairly and completely discussed by both of these speakers. The objections of the government were more of detail: that the means were too costly for a very limited end; that the extent of employment assumed by this measure was not by any means equal to the occasion, and that probably not a moiety even of that assumed would be realised by it; that especially the financial condition of the country did not justify such an undertaking. The first minister concluded the debate at half-past three o'clock in the morning, in a short but gloomy speech, the prelude of those terrible financial disasters that were then impending over the country. His announcement of the last official bulletin from Ireland diffused through the house a feeling of almost awful apprehension. 'I believe in the last week,' he said, 'that not less than six hundred thousand persons have received wages on the public works in Ireland, representing probably three millions of the population. One hundred thousand persons more are in the workhouses, maintained by the rates. Thousands and thousands more are maintained by private charity. . . . The consequence of enabling the people of Ireland in such large numbers to buy food is this, that the price of food in this and in foreign countries has been greatly enhanced. But not only are the consequences of the high prices of food beginning to be felt, and very severely felt, but a depression in the manufacturing interests of the country has also taken place; together with the want of sufficient wages for industry, upon which the great bulk of the population is maintained.'

Having shown according to his views that the plan of Lord George Bentinck was not competent to deal with the state of things in Ireland, and would in all probability aggravate the general pressure on the imperial resources, Lord John Russell vindicated in conclusion the constitutional character of his conduct in notifying to his party preliminarily to the debate the consequences of their decision.

' I am far from making any complaint of my noble friend bringing a measure before the house which he conscientiously believes will be of great service to Ireland and will tend to relieve the misery of that country; but he must at the same time see that it was not equally reasonable in him to expect, that if the ministers of the queen did not take the same view as he takes of the utility of this measure, they should adopt a measure of which they did not approve. He might have brought it forward, and have laid it on the table as a measure to be taken or not by the government, but he thought it so important as to proceed with the measure, and elicit the opinion of parliament with regard to it. But it is quite impossible for any government to allow the finances of the country to be taken out of their hands, and placed under the direction of the noble lord, or any other person. Therefore, while I quite concede that he had the best motive for bringing forward this measure, and though I think he was quite right in saying that if he succeeded with the measure he would himself be responsible for carrying it into execution—though I think he showed great spirit in expressing that determination—yet, on the other hand, I must say, feeling myself responsible for the conduct of affairs in this very important crisis, all I can do, is to bring forward those measures which I in my heart believe will tend most to the relief of destitution in Ireland, and ask parliament to consent to those measures. If I am supported by parliament,

I shall then feel courage to go on, and to brave all the difficulties with which I am encompassed; but I hold it would be most injurious to this country to have at this moment any minister at the head of affairs who may be baffled in any effort he may make; whose opinions are not in accordance with the ruling opinions of the members of the house of commons; and whose position is still further embarrassed by having to carry out measures of which he does not approve. I must repeat, therefore, that I do not think I was taking any other than a constitutional course, when I intimated to those who, I believed, were disposed to support the government, that with respect to the management of the finances of this country in this great crisis, we must have the majority of the house of commons with us, or we cannot be competent to conduct the government of this country.'

The conjuncture of many critical circumstances had for some time made it evident that the division would be very unfavourable, and in a house of four hundred and fifty members, only one hundred and eighteen voted for the second reading of that bill which had been so generally welcomed on its introduction.

The period was not propitious for the particular measure proposed by Lord George Bentinck, but the general policy which he recommended must not be decided upon by a mere reference to the specific provisions of this bill. That policy must be viewed in relation to the system then pursued by the government. The real question raised was, whether the employment of the Irish people by the state should be for profitable purposes of permanent advantage to the country, or solely as a machinery to regulate the distribution of doles, either in the shape of rations or wages. What would have been the effect upon Ireland if the plan of Lord George Bentinck had been adopted at the commencement of the year '46 instead of being rejected at the commencement of the year '47? There is scarcely any one who can doubt that the pressure of the famine must have been greatly mitigated by such means being in readiness to sustain the labour of the country. In that case it would not have been necessary for a government just acceding to office suddenly to have plunged into a system which disheartened and dispirited every class in Ireland; which demoralised the labouring class by employing them like slaves under the superintendence of a host of strangers without the animating consciousness of usefulness; which depreciated permanently the value of property by charging it with an annuity equivalent to one-half the cost of these useless works; and which increased the anti-Irish prejudice in England by superadding the disgust with which every Englishman regards the squandering of public money. Looking at the project of Lord George Bentinck in this aspect, the largeness of his demand only proved his sagacity and prudence, and perhaps it might be shown, that even if the whole of the sixteen millions had been required, which by no means followed from his scheme, the position of England would not have been worse financially, while that of Ireland would have been incalculably better than it now.is.

In the present altered state of affairs it would be useless to inquire and impossible to ascertain whether the estimates Lord George formed of the remunerative character of the undertakings he recommended would have been realised, but one can hardly doubt, with the experience of the last four years to aid us, that the regular employment of more than one hundred thousand men at high wages would have greatly relieved every union in Ireland from the pressure of poor rates; that such employment would have had a strong tendency to convert the cottier tenantry into independent labourers; that English capital would have been attracted to the undeveloped mineral treasures of Ireland; and that the emigration of the industrious, if not entirely arrested, would have been sensibly checked.

When the Devon commissioners made their report in '45, they represented all classes in Ireland, except the lowest class of labourers, as in a state of rapid improvement, and they recommended measures which, had they been adopted promptly, would have improved the condition of that class. What is the condition of Ireland now?

The certified circulation of Ireland in April, '46, was seven millions and a half sterling; in March, '51, it was four millions and a half. The population in '46 was eight millions and a half; in '51 it was six millions and a half. So great a diminution of population in so short a time is not to be found in the history of any civilised people, and fills the mind of the statesman with almost appalling thoughts.

Lord George Bentinck was too proud to express the mortification which he felt from the division on his Irish bill. Some of the members from the sister kingdom, who had deserted him, excused their tergiversation on the plea, that, if the 'prompt and profitable employment' scheme had been carried, the plan of the government for the redemption of the waste lands in Ireland might have been endangered. As very shortly after this the government abandoned this redemption project without remorse and scarcely with decency, for the leader of the house of lords was eulogising its virtues almost at the moment it was cast away by the chancellor of the exchequer, these Irish members were left in a position not altogether grateful to the feelings, of which Lord George took care to remind them. For himself, he, according to his wont, tried to forget his disappointment in continued and increased exertions, but a long time did not elapse before the subject was again brought back to his memory and consideration, and that in a manner most agreeable and satisfactory to his feelings.

The financial disasters which were apprehended by the government at the commencement of the session, and the fear of which was perhaps the principal reason of their not embarking at that time in the construction of reproductive works in Ireland, were grievously rife about the end of the month of April. It was said in the house of commons on the 26th of that month ('47) by Mr. Hume, that 'since '25 there had never been such a day in the city.' A drain of bullion had reduced the amount of gold in the bank to the extent of four millions sterling. Consols had fallen that day as low as 85⅞; exchequer bills, which in February were fourteen premium, were at four discount; mercantile bills, except at short dates, could not be discounted. The house had been occupied that day in a protracted debate on the government plan of education; it was long past midnight when the chancellor of the exchequer rose, and after some prelude—reminding the house that in his opposition to the plan of Lord George Bentinck in February, he had not expressed any opinion adverse to the construction of railways in Ireland, on the contrary, had expressed an opinion that their construction would be beneficial, but did not think it expedient, as he had to raise a large loan applicable to the relief of the existing distress in Ireland, to propose a further loan of sixteen millions;—astonished the house by recommending to them a vote for the purpose of assisting Irish railways to the amount of £620,000. There was a great clamour. Mr. Hume and Mr. Goulburn recommended that the chairman should report progress and the proposition be postponed. Mr. Roebuck said, he should take the sense of the house in every stage on the advance. 'Talk about the fearful state of Ireland!' he exclaimed, 'it would be necessary soon to talk about the state of England too.' Lord George Bentinck would not object to proceeding with the vote. 'There was more joy over one sinner that repenteth, than over ninety and nine just persons.' He greatly rejoiced to find that ministers had at length discovered, that it was cheaper for England to lend her money, receiving interest for it upon reproductive works, than upon those useless relief works which were to return no interest and produce no fruit. He greatly rejoiced also to hear from the chancellor of the exchequer, that in the course of the last two months he had become better instructed upon the subject of the number of men to whom the construction of railways would give employment. Lord George Bentinck had proposed to employ one hundred and ten thousand men a year with £6,000,000; but the chancellor of the exchequer then told the house that £6,000,000 laid out in railways would only furnish employment for forty-five thousand labourers. Now the chancellor of the exchequer told the house that £600,000 would employ fifteen thousand labourers; so that upon his calculations, £6,000,000 would afford employment not merely for one hundred and ten thousand, as Lord George Bentinck had stated, but for one hundred and fifty thousand able-bodied labourers. When it suited the purpose of the chancellor of the exchequer, a million of money would give employment to half as many more able-bodied labourers as it could when it suited his purpose to resist a motion proposed by his opponents. Then as to the money market; what was the state of the money market now? Had the government made a proper proposition on this subject four months ago, they could have saved a great portion of that million sterling a month which had been since expended, and was now expending in unproductive labour. 'Let it be remembered, the chancellor of the exchequer argues,' observed Lord George, 'in favour of this measure, that the money he asks for will certainly be paid back, while only one-half, he tells you, of the money advanced on relief works is sought to be reclaimed. Why, sir, that was just my argument three months ago!'

The question was again introduced by the government on the first occasion at their command, namely, Friday the 30th of April, and a long and animated debate ensued. Mr. Roebuck denounced the government scheme. 'The proposition of Lord George Bentinck was at all events not a peddling measure; it was a bold if not wise plan; but the present scheme possessed nothing of the recommendations which attached to that of Lord George Bentinck.' Mr. Osborne 'wished the government had not been deterred by any false pride from taking up the plan of Lord George Bentinck'; even Sir Robert Peel said that 'the measure of Lord George Bentinck was free from some of the objections which forcibly applied to the present measure.'

The chancellor of the exchequer made a statement this night with respect to the employment on the public works, which ought to be preserved. It appeared by his account, that the number of persons employed on the public works in the month of March ('47) was seven hundred and thirty-four thousand. A reduction of twenty per cent. was made at the latter end of that month, which was effected without the least difficulty, and which reduced the number to five hundred and seventy-nine thousand. A further reduction also took place without any difficulty, and another reduction was arranged for the 1st of May, which, when effected, would bring down the number of persons thus employed in Ireland to about two hundred and eighty thousand. It is scarcely necessary to add that the number in March was the maximum number.

After a strong opposition from Sir Robert Peel, and an exulting speech from Lord George Bentinck, the resolution was carried at two o'clock in the morning by a large majority.

In justifying the prudence of the proposed advance in the present financial difficulties, tracing the different influence on the money market of calls for capital to be employed in productive works at home from that which is produced by capital sent out of the country to purchase the produce of other climes, Lord George entered into a calculation to which we may have occasion to advert and which deserves attention. 'It must be clear,' he said, 'to any reflecting man that every sovereign that goes out of this country must operate in a pressure of at least ten-fold, if not twenty-fold degree, more than the sovereign which is borrowed to be expended in this country. I believe it is commonly reckoned that £5 bank notes, upon an average, are turned over thirteen times at least in the course of a year; and if this be so, a sovereign, at all events, must be turned over much oftener than that. The sovereign we send out of the country to purchase corn or sugar, or any other commodity, the produce of foreign countries, cannot return, and does not in fact return for twelve months at the least, and during that time visits no English pocket. Let any one follow in his own mind the course of a sovereign which is sent to America. When shall we get that sovereign back? Certainly not for a year at least. Well, sir, if I am right in these views—and I believe they are those generally entertained by reflecting men—I am justified in saying that a loan of £620,000 to be employed in Ireland would create no greater pressure in the money market, would diminish the circulation of money at home no more than a thirteenth part of that sum were it sent abroad to purchase the produce of foreign countries.'

The government could not succeed in bringing forward the second reading of their bill on Irish railways, which was introduced in pursuance of the resolution of the committee of the whole house of the 30th of April, until so late as the 28th of June, and on the eve of a general election. A strong opposition was arrayed against it, if not in numbers, at least in parliamentary reputation. An amendment that the bill should be read that day three months was moved by Sir William Molesworth in one of those speeches, highly finished and full of thought and information, for which he is distinguished. He said that 'compared with the bill of the government, the scheme of Lord George Bentinck had the outward semblance of a comprehensive and imposing plan. It did at first sight appear not unlike the project of a statesman—a bold and vigorous measure calculated, perhaps, to meet a great and sudden emergency. It had been proposed when there seemed to be a pressing necessity to do something for Ireland; when they were assailed on every side by clamours of distress, by tales of hideous misery and suffering, by begging landlords, by imploring priests, by penitent repealers and agitators, all calling aloud for assistance from England. Then it was supposed that thousands were dying of hunger, that myriads would perish if unassisted. Men were at their wits' ends as to what ought to be done for Ireland, and no two were agreed upon the subject. At that period Lord George Bentinck had stood forward. He had manfully submitted his plan, such as it was, to the house; he supported it by every argument he could think of; it was patiently discussed, without party feeling; his arguments were carefully examined, ably met, and refuted; he was therefore abandoned by half of those whom he had looked upon as his party, and his scheme was rejected by a majority of three to one. After so signal a defeat, who had expected to hear again of the measure of the noble lord ? '

Sir James Graham touched upon the financial condition of the country. The prospects, he said, might be somewhat better than when this subject was last under discussion. The exchanges were not so unfavourable, the drain of bullion seemed to have ceased. But, on the other hand, the importation of corn within the last month had been greater than at any former period of the commercial history of this country. That large importation must be met by payment either in specie, or by export of our manufactures. But co-incident with the extraordinary difficulty of the present moment, the high price of provisions, there was the most unfortunate circumstance of an extraordinary high price of the raw material of the staple article of our manu- facture—cotton. Therefore it was to be anticipated that we should have great difficulty in paying for our food by extending the export of our manufactures; and it was to be apprehended that an export of specie to a considerable extent must even yet take place.

It had been the intention of Lord George Bentinck to move an amendment to the ministerial measure, that all other railways in Ireland similarly situated as those which the government had resolved to assist, should participate in the advantage, but on the assurance of the first minister, that when those railways had put themselves in a position equivalent to that in which the assisted railways stood, namely, paying up half the amount of their subscribed capital, a corresponding advance would be made to them, he relinquished his purpose. Irrespective of a triumphant vindication of his own plan in which he again naturally indulged, he made on this occasion a speech full of novel and interesting details. Referring to some renewed appre- hensions respecting the coming potato crop, he said: 'I am not one of those who apprehend a recurrence of the blight of last year. The potato is a crop of the most delicate and hazardous description, and always has been subject to many calamities. The hot blast which passed over Ireland and England in the month of August last (1846), which in the course of forty-eight hours burnt up the crop of potatoes and deprived the root of its nourishment, bore no resemblance to the rot of the year before. The rot of 1845 did not come in with a hot blast; for it will be remembered that the year '45 was of a very sunless character, and remarkable for wet and cold. The potato rot of '45 was accompanied in all respects by circumstances and characteristics the very opposite from the destruction of last season. The rot of that year came not early in August, but in October; it came upon a crop which preserved its greenness to the latest period; it came partially only upon a crop which was unprecedented not only in the numbers but in the largeness of the bulbs, and bore no more resemblance to the blast of last year than the wire-worm in wheat does to the blight, or the cause of the famine in 1800 to that of 1799, one crop being drowned, and the other burnt up with excessive drought. We hear these accounts to-night from Ireland of a renewal of the potato disease; but recollecting that it is written that "while the earth remaineth, seed time and harvest shall not cease," I for one feel no apprehension of the habitual or frequent return of this extraordinary potato calamity.'

His observations on an opinion then becoming rife that the construction of railways had a tendency to convert floating into fixed capital are very ingenious, and well worthy attention.

'When it is alleged that the effect of this lending money to Irish railways is to destroy the finances of this country, and to convert floating capital into fixed capital, and by thus locking it up make it a permanent pressure upon England, I think far from locking up capital it can be easily shown that the result of these outlays on railways is to set capital at liberty. It is only necessary to calculate the value of the capital engaged in trade which was formerly held in suspense by the slowness of communication, and compare it with the economy effected in these days through the instrumentality and speed of railways in the conveyance of goods. A greater fallacy never existed than the supposition that money laid out in railways is so much fixed capital locked up and lost to the trade of the country. We have £96,000,000 already expended in railways. I believe the gross returns of profit amount to eight millions a year. Of this £5,000,000 is derived from passengers' traffic, and £3,000,000 from goods' traffic. But we have only to look at the ancient charges to find, that over and above the time saved, the cost of passenger-travelling has been reduced at least to one-third, while the carriage of goods, as compared with canal conveyance, has been reduced to one-half. Thus the goods' and passengers' traffic, to which I have referred as having been carried by railroad, at the former rates of land and water carriage, would have come to £21,000,000 instead of £8,000,000 in the last year; and the public gains the difference between these two sums. That proposition no man I think can deny; and as regards the public and the money market, instead of floating capital to the amount of £96,000,000 being converted into locked-up capital, no less than £13,000,000 a year is economised, which reckoning it at 5 per cent. represents £260,000,000. So that far from losing, the public are absolute gainers of £260,000,000 in the economy of the inland traffic and carrying-trade of the country.'

Perhaps the advantages which a community gains by railroads in the saving of their time and money were never illustrated in a more striking manner than by the picture which he presented of their consequences in these respects on the life of an active public servant.

Mr. Robert Weale was twelve years employed as an assistant poor-law commissioner, during which time he travelled in the public service ninety-nine thousand six hundred and seven miles. Sixty-nine thousand of these miles were travelled by the old conveyance, and thirty thousand by railway. By the old mode the cost of travelling was 1s. 6¾d. per mile, and by railway it was only 3¼d.; so that virtually the country saved by the new mode of conveyance five-sixths of the cost of travelling. But the saving of time was still more remarkable. If the whole distance had been performed by railway, it would have occupied one year, thirty weeks, and six days ; if the whole had been performed by the superseded method, it would have occupied four years, thirty-nine weeks, and one day. The result is that three years and nine weeks of Mr. Weale's life would have been saved, while the advantage to the public would have been that the whole cost would only have been £1344, instead of £7735. So that this active public servant would have saved three years and a half of his life, and the country £5390 in his travelling expenses alone.

The bill was read a second time, at one o'clock, by a very large majority.

CHAPTER XXI

WHATEVER may have been the cause of the monetary malady of 1847, one thing is evident, that it was not anticipated by those who would be deemed most competent to form an accurate judgment on such a topic. The ministers themselves were clearly taken by surprise; indeed, with a commendable ingenuousness, they omitted no opportunity of impressing upon the country their astonishment and perplexity. It was clearly with them a state of things which ought not to have occurred, and which must be transient. Never, according to ministers, was trade in a sounder state; commerce legitimate, speculation dormant, stocks low. The disasters terminated by a committee of inquiry into the causes of commercial distress, moved for by the chancellor of the exchequer, who himself drew the report of the committee which represented to the house that one of the causes of this distress was reckless commercial speculation.

On the 1st of March (1847), the government raising a loan of eight millions to meet their Irish expenditure, the contractors of the loan proposed to discount their instalments, which would have immediately placed the exchequer in the possession of ample funds; the ministry confident in their resources rejected at once the proposition. On the 7th of May, the chancellor of the exchequer with an empty treasury had to appeal to parliament for an act to authorise an advance of interest by way of discount for prompt payments on the loan, which he had ultimately to receive on much less advantageous terms than those rejected two months previously.

On the 30th of April, when proposing the vote of money for the construction of Irish railways, the chancellor of the

exchequer alluded to 'the panic and alarm which had prevailed for some days past in the city, and also in several
parts of the country,' and which he gave it as his opinion
to be 'utterly and altogether without foundation.' He said
also on that occasion, 'It is clear that the effort which the
bank of England thought it necessary to make has been
made. It is now over.' Little more than a week after he
was himself in a state of 'panic and alarm' in the house of
commons, proposing for the second time in the course of the
session to raise the rate of interest on exchequer bills, 'as
indispensably necessary for the sake of the credit of the
government.'

Throughout the spring the government repeated their
resolution, amid the cheers of Sir Robert Peel, not to interfere with the provisions of the bank act of 1844; 'they were
more and more convinced by the discussions which took
place upon it of the policy and expediency of maintaining
that act,' although the merchants of London informed them
'that for ten days there was a total want of the means of
obtaining accommodation by the most solvent houses upon
the most undoubted security,' and when not one shilling
could be raised upon £60,000 worth of silver, which was a
legal tender in most parts of the civilised world. Nevertheless, in the autumn of the same year, after houses had fallen
to the amount of £15,000,000, and a reign of terror prevailed,
the governor of the bank representing to the treasury that
he could be no longer responsible for the consequences, the
ministers suddenly changed their resolution and authorised
the directors of the bank to violate the law.

It may be questioned whether Sir Robert Peel and his
followers were more clear and correct in their perception of
the cause of the convulsion. It was Mr. Goulburn who, in
the debate of the 30th of April on the government grant for
Irish railways, first threw out the idea in parliament, that
the 'monetary difficulty' was mainly occasioned by the conversion of the floating capital of the country into fixed
capital, the consequence, as he said, of the extraordinary and
undue prevalence of the railway system. But no persons

were more responsible for the extraordinary and undue prevalence of the railway system than the ministry of Sir
Robert Peel. The speech which most stimulated those
speculations was made in parliament in 1845, by that eminent statesman himself. It encouraged what even in those
riotous days was looked upon with distrust by many—the
reckless construction of competition lines. These sentiments
were repeated by the same minister in not certainly so
august a place, but with circumstances perhaps still more
calculated to influence opinion, when he himself cut the
first sod of one of the most considerable and the most im-
prudent of these undertakings. Sir Robert Peel even as
minister sanctioned a violation of the rules of the house of
commons, and made attendance on railway business compulsory, that no time should be lost in forwarding these
projects: himself too particularly impressing on the youth
of England, some of whom were then beginning to show
symptoms of insubordination, that they should devote
their energies to railway committees and not to empty
rhetoric. Was Sir Robert unaware of the danger of converting floating into fixed capital in 1845 ? If so, it must
be acknowledged as a remarkable want of prescience in a
man of such great capacity, who for forty years one would
have supposed had been meditating on the nature of capital
and currency.

But on the 30th of April ('47), notwithstanding his condemnation of this 'locking up of this floating capital, and
withdrawing it thereby from the manufacture of exportable
articles, leading to a still greater demand for bullion to pay
for the commodities, which we are obliged to import,' Mr.
Goulburn did not appear to apprehend any very grievous
consequences from the process, for he agreed with the
chancellor of the exchequer, that 'the present was an
exaggerated alarm arising from some misconduct on the
part of those to whom the management of the monetary
transactions of this country are committed.' This would
clearly rather hint at an ill-management of currency than
of capital. Sir Robert Peel also threw all the blame upon

the bank; but the bank deals with the currency of the country, not the capital.

The Irish loan was taken on the 1st of March by the two most eminent commercial houses in the world. They of course did not anticipate when they gave 89½ for £100, three per cent. consols, that their scrip within a fortnight would be at a discount, and that the prices of £100 three per cent. consols at the end of April would be 85⅞. Yet was it probable that the contractors for the loan entered into such vast engagements without a due estimate of the amount of floating capital in the monetary world? Is it to be supposed that the effect of investments in railroads had not been narrowly watched and duly considered by individuals habituated to such observations on the most extensive scale? That men with such varied means of information as Mr. Rothschild and so prudent and acute as Mr. Thomas Baring, should have remained in such deplorable ignorance of the resources of the money market?

The seed sown by Mr. Goulburn on the 30th of April was not lost, and on the 10th of May following we find the chancellor of the exchequer, among other ingenuous observations, assuring the house 'on authority upon which he could rely, that the large sum of money which has been advanced on railroad shares has affected to a considerable extent the amount of available capital, which would otherwise have been employed in discounting bills.'

Lord George Bentinck was greatly opposed to this view, that the 'monetary difficulty' was occasioned by investments in railway enterprise. He broke ground upon this head on the night of the 25th of April, when the chancellor of the exchequer made his first and unsuccessful attempt to pass the vote for the Irish railways. Adverting to exchequer bills being then at a discount, when matters, he said, had been brought to such a pass, it might well be asked if this could truly be ascribed to the effect of railway advances, or whether it were not with better foundation to be ascribed to the exportation of gold, which was sent instead of manufactures out of the country, as had always been predicted, to pay for unrestricted imports? Had railway speculation brought exchequer bills to four per cent. discount? The bank of England encountered no such difficulties in August last, when it was freely discounting at 2½ per cent., though railway bills had just then passed parliament, which involved an expenditure of £120,000,000. It was the bank act which was grinding the trade and commerce of the country to dust, by forcing the bank to contract its issues against the wish of the bank directors. It was a fair-weather law not suited to times like these. He advised the government to give the bank directors a proper discretion before thousands of bankrupts came knocking at their doors. On the 30th of April, he followed up the same train of thought, making the calculation which we have noticed as to the number of times capital is turned in a domestic investment compared with a foreign one, and the comparative pressure on the money market of investments for the respective purposes.

It was then also, vindicating the directors of the bank of England from the criticism of the chancellor of the exchequer, he said: 'It is said "corporations have no souls"; I know not how this may be; but if corporations have no souls I am sure cabinets have no hearts.' And then he asked the chancellor of the exchequer if the bank of England had restricted their issues at an earlier period, what would have been the price of his exchequer bills, and still more, what would have been the price at which he would have raised his eight million loan. 'It can be no more right,' he concluded, 'that the bank of England should be tied down beforehand to a particular amount of issues under various circumstances, than it would be right to pass a law obliging ships at all times and in all weathers to carry either studding-sails or tri-sails. By this law we are placed in this extraordinary position, that though trade is in danger of being destroyed for want of the assistance of the bank, and though the bank is most willing and anxious to give trade that assistance, she is shackled by the operation of this law. It is just as though when one strong man were standing on the bank of a river in which another was drowning, the law were to step in and bind the willing and ready arms of him on the bank to make it impossible to save the other who was drowning.'

On the 2nd May he wrote thus to Mr. Ichabod Wright, an eminent country banker and also the accomplished translator of Dante: 'Your "exposition of Sir Robert Peel's bank charter act" puts the matter in a more concise form and in a more clear point of view than anything I have yet heard spoken or seen written.

'If it be not taking too great a liberty, I would venture to ask your opinion of the comparative pressure created upon the money-market here by a million sterling borrowed to be employed in railways in England or Ireland, with that created by a million of sovereigns in gold sent to the United States to pay for corn and cotton, to Cuba, Porto Rico or Bahia, to pay for sugar; or to Odessa for grain, or to St. Petersburg for hemp or tallow.

'I have ventured in the house of commons to assert that a £5 note kept at home is turned over thirteen times upon a rough average in the course of a year, and that assuming this to be anything near the mark as regards a £5 note, a sovereign kept at home would probably change hands twenty times in the same time, whilst a sovereign which goes to the United States, to Brazil, or to Russia, in payment for the produce of those countries, would not find its way back maybe for twelve months or more, whilst under the bank charter act each exported million of sovereigns virtually, by causing them to be withdrawn from circulation, takes a million sterling in bank of England notes upon its back; and from this I argue, that, assuming thirteen as the basis of my calculation, the pressure of each million of sovereigns exported would be equal to that created by twenty-six millions borrowed to be expended in reproductive works, such as railways, drainage, etc., in Great Britain or Ireland.

'Assuming the sovereign employed at home to be turned over twenty times in the course of the year, and the exported sovereign engaged in the purchase of foreign commodities to be absent twelve months, I argue that a million of sovereigns sent to foreign countries with the million in bank notes simultaneously withdrawn under Sir Robert Peel's bank charter act would make money as scarce at home for general purposes as £40,000,000 borrowed to be expended, and expended as soon as borrowed, on domestic works of railway constructions or drainage.

'A right solution of this important question would be a most valuable piece of knowledge, and must plead my excuse for venturing to trouble you and to intrude upon you with the inquiry.

'The first estimate to be made is how often a sovereign employed at home, is turned over in the course of a year.

'The second, how long upon an average, under such circumstances as the present, will it be before the sovereigns weekly exported in payment for corn, cotton, hemp, sugar, and tallow, return home; and thirdly, whether the comparative pressure upon the money market at home may justly be estimated upon this basis.'

On the 7th May, on which day the chancellor of the exchequer made his first formal statement respecting the monetary pressure, preliminary to his proposing on the following Monday his two measures, viz., that the interest on exchequer bills should be raised to 3 per cent., and that the contractors for the loan should have the power of discounting their instalments, Lord George wrote again to the same gentleman.

'I am extremely obliged to you for your letter of Tuesday, which handles the matter with your usual perspicuity.

'Of course any such calculation as that which I asked you to make must necessarily be a very rough and vague estimate; all practical and commercial men whom I have consulted agree with you in thinking that the estimate, that a £5 note is turned over thirteen times, and a sovereign upon an average, when kept at home, twenty times, is underrated. This makes my argument the stronger; it was my wish not to exaggerate, the proposition being in itself a novel and a startling one, and I rejoice to find all whose opinions are worth having are agreed in thinking the basis of my argument is sound.

'There must be an immense number of sovereigns and £5 notes laid by in labourers, mechanics, and little farmers' houses for many weeks for rent. I imagine a large portion of these persons never are at the trouble to put these weekly surplus earnings in any bank, but keep them in a drawer, in their pockets, or in an old stocking; in Ireland in the thatch of their cabins.

'You are quite right: I made an oversight in calculating the notes withdrawn upon the backs, or rather in the retinue of the sovereigns as equal to sovereigns. I forgot they were £5 notes, and not £1 notes.

'This question of the bank charter and the drain of gold to pay for unreciprocated free-trade importations from foreign countries are the subjects which must necessarily engross public attention for the next twelve months.'

We have adverted to the debate of the 10th of May. It was an extremely interesting one. Notwithstanding the renewed assurances of the chancellor of the exchequer, that 'things were easier in the money market than they were,' Lord George Bentinck again attacked the restrictions on the discretion of the directors of the bank of England contained in the act of 1844, and said that unless they at once enabled the government to establish that discretion, he saw greater evils ahead. Illustrating the influence of credit in all monetary transactions, he said: 'I will give an instance of the effect of credit, and the way in which it would be affected by a repeal of the restrictive clause in the bank act. Lately the bank of France and the trade of France were very much in the same predicament as that in which we now are; the bank of France then succeeded in obtaining a loan of £800,000 from this country. Well, no sooner was that known than confidence was restored, and trade revived so much that the bank of France was enabled to forego the last instalment of that loan.'

The most remarkable speech, however, that was made in the course of these debates was that of Mr. Thomas Baring;

viewed both with reference to the point at issue, the discretion of the bank, and to the consequences of our not mitigating the present system. His observations showed in the first place that, as a financier, he had well considered the influence on the money market of all those circumstances which now were alleged by the ultra-bullionists as the causes of its disorder: large foreign imports, domestic speculation, even the mismanagement of the bank. All these, if they had happened now, had happened before; but ' there never had happened before that total want of means upon even the best possible security to meet the pressing engagements of the day which had lately been experienced.' Mr Baring said, ' that he did not know that he should ever be able to answer the question put by Sir Robert Peel " what is a pound ? " but this much he could say, that having for a long time been engaged in commercial affairs, and having rather attentively considered them, he could state what facts were; and he knew that for ten days there was a total want of the means of obtaining accommodation by the most solvent houses upon the most undoubted security, and that because the bank of England by its charter was not permitted to afford it.' He noticed the instance of the possessor of £60,000 of silver, who was unable to obtain the slightest advance upon it. ' They came to the bank to sell and the bank refused to buy.' It was not a question of price with the bank, but a question affecting its own safety. The bank could only issue notes upon silver to the extent of one-fifth of the bullion in the bank. ' But it might be said, " Why not ship the metal to Paris or Hamburg and draw against it ? " But no one had money wherewith to take a bill of exchange. Then it might be said, " Send it and get returns for it." But suppose that bills having a fortnight to run were sent in return to London, they would be refused discount. If such proceedings on the part of this country were not productive of so much inconvenience they would be held up to ridicule by foreign countries.'

It was the opinion of Mr. Baring, that either there should be a discretion placed somewhere, or in a great emergency like the present, when there was a drain of gold to meet an unavoidable want, the bank should have a greater liberty of using its securities for the issue of notes. At present, he showed, the country had exported £7,000,000 in gold, and the property of the country had been depreciated £100,000,000 in value. When they made the interest of money 3 per cent. in August and 13 per cent. in April, they made trade the greatest lottery in the world. It was not because we had eight or ten millions to pay to foreign countries that such an effect ought to be produced upon our commerce as to make our most solid and prudent institutions tremble.

When we consider the position of the speaker, not only as the first merchant of Great Britain but as a director of the very institution whose conduct was called in question, and recall the terrible vicissitudes of the following autumn, there is something very striking when he observed, 'Hitherto there has been a real pressure, but not yet a panic. But there may be a panic, if credit be still refused. Hitherto there has not been a whisper of discredit against the commercial body. But the house must not fancy that their resources have not been disturbed and that great sacrifices have not been made to meet difficulties which have not been of their own creation.'

That panic came, and the ministry took the responsibility of authorising the non-observance of the stern law which had occasioned a financial reign of terror. The law was broken, but after having accomplished awful devastation. The bank act was not planned by men learned in human nature. The passions have something to do even with the mart and the exchange. Mankind is governed by hope and fear; and if a law deprives a community of confidence, the minister will tremble before a nation in despair and will himself violate the enactment which he has been most obstinate to enforce.

CHAPTER XXII

THOSE who throw their eye over the debates of the session of '47 cannot fail to be struck by the variety of important questions in the discussion of which Lord George Bentinck took a leading or prominent part. And it must be borne in mind that he never offered his opinion on any subject which he had not diligently investigated and attempted to comprehend in all its bearings. His opponents might object to his principles or challenge his conclusions, but no one could deny that his conclusions were drawn from extensive information and that his principles were clear and distinct. He spared no pains to acquire by reading, correspondence, and personal research, the most authentic intelligence on every subject in debate. He never chattered. He never uttered a sentence in the house of commons which did not convey a conviction or a fact. He was too profuse indeed with his facts: he had not the art of condensation. But those who have occasion to refer to his speeches and calmly to examine them, will be struck by the amplitude and the freshness of his knowledge, the clearness of his views, the coherence in all his efforts, and often, a point for which he never had sufficient credit, by his graphic idiom.

The best speech on the affairs of Cracow, for example, the most vigorous and the best informed, touching all the points with a thorough acquaintance, was that of Lord George Bentinck. The discussion on Cracow, which lasted several nights and followed very shortly after the defeat of his Irish bill, appeared to relate to a class of subjects which would not have engaged his attention; but on the contrary, he had given days and nights to this theme, had critically examined all the documents, and conferred with those qualified to

supply him with any supplementary information requisite.
He spoke several times this session on questions connected
with our foreign affairs, and always impressed the house
with a conviction that he was addressing it with a due study
of his subject: as, for example, his speech against our interference in Portugal, and the statement in which he brought
forward the claims of the holders of Spanish bonds on the
government of Spain before the house of commons.   In the
instance of Portugal, a motion of censure on the conduct of
ministers had been introduced by Mr. Hume, and the government were only saved from a minority by the friendly interposition of Mr. Duncombe, who proposed an amendment to
the motion of Mr. Hume which broke the line of the liberal
force.   Lord George Bentinck in this case followed Mr.
Macaulay, whose speech, as was his wont, had been rich in
historical illustration.   'The right honourable and learned
member for Edinburgh,' Lord George replied, 'had entered
into a very interesting history of various interferences which
had taken place in the affairs of Portugal; but in making
that statement, he forgot to mention one circumstance which
had occurred in that history; and it was this—that when
Philip ii. of Spain sought to conquer Portugal, the method
he had recourse to for that purpose was one which he thought
her majesty's ministers had successfully practised on the
present occasion—he persuaded the leaders in Portugal to
mix sand with the powder of their troops.   And so, on this
occasion, her majesty's ministers had prevailed on the member for Finsbury, and those other members who were so
ready to profess a love of liberty, to mix sand with their
powder.'

In the last chapter but one we have treated at some length
of the means proposed or adopted by the parliament for the
sustenance and relief of the people of Ireland.   The new
poor law for that country also much engaged the attention
of both houses this session.   Lord George Bentinck took a
very active part in these transactions, and moved the most
important of all the amendments to the government measure,
namely, an attempt to assimilate the poor law of Ireland as

much as possible to that of England, and make the entire rates be paid by the occupying tenant. His object, he said, was to 'prevent lavish expenditure and encourage profitable employment to the people.' This amendment was only lost by a majority of 4.

On the 26th of March, on the government bringing forward their bill on the rum duties, Lord George Bentinck brought before the house the case of the British and Irish distillers, not with any preference or partiality towards English, Scotch, or Irish distillers over the colonial producer. 'I am no advocate of any monopoly whatever. I desire only equal and exact justice between both parties; and the only way in which that end can in my opinion be properly attained is in a select committee upstairs consisting of impartial members of this house.'

He often used to say that no subject ever gave him more trouble thoroughly to master than the spirit duties, and he noticed the character of the theme at the beginning of his speech. He said he required not only the most especial indulgence but even the toleration of the house, 'for of all the dry and dull subjects which could possibly be introduced, the question which it is now my misfortune to bring under the consideration of the house is the driest and the dullest. If this question had been one merely of pounds, shillings, and pence, it would have been dull and complicated enough; but this is a question in which are concerned not pounds and shillings, but pence, and halfpence, and farthings.'

The Whitsuntide holidays occurred at the end of May. It had originally been the intention of Lord George Bentinck, at the request of leading merchants and manufacturers of all parties and opinions, to have brought forward the question of the bank act after these holidays and to move a resolution that some discretionary power should be established as to the issue of notes. He thus alludes to this point in a letter to Mr. Wright of the 24th of May.

'I return you No. 1019 of the Banker's Circular with many thanks.

'This delightful and timely change in the weather will do

wonders for the country, and by producing an abundant and seasonable harvest will save the country and *may save the bank charter act*; but it is pretty well settled that I am to give notice immediately after the holidays of a resolution very much in the spirit of the memorial contained in the paper I am returning to you.

'Things are better in the city and at Liverpool, and with this weather will continue to improve; but it seems to me any reverse in the weather such as would occasion a late and deficient harvest could not fail to bring the commerce of the country to a deadlock.

'The opinion is gaining ground that in the present state not only of Ireland but of many districts in England the government will not venture upon a general election till after the harvest, and not then, unless the harvest should prove favourable.

'I am glad to read your opinion in opposition to Lord Ashburton's that railways keep the gold in the country, and do not send it out. Glyn gave strong evidence last year to this effect before the railway committee.'

Neither of the prospects in this letter was realised. The commercial and manufacturing interest, after the Whitsun recess, thought it advisable for reasons of great weight that Lord George Bentinck should postpone for a month or six weeks his intended motion on the bank charter, and the ministers resolved to dissolve parliament before the harvest; thus it happened that the merchants and manufacturers lost their chance of relief from the yoke, and experienced the reign of terror in the autumn, the terrible events of which ultimately occasioned the assembling of the new parliament in November.

Anticipating the immediate dissolution of parliament, Sir Robert Peel had issued an address to the electors of Tamworth, justifying his commercial policy. In the opinion of Lord George Bentinck it set forth a statement as to the effect and operation of those financial measures which had taken place in the course of the last six years, which if left altogether unrefuted might have a dangerous tendency at the coming elections. The general effect of that statement was, that by the reduction of duties to a large extent it was possible to relieve the people of this country of burdens amounting to more than seven millions and a half sterling with little or no loss whatever to the revenue. But the truth was Sir Robert Peel in his reductions had dealt only with little more than ten millions sterling of the revenue of the country, and had left the remaining thirty-seven millions untouched. Now on that portion of the revenue with which alone he had dealt, there was a deficiency through his changes to the amount of five millions sterling, which loss was compensated by the increase on those very articles which Sir Robert had left untouched. It was the opinion of Lord George Bentinck that the conclusion which Sir Robert Peel had drawn from the comparatively barren results of the increased duties on imports, carried by the whigs in 1840, viz., that indirect taxation had reached its limit, and which was indeed the basis of his new system, was a fallacy, and that the anticipated increase of import duties had not accrued in 1840, in consequence of our having had three successive bad harvests, 'and a bad cotton crop to boot,' all of which had checked the consuming power of the community. Sir Robert Peel had been favoured by three successive good harvests, and nearly £100,000,000 invested in six years in domestic enterprise. 'The interposition of Providence,' said Lord George, 'is never a part of our debates.'

Under these circumstances Lord George took occasion to review the commercial policy of Sir Robert Peel on the 20th July, in the house of commons, only three days before the prorogation, and in one of his most successful speeches. He was much assisted by the fact that the exports of all our staple manufactures had then greatly diminished, and of course he urged this point triumphantly. 'If we had been indemnified for the dead loss of £650,000 on cotton wool by any great impulse given to our manufacturers, it would be a consolation which unfortunately we could not enjoy.' He traced all the consumption to railway enterprise, and showed

that it alone had compensated for the fruitless loss of
revenue, which we had incurred in vainly stimulating the
exports of our manufactures, which had actually diminished.
He was so impressed with the importance that, 'on the eve
of a dissolution, such a statement as that of Sir Robert Peel
should not go forth to the country uncontroverted, as in
that case the necessary result would be that the people
would come to the opinion that they might abolish taxes
altogether and yet maintain the revenue,' that he sat up all
night writing an address to his constituents, the electors of
King's Lynn, which took up nearly two columns of the
newspapers, in which he presented his refutation to the
public of the commercial manifesto of Tamworth, illustrated
by the necessary tables and documents.

There is a sentence in this speech which as a distinct
expression of policy should perhaps be quoted:—

'Sir, I am one of those who seek for the repeal of the
malt tax and the hop duties. I am one of those who think
that the excise duties ought to be taken off. But, sir, I do
not pretend that you can repeal the malt tax, or the hop
duties, or remove the soap tax without commutation for
other taxes. I will not delude the people by pretending
that I could take off more than seven millions and a half of
taxes without replacing them by others, and not leave the
nation bankrupt. But I think these reforms of Sir Robert
Peel have been in a mistaken direction; I think that revenue
duties on all foreign imports ought to be maintained, and
that a revenue equal to those excise duties which I have
mentioned can be levied upon the produce of foreign
countries and foreign industry, without imposing any greater
tax than one which shall fall far short of Mr. Walker's
" perfect revenue standard of 20 per cent." I say that by
imposing a tax far less than 20 per cent. upon all articles of
foreign import, a revenue might be derived far less burden-
some to this country than that of excise, a revenue of which
the burden would be largely shared in by foreign countries,
and in many cases paid altogether by foreign countries.'

Lord George at this time watched with great interest a

novel feature in our commercial transactions. He wrote on the 29th May (1847) to Mr. Burn, the editor of the *Commercial Glance*, and an individual of whose intelligence, accuracy, and zeal he had a high and just opinion, 'Could you inform me how the raw cotton purchased for exportation stands in the first three weeks of the present month of May, as compared with the corresponding periods of '46—5—4—3?

'I observe from a cotton circular sent to me the other day, that seven thousand five hundred bags of cotton had been purchased for exportation between the 1st and 21st of May. If with reduced stocks of raw cotton we are commencing a career of increased exportation, it appears to me to involve very serious consequences for our cotton manufactures, as growing out of the existing monetary difficulties of the manufacturers.

'If you could answer me these queries within the next three or four days, I should feel greatly obliged to you.'

Again, on the 22nd July, on the point of going down to his constituents, he was still pursuing his inquiries in the same quarter. 'I want particularly to compare,' he says to Mr. Burn, 'the export of the last ten weeks of raw cotton with the corresponding ten weeks of '46 and '45, and at the same time to compare the importations and deliveries into the hands of the manufacturers during these same periods.

'Pray address me, Lynn, Norfolk, where I go on Saturday, and shall remain till after my election on Thursday.'

He writes again from Lynn, with great thanks for the information which had been accordingly forwarded to him there. 'Might I ask you to give me an account of the cotton wool imported weekly into Liverpool, and also the quantity sold to dealers, exporters, and speculators in the three corresponding weeks of '45—46.

'This information by return of post would greatly oblige me.'

On the 23rd of July 1847, the last day of the second parliament of Queen Victoria, Lord George went down to the house of commons early, and took the opportunity of making a statement respecting the condition of our sugar-producing colonies, which were now experiencing the consequences of the unjustifiable legislation of the preceding year. He said there were appearances in the political horizon which betokened that he should not be able to obtain a select committee in the present session, and therefore, if he had the honour of a seat in the next parliament, he begged to announce that he would take the earliest occasion to move for a committee to inquire into the present power of our colonies to compete with those countries which have still the advantage of the enforced labour of slaves. The returns just laid upon the table of the house could leave no doubt, he thought, on any man's mind on that point. Since the emancipation, the produce of sugar by the colonies from '31 to '46 had been reduced one-half, and of rum and coffee had been reduced to one-fourth. When the act of last year, which admitted slave-grown sugar, was introduced, the allegation of the English colonies that they could not compete with the labour of slaves was denied. The proof of that allegation was that they were already overwhelmed.

When one recalls all to which this speech led, the most memorable effort of that ardent, energetic life, to which it was perhaps fatal, one can scarcely observe the origin of such vast exertions without emotion.

The under-secretary of state replied to Lord George, making a cry of cheap sugar for the hustings which were before everybody's eyes, but making also this remarkable declaration, that 'the island of Mauritius was in a state of the greatest prosperity.' While Lord George was speaking the cannon were heard that announced the departure of her majesty from the palace.

Then followed a motion of Mr. Bankes about the sale of bread, which led to some discussion. Mr. Bankes threatened a division. Lord Palmerston, who on this occasion was leading the house, said it would be acting like a set of schoolboys, if when the black rod appeared they should be in the lobby instead of attending the speaker to the other house.

But as the members seemed very much inclined to act like schoolboys, the secretary of state had to speak against time on the subject of baking. He analysed the petition, which he said he would not read through, but the last paragraph was of great importance.

At these words the black rod knocked at the door, and duly making his appearance, summoned the house to attend the queen in the house of lords, and Mr. Speaker, followed by a crowd of members, duly obeyed the summons.

In about a quarter of an hour Mr. Speaker returned without the mace, and standing at the table read her majesty's speech to the members around, after which they retired, the parliament being prorogued. In the course of the afternoon the parliament was dissolved by proclamation.

CHAPTER XXIII

THE general election of 1847 did not materially alter the position of parties in the house of commons. The high prices of agricultural produce which then prevailed naturally rendered the agricultural interest apathetic, and although the rural constituencies from a feeling of esteem again returned those members who had been faithful to the protective principle, the farmers did not exert themselves to increase the number of their supporters. The necessity of doing so was earnestly impressed upon them by Lord George Bentinck, who warned them then that the pinching hour was inevitable, but the caution was disregarded, and many of those individuals, who are now the loudest in their imprecations on the memory of Sir Robert Peel, and who are the least content with the temperate course which is now recommended to them by those who have the extremely difficult office of upholding their interests in the house of commons, entirely kept aloof, or would smile when they were asked for their support with sarcastic self-complacency, saying, ' Well, sir, do you think after all that free trade has done us so much harm?' Perhaps they think now, that if they had taken the advice of Lord George Bentinck and exerted themselves to return a majority to the house of commons, it would have profited them more than useless execrations and barren discontent. But it is observable, that no individuals now grumble so much as the farmers who voted for free traders in 1847, unless indeed it be the shipowners, every one of whom for years, both in and out of parliament, supported the repeal of the corn laws.

The protectionists maintained their numbers, though they did not increase them, in the new parliament. Lord George

Bentinck, however, gained an invaluable coadjutor by the reappearance of Mr. Herries in public life, a gentleman whose official as well as parliamentary experience, fine judgment and fertile resource, have been of inestimable service to the protectionist party. The political connection which gained most were the whigs; they were much more numerous and compact, but it was in a great measure at the expense of the general liberal element, and partly at the cost of the following of Sir Robert Peel. The triumphant conservative majority of 1841 had disappeared, but the government with all shades of supporters had not an absolute majority.

Had the general election been postponed until the autumn, the results might have been very different. That storm, which had been long gathering in the commercial atmosphere, then burst like a typhoon. The annals of our trade afford no parallel for the widespread disaster and the terrible calamities. In the month of September fifteen of the most considerable houses in the city of London stopped payment for between five and six millions sterling. The governor of the bank of England was himself a partner in one of these firms; a gentleman who had lately filled that office was another victim; two other bank directors were included in the list. The failures were not limited to the metropolis, but were accompanied by others of great extent in the provinces. At Manchester, Liverpool, and Glasgow large firms were obliged to suspend payments. This shock of credit arrested all the usual accommodation, and the pressure in the money market, so terrible in the spring, was revived. The excitement and the alarm in the city of London were so great, that when the chancellor of the exchequer hurried up to town on the 1st of October he found that the interest of money was at the rate of 60 per cent. per annum. The bank charter produced the same injurious effect as it had done in April; it aggravated the evil by forcing men to hoard. In vain the commercial world deplored the refusal of the government to comply with the suggestion made by Lord George Bentinck and Mr.

Thomas Baring in the spring; in vain they entreated them at least now to adopt it, and to authorise the bank of England to enlarge the amount of their discounts and advances on approved security without reference to the stringent clause of the charter.   The government, acting it is believed with the encouragement and sanction of Sir Robert Peel, were obstinate, and three weeks then occurred during which the commercial credit of this country was threatened with total destruction.   Nine more considerable mercantile houses stopped payment in the metropolis; the disasters in the provinces were still more extensive.   The royal bank of Liverpool failed; among several principal establishments in that town, one alone stopped payment for upwards of a million sterling.   The havoc at Manchester was also great. The Newcastle bank and the north and south Wales bank stopped.   Consols fell to 79¼, and exchequer bills were at last at 35 per cent. discount.   The ordinary rate of discount at the bank of England was between 8 and 9 per cent., but out of doors accommodation was not to be obtained.   In such a state of affairs, the small houses of course gave way. From their rising in the morning until their hour of retirement at night, the first lord of the treasury and the chancellor of the exchequer were employed in seeing persons of all descriptions, who entreated them to interfere and preserve the community from universal bankruptcy. 'Perish the world, sooner than violate a principle,' was the philosophical exclamation of her majesty's ministers, sustained by the sympathy and the sanction of Sir Robert Peel. At last, the governor and the deputy-governor of the bank of England waited on Downing Street and said it could go on no more.   The Scotch banks had applied to them for assistance. The whole demand for discount was thrown upon the bank of England.   Two bill-brokers had stopped; two others were paralysed.   The bank of England could discount no longer. Thanks to the bank charter they were safe and their treasury full of bullion, but it appeared that everybody else must fall, for in four-and-twenty hours the machinery of credit would be entirely stopped.   The position was frightful and the government gave way. They did that on the 25th of October, after houses had fallen to the amount of fifteen millions sterling, which they had been counselled to do by Lord George Bentinck on the 25th of April. It turned out exactly as Mr. Thomas Baring had foretold. It was not want of capital or deficiency of circulation which had occasioned these awful consequences. It was sheer panic occasioned by an unwisely stringent law. No sooner had the government freed the bank of England from that stringency than the panic ceased. The very morning the letter of licence from the government to the bank of England appeared, thousands and tens of thousands of pounds sterling were taken from the hoards, some from boxes deposited with bankers, although the depositors would not leave the notes in their bankers' hands. Large parcels of notes were returned to the bank of England cut into halves, as they had been sent down into the country; and so small was the real demand for an additional quantity of currency, that the whole amount taken from the bank, when the unlimited power of issue was given, was under £400,000, and the bank consequently never availed itself of the privilege which the government had accorded it. The restoration of confidence produced an ample currency, and that confidence had slowly been withdrawn from the apprehension of the stringent clauses of the bank charter act of 1844.

These extraordinary events had not occurred unnoticed by Lord George Bentinck. The two subjects that mostly engaged his attention after the general election were the action of the bank charter and the state of our sugar colonies. Perhaps it would be best to give some extracts from his correspondence at this period. He was a good letter-writer, easy and clear. His characteristic love of details also rendered this style of communication interesting. It is not possible to give more than extracts, and it is necessary to omit all those circumstances which generally in letter-reading are most acceptable. His comments on men and things are naturally free and full, and he always endeavoured for the amusement of his correspondents to communicate the social gossip of the hour. But although all this must necessarily be omitted his letters may afford some illustrations of his earnestness and energy, the constancy of his aim and the untiring vigilance with which he pursued his object—especially those which are addressed to gentlemen engaged in commercial pursuits who co-operated with him in his investigations.

To a Friend.

HARCOURT HOUSE, *August* 30, 1847.

An answer is come out to my address to my constituents at King's Lynn, and to my speech in answer to Peel's manifesto. Pray read it. At first I thought I could swear to its being ****. I now think I can swear to its being ****; the servility to Peel, and the official red-tape style would equally do for either; but the no popery page I think fixes it on ****.

I think it wretchedly weak, and have written some notes on the margin, showing up the principal points. The nine months' famine of 1846-47 as contrasted with Peel's famine, shows a difference of between £6,000,000 and £7,000,000; that is to say, on the balance in the nine months 1845-46, Ireland exported about three millions' worth of breadstuffs, and not a soul died of famine. In the nine months, 1846-47, she imported three millions' sterling worth of breadstuffs, which insufficed to prevent one million—or say half a million—of the people from dying of starvation.

At present I have seen no notice of the pamphlet in any of the newspapers: if it is either ****'s, or ****'s, or ****'s, we shall see it reviewed in *Times, Chronicle*, and *Spectator*.

The bank of England have raised the interest on ****'s mortgage one-third per cent., making an additional annual charge of £1500 a year to him. I am very sorry for him, but I know nothing so likely to rouse the landed aristocracy from their apathy and to weaken their idolatry of Peel so much, as this warning note of the joint operation of his free trade and restrictive currency laws.

To a Friend.

HARCOURT HOUSE, *September* 2, 1847.

I think it is ****.   The trickster, I observe, has carefully reduced the pounds of cotton to cwts., in the hopes of concealing a great fraud to which he has condescended; taking, in the whig year of 1841, the home consumption of cotton, whilst in Peel's year he gives entire importation as the home consumption, representing both as home consumption.

In Peel's year, 1846, officially we have only the gross importation; but in the whig year, 1841, the entire importation and the home consumption are given separately : the importation exceeding the home consumption by fifty million pounds.   Burn's *Glance*, however, gives the importation and home consumption for both years—unfortunately, however, not in lbs. or cwts., but in bags. ****'s fraud, however, is not the less apparent.   These are the figures :—

		Imported.	Consumed at Home.
		Bags.	Bags.
1840		1,599,343	1,274,729
1841	. . Whig years . .	1,341,659	1,118,717
1842		1,384,894	1,221,693
1843		1,556,982	1,357,662
1844	. . Peel's years . .	1,479,331	1,427,482
1845		1,855,660	1,577,617
1846		1,243,706	1,561,232

So that he selects a whig year when the home consumption was 220,000 bags under the importation, and a year for Peel when the importation exceeded the home consumption by 280,000 bags, and claps down the figures as alike describing the home consumption.

None of the Peel papers have taken up the subject—if they should the *Morning Post* will answer the pamphlet; but I should like to have mine back again in order that I may furnish them with the notes.

**** was with me this morning, and called my attention to the circumstance that the author starts with 'We,' but drops into the singular number; **** fancies it is Peel himself, but the page on endowment fixes it on *****.

Lord L**** means, I presume, that Peel's savage hatred is applied to the protectionist portion of his old party, not of course to the janissaries and renegade portion.

The following letter was in reply to one of a friend who had sent him information, several days before they occurred, of the great failures that were about to happen in the city of London. The list was unfortunately quite accurate, with the exception indeed of the particular house respecting which Lord George quotes the opinion of Baron Rothschild.

To a Friend.

WELBECK, *September* 17, 1847.

A thousand thanks for your letter, the intelligence in which created a great sensation at Doncaster.

As yet none of the houses appear to have failed except S****. Baron Rothschild was at Doncaster. I talked with him on the subject; he seemed not to doubt the probable failure of any of the houses you named, except ******. He declared very emphatically 'that ****** house was as sound as any house in London.'

Lord Fitzwilliam declares 'it is no free trade without free trade in money.'

Lord Clanricarde is here—laughs at the idea of parliament meeting in October; but talks much of the difficulties of Ireland—says he does not see how the rates are to be paid.

Messrs. Drummond are calling in their mortgages. I expect to hear that this practice will be general; money dear, corn cheap, incumbrances enhanced, and rents depressed, what will become of the apathetic country gentlemen? I judge from *******'s language that Lord John Russell will stand or fall by the bank charter act; but that he feels very apprehensive of being unable to maintain it.

I agree with Bonham in thinking that the protectionist party is smashed for the present parliament; but I must say I think protectionist principles and policy are likely to come into repute again far sooner than was expected; and though Peel's party be a compact body and formidable in the house of commons, I cannot think that there appears that in the working of his measures to make it likely that he should be soon again carried into power on the shoulders of the people. I think his political reputation must ebb further before it can rise again, if it should ever rise again. ****** thought him 'broken and in low spirits' when he met him at Longshaw; but Lord ***** who was there at the same time came away more Peelite than ever, and told them at Bretby that Sir Robert said, 'That he was quite surprised at the number of letters he got every day from members returned to parliament, saying they meant to vote with him.'

You may rely upon it the Peelites are very sanguine that they will be in power again almost directly. We must keep them out.

To Mr. Burn, Editor of the *Commercial Glance*.

WELBECK, *September* 28, 1847.

To the many courtesies you have already bestowed upon me, I will sincerely thank you to add that of informing me what have been the estimated cotton crops in the United States in each of the last four years. I would also thank you to inform me the comparative importation, home consumption, re-exportation, and stocks on hand of cotton of the first seven months of the current and three preceding years.

To Mr. Burn.

WELBECK, *October* 4, 1847.

Your statistics have reached me in the very nick of time, and are invaluable. I care nothing about 'outsides,' it is 'insides' I look to; give me a good 'heart,' and I don't care how rough the '*bark*' is.

Anything so good I fear to spoil by suggesting the most trivial addition, else I should say it would be an interesting feature to classify the exports of cotton goods, etc. etc., under three heads :

1st. To the British colonies and British possessions abroad.

2nd. To the northern States of Europe, France, Spain, Germany,

Italy, etc. etc. The United States of America, and other countries having high tariffs.

3rd. To China, Turkey, Africa, and the southern States of America, and countries with low tariffs.

I fear these failures of East and West India houses must entail great distress upon Manchester, and the manufacturing interests generally. You have given an account of the bankruptcies in the cotton trade during a long series of years till last year inclusive; are you able to say how the first nine months of the current year stands in comparison with its predecessors?

I so highly prize your new work that I must ask for a dozen copies to distribute among my friends.

PS.—I have already parted with the copy you sent me; may I therefore beg another without waiting for any other binding.

To a Friend.

WELBECK, *October* 5, 1847.

I shall go up to town on Friday evening, in my way to Newmarket, and shall be at Harcourt House all Saturday and Sunday, and shall be delighted to see you, and have a thorough good talk with you. Free trade seems working mischief faster than the most fearful of us predicted, and Manchester houses, as I am told, 'failing in rows,' ashamed to do penance in public are secretly weeping in sackcloth and ashes, and heartily praying that Peel and Cobden had been hanged before they were allowed to ruin the country.

Money at Manchester is voted one and a quarter per cent. for ten days: £45, 12s. 6d. per cent. per annum!

To a Friend.

HARCOURT HOUSE, *October* 22, 1847.

I have this moment got a note from Stuart, telling me that 'the chancellor has this afternoon sent out his notice of the business to be taken in his own court during Michaelmas term, that is, from the 2nd of November till the 26th, and *below it* THERE IS THIS NOTICE—*except those days on which the lord chancellor may sit in the house of lords ! ! !* '

Surely this must portend a November session.

To a Friend.

Harcourt House, *October* 23, 1847.

The fat banker's gossip is all stuff. Peel goes to Windsor to-day, I believe on an invitation of some standing. *****, who had been dining at Palmerston's last night, tells me that he does not think that ministers mean calling parliament together, and is confident they mean to maintain the bank charter act. There have been some first-rate articles and letters in the *Morning Chronicle* lately on this subject.

To a Friend.

Harcourt House, *November* 6, 1847.

I will stay over Tuesday that I may have the pleasure of a thorough talk with you.

I am told things are gradually getting better. I expect, however, a fresh reverse about six weeks or two months hence, when the returned lists of the stoppages in the East and West Indies, consequent upon the late failures here, come home. The western bank of Scotland is whispered about. If that were to fail, it might bring the canny Scots to their senses; but they are a head-strong race.

To Mr. Burn.

Harcourt House, *November* 11, 1847.

I thank you for your very valuable information, which presents a frightful picture of the cotton trade, unless as winter (the season for warm clothing) approaches, the exports of cotton goods, as a matter of course, concede their place to woollens; but this should not affect India and China. It may be, however, that July and August are always great months of exports, which diminish in September, and fall off still more extensively in October.

If it were not trespassing too much upon your time and courtesy, I would ask you for the comparative accounts of 1844, '45, and '46. The report you have sent me does not include Europe. The exports to the north of Europe have, I presume, ceased for the winter; but the south of Europe, France, Belgium,

Holland, and Germany, remain open to our trade. How shows the picture of the trade with those countries?

The foreign West Indies alone display a flattering result of trade; but the falling off in the trade to the United States, unless it be accounted for by the approach of winter, seems otherwise quite unaccountable, considering the unprecedented importations of produce from that country. The opening of the sugar trade with the foreign West Indies, and the transfer of the sugar trade from the East Indies, Mauritius, and British West Indies, to Cuba and Brazil, would naturally account for the increase of exports to the foreign West Indies; but why has not the same rule favourably affected the trade with the United States in the same way? Is it the high protective tariff of the United States, or is it that money being scarce and dear in England, and comparatively plentiful and cheap in the United States, the American manufacturers having stepped into the vacated shoes of British capitalists, are now beating us with our old weapons? We used to beat the world by means of our superior and commanding capital. The unfavourable balance of trade has transferred our capital to the other side of the Atlantic. Are American mill-owners successfully setting up rival factories with £7,000,000 of English gold? I fear it looks like it.

Another important and lamentable circumstance in the report you send me is the increased export, in the face of diminished stocks and diminished home consumption, of raw cotton; to which it would appear that the further misfortune seems to be added of an enormous export at a loss. I make out that in the course of the present year one hundred and seventeen thousand nine hundred and forty bales of raw cotton, or thereabouts, have been exported under a continuance of falling prices, and of prices lower at Liverpool than at New Orleans. If I am right in this conjecture, and that the loss averages but $\frac{1}{2}$d. per pound, the Liverpool merchants must this year have lost on this portion of their trade full £120,000, sacrificed to the advantage of the foreigner, to operate hereafter absolutely as a bounty upon foreign manufactures. Am I right or am I wrong in this surmise, and the conclusion I come to upon it?

My Liverpool correspondents assure me that at this moment they are selling 1$\frac{1}{2}$d. below the price at New Orleans, and 2d. per pound below the *actual cost price!* If this, however, be not an exaggerated view of the present doings, I presume it would certainly not afford any correct view of the average transactions of the year as regards the export of raw cotton.

Without giving yourself too much trouble, could you ascertain for me the comparative expenditure for the relief of the poor in Manchester in the first weeks respectively of November 1826, 1838, 1840, 41, 42, 43, 44, 45, 46, and 47. I should like also very much to know what number of persons are employed in Manchester in the construction of locomotive engines and railway carriages, and the existing state of that trade as regards prosperity or slackness. A great cry is raised for the stoppage of railway works; but it does seem to me that if one hundred thousand railway navigators were thrown out of work, and the manufacture of locomotives and railway carriages was to be proportionably diminished, not only a great branch of the home consumption of Manchester goods would be disabled, but there would be too much reason to fear another great class of operatives would be thrown out of work, and upon the poor rates of Manchester, even in aggravation of the existing and appalling distress.

If it is not too much abusing your willing courtesy, I should like very much to be practically instructed on the various points on which I have treated in this letter. One other point I would inquire about. It is this. How are the goods exported to the British West Indies and to the East Indies in October to be paid for, the East India and West India bills having all gone back dishonoured? It seems to me the mischief will not be over till we hear what has been the fate of these consignments to the British colonies in East and West Indies.

Canada's 'time' too must be near at hand. Her flour trade superseded by that of New York, and her timber beaten down in price by that of the Baltic, she will be placed in very much the same position with the Mauritius and Dominica. I always expected the sugar-planting colonies would fall first, and I placed the British Canadas second, the recoil of their ruin falling upon Manchester and the West Riding of Yorkshire. I scarcely expected that the manufacturing interests would take precedence in the march of ruin of the British colonies and British agriculture. This last has been saved for a time by the potato failure in Ireland. A couple of years more of favourable harvests over the world will bring the English corn grower into the condition of the

British sugar planter. Then will follow the diminished home consumption of British manufactures in the track of colonial export. And then will come such a state of things as every man who loves England may well shudder to think of. The strong convictions I have on this subject must plead my excuse to you for presuming to tax your time, which I know is your income and fortune, by asking you for so much information.

To a Friend.

WELBECK, *November* 14, 1847.

I estimate the rise of one and a half per cent. in the interest of money as equivalent to an increased annual charge upon the land alone of the three kingdoms of £12,000,000 at the lowest, and taking houses, mills, mines, trade, and commerce, £25,000,000 at the least, to be annually transferred from the land, house, and mineral property, the trade, commerce, and manufactures of the country, to the monied interest—to the money-changers and usurers—to Jones Lloyd, Peel and Co. This must be well scrutinised, and if it bears examination, it must be constantly dinned into the ears of the British people.

I send you back John Manners's sensible and spirited letter. I am low-spirited for want of such comrades in arms as this very John Manners. I am low-spirited at seeing the party occupying itself about the admission or exclusion of an individual from parliament, at a moment when the greatest commercial empire of the world is engaged in a life and death struggle for existence. It is tea-table twaddling, more becoming a pack of old maids than a great party aspiring to govern an empire upon which the sun never sets.

I think the East and West India question must prove a puzzle for the government—Lord Grey's government bank in the Mauritius, with his 10s. assignats! The Mauritius fed by the government, and the West Indies in no better plight, will bring the country to its senses.

In consequence of the government having authorised the infringement of a law, the new parliament was summoned to meet on the 8th of November. The choice of a speaker and the swearing in of members occupied the house of commons until the 23rd, when a speech by command of her majesty was delivered by the lords commissioners. It was the wish of Lord George Bentinck that there should be an amendment to the address with reference to the bank charter, but amendments to the address are generally so unfortunate, and the effort of the protectionist part in this respect in the last session of the late parliament not having proved an exception to the rule, he was dissuaded from the attempt, which he always very much regretted. He took the opportunity, however, of bringing forward the condition of the country in a comprehensive speech.

He said that 'so gloomy a speech had never been made by any sovereign to her people as that which they were then considering'; that the disappointment of the country would be bitter if the address to the crown were assented to without a full explanation by the government of all the circumstances which led to their letter of licence to the bank of England. In an early period of the last session of the late parliament, the chancellor of the exchequer, in bringing his financial budget before the house, pronounced a high eulogium on the bank charter act. The house would recollect that the chancellor was loudly called upon in the spring by many on the opposition benches, by a petition from the merchants of London, and by various petitions from the merchants and manufacturers of almost every city throughout England and Scotland to relax the restrictions of that act, but the answer of the chancellor of the exchequer was that the worst was over, and though it had been the intention of Lord George Bentinck to have moved the repeal or the mitigation of that act, the unexpected announcement of an early dissolution of parliament left no time for such a course. It would also be recollected that towards the end of September, a deputation from Newcastle waited on the chancellor of the exchequer at a period when already the value of the property of the houses that had failed in London, Liverpool, and Glasgow approached nearly ten millions sterling, that they, foreseeing that increased difficulties were coming, applied to the government to remove this bank restriction which made it difficult to get the best bills discounted. The answer of the chancellor of the exchequer was, that he could not be expected to guard against the consequences of over trading and over speculation, and that everybody knew there was no undue pressure in the money market as regarded houses on good credit. This at the very time when exchequer bills were at 25 per cent. discount, when the power of the bank of England to continue its payments began to be doubted, when among the houses in bad credit was the exchequer office itself, whose bills ultimately went down to 40 per cent. discount. But still the government was obdurate. On the 19th of October another deputation from Liverpool. What said the first minister to them? Why, that he gave them no hopes. Time went on. Suddenly on Saturday the 23rd of October certain bankers from the city of London called at the treasury, and then, when houses to the amount of nearly fifteen millions sterling had fallen, the government changed their minds, and did that which they had hitherto peremptorily refused to do. Why did they change their minds? What were the immediate causes that induced them at this particular period to give way, which they refused to do at three earlier periods, when, if they had been more conceding, they might have warded off a very large portion of this distress and disaster? The house had a right to know why the government had postponed so long this urgent measure of relief.

It cannot be denied that this was a very legitimate question, though one probably not very easy to answer. On the present occasion the first minister made a general reply to Lord George Bentinck's ‘song of triumph over the calamities of the country,’ and denied that he had made out any connection between our existing distress and our currency laws and new commercial system. The minister gave notice that on the 30th instant the whole question of our commercial and monetary position would be brought forward by the chancellor of the exchequer. The speech from the throne gave a prominent place to this topic and a full discussion of it could not be evaded.

Accordingly, on the appointed day the chancellor of the exchequer, in a very able and argumentative statement, which lasted two hours and a half, reviewed the past transactions of the year and vindicated the policy of the government. The proposition of the ministry was a secret committee to inquire into the causes of the recent commercial distress, and how far it had been affected by the laws for regulating the issue of bank notes payable on demand. Unhappily, Lord George Bentinck, who was prostrate from illness, could not be present during this important debate of three days, but the views of those who attributed to the bank charter an aggravating influence over the recent disasters were vindicated by Mr. Thomas Baring, in a speech which may be safely referred to as containing the essence of the question conveyed in the most popular form. An abstruse subject was never put before an assembly in a more practical and animated style. Mr. Baring was opposed to a committee of inquiry into the bank act: 'Why,' he exclaimed, 'the country has already sat as a committee upon it. The pressure and the suffering endured by the country were the witnesses, and the letter of the 25th of October was all the report that was necessary.'

The strongest condemnation of the act according to Mr. Baring was that it had not prevented the crisis; that it had not checked it after it had occurred; and that an infringement of its provisions had become absolutely necessary. 'What the commercial body wished to know was, if the power which had lately been exerted on their behalf would never be exerted again till ruin was complete.' Without the bill of 1844, he said very truly, there was ample power in the bank of England to save itself and its gold, while it spread desolation around. The severest criticism on the stringency of the act was the success of the trifling measure of relaxation.

To Mr. Burn.

Harcourt House, *November* 25, 1847.

It seems to me that your invaluable Glance at the Cotton Trade affords a complete and effective key to the inquiry : what is the sum of money England receives from foreign countries in each year for converting the raw material into yarn, and into every other description of cotton goods ?   Yarn is a very simple affair ; it is only adding 11 per cent. for waste to the weight of the yarn, which gives the amount of the raw cotton consumed.   Having ascertained the amount consumed of raw cotton, nothing remains but to multiply the pounds of raw cotton by the price of cotton in each year, and deduct the product from the declared value of yarn exported, and the remainder gives the money paid by foreign countries to England for working up the raw cotton into yarn. Getting at the payment to England for the manufacture of calicoes, cambrics, etc. etc., is rather more complicated, but still very simple.

Take for example 1844.   Page 7 gives the price of plain calicoes, viz., 6s. 6d. per piece, as well as the weight of each piece, which appears to be 5 lbs. 12 oz.   Add to this eleven per cent. for waste in working the raw cotton originally into yarn, and we get at the entire weight of the raw cotton wrought up into plain calicoes.

The price of raw cotton is given in another page as 4d. in 1844. The weight in cotton multiplied by the price gives the money value of the raw material consumed in the manufacture of each article each year, and deducting in each case the value of the raw material from the declared value of the several manufactured articles exported, in the difference we learn what England in each year received from the foreigner as a recompense to our manufacturers and working men for converting the raw material into the manufactured article.   I have set on an accountant to make this statement out up to 1846 inclusive.   If you could make it out for me for the first ten months of the present year it would be a great service.

Enclosed I send you a rough calculation I have made as regards yarn for three years.   You will observe that England's profit, in 1844, on working up 144,000,000 lbs. of raw cotton into yarn, to sell to the foreigner, exceeded by £280,000 her profit in 1846, in working up 174,000,000 lbs. I have to thank you for your communications of to-day. As yet I have not had a moment to look into them, but I doubt not they will be very valuable.

To Mr. Wright, of Nottingham.

HARCOURT HOUSE, *November* 26, 1847.

We are to settle on Monday what course we are to take in regard to the bank charter act.

I believe we shall decide upon a motion to suspend the act until the committee have reported.

I wish you would publish a new edition of your old pamphlet, reviewing the late occurrences and disasters. I can only say that I never fairly understood the question until I read your former pamphlet.

To Mr. Burn.

HARCOURT HOUSE, *November* 27, 1847.

Enclosed I send you an extract from a letter I have this morning received from Mr. Haywood, of Liverpool. Pray consider it. He appears to estimate the loss on stock on hand much higher than you do, but to ascribe no loss to the sales prior to the 17th of September, though he does not mention the subject in any way.

I will to-morrow send you the entire table of cotton exports made out as I suggested in my letter of yesterday.

To Mr. Burn.

HARCOURT HOUSE, *November* 28, 1847.

I have only got your plain and printed calicoes made out, which I send you for your observations and future use if you think the table a valuable one. It shows that all is not gold that glitters, and that the profit to England can be very ill appreciated by an imposing array of figures, showing the declared value of the exports. England received £4,000,000 sterling more in 1845, and £3,000,000 sterling more in 1844, for manufacturing a less quantity of cotton than she did in 1846, and within £400,000 as much in 1836 as she did in 1846 for working up three-fifths of the quantity made in 1846.

I will send you the other items as soon as they are made out for me. If you supply me with the first nine or ten months of this year the account would be of still greater interest.

To Mr. Burn.

HARCOURT HOUSE, *November* 29, 1847.

Accompanying I send you the remainder of the cotton exports dissected. Altogether they will form a most curious statistical table, showing how much work England did in 1846 for very little profit. How have prices been in the home market? Does the foreign market govern the home prices, or *vice versâ*? Do the two markets keep level, or having to a certain extent a protected home market and a taxed foreign market, are our manufacturers enabled to obtain a better price in the home than they are unfortunately obtaining in the foreign market?

The statement you furnished me with as regards the loss of British merchants on cotton seems to have made a considerable sensation. Your member, Mr. W. Brown, and I believe Mr. M'Gregor, both assured Sir Charles Wood that £380,000 was the utmost of the loss sustained.

I understand Mr. Brown has been told a different story through his Liverpool correspondents. He has been told I was under the mark.

To Mr. Burn.

HARCOURT HOUSE, *December* 1, 1847.

It is fortunate indeed I sent the statement to you for inspection. The blunder of the accountant employed was quite inexcusable, as he had your book before him. Page 23 was pointed out to him. He had previously been employed to get at the money value of cotton imported from the United States, through table page 23, and had done so, and then he goes to work stupidly on page 13 !!! It is very provoking. I was myself confined to my bed with illness, and trusted to his work being faithfully done, and did not try the basis of the calculation by the test of comparing his price column of cotton with your prices in page 23. I have now set him to do his work over again, and when complete I will send it to you.

It is very satisfactory to find that the fidelity of the picture I drew of the state of trade, and especially of the cotton trade, is sanctioned by those best acquainted with it. For that part of it which has most struck and surprised the mind of the mercantile community, the statement with regard to England's loss on cotton in 1847, I am entirely indebted to you.

Your rough notes of the loss on raw cotton made here were pretty much what you now estimate it at, but then there was an unknown quantity to be deducted on account of American consignments. This we understood to be 'certainly less than 30 per cent.' That I might be safe from any charge of exaggeration, I assumed it to be one-third, and so I called the loss upwards of £2,000,000 to British merchants. What the Americans lose is no concern of ours ; in fact, in such transactions their loss is our gain.

To Mr. Burn.

Harcourt House, *December* 4, 1847.

The slave-grown sugar admission bill passed, I think, on the 18th of August last year. If you could furnish me with a statement of the exports of cotton goods, with their money value, from the 10th of September 1846 to the 10th of November 1847, to Cuba, Porto Rico, and the Brazils on the one side, and to Bombay, Calcutta, Madras, the Mauritius, and the British West Indies on the other, as compared with the exports to these same countries in the corresponding period of 1845-46, I should be more obliged to you than I can express.

Mr. Heywood, your member, has challenged me to show that England has not gained by the transfer of the sugar trade from her own colonies to the foreigners, and I have accepted his challenge, relying upon your kindness to procure me the information. The return you last sent me for the month ending November this year, as compared with the corresponding month last year, is what I want, only extended to the period I have before named, and with the money value added.

I bring forward my motion on Thursday.

To Mr. Burn.

HARCOURT HOUSE, *December* 7, 1847.

I know not how sufficiently to thank you for your enthusiastic zeal and devotion in my service.

Had your labours on my account been limited to work by day, I should have felt myself ill able enough to thank you for your exertions. When the night as well as the day are sacrificed by you on my account, I am utterly at a loss to find words to express how highly I appreciate such extraordinary devotion.

To Mr. Burn.

HARCOURT HOUSE, *December* 10, 1847.

In consequence of Lord John's illness I was obliged to postpone my motion last night.

Your return is admirable, fulfils every expectation I entertained of it, and will be invaluable in the house. How it proves the folly of letting slip an old customer in the vain hope of obtaining a better. So completing the old fable.

Can you make out how many bankruptcies or failures there have been in the cotton trade up to the present time ?

You wrote to me that between the 1st of September and the 7th of November sixteen firms, consisting of forty partners, had failed in the cotton trade. This I presume included Glasgow and Paisley, or do you restrict yourself to England ?

PS.—Since writing the foregoing it occurs to me that these will be held to be a flaw in my case. I have got in this comparative return the two months from the 12th of September to the 10th of November 1846, twice over ! And it will be objected to my return that on this account it is no fair comparison at all. My opponents will at once say (whether true or not) your return of 1845-46 owes its magnitude entirely to those very two months of 1846, which were the two first months of the admission of slave-grown sugar. If therefore it were not too unreasonable, I would ask you to pick out of the return of 1845-46 the two months from the 12th of September to the 10th of November, and to insert instead the two months of 1845, commencing with the 12th of July and ending the 12th of September. Then no one can say a word against the return, and a most valuable one it will be.

To Mr. Wright, of Nottingham.

December 12, 1847.

I was sorry to miss you as you passed through London. I was laid up, confined to my bed with the influenza, when you called. You will have seen Herries' motion. It seems to meet pretty general concurrence from those opposed to the bank charter act, but parliament will be adjourned next Friday, I hear, till the end of January, so Herries' motion will not come on till after the recess; in short, some time the first week in February. I rather fear we have missed our opportunity. We ought to have moved an amendment to the address. The immediate pressure of the bank charter act's restrictions having passed away, the iron which was hot and malleable is fast growing cold and callous.

To Mr. Burn.

Harcourt House, *December* 30, 1847.

You must begin to think me very ungrateful for your extraordinary exertions on my behalf. The truth is an immense press of business and illness together have thrown me terribly into arrear.

I now stand positively to come on with my East and West India and Mauritius motion on Thursday the 3rd of February. If you could make up for me by that time the return, say to the 12th or 15th of January 1848, and going back with the corresponding return for 1845-46, so as to make the periods correspond, it would be a great obligation. I imagine December and January will expose a terrible decay in the cotton trade with the ruined sugar-planting colonies; whilst I apprehend as I go back into 1845 I shall meet a very prosperous trade with the East Indies at any rate. I think there is no doubt we are bound, though it tells against my argument, to put on the $5\frac{1}{2}$ per cent. increased price in 1847; but on the other hand, if it were not too much trouble, I think we might in each case accompany the statement of the value of the exports with a memorandum of the cost of raw cotton in each case to be deducted from England's profit.

Let me wish you with all my heart a happy new year, and a prosperous one.

To Mr. Burn.

HARCOURT HOUSE, *January* 16, 1848.

I have to thank you for a letter full of interesting information.

The way in which foreigners are apparently giving us the 'go by' is very alarming; it is that they are getting first our gold, and then with it our goods at 20, 30, and 50 per cent. under prime cost. An abundant harvest, cheap cotton, cheap sugar, and cheap tea, for the first time in our history appear to be of no use to us.

If I get the returns by the 31st of this month, it will be quite time enough for me; perhaps by taking ten days more time you might add another week's exports. The game I imagine is showing itself now more and more every month and week.

I should like to have the name of the West Indian to whom your letter refers, perhaps he would give me leave to mention his name, as I am fighting their cause for them? I make out that in the last six years ending 31st December 1846, upwards of £800,000 worth of machinery went out to the East and West Indies and the Mauritius. It is quite clear that this export to British possessions is now to be stopped, and a large part of it transferred to slave-holding countries.

Do you think your friend in Manchester could give any account of the exports of millwork and machinery to the East and British West Indies, and to Mauritius, to Cuba, Porto Rico, and Brazil, in 1847? I have the returns for the six years previous. If I could obtain this it would make an excellent companion to the return you are making for me.

In a former letter you asked me if I should like to have a statement of Scotch sequestrations in the cotton trade. I should very much; and more especially if I could get a comparison with former years. I observe that there are notices of eleven sequestrations in Glasgow alone in the last week's *Gazette*.

The account you are preparing for me of colonial produce will be very valuable.

I make out that directly and indirectly, that is to say, squadrons on the African coast and elsewhere, judicial commissions, establishments on the African coast, payments to foreign powers for putting down slave-trading, compensations for illegal detentions of foreign ships, maintenance of captured slaves, head-money to the captors, etc., has cost since 1808, . . . £29,000,000

Slavery compensation, ... 20,000,000

Increased cost of sugar, rum, and molasses, in twelve years, from 1834 to 1846, as compared with last twelve years of slavery, . . . 33,000,000

£82,000,000

The average price of sugar was 29s. per cwt. for the twelve years antecedent to emancipation. In consequence of the diminished production through the idleness of the slaves after emancipation, the average price of sugar, EX DUTY, rose 10s. 0½d. per cwt. in the twelve years subsequent to August 1834. Multiplying the colonial sugar consumed in Great Britain in those twelve years of freedom by 10s. 0½d., and allowing one-third more for rum and molasses, I find that the British nation paid in those twelve years £33,000,000 extraordinary for their sugar; but notwithstanding this enormously enhanced price of sugar, the quantities produced were so much more diminished that the planter's *gross* receipts were upwards of £5,000,000 sterling less than they had been in the corresponding period of slavery! So that the blacks squeezed £33,000,000 in those twelve years out of John Bull.

The nett profits of the planters in the twelve years subsequent to emancipation were diminished beyond the amount of these two sums together. The free labourers, whilst they produced 25 per cent. *less sugar* and *rum*, upon an average have earned 6s. a week where before they cost the planter (according to Lord Grey's statement in 1833) but 2d. a day. They now work upon an average six hours a day, *seven days* in a *fortnight*, whereas under the mitigated slavery of latter times they worked *nine* hours a day, *eleven days* in a fortnight. They now get, according to Lord Grey's statement in 1833, six times the money for forty-two hours' work in a fortnight, they used under slavery to cost doing ninety-nine hours' work. I am assured that 60 per cent. of the free labourers in Jamaica *ride their horses!!!* I don't think when John Bull paid £20,000,000 to knock off their chains, he meant to make idle gentlemen of the emancipated negroes; but practically that is what he has done.

The Yankee recruiting in Manchester for female silk manufacturers is another ominous feature of the times.

Somehow the silk manufacture does not appear to suffer so much as other trades—how comes this?

To Mr. Burn.

HARCOURT HOUSE, *January* 20, 1848.

It is excessively difficult to get at the aggregate expense of putting down slave-trading; but though I am aware that some of the journals have set it down at £1,500,000 a year, I cannot myself make out that it has ever cost in any one year more than £1,000,000. The house of commons' return this year gives the expense of the African squadron for 1847 at £300,000 or £305,000, I forget which, whilst two years ago a similar return gave the expense £720,000! But then there is the slave commission, maintenance of slaves at Sierra Leone, head-money for captured slaves, the cost of the various military and civil establishments on the African coast, payments to foreign powers, £300,000 or £400,000 to Portugal for an engagement to sign a treaty, etc.

You ask me how quakers will manage to reconcile their free trade and their anti-slavery morality on this occasion? I think a letter I got from Bristol dated the 27th of last December gives a good insight into their practice. I quote from it:

'The parties who imported the first foreign sugar here (*i.e.* Bristol) were John Thomas, Sons and Co., wholesale grocers, 19th October 1846, in the *Unity*, from Havannah, consisting of 520 boxes. They were purchased of a house in London while the vessel lay at Cowes. Another house, also quakers, of the firm of Wedmore and Claypole, wholesale grocers, imported direct from Porto Rico, 12th April 1847, 158 hogsheads 122 barrels per *Brilliant*. We have had several other cargoes imported, but they have been consignments to brokers for sale.'

If I recollect right the quakers voted against the payment of any compensation to slave-owners. Theirs was a costless christianity and a cheap philanthropy.

To Mr. Burn.

HARCOURT HOUSE, *January* 25, 1848.

I have got a very good return from Calcutta. The commercial year at Calcutta, I suppose, begins and ends the 1st of July. Is it so?

If it is, if you could give me an account of the value of cotton goods and yarn exported from Great Britain to Calcutta for the six months commencing the 1st of July and ending the 31st of December, it would supply me with an additional argument. Mr. James's statement having already been made in the house of commons by himself does not matter. The great argument will be derived from the two returns you are making out for me.

If you can lay your hands upon any old and remarkable prophecies of the great increase of the cotton trade to ensue from opening up Brazil and Cuba made by Cobden, Bright, or Milner Gibson in former years, I should like to have them. I well remember the general purport of them was that free trade in corn was almost of inferior importance to cheap sugar and opening out the boundless markets of Brazil and Cuba. Let me have the *Calcutta Trade Circular* again.

When you have done the job you are now about I wish you would sift Du Fay's grand finance statement of the cotton trade of the last year. I have not the paper now before me, but my impression is that he has miscalculated the home consumption of cotton goods by some 100,000,000 lbs. weight in every year, besides which his average price of raw cotton differs most materially. I think you should dissect and anatomise Du Fay in the *Glance*.

To Mr. Burn.

WIMPOLE, *January* 29, 1848.

I received your account of exports to the sugar-growing countries yesterday just before I left London for this place, and return you my warm thanks for it. Lord Ashburton, who is here, tells me that no sugar is cultivated about Rio Janeiro—that the sugar of Brazil is all cultivated in the neighbourhood of Pernambuco and Bahia. He is curious to know, and so am I, if you have the means at hand readily (not otherwise), whether the increased exports of cottons to Brazil are exclusively to Bahia and Pernambuco, or whether Rio Janeiro, not engaged in the sugar trade, shares equally with or in part with Bahia and Pernambuco.

With regard to the exports to Calcutta, though the Calcutta commercial year commences in May, I think I will only take half the year, viz., from July to December both inclusive : half a year is a more even period ; besides the last half-year is just the period when the injury to the Calcutta sugar trade had come into practical operation. I return on Monday morning to London, so pray continue to address my letters as heretofore.

Can you tell me what proportion the value of raw cotton in each period bears to the whole value?

I imagine that after deducting the value of raw cotton in the two periods from the 12th of September 1846 to the 12th of January 1848, with that from the 12th of May 1845 to the 12th of September 1846, the case will appear much stronger as regards the balance of wages, etc., lost in the period from the 12th of September 1846 to the 12th of January 1848.

TO MR. BURN.

February 1, 1848.

Some of your quotations from Turnbull are very happy, and I shall make use of them. I propose to take this line but as a preliminary. I want you to tell me how many men, women, and children there are in Great Britain (*i.e.* including Scotland) dependent for their subsistence on the cotton trade. I think according to the last census there were about 260,000 employed. Bright last year in the house of commons estimated them, if I recollect right, at 310,000. Assuming them to be 310,000 employed, I suppose in the cotton trade, where so large a proportion of women and children are employed, it would be sufficient to allow 190,000 unemployed as dependent on the 310,000 employed for their subsistence. Having assumed those dependent for their subsistence on the cotton trade to be 500,000 and the average consumption of the empire at $23\frac{1}{5}$ lbs. per mouth per annum, these 500,000 persons in sixteen months would eat 6904 tons 14 cwt. of sugar, and at £10 per ton would have saved in the sixteen months £69,046, 1s. 8d.; but whilst they have this much on the credit side of the account, they have on the debtor sheet their share of the profits and wages of converting that raw cotton into manufactures, on which there has been a diminution in the exports to the sugar-growing colonies of £1,171,142 during the same period. I wait for you to tell me what portion of this would be wages to the operatives and profits to the manufacturers. Say half, and still on the balance those dependent for subsistence on the cotton trade lose upwards of half a million by the transaction.

The committee on commercial distress having been appointed, the principal reason for the summoning of the new parliament in the autumn had been satisfied, and an adjournment until a month after Christmas was in prospect. Before, however, this took place a new and interesting question arose which led to considerable discussion, and which ultimately influenced in no immaterial manner the parliamentary position of Lord George Bentinck.

The city of London at the general election had sent to the house of commons, as a colleague of the first minister, a member who found a difficulty in taking one of the oaths appointed by the house to be sworn preliminarily to any member exercising his right of voting. The difficulty arose from this member being not only of the Jewish race, but unfortunately believing only in the first part of the Jewish religion.

CHAPTER XXIV

THE relations that subsist between the Bedoueen race that under the name of Jews is found in every country of Europe, and the Teutonic, Sclavonian, and Celtic races which have appropriated that division of the globe, will form hereafter one of the most remarkable chapters in a philosophical history of man.

The Saxon, the Sclave, and the Celt have adopted most of the laws and many of the customs of these Arabian tribes, all their literature and all their religion. They are therefore indebted to them for much that regulates, much that charms, and much that solaces existence. The toiling multitude rest every seventh day by virtue of a Jewish law; they are perpetually reading, 'for their example,' the records of Jewish history and singing the odes and elegies of Jewish poets; and they daily acknowledge on their knees, with reverent gratitude, that the only medium of communication between the Creator and themselves is the Jewish race. Yet they treat that race as the vilest of generations; and instead of logically looking upon them as the human family that has contributed most to human happiness, they extend to them every term of obloquy and every form of persecution.

Let us endeavour to penetrate this social anomaly that has harassed and perplexed centuries.

It is alleged that the dispersion of the Jewish race is a penalty incurred for the commission of a great crime: namely, the crucifixion of our blessed Lord in the form of a Jewish prince, by the Romans, at Jerusalem, and at the instigation of some Jews, in the reign of Augustus Cæsar. Upon this, it may be observed, that the allegation is neither historically true nor dogmatically sound.

1. *Not historically true.* It is not historically true, because at the time of the advent of our Lord, the Jewish race was as much dispersed throughout the world as at this present time, and had been so for many centuries. Europe, with the exception of those shores which are bathed by the midland sea, was then a primæval forest, but in every city of the great Eastern monarchies and in every province of the Roman empire, the Jews had been long settled. We have not precise authority for saying that at the advent there were more Jews established in Egypt than in Palestine, but it may unquestionably be asserted that at that period there were many more Jews living, and that too in great prosperity and honour, at Alexandria than at Jerusalem. It is evident from various Roman authors that the Jewish race formed no inconsiderable portion of the multitude that filled Rome itself, and that the Mosaic religion, undisturbed by the state, even made proselytes. But it is unnecessary to enter into any curious researches on this head, though the authorities are neither scant nor uninteresting. We are furnished with evidence the most complete and unanswerable of the pre-dispersion by the sacred writings themselves. Not two months after the crucifixion, when the Third Person of the Holy Trinity first descended on Jerusalem, it being the time of the great festivals, when the Jews according to the custom of the Arabian tribes, pursued to this day in the pilgrimage to Mecca, repaired from all quarters to the central sacred place, the holy writings inform us that there were gathered together in Jerusalem, 'Jews, devout men, out of every nation under heaven.' And that this expression, so general but so precise, should not be mistaken, we are shortly afterwards, though incidentally, informed, that there were Parthians, Medes, and Persians at Jerusalem, professing the Mosaic faith; Jews from Mesopotamia and Syria; from the countries of the lesser and the greater Asia; Egyptian, Libyan, Greek, and Arabian Jews; and especially Jews from Rome itself, some of which latter are particularly mentioned as Roman proselytes.

Nor is it indeed historically true that the small section of the Jewish race which dwelt in Palestine rejected Christ. The reverse is the truth. Had it not been for the Jews of Palestine the good tidings of our Lord would have been unknown for ever to the northern and western races. The first preachers of the gospel were Jews, and none else; the historians of the gospel were Jews, and none else. No one has ever been permitted to write under the inspiration of the Holy Spirit except a Jew. For nearly a century no one believed in the good tidings except Jews. They nursed the sacred flame of which they were the consecrated and hereditary depositories. And when the time was ripe to diffuse the truth among the ethnics, it was not a senator of Rome or a philosopher of Athens who was personally appointed by our Lord for that office, but a Jew of Tarsus, who founded the seven churches of Asia. And that greater church, great even amid its terrible corruptions, that has avenged the victory of Titus by subjugating the capital of the Cæsars and has changed every one of the Olympian temples into altars of the God of Sinai and of Calvary, was founded by another Jew, a Jew of Galilee.

From all which it appears that the dispersion of the Jewish race, preceding as it did for countless ages the advent of our Lord, could not be for conduct which occurred subsequently to the advent, and that they are also guiltless of that subsequent conduct which has been imputed to them as a crime, since for Him and His blessed name they preached, and wrote, and shed their blood 'as witnesses.'

But is it possible that that which is not historically true can be dogmatically sound? Such a conclusion would impugn the foundations of all faith. The followers of Jesus of whatever race need not, however, be alarmed. The belief that the present condition of the Jewish race is a penal infliction for the part which some Jews took at the crucifixion is not dogmatically sound.

2. *Not dogmatically sound.* There is no passage in the sacred writings that in the slightest degree warrants the penal assumption. The imprecation of the mob at the cruci-

fixion is sometimes strangely quoted as a divine decree. It is not a principle of jurisprudence, human or inspired, to permit the criminal to ordain their own punishment. Why too should they transfer any portion of the infliction to their posterity? What evidence have we that the wild suggestion was sanctioned by Omnipotence? On the contrary, amid the expiating agony, a divine voice at the same time solicited and secured forgiveness. And if unforgiven, could the cry of a rabble at such a scene bind a nation?

But, dogmatically considered, the subject of the crucifixion must be viewed in a deeper spirit. We must pause with awe to remember what was the principal office to be fulfilled by the advent. When the ineffable mystery of the Incarnation was consummated, a divine person moved on the face of the earth in the shape of a child of Israel, not to teach but to expiate. True it is that no word could fall from such lips, whether in the form of profound parable, or witty retort, or preceptive lore, but to guide and enlighten, but they who in those somewhat lax effusions, which in these days are honoured with the holy name of theology, speak of the morality of the gospel as a thing apart and of novel revelation, would do well to remember that in promulgating such doctrines they are treading on very perilous ground. There cannot be two moralities; and to hold that the Second Person of the Holy Trinity could teach a different morality from that which had been already revealed by the First Person of the Holy Trinity, is a dogma so full of terror that it may perhaps be looked upon as the ineffable sin against the Holy Spirit. When the lawyer tempted our Lord, and inquired how he was to inherit eternal life, the great master of Galilee referred him to the writings of Moses. There he would find recorded 'the whole duty of man'; to love God with all his heart, and soul, and strength, and mind, and his neighbour as himself. These two principles are embalmed in the writings of Moses, and are the essence of christian morals.[1]

---

[1] 'Thou shalt love thy neighbour as thyself: I am the Lord.'—*Leviticus*, c. xix, v. 18.

It was for something deeper than this, higher and holier than even Moses could fulfil, that angels announced the Coming. It was to accomplish an event preordained by the Creator of the world for countless ages. Born from the chosen house of the chosen people, yet blending in his inexplicable nature the divine essence with the human elements, a sacrificial mediator was to appear, appointed before all time, and purifying with his atoning blood the myriads that had preceded and the myriads that will follow him. The doctrine embraces all space and time, nay, chaos and eternity; divine persons are the agents and the redemption of the whole family of man the result. If the Jews had not prevailed upon the Romans to crucify our Lord, what would have become of the Atonement? But the human mind cannot contemplate the idea that the most important deed of time could depend upon human will. The immolators were preordained like the victim, and the holy race supplied both. Could that be a crime which secured for all mankind eternal joy? Which vanquished Satan, and opened the gates of Paradise? Such a tenet would sully and impugn the doctrine that is the corner-stone of our faith and hope. Men must not presume to sit in judgment on such an act. They must bow their heads in awe and astonishment and trembling gratitude.

But though the opinion that the dispersion of the Jewish race must be deemed a penalty incurred for their connection with the crucifixion has neither historical nor doctrinal sanction, it is possible that its degrading influence upon its victims may have been as efficacious as if their present condition were indeed a judicial infliction. Persecution, in a word, although unjust, may have reduced the modern Jews to a state almost justifying malignant vengeance. They may have become so odious and so hostile to mankind, as to merit for their present conduct, no matter how occasioned, the obloquy and ill-treatment of the communities in which they dwell, and with which they are scarcely permitted to mingle.

Let us examine this branch of the subject, which, though of more limited interest, is not without instruction.

In all the great cities of Europe, and in some of the great cities of Asia, among the infamous classes therein existing there will always be found Jews. They are not the only people who are usurers, gladiators, and followers of mean and scandalous occupations, nor are they anywhere a majority of such, but considering their general numbers, they contribute perhaps more than their proportion to the aggregate of the vile. In this they obey the law which regulates the destiny of all persecuted races: the infamous is the business of the dishonoured; and as infamous pursuits are generally illegal pursuits, the persecuted race which has most ability will be most successful in combating the law. The Jews have never been so degraded as the Greeks were throughout the Levant before their emancipation, and the degradation of the Greeks was produced by a period of persecution, which, both in amount and suffering, cannot compare with that which has been endured by the children of Israel. This peculiarity, however, attends the Jews under the most unfavourable circumstances; the other degraded races wear out and disappear; the Jew remains, as determined, as expert, as persevering, as full of resource and resolution as ever. Viewed in this light, the degradation of the Jewish race is alone a striking evidence of its excellence, for none but one of the great races could have survived the trials which it has endured.

But though a material organisation of the highest class may account for so strange a consequence, the persecuted Hebrew is supported by other means. He is sustained by a sublime religion. Obdurate, malignant, odious, and revolting as the lowest Jew appears to us, he is rarely demoralised. Beneath his own roof his heart opens to the influence of his beautiful Arabian traditions. All his ceremonies, his customs, and his festivals are still to celebrate the bounty of nature and the favour of Jehovah. The patriarchal feeling lingers about his hearth. A man, however fallen, who loves his home, is not wholly lost. The trumpet of Sinai still sounds in the Hebrew ear, and a Jew is never seen upon the scaffold, unless it be at an *auto-da-fé*.

But having made this full admission of the partial degradation of the Jewish race, we are not prepared to agree that this limited degeneracy is any justification of the prejudices and persecution which originated in barbarous or mediæval superstitions. On the contrary, viewing the influence of the Jewish race upon the modern communities, without any reference to the past history or the future promises of Israel, dismissing from our minds and memories, if indeed that be possible, all that the Hebrews have done in the olden time for man, and all which it may be their destiny yet to fulfil, we hold that instead of being an object of aversion, they should receive all that honour and favour from the northern and western races which, in civilised and refined nations, should be the lot of those who charm the public taste and elevate the public feeling. We hesitate not to say that there is no race at this present, and following in this only the example of a long period, that so much delights, and fascinates, and elevates, and ennobles Europe, as the Jewish.

We dwell not on the fact, that the most admirable artists of the drama have been and still are of the Hebrew race; or, that the most entrancing singers, graceful dancers, and exquisite musicians are sons and daughters of Israel: though this were much. But these brilliant accessories are forgotten in the sublimer claim.

It seems that the only means by which in these modern times we are permitted to develop the beautiful is music. It would appear definitively settled that excellence in the plastic arts is the privilege of the earlier ages of the world. All that is now produced in this respect is mimetic, and, at the best, the skilful adaptation of traditional methods. The creative faculty of modern man seems by an irresistible law at work on the virgin soil of science, daily increasing by its inventions our command over nature, and multiplying the material happiness of man. But the happiness of man is not merely material. Were it not for music, we might in these days say, the beautiful is dead. Music seems to be the only means of creating the beautiful in which we not only equal but in all probability greatly excel the ancients. The music of modern Europe ranks with the transcendent creations of human genius; the poetry, the statues, the temples of Greece. It produces and represents as they did whatever is most beautiful in the spirit of man, and often expresses what is most profound. And who are the great composers, who hereafter will rank with Homer, with Sophocles, with Praxiteles, or with Phidias? They are the descendants of those Arabian tribes who conquered Canaan, and who by favour of the Most High have done more with less means even than the Athenians.

Forty years ago—not a longer period than the children of Israel were wandering in the desert—the two most dishonoured races in Europe were the Attic and the Hebrew, and they were the two races that had done most for mankind. Their fortunes had some similarity: their countries were the two smallest in the world, equally barren and equally famous; they both divided themselves into tribes; both built a most famous temple on an acropolis; and both produced a literature which all European nations have accepted with reverence and admiration. Athens has been sacked oftener than Jerusalem, and oftener rased to the ground; but the Athenians have escaped expatriation, which is purely an oriental custom. The sufferings of the Jews, however, have been infinitely more prolonged and varied than those of the Athenians. The Greek, nevertheless, appears exhausted. The creative genius of Israel, on the contrary, never shone so bright; and when the Russian, the Frenchman, and the Anglo-Saxon, amid applauding theatres or the choral voices of solemn temples, yield themselves to the full spell of a Mozart or a Mendelssohn, it seems difficult to comprehend how these races can reconcile it to their hearts to persecute a Jew.

We have shown that the theological prejudice against the Jews has no foundation, historical or doctrinal; we have shown that the social prejudice, originating in the theological but sustained by superficial observations irrespective of religious prejudice, is still more unjust, and that no existing race is so much entitled to the esteem and gratitude of society as the Hebrew. It remains for us to notice the injurious consequences to European society of the course pursued by the communities to this race, and this view of the subject leads us to considerations which it would become existing statesmen to ponder.

The world has by this time discovered that it is impossible to destroy the Jews. The attempt to extirpate them has been made under the most favourable auspices and on the largest scale; the most considerable means that man could command have been pertinaciously applied to this object for the longest period of recorded time. Egyptian pharaohs, Assyrian kings, Roman emperors, Scandinavian crusaders, Gothic princes, and holy inquisitors, have alike devoted their energies to the fulfilment of this common purpose. Expatriation, exile, captivity, confiscation, torture on the most ingenious and massacre on the most extensive scale a curious system of degrading customs and debasing laws which would have broken the heart of any other people, have been tried, and in vain. The Jews, after all this havoc, are probably more numerous at this date than they were during the reign of Solomon the wise, are found in all lands, and unfortunately prospering in most. All which proves, that it is in vain for man to attempt to baffle the inexorable law of nature which has decreed that a superior race shall never be destroyed or absorbed by an inferior.

But the influence of a great race will be felt; its greatness does not depend upon its numbers, otherwise the English would not have vanquished the Chinese, nor would the Aztecs have been overthrown by Cortez and a handful of Goths. That greatness results from its organisation, the consequences of which are shown in its energy and enterprise, in the strength of its will and the fertility of its brain. Let us observe what should be the influence of the Jews, and then ascertain how it is exercised. The Jewish race connects the modern populations with the early ages of the world, when the relations of the Creator with the created were more intimate than in these days, when angels visited the earth, and God himself even spoke with man. The Jews represent the Semitic principle; all that is spiritual in our nature. They are the trustees of tradition, and the conservators of the religious element. They are a living and the most striking evidence of the falsity of that pernicious doctrine of modern times, the natural equality of man. The political equality of a particular race is a matter of municipal arrangement, and depends entirely on political considerations and circumstances; but the natural equality of man now in vogue, and taking the form of cosmopolitan fraternity, is a principle which, were it possible to act on it, would deteriorate the great races and destroy all the genius of the world. What would be the consequence on the great Anglo-Saxon republic, for example, were its citizens to secede from their sound principle of reserve, and mingle with their negro and coloured populations? In the course of time they would become so deteriorated that their states would probably be reconquered and regained by the aborigines whom they have expelled, and who would then be their superiors. But though nature will never ultimately permit this theory of natural equality to be practised, the preaching of this dogma has already caused much mischief, and may occasion much more. The native tendency of the Jewish race, who are justly proud of their blood, is against the doctrine of the equality of man. They have also another characteristic, the faculty of acquisition. Although the European laws have endeavoured to prevent their obtaining property, they have nevertheless become remarkable for their accumulated wealth. Thus it will be seen that all the tendencies of the Jewish race are conservative. Their bias is to religion, property, and natural aristocracy: and it should be the interest of statesmen that this bias of a great race should be encouraged, and their energies and creative powers enlisted in the cause of existing society.

But existing society has chosen to persecute this race which should furnish its choice allies, and what have been the consequences?

They may be traced in the last outbreak of the destructive principle in Europe. An insurrection takes place against tradition and aristocracy, against religion and property. Destruction of the Semitic principle, extirpation of the Jewish religion, whether in the mosaic or in the christian form, the natural equality of man and the abrogation of property, are proclaimed by the secret societies who form provisional governments, and men of Jewish race are found at the head of every one of them. The people of God cooperate with atheists; the most skilful accumulators of property ally themselves with communists; the peculiar and chosen race touch the hand of all the scum and low castes of Europe! And all this because they wish to destroy that ungrateful Christendom which owes to them even its name, and whose tyranny they can no longer endure.

When the secret societies, in February 1848, surprised Europe, they were themselves surprised by the unexpected opportunity, and so little capable were they of seizing the occasion, that had it not been for the Jews, who of late years unfortunately have been connecting themselves with these unhallowed associations, imbecile as were the governments the uncalled-for outbreak would not have ravaged Europe. But the fiery energy and the teeming resources of the children of Israel maintained for a long time the unnecessary and useless struggle. If the reader throws his eye over the provisional governments of Germany, and Italy, and even of France, formed at that period, he will recognise everywhere the Jewish element. Even the insurrection, and defence, and administration of Venice, which, from the resource of statesmanlike moderation displayed, commanded almost the respect and sympathy of Europe, were accomplished by a Jew—Manini, who by the bye is a Jew who professes the whole of the Jewish religion, and believes in Calvary as well as Sinai, ' a converted Jew,' as the Lombards styled him, quite forgetting, in the confusion of their ideas, that it is the Lombards who are the converts—not Manini.

Thus it will be seen that the persecution of the Jewish race has deprived European society of an important conservative element and added to the destructive party an influential ally. Prince Metternich, the most enlightened of modern statesmen, not to say the most intellectual of men, was, though himself a victim of the secret societies, fully aware of these premises. It was always his custom, great as were the difficulties which in so doing he had to encounter, to employ as much as possible the Hebrew race in the public service. He could never forget that Napoleon in his noontide hour had been checked by the pen of the greatest of political writers; he had found that illustrious author as great in the cabinet as in the study; he knew that no one had more contributed to the deliverance of Europe. It was not as a patron, but as an appreciating and devoted friend, that the high chancellor of Austria appointed Frederick Gentz secretary to the congress of Vienna—and Frederick Gentz was a child of Israel.

It is no doubt to be deplored that several millions of the Jewish race should persist in believing in only a part of their religion; but this is a circumstance which does not affect Europe, and time, with different treatment, may remove the anomaly, which perhaps may be accounted for. It should be recollected that the existing Jews are perhaps altogether the descendants of those various colonies and emigrations which, voluntary or forced, long preceded the advent. Between the vast carnage of the Roman wars from Titus to Hadrian, and the profession of Christ by his countrymen which must have been very prevalent, since the christian religion was solely sustained by the Jews of Palestine during the greater part of its first century, it is improbable that any descendants of the Jews of Palestine exist who disbelieve in Christ. After the fall of Jerusalem and the failure of Barchochebas, no doubt some portion of the Jews found refuge in the desert, returning to their original land after such long and strange vicissitudes. This natural movement would account for those Arabian tribes of whose resistance to Mohammed we have ample and authentic details, and who, if we are to credit the accounts which perplex modern travellers, are to this day governed by the Pentateuch instead of the Koran.

When christianity was presented to the ancestors of the present Jews, it came from a very suspicious quarter and was offered in a very questionable shape. Centuries must have passed in many instances before the Jewish colonies heard of the advent, the crucifixion, and the atonement, the latter, however, a doctrine in perfect harmony with Jewish ideas. When they first heard of christianity, it appeared to be a gentile religion, accompanied by idolatrous practices, from which severe monotheists like the Arabians always recoil, and holding the Jewish race up to public scorn and hatred. This is not the way to make converts.

There have been two great colonies of the Jewish race in Europe: in Spain and in Sarmatia. The origin of the Jews in Spain is lost in the night of time. That it was of great antiquity we have proof. The tradition, once derided, that the Iberian Jews were a Phœnician colony has been favoured by the researches of modern antiquaries, who have traced the Hebrew language in the ancient names of the localities. It may be observed, however, that the languages of the Jews and the Philistines, or Phœnicians, were probably too similar to sanction any positive induction from such phenomena, while on the other hand, in reply to those who have urged the improbability of the Jews who had no seaports colonising Spain, it may be remarked that the colony may have been an expatriation by the Philistines in the course of the long struggle which occurred between them and the invading tribes previous to the foundation of the Hebrew monarchy. We know that in the time of Cicero the Jews had been settled immemorially in Spain. When the Romans, converted to christianity and acted on by the priesthood, began to trouble the Spanish Jews, it appears by a decree of Constantine that they were owners and cultivators of the soil, a circumstance which alone proves the antiquity and the nobility of their settlement, for the possession of the land is never conceded to a degraded race. The conquest of Spain by the Goths in the fifth and sixth centuries threatened the Spanish Jews, however, with more serious adversaries than the Romans. The Gothic tribes, very recently converted to their Syrian faith, were full of barbaric zeal against those whom they looked upon as the enemies of Jesus. But the Spanish Jews sought assistance from their kinsmen the Saracens on the opposite coast; Spain was invaded and subdued by the Moors, and for several centuries the Jew and the Saracen lived under the same benignant laws and shared the same brilliant prosperity. In the history of Spain during the Saracenic supremacy any distinction of religion or race is no longer traced. And so it came to pass that when at the end of the 14th century, after the fell triumph of the Dominicans over the Albigenses, the holy inquisition was introduced into Spain, it was reported to Torquemada that two-thirds of the nobility of Arragon, that is to say of the proprietors of the land, were Jews.

All that these men knew of christianity was that it was a religion of fire and sword, and that one of its first duties was to revenge some mysterious and inexplicable crime which had been committed ages ago by some unheard-of ancestors of theirs in an unknown land. The inquisitors addressed themselves to the Spanish Jews in the same abrupt and ferocious manner in which the monks saluted the Mexicans and the Peruvians. All those of the Spanish Jews who did not conform after the fall of the Mohammedan kingdoms were expatriated by the victorious Goths, and these refugees were the main source of the Italian Jews, and of the most respectable portion of the Jews of Holland. These exiles found refuge in two republics: Venice and the United Provinces. The Portuguese Jews, it is well known, came from Spain, and their ultimate expulsion from Portugal was extended by the same results as the Spanish expatriation.

The other great division of Jews in Europe are the Sarmatian Jews, and they are very numerous. They amount to nearly three millions. These unquestionably entered Europe with the other Sarmatian nations, descending the Borysthenes and ascending the Danube, and are according to all probability the progeny of the expatriations of the times of Tiglath-Pileser and Nebuchadnezzar. They are the posterity of those 'devout men,' Parthians, Medes, and Elamites, who were attending the festivals at Jerusalem at the time of the descent of the Holy Spirit. Living among barbarous pagans who never molested them, these people went on very well, until suddenly the barbarous pagans, under the influence of an Italian priesthood, were converted to the Jewish religion, and then as a necessary consequence the converts began to harass, persecute, and massacre the Jews.

These people had never heard of Christ. Had the Romans not destroyed Jerusalem, these Sarmatian Jews would have had a fair chance of obtaining from civilised beings some clear and coherent account of the great events which had occurred. They and their fathers before them would have gone up in customary pilgrimage to the central sacred place, both for purposes of devotion and purposes of trade, and they might have heard from Semitic lips that there were good tidings for Israel. What they heard from their savage companions, and the Italian priesthood which acted on them, was, that there were good tidings for all the world except Israel, and that Israel, for the commission of a great crime of which they had never heard and could not comprehend, was to be plundered, massacred, hewn to pieces, and burnt alive in the name of Christ and for the sake of christianity.

The eastern Jews, who are very numerous, are in general the descendants of those who in the course of repeated captivities settled in the great eastern monarchies, and which they never quitted. They live in the same cities and follow the same customs as they did in the days of Cyrus. They are to be found in Persia, Mesopotamia, and Asia Minor; at Bagdad, at Hamadan, at Smyrna. We know from the Jewish books how very scant was the following which accompanied Esdras and Nehemiah back to Jerusalem. A fortress city, built on a ravine, surrounded by stony mountains and watered by a scanty stream, had no temptations after the gardens of Babylon and the broad waters of the Euphrates. But Babylon has vanished and Jerusalem remains, and what are the waters of Euphrates to the brook of Kedron! It is another name than that of Jesus of Nazareth with which these Jews have been placed in collision, and the Ishmaelites have not forgotten the wrongs of Hagar in their conduct to the descendants of Sarah.

Is it therefore wonderful, that a great portion of the Jewish race should not believe in the most important portion of the Jewish religion? As, however, the converted races become more humane in their behaviour to the Jews, and the latter have opportunity fully to comprehend and deeply to ponder over true christianity, it is difficult to suppose that the result will not be very different. Whether presented by a Roman or Anglo-Catholic, or Genevese, divine, by pope, bishop, or presbyter, there is nothing one would suppose very repugnant to the feelings of a Jew when he learns that the redemption of the human race has been effected by the mediatorial agency of a child of Israel; if the ineffable mystery of the Incarnation be developed to him, he will remember that the blood of Jacob is a chosen and peculiar blood, and if so transcendent a consummation is to occur he will scarcely deny that only one race could be deemed worth of accomplishing it. There may be points of doctrine on which the northern and western races may perhaps never agree. The Jew, like them, may follow that path in those respects which reason and feeling alike dictate; but nevertheless it can hardly be maintained that there is anything revolting to a Jew to learn that a Jewess is the queen of heaven, or that the flower of the Jewish race are even now sitting on the right hand of the Lord God of Sabaoth.

Perhaps too in this enlightened age, as his mind expands and he takes a comprehensive view of this period of progress, the pupil of Moses may ask himself, whether all the princes of the house of David have done so much for the Jews as that prince who was crucified on Calvary? Had it not been for Him, the Jews would have been comparatively unknown, or known only as a high oriental caste which had lost its country. Has not He made their history the most famous in the world? Has not He hung up their laws in every temple? Has not He vindicated all their wrongs? Has not He avenged the victory of Titus and conquered the Cæsars? What successes did they anticipate from their Messiah? The wildest dreams of their rabbis have been far exceeded. Has not Jesus conquered Europe and changed its name into Christendom? All countries that refuse the cross wither while the whole of the new world is devoted to the Semitic principle and its most glorious offspring the Jewish faith, and the time will come when the vast communities and countless myriads of America and Australia, looking upon Europe as Europe now looks upon Greece and wondering how so small a space could have achieved such great deeds, will still find music in the songs of Sion and solace in the parables of Galilee.

These may be dreams, but there is one fact which none can contest. Christians may continue to persecute Jews and Jews may persist in disbelieving Christians, but who can deny that Jesus of Nazareth, the Incarnate Son of the Most High God, is the eternal glory of the Jewish race?

CHAPTER XXV

THE views expressed in the preceding chapter were not
those which influenced Lord George Bentinck in forming his
opinion that the civil disabilities of those subjects of her
majesty who profess that limited belief in divine revelation
which is commonly called the Jewish religion, should be
removed. He had supported a measure to this effect in the
year 1833, guided in that conduct by his devoted attachment to the equivocal principle of religious liberty, the
unqualified application of which principle seems hardly
consistent with that recognition of religious truth by the
state to which we yet adhere, and without which it is highly
probable that the northern and western races after a disturbing and rapidly degrading period of atheistic anarchy
may fatally recur to their old national idolatries, modified
and mythically dressed up according to the spirit of the age.
It may be observed that the decline and disasters of modern
communities have generally been relative to their degree
of sedition against the Semitic principle. Since the great
revolt of the Celts against the first and second testament, at
the close of the last century, France has been alternately
in a state of collapse or convulsion. Throughout the awful
trials of the last sixty years, England, notwithstanding her
deficient and meagre theology, has always remembered Sion.
The great transatlantic republic is intensely Semitic and
has prospered accordingly. This sacred principle alone has
consolidated the mighty empire of all the Russias. How
omnipotent it is cannot be more clearly shown than by the
instance of Rome, where it appears in its most corrupt form.
An old man on a Semitic throne baffles the modern Attilas,
and the recent invasion of the barbarians, under the form of

red republicans, socialists, communists, all different phases which describe the relapse of the once converted races into their primitive condition of savagery. Austria would long ago, have dissolved but for the Semitic principle, and if the north of Germany has never succeeded in attaining that imperial position which seemed its natural destiny, it is that the north of Germany has never at any time been thoroughly converted. Some perhaps may point to Spain as a remarkable instance of decline in a country where the Semitic principle has exercised great influence. But the fall of Spain was occasioned by the expulsion of her Semitic population: a million families of Jews and Saracens, the most distinguished of her citizens for their industry and their intelligence, their learning and their wealth.

It appears that Lord George Bentinck had offended some of his followers by an opinion expressed in his address to his constituency in '47, that in accordance with the suggestion of Mr. Pitt, some provision should be made for the roman catholic priesthood of Ireland out of the land. Although this opinion might offend the religious sentiments of some, and might be justly looked upon by others as a scheme ill-suited to the character of an age adverse to any further religious endowments, it must be acknowledged that no member of the protectionist party had any just cause of complaint against Lord George for the expression of an opinion which he had always upheld, and of his constancy to which he had fairly given his friends notice. This was so generally felt that the repining died away. The Jewish question, as it was called, revived these religious emotions. These feelings, as springing from the highest sentiment of our nature, and founded, however mistaken in their application, on religious truth, are entitled to deep respect and tenderness; but no one can indulge them by the compromise of the highest principles or by sanctioning a course which he really believes to be destructive of the very object which their votaries wish to cherish.

As there are very few Englishmen of what is commonly called the Jewish faith, and as therefore it was supposed that political considerations could not enter into the question, it was hoped by many of the followers of Lord George Bentinck that he would not separate himself from his party on this subject, and very earnest requests and representations were made to him with that view. He was not insensible to them; he gave them prolonged and painful consideration; they greatly disquieted him. In his confidential correspondence he often recurs to the distress and anxiety which this question and its consequences as regarded his position with those friends to whom he was much attached occasioned him. It must not therefore be supposed that in the line he ultimately took with reference to this question he was influenced, as some have unkindly and unwarrantably fancied, by a self-willed, inexorable, and imperious spirit. He was no doubt by nature a proud man, inclined even to arrogance and naturally impatient of contradiction, but two severe campaigns in the house of commons had already mitigated these characteristics: he understood human nature, he was fond of his party, and irrespective of other considerations it pained his ardent and generous heart to mortify his comrades. It was therefore not in any degree from temper, but from principle, from as pure, as high, and as noble a sense of duty as ever actuated a man in public life, that Lord George Bentinck ultimately resolved that it was impossible for him to refuse to vote for the removal of what are commonly called Jewish disabilities. He had voted in this particular cause shortly after his entrance into public life; it was in accordance with that general principle of religious liberty to which he was an uncompromising adherent; it was in complete agreement with the understanding which subsisted between himself and the protectionist party, when at their urgent request he unwillingly assumed the helm. He was entreated not to vote at all; to stay away, which the severe indisposition under which he was then labouring warranted. He did not rudely repulse these latter representations, as has been circulated. On the contrary, he listened to them with kindness, and was not uninfluenced by them. Enfeebled by illness, he had nearly brought himself to a compliance with a request urged with affectionate importunity, but from which his reason and sense of duty held him aloof. After long and deep and painful pondering, when the hour arrived, he rose from his bed of sickness, walked into the house of commons, and not only voted, but spoke in favour of his convictions.   His speech remains, one of the best ever delivered on the subject, not only full of weighty argument, but touched with a high and even tender vein of sentiment.

This vote and speech of Lord George Bentinck no doubt mortified at the moment a considerable portion of his followers, and occasioned great dissatisfaction among a very respectable though limited section of them.   This latter body must either have forgotten or they must have been strangely unacquainted with the distinct understanding on which Lord George had undertaken the lead of the party, or otherwise they could not have felt authorised in conveying to him their keen sense of disapprobation.   Unfortunately he received this when the house had adjourned for the holidays, and when Mr. Bankes, who had been the organ of communication with him in '46, was in the country, and when the party was of course generally dispersed. Lord George did not take any pains to ascertain whether the representation which was made to him was that of the general feeling of a large party, or that only of a sincere, highly estimable, but limited section.   He was enfeebled and exhausted by indisposition; he often felt, even when in health, that the toil of his life was beyond both his physical and moral energies; and though he was of that ardent and tenacious nature that he never would have complained but have died at his post, the opportunity of release coming to him at a moment when he was physically prostrate was rather eagerly seized, and the world suddenly learnt at Christmas, with great astonishment, that the renowned leader of the protectionist party had relinquished his trust.

The numerous communications which he received must

have convinced him that the assumed circumstances under which he acted had not been accurately appreciated by him. He was implored to reconsider his course, as one very detrimental to the cause to which he was devoted, and which would probably tend to the triumph of those whose policy he had attempted to defeat, and whose personal conduct he had at least succeeded in punishing.

'The prophesied time has come,' he wrote to his friend, Mr. Bankes, on the 23rd of December 1847, 'when I have ceased to be able to serve the party, the great cause of protection, or my country, by any longer retaining the commission bestowed on me in the spring of 1846. You will remember, however, that when unfeignedly and honestly, but in vain, trying to escape from being raised to a position which I foresaw I must fail to maintain with advantage to you or honour to myself, I at last gave my consent, I only did so on the express understanding that my advancement should be held to be merely a *pro tempore* appointment, waiting till the country should have the opportunity of sending to parliament other men better fitted to lead the country gentlemen of England. I have recalled these circumstances to your mind with no other purpose than that the party may feel how entirely free they are, without even the suspicion of doing an injustice to me or of showing me in this any disrespect, to remodel their arrangements, and to supersede my lieutenancy by the appointment of a superior and permanent commander.'

And again on Christmas day to the same gentleman, in reply to an acknowledgment of the preceding, while thanking Mr. Bankes 'for his warm-hearted letter as very grateful to his feelings,' he says, 'Confidentially I tell you, that far from feeling in the least annoyed, I shall feel greatly relieved by a restoration to privacy and freedom. I worked upon my spirit in '46 and '47; but I have learnt now that I have shaken my constitution to the foundation, and I seriously doubt my being able to work on much longer.'

He wrote on the 24th of December to one of his most

intimate friends and warmest supporters, Mr. Christopher, the member for Lincolnshire, who had remonstrated with him as to his decision: 'It is not in my nature to retain a station one moment after I get a hint even that any portion of those who raised me to it are wearied of seeing me there. The old members of the party will all recollect how clearly I foresaw and foretold that I should be found a very inconvenient as well as a very inefficient leader, so soon as the great protection battle was brought to a close. I predicted all that has since occurred; and no one more cordially agrees than I do in the wisdom of the present decision, the spirit I presume of which is that no great party or large body of men can be successfully, or to any good purpose, led except by a man who heart and soul sympathises with them in all their feelings, partialities, and prejudices. Cold reason has a poor chance against such influences. There can be no *esprit de corps* and no zeal where there is not a union of prejudices as well as of commercial opinions. The election of a leader, united with the great body of the party in these respects, will tend greatly to reunite its scattered particles, even on those questions where I shall be able to give my aid with all my wonted zeal, which will not be the less spirited because it will be free and independent.'

At a later period, acknowledging an address signed by the great body of the protectionist party, and presented to him by the present Earl Talbot, then a member of the house of commons, Lord George wrote, 'The considerations which obliged me to surrender a post of honour which every independent and high-minded English gentleman has at all times prized above the highest rewards in the gift of the crown, "the leadership of the country gentlemen of England," will never influence me to swerve from any endeavours of which my poor abilities and bodily energies are capable in the promotion of the prosperity of all classes in the British empire at home and in the colonies, any more than they can ever make me forget the attachment, the friendship, and the enthusiastic support of those who stood by me to the end of the death-struggle for British interests and for English good faith and political honour, and to whose continued friendship and constancy I know I am indebted for this graceful and grateful compliment.'

If Lord George Bentinck were inexorable to the entreaties of his friends, it must not be supposed that he was influenced in the course which he pursued, as was presumed by many at the time not acquainted with the circumstances, by any feeling of pique or brooding sullenness. No high-spirited man under vexatious and distressing circumstances ever behaved with more magnanimity. In this he was actuated in a great degree by a sense of duty, but still more by that peculiar want of selfishness which was one of the most beautiful traits of his character. The moment he had at all recovered from the severe attack by which, to use his own language, he had been 'struck down in the first week of the session,' and from the effects of which it may be doubted whether he ever entirely recovered, he laboured zealously to induce some competent person to undertake the office which he had thought it expedient to resign, offering in several instances to serve in the ranks, and to assist with his utmost energies, both in and out of the house, the individual who would undertake the responsible direction in the commons.

These efforts, though indefatigable, were not successful, for those who were competent to the office cared not to serve under any one except himself. About this time a personage of great station, and who very much admired Lord George Bentinck, wrote to him, and recommended him not to trouble himself about the general discipline of the party, but to follow his own course, and lead that body of friends who under all circumstances would adhere to him, instancing the case of Mr. Canning, under circumstances not altogether dissimilar. Lord George replied: 'As for my rallying a personal party round myself as Mr. Canning did, I have no pretension to anything of the kind; when Mr. Canning did that, the house of commons, and England too, acknowledged him to be the greatest orator who had survived Pitt and Fox; he had been secretary of state for foreign affairs, and had taken a conspicuous part in rousing the country to carry on the war against France.'

The nature of the subject, dealing as it necessarily does with so many personal details, renders it impossible to make public the correspondence in which Lord George Bentinck was engaged at this time in his attempts to place the protectionist party under the guidance of one who would unite all sympathies; but were that publication possible, it would place Lord George Bentinck in a very noble and amiable light, and prove a gentleness and softness in his nature for which those who were not very intimate with him did not give him credit. Not that it must be for a moment supposed that he was insensible to what was occurring. He was the most sensitive as well as the proudest of men. When the writer called at Harcourt House to bid him farewell before the Christmas holidays, and conversing very frankly on the course which he was then pursuing, inquired as to his future proceedings, Lord George said with emotion: 'In this cause I have shaken my constitution and shortened my days, and I will succeed or die.' In the course of the year 1848, walking home together from the house of commons, he twice recurred to this terrible alternative.

But all considerations were merged at this moment in the predominant one which was to keep the party together. He wrote to a friend at the end of January, who urged him, as the hour of work approached and the injurious inconveniences of his abdication would be more felt, to confer with his former followers and reconsider his position, that no personal feeling prevented his taking that course, but that he felt any resumption of responsibility on his part would not be pleasing to a section of those who formerly served with him, and that there would be a 'split' in the ranks. 'As far as I am personally concerned,' he added, 'I could submit to anything short of having my ears cut off and appearing as a "Croppy," to be free again. My pride cannot stand leading an unwilling party; I would just as soon thrust myself into a dinner-room, where I was at once an uninvited and an unwelcome guest.'

In the meantime, according to his custom, the moment that he had sufficiently recovered from his illness, he prepared with the utmost zeal for the coming struggle respecting the fate of our sugar colonies, in which subject he was soon absorbed.

'The other subject on which I am going to bother you,' he wrote to a friend towards the end of January, 'is the sugar question. I move for my committee on Thursday next, but although government grant the committee, I plainly see that a very spirited debate will be got up on the question, and not unlikely an amendment in some shape moved recording the opinion of the house that some relief should be immediately given or guaranteed.

'It is a subject on which you, Granby, and I have good reason to pride ourselves, and I clearly perceive that it is the question now upon which the commerce of the country is most alive, and the weak point in the defences of free trade. There is no use speaking to the country on matters about which it does not feel, but its nerves are just now very sensitive upon this subject, and if well managed are very assailable to new impressions.

'The West Indian and colonial interests are strongly impressed with a notion that Peel means to pirouette again and fly to their rescue. If so, he would lay himself open to a most terrific and cruel dissection at your hands. Free trade will break down and protection eventually triumph through the sugar duties.

'Pray give your mind a little to this subject, and let us be prepared for all comers and rouse the country.

'*P.S.*—Recollect, however, that we cannot deny that in the first instance the revenue has gained £400,000, and that the consumers have saved nearly two millions and a half in the price of their sugar; but with all this the balance of imperial ruin is so great as to be intolerable.'

He wrote also to Mr. C. Henry Chapman, of Liverpool: 'My motion for a committee to inquire into the state of the sugar-planting colonies will come on the day parliament meets. I must write to * * * * *. My own illness, the arrear I fell into with business, and since the adjournment the bother of correspondence about the leadership, have combined to prevent my doing so earlier. I propose beginning with the East Indies, which I expect will be only two or three days' business; then taking the Mauritius, which cannot be a long affair; and concluding with the West Indies, which I suppose may take a good while.'

He wrote also to Mr. Wright, of Nottingham, on the 1st of February.

'I am just now engaged with the sugar question, but after Thursday I shall be happy to see you any day you happen to come to town.

'The anti-gold league goes further than I should like to accompany them, and I have avoided mixing myself up with them.

'Perhaps a private circulation of your pamphlet might be better than publishing for sale, but why not combine both? Privately circulating it to all members of parliament, newspaper and periodical writers, and letting the multitude have the chance of purchase.

'Herries has some resolutions which stand for the 8th, but with thirteen millions of gold and silver in the bank coffers, consols bordering on 90, and money a drug in the city, we may be said to have let the bird get out of shot before we pulled the trigger. We ought to have moved an amendment on the address; when the bank usury was eight per cent., and half the world doubted if the next dividends would be paid.

'We are always two months too late in every move we make.'

Parliament reassembled on the 3rd of February, and on that night Lord George Bentinck brought forward his motion for 'a select committee to inquire into the present condition and prospects of the interests connected with and dependent on sugar and coffee planting in her majesty's East and West Indian possessions and the Mauritius, and to consider whether any and what measures can be adopted by parliament for their relief.' When he entered the house Lord George walked up to the head of the second bench below the gangway on the opposition side, and thus significantly announced that he was no longer the responsible leader of the protectionist party. It was the wish of the writer of these pages, who had resolved to stand or fall by him, to have followed his example and to have abdicated the prominent seat in which the writer had been unwillingly and fortuitously placed; but by the advice or rather at the earnest request of Lord George Bentinck this course was relinquished as indicative of schism, which he wished to discourage; and the circumstance is only mentioned as showing that Lord George was not less considerate at this moment of the interests of the protectionist party than when he led them with so much confidence and authority. The session, however, was to commence without a leader, without any recognised organ of communication between parties, or any responsible representative of opinion in debate. All again was chaos. There is, however, something so vital in the conservative party that it seems always to rally under every disadvantage.

Lord George spoke well to his resolution; the house soon recognised he was master of his case, and though few foresaw at the moment the important consequences to which this motion would lead, the house was interested from the first, and though there was no division the debate lasted two days and was sustained on both sides with great animation.

The mover vindicated himself very successfully for only proposing a committee of inquiry. 'It has been represented to me,' he said, 'by the colonies and by persons in this country who are interested in them, that the course which I am proposing is not consistent with the necessities of the case, that there is something pusillanimous in the motion which I am going to make, that in point of fact the interests connected with sugar and coffee planting are *in extremis*, and that while the question of their redress is discussing in a committee above-stairs these great interests will perish.

They say to me that a committee of inquiry will be to them of the nature of that comfort which,

"Like cordials after death, come late,"

and that before the committee shall have reported the West Indian interest will be altogether past recovery. But, sir, it is for me to consider what my power is to obtain any substantial relief by a direct vote of this house, and when I remember that in July 1846 I moved a resolution the purport of which was to maintain the protection for the West Indian and the East Indian free-labour colonies which they now seek, and that I had but one hundred and thirty gentlemen to support me, while two hundred and sixty-five votes were recorded in favour of the measure of the government admitting slave-labour sugar, I feel that it is hopeless for me to endeavour in this house, where I have no reason to suppose any addition has been made to the members acquiescing in my views, to convert that minority into a majority, and more especially, when I recollect that on that occasion but five gentlemen connected with the West Indian and East Indian interests recorded their votes with me, I think the West Indian interest has not a good case against me when they blame me for not taking a more resolute step on this occasion.'

He was not, however, without hope from the course which he had decided to pursue. 'Looking as I have done at the deplorable state of the West Indies, the East Indies, and the Mauritius, and holding as I do in my hand a list of forty-eight great houses in England—twenty-six of the first commercial houses in London, sixteen in Liverpool, and six elsewhere—which have failed, and whose liabilities amount in the whole to £6,300,000 and upwards, none of which I believe would have fallen had it not been for the ruin brought upon them by the change in the sugar duties and the consequent reduction in the price of their produce, I do hope through the intervention of a committee of this house I may be able to prevail upon the house to change its policy with regard to this great question.'

Lord George was supported in this debate by Mr. Thomas Baring in one of the best speeches ever made in the house of commons. Few more combine mastery of the case with parliamentary point than this gentleman. It is not impossible to find a man capable of addressing the house of commons who understands the subject, it is not impossible to find a man who can convey his impressions on any subject to the house in a lively and captivating manner, though both instances are rarer than the world would imagine; but a man who at the same time understands a question and can handle it before a popular assembly in a popular style, who teaches without being pedantic, can convey an argument in an epigram, and instruct as the Mexicans did by picture, possesses a talent for the exercise of which he is responsible to his sovereign and his country.

Mr. Baring said that he could not perfectly agree either with Lord John Russell or Lord George Bentinck that protection or free trade must be in what they called a circle round which in their legislation they must always move; that they must either give protection to everything or free trade to everything. He could not say that because sugar claimed protection coals must have protection also. Neither would he on the other hand apply free trade to every article. He acknowledged the advantage of competition as a stimulus, he thought that, placing things on equal grounds, competition was undoubtedly a great advantage. He could understand a competition to try the mutual speed of racehorses, but there could be no competition between a racehorse and a steam-engine, for the power of the animal could bear no comparison with that of the machine.

Mr. Baring could look back to no legislation more humiliating than the legislation regarding our colonies. No great interest was ever so much trifled with, so much sacrificed to the cry of the day; at one moment to no slavery and another to cheap sugar.

The committee was granted, and it was generally felt that the question was consequently quieted for the session. Let us see whether that anticipation were realised.

CHAPTER XXVI

When Lord John Russell, in 1846, endeavoured to reconcile our sugar-producing colonies to the inferior position in which his government placed them by representing to them that the duties under the new law would be permanent, not leaving the question to yearly debate with all the uncertainty and anxiety which then attended it, he could have little anticipated that before twelve months had elapsed the consideration of parliament would again be challenged to the subject, and under circumstances which made almost all persons feel that renewed deliberation was required. The dissolution of parliament then prevented Lord George Bentinck from bringing the subject of these colonies before the house. The black rod arrived on the very day that he made a statement of their condition, and time was only afforded to receive from the lips of the minister who represented in the house of commons the colonial office a report of the prosperous condition of the island of Mauritius.

The session of 1848, one of the longest on record, may be said to have commenced with sugar and to have concluded with sugar; and although in the course of that session the whole world was involved in revolution, though the navigation laws were vainly attacked, and the income tax threatened to be nearly doubled, though at such a crisis the government were discomfited in their financial policy, sugar was the subject which really shook them in their saddles, and from the consequences of which they escaped in a full house and after protracted debates by only a bare majority.

Singular article of produce! What is the reason of this influence? It is that all considerations mingle in it; not merely commercial, but imperial, philanthropic, religious; confounding and crossing each other, and confusing the legislature and the nation lost in a maze of conflicting interests and contending emotions.

It was expected, we will not say it was hoped, that the committee would have disposed of the question for the year, and so it would have done under ordinary circumstances and with an ordinary man. The committee was named on the 7th February. It consisted, besides the chairman, of three members of the protectionist party, Mr. Miles, of Bristol, Sir John Pakington and Lord George Manners, and of a sugar protectionist, Sir Edward Buxton; of two followers of Sir Robert Peel, namely, Mr. Goulburn and Mr. Cardwell; of a cabinet minister, Mr. Labouchere, and six followers, Sir Thomas Birch, Mr. Villiers, Mr. Milner Gibson, Mr. Wilson, Mr. Ewart, and Mr. Matheson, and of a free-trader not connected with any section, Mr. Henry Hope: of these fifteen gentlemen only three had voted against the act of 1846, namely the chairman, Mr. Miles, and Sir John Pakington; five had voted for it, namely Mr. Goulburn, Mr. Labouchere, Mr. Gibson, Mr. Villiers, and Mr. Ewart. The other members had not sat in the parliament of '46, with the exception of Mr. Cardwell, who, we believe, was absent from the division of that year.

The committee commenced its sittings on the 9th of February, and received evidence until the 22nd of May, during which period it sat thirty-nine days, always three times a week, and on one or two occasions four times a week. The committee sat long beyond the parliamentary hours, and sometimes so late as six o'clock. Eighty-three witnesses were called, of which sixty-five were summoned by Lord George Bentinck, individuals of every class connected with the subject: merchants, planters, brokers, distillers, members of parliament, secretaries of state, East India directors. More than seventeen thousand questions were asked, and it is agreed on all hands that the examination was never permitted for a moment to wander from the point at issue. The minutes of evidence were reported from time to time to the house, and ultimately took the shape of seven folio volumes.

The efficient conduct of a parliamentary committee mainly depends upon its chairman. A body of men, however zealous and intelligent, of peculiar views and injudicial habits, are soon lost in idle controversies on trifling questions if there be no dominant spirit who by his complete acquaintance with the subject and by the firmness, precision, and vigilance of his character, is capable and resolved to guide them. Lord George Bentinck in the present instance had mastered all the facts of a case involving a vast amount of details with which he had not been previously familiar; and those only who have busied themselves with a great commercial question can know what correspondence, what interviews, what communications of all kinds, such an undertaking entails upon a member of parliament; he had to preside over an inquiry admitting a great variety of evidence of very conflicting character; he was resisted in the purpose of the investigation by the government, and strongly also by the free-trade party, and he was not cordially supported by those whom he intended to serve. But he succeeded in establishing from the first good order and discipline in the committee. He prevailed upon them in the beginning to consent to certain rules as to the order in which the inquiry should be taken and the witnesses examined, and to make it clear for what purpose any evidence was to be called, and then he never allowed any member, whether friend or foe, to depart in the least from what had been agreed upon. Nor did he in his own conduct of the business manifest any of those deficiencies which are too often apparent in the chairman of committees. He was intelligent, just, and firm, aiding instead of puzzling the group over which he presided in doing their work. Although the proceedings were, in fact, a race against time, in order that their report might form the foundation of measures to be adopted within the session, Lord George never hurried the inquiry. He endeavoured to obtain his object of a comparatively speedy report by punctuality of attendance, strictness of reference, and indefatigable energy in getting through with the work. Never was so much evidence taken by a committee in so short a space of time—never was such a degree of exhaustion experienced by shorthand writers, clerks, and members, all sustained by the energy of their chief.

The writer of these remarks was not a member of the committee on sugar and coffee planting, upon which he had felt it his duty, though unwillingly, to decline to act, as he had been appointed a member of the secret committee on commercial distress, and also at that time was subject in the house to a greater pressure in debate than his experience warranted; but although therefore he had not the advantage of personal observation in the details which he has given of the sugar and coffee planting committee, he has great confidence in their truth and justness. For he sought the aid under the circumstances of two of his friends who were members of that committee, and neither of whom were political adherents of Lord George Bentinck; one of them indeed a most eminent member of the free-trade party. Independently of their opportunities of forming an opinion, both of these gentlemen are particularly qualified for adopting a sound one, one of them being distinguished for his quick perception and the other for the accuracy of his judgment. The writer therefore has had the advantage of being guided in his narrative by the impressions of Mr. Charles Villiers and Mr. Henry Hope.

It should here perhaps be remarked as illustrative of the capacity of labour by which Lord George Bentinck was distinguished, that the conduct of the sugar and coffee committee, which seemed alone to require the devotion of his time, did not prevent him from simultaneously acting as a member of the secret committee on commercial distress of which he was a regular attendant, and where he examined at great length the governor of the bank of England. Nor was he ever more regular in his attendance in the house than throughout this laborious spring, always ready in his place to vindicate his own peculiar views, or to assail those who differed from him whenever the opportunity arose. It should also be recollected that every morning before he attended the committee he had preliminarily to receive at home and to hear the statements of those who were to give their evidence, and whom in the great majority of instances he had afterwards to examine in chief. None of these witnesses left him without being impressed with admiration and astonishment at his knowledge of the subject and the perseverance which he displayed. Nor must it be omitted that during all this period he was also laboriously digesting the evidence received, and preparing that remarkable report which remains one of the most singular and valuable productions of our parliamentary literature, pouring a flood of light upon the position of our sugar colonies which they never had received, and which concluded with no less than two hundred and thirty-four resolutions, in none of which is there any repetition, and in all of which are references to the evidence where anything, however minute, is alleged or asserted. This was the period of his life when he was frequently in the habit of working eighteen hours a day. That might indeed be said of Bentinck which Tully said of Marcus Brutus, *quidquid vult, valde vult.*

After the evidence was concluded on the 22nd of May, the committee on sugar and coffee planting sat for one week on their report. The resolutions of the chairman, which as regards sugar recommended that the duty on foreign sugar should be maintained at 20s. per cwt., and the duty on British colonial sugar should be reduced to 10s., were negatived by a majority of nine to five. This would not have been a disappointment to any one less sanguine than Lord George Bentinck, but notwithstanding the elements of the committee, he had indulged in hopes, and he frequently mentioned that he never knew a committee of which the members were universally so anxious to ascertain the truth and to arrive at a just conclusion without reference to their preconceived opinions. On the resolutions moved by Mr. Wilson, which recommended relief, but threw the selection of the remedies on the government, the numbers were equal, and they were negatived by the casting vote of the chairman. The draft of resolutions moved by Mr. Goulburn, conceived generally in the spirit of the preceding ones, was then read a second time by a majority of eight to six against the free-trade party; but after two days' severe discussion the numbers became equal on the vital point of these resolutions, and they were negatived by the casting vote of the chairman. The exercise of this peculiar suffrage was invoked during this committee on five or six critical occasions, and ultimately on the 29th of May the casting vote of the chairman carried the resolution of Sir Thomas Birch, recommending a differential duty of 10s. in favour of sugar the produce of British possessions, for a period of six years; 'being of opinion that this temporary encouragement would have the effect of preventing the immediate and otherwise inevitable abandonment of the majority of the estates, and secure time for bringing into operation the intended measures of relief.'

During the first six weeks of this famous committee the attendance of its members was not very regular and its labours attracted little attention. The evidence on the East India part of the question was closed and reported to the house by the end of February; after that period the evidence was reported to the house every week or ten days. Towards the end of March rumours began to circulate of the extraordinary vigour and ability with which this investigation was pursued, and of the novel, authentic, and striking evidence that had been elicited. The proceedings were talked of in the house of commons and on the royal exchange; the city men who were examined went back to their companions with wondrous tales of the energy and acuteness of Harcourt House, and the order, method, and discipline of the committee-room at Westminster. As time elapsed the hopes of the colonial interest again revived. It was generally felt that Lord George had succeeded in establishing an irresistible case. It was rumoured that the government could not withstand it. Those who had originally murmured at the course which he had adopted of moving for a committee of inquiry instead of proposing a specific measure of relief, and had treated an investigation as a mere means of securing inaction, now recanted their rash criticism and did justice to his prescience and superior judgment as well as to his vast information and indefatigable exertions. The week during which the committee sat on their report was a very anxious one; the divisions were known every day in the house of commons; the alternations of success and discomfiture, and the balanced numbers that so often called for the interposition of the chairman, were calculated to sustain the excitement; and when on the 29th of May it was known that the report was at length agreed to, and that a committee of free-traders had absolutely recommended a differential duty of 10s. in favour of our own produce, one might have fancied from the effect visibly produced that a government was changed.

A few days before, it was the day after the Derby, May 25th, the writer met Lord George Bentinck in the library of the house of commons. He was standing before the bookshelves, with a volume in his hand, and his countenance was greatly disturbed. His resolutions in favour of the colonial interest after all his labours had been negatived by the committee on the 22nd, and on the 24th his horse Surplice, whom he had parted with among the rest of his stud solely that he might pursue without distraction his labours on behalf of the great interests of the country, had won that paramount and Olympian stake to gain which had been the object of his life. He had nothing to console him, and nothing to sustain him except his pride. Even that deserted him before a heart which he knew at least could yield him sympathy. He gave a sort of superb groan:

'All my life I have been trying for this, and for what have I sacrificed it!' he murmured.

It was in vain to offer solace.

'You do not know what the Derby is,' he moaned out.

'Yes, I do; it is the blue ribbon of the turf.'

'It is the blue ribbon of the turf,' he slowly repeated to himself, and sitting down at the table, he buried himself in a folio of statistics.

But on Monday, the 29th, when the resolution in favour of a 10s. differential duty for the colonies had at the last moment been carried, and carried by his casting vote, 'the blue ribbons of the turf' were all forgotten. Not for all the honours and successes of all the meetings, spring or autumn, Newmarket, Epsom, Goodwood, Doncaster, would he have exchanged that hour of rapture. His eye sparkled with fire, his nostril dilated with triumph, his brow was elate like a conqueror, his sanguine spirit saw a future of continued and illimitable success.

'We have saved the colonies,' he said, 'saved the colonies. I knew it must be so. It is the knell of free trade.'

A few days after the report of the committee on sugar and coffee planting was presented by its chairman to the house, the first minister announced that immediately after the Whitsun holidays, then impending, he would state on the part of the government the course they proposed to take 'with respect to the West Indian distress.' Thus was the prophecy of reaction made in 1846 with respect to the sugar duties act fulfilled, and fulfilled too in the person of the author of that act.

The house adjourned on the 9th until the 15th of June, and on the following day, pursuant to his notice, the first minister made the promised statement. He acknowledged that with respect to the West Indies, 'the operation of the act of '46 had been too rapid.' The proposition of the minister, though it fell short of the wishes, and perhaps the hopes, of the colonial interest, and though it did not fully realise the recommendation of the committee, was, considering the antecedents of the ministry and the general principles which they represented, a temperate and statesmanlike one. Its pith was to maintain the scale of '46 as to the duty on foreign sugar, but to reduce immediately the duty on colonial sugar, so that a differential duty might be secured to the colonies without raising the price to the consumer. This differential duty, however, gradually diminishing, was to cease altogether in the year 1855, when both foreign and colonial sugar would be admitted at a duty of 10s. per cwt. This latter part of the scheme seemed very objectionable.

The plan of the government seemed to please no one; the protectionists and the free-traders alike assailed it. Mr. Hume 'confessed he could not understand how the government, after protesting as they had repeatedly done that nothing would induce them to alter or meddle with that act, could now come down to the house and unblushingly propose an alteration almost equivalent to its repeal.'

Mr. Herries noticed later in the evening that not a single member who had spoken had approved of the proposition of the government. Every one of them had intimated his intention of opposing it on one ground or another. 'After a committee, conducted with such extraordinary ability by Lord George Bentinck, had sat for such a length of time, and had produced such a mass of information as never yet had been laid on the table of the house on any one subject, after it had issued reports and come to resolutions, the government brought forward a measure which did not meet one of the requisites they recommended.'

It was on this night that Lord George Bentinck made 'a grave charge' against the colonial office, which led to very warm and repeated discussions. It appeared that on the 27th of March a despatch had been received by the secretary of state from a free-trade governor of Jamaica, recommending, 'upon the most comprehensive and painstaking review of the whole subject,' a permanent differential duty of 10s. per cwt. in favour of the sugar of our West Indian colonies. Without this the governor 'firmly believed that the greater portion of the sugar cultivation of Jamaica would be abandoned.' The under-secretary of the colonies had been a witness before the sugar and coffee committee on the 5th of April following the receipt of this despatch, and had been asked by Mr. Goulburn whether any despatch had been received from the governor of Jamaica respecting the state of that island. The under-secretary had replied 'that he was not aware of any despatch from the governor of any importance which had been withheld from the committee.'

Now this despatch was of paramount importance. ' It was,' as Lord George Bentinck observed, ' to this point, as to the requisite amount of differential duty necessary to save the colonies, that for three months I may say, morning, evening, and night, we gave our study: and fortified by such evidences as that of the governor of Jamaica, without any concert of course with us, and himself a free-trader, I cannot doubt that the majority in the committee would have been much greater, and would have had proportionably greater influence in the country.'

On the 5th of April, though subject to a strict examination, the under-secretary persisted in his statement that there was no important despatch from the governor of Jamaica which had not been placed before the committee. The committee remained sitting, and came to no vote whatever until eight weeks after the receipt of the 'missing despatch,' but nothing was heard from the colonial office, while on the 9th of June, after the proceedings of the committee had closed, a volume of papers was laid before the house, in which the despatch from Sir Charles Grey, governor of Jamaica, of the 25th March appeared for the first time. ' I repeat my conviction,' said Lord George Bentinck, ' that if that despatch of Sir Charles Grey had not been withheld at the critical moment for fifty-six days, instead of the narrow majority by which our resolution was carried, the report of the committee would have come out backed by a very considerable number.' He said ' it was a repetition of the trick played in the earlier part of the session. The sugar-planting interest has not had fair play in this transaction, and it has not been intended that it should have fair play. I now ask why that despatch was held back from the committee till their sittings were brought to an end ? '

The under-secretary was unable without inquiry to communicate satisfactorily to the house on the subject, but on the next night of the house meeting, which was Monday the 19th, he informed the house that he had made the requisite inquiries, that the despatch in question, ' the missing despatch,' had been minuted by himself when received to be laid before the committee and also minuted to that effect by the secretary of state, but that unfortunately, through the inadvertence of a subordinate officer, it had not been transmitted to the committee. After this statement Sir John Pakington, who had undertaken the office at the request of Lord George Bentinck and which he very effectively fulfilled, proposed in a comprehensive speech a counter-resolution on the sugar duties, expressing the opinion of the house, that considering the evidence taken before the sugar and coffee planting committee the remedies proposed by the government for the great distress of the sugar-growing possessions of the crown which the committee had unanimously declared to require an immediate application of relief would neither effect that object nor check the stimulus to the slave-trade, which a diminution of the production of sugar in those possessions must inevitably occasion. This amendment was seconded by Sir Edward Buxton, and was prolonged with great oratorical display on all sides for five nights.

On the third night, Mr. Hawes, the under-secretary of state for the colonies, spoke, and his speech, among many other things, was remarkable for the frank admission that the change of policy on the part of the government had been greatly influenced by the investigation and the opinion of the committee presided over by Lord George Bentinck. On the same night also Lord George spoke, and reiterated in detail his charge against the colonial office of suppressing the missing despatch. Nettled at these observations, and partly perhaps executing a design contemplated, the first minister took advantage of the motion for the adjournment of the debate to make a severe personal attack on Lord George Bentinck. The minister said that these mean frauds, these extremely dishonourable tricks, which Lord George Bentinck imputed, were not the faults and characteristics of men who are high in public office in this country; they were characteristics of men who were engaged in pursuits which Lord George Bentinck long followed.

Upon this there was a burst of disapprobation from all sides, in the midst of which the minister, feeling perhaps that the drift of his retort had been somewhat misapprehended, went on to say that Lord George Bentinck some years ago had greatly distinguished himself in detecting a fraud of that nature with respect to the name or the age of a horse, in which he showed very great quickness of apprehension. But the house would not be diverted from its first impression, and the minister, though he pursued his observations for some minutes, was continually interrupted. It was clear that the taste and feeling of the house were both offended.

This unusual indiscretion from so eminent a personage, and one who both by temper and discipline is acknowledged to be superior to passion, called forth a rejoinder from a friend of Lord George Bentinck, who reminded the minister that his brother, the Duke of Bedford, had taken the lead in honouring Lord George Bentinck for his great services to public morality in this very instance. A scene of great and prolonged excitement occurred which did not terminate until half-past two o'clock on Saturday morning. Two cabinet ministers endeavoured to palliate the position of their chief, but the house was not appeased, and it was observed that Sir Robert did not come to the rescue of his successor. It was thought that if the division had been taken under the circumstances, the ministry would have been beaten. As it was, the debate was again adjourned until Monday, when the under-secretary of state again preceded the business of the night by an explanatory statement, and on this occasion, though with reluctance, gave the name of the gentleman through whose neglect the direction in the official minute had been disregarded. Lord George Bentinck following, substantially retracted nothing, enforced his original charge, and then, as illustrative of the system pursued by the colonial office, introduced a new one into the debate of a very grave character. He charged Lord Grey in the house of lords with reading an important memorial to prove the prosperous state of Jamaica and omitting the sequel of the same document, in which the memorialists declared that they were in a ' desperate position.' This unexpected discussion was not calculated to cool the fervid atmosphere of Saturday, and occupied several hours, and the subject was considered so grave that Lord Grey felt it necessary on the next night (the 27th) to vindicate his conduct in the house of lords, whereupon Lord Stanley, who was master of the case, enforced the charges of Lord George Bentinck against the colonial office, and vindicated his conduct and motives throughout these discussions in a manner which was felt and much appreciated by his friend.

On the 29th, the fifth and last night of the debate, Sir Robert Peel spoke, and although the greater part of his followers, including Mr. Goulburn, Mr. Gladstone, Mr. Herbert, Sir George Clerk, and Mr. Cardwell voted for the counter-resolution of Sir John Pakington, he thought fit to oppose it. It is due to the memory of two remarkable men that we should quote here a passage in the speech of Sir Robert Peel, which was delivered with marked emphasis, turning as he spoke to Lord George Bentinck:

' I have read,' said Sir Robert Peel, ' the proceedings of the committee on sugar and coffee planting. Occupied as I have been by other committees and by other business, yet from the great importance of the noble lord's committee, I have read the whole of the evidence taken; and no consideration shall prevent me from expressing the opinion that a flood of light has been thrown upon the position of the West Indian colonies which could not have been thrown upon it unless that committee had been presided over by a chairman bringing to the performance of his duty the assiduity, the zeal, and the knowledge which were displayed by the noble lord.'

The division was called at two o'clock, and the government had only a majority of 15 in a house of 509 members.

The house sat four days in committee on the ministerial resolutions. On the fourth day, the 10th of July, Lord George Bentinck delivered a speech on the question in all its bearings, which took three hours and a half in its delivery. This speech has been published, and is a repertory of all the facts of the case lucidly arranged. One of his great points was that our manufacturers were suffering not so much from the disturbed state of Europe as from the ruin of our own colonies. The results of his active correspondence with Mr. Burn, the editor of the *Commercial Glance*, may be traced in this speech, whom he quoted with that respect which he sincerely felt for that painstaking and accurate commercial statistician.

On the 15th of July the report of the resolutions was brought up, and a bill in pursuance of them brought in. Four days afterwards Lord George found an informality in the bill, which the chancellor of the exchequer disregarded. Nevertheless, on the 21st Lord George returned to the conflict, and entering into many impugning details, said the bill must be withdrawn. Ten days after this the government withdrew their bill and introduced a new one. Under these circumstances it may be easily credited that Lord George Bentinck did not spare his opponents. Finally the famous sugar bill of 1848 was not read a third time and passed until the 22nd of August, when Lord George Bentinck, true to his mission, brought forward an additional clause, 'the effect of which would be to place the English refiner on the same footing with foreigners.'

CHAPTER XXVII

THE ministers had commenced their financial career of 1848 with a proposition greatly to increase the income tax, chiefly on the plea of the necessity of considerably enlarging our means of defence and armaments. It was understood, but sceptically received, that the dangerous designs of the French Bourbons occasioned this anxiety and justified this expenditure. The house of commons, and no one more actively than Lord George Bentinck, could not, however, tolerate so great and so odious an increase of taxation from a government without a parliamentary majority. The ministerial propositions were withdrawn, but strange to say, before this retreat was sounded, the throne of the French Bourbons had fallen; and in the midst of general convulsion, with four pitched battles fought in Europe in eight weeks, and the Adriatic and the Baltic both blockaded, the government discovered that without the increased tax our armaments were sufficiently strong and our means of defence adequate.

The subversion of the Orleans dynasty was a great misfortune for France and for Europe. After the overthrow of the king of the French, his former admirers in this country very freely criticised his conduct, and very satisfactorily accounted for his calamities. One eminent politician informed us that the basis of the suffrage in France was too narrow; it has been broad enough since, without producing an assembly more entitled to public respect; another statesman deplored the parliamentary corruption by which the chamber of deputies was managed as fatal to the dynasty, which, however, was not so flagrant as our own system in the early part of the last century, and which then saved the dynasty. The economists traced the catastrophe in the most scientific manner to bad harvests and a restricted commerce. All these are the conclusions of superficial observers and of pedants. It was neither parliaments nor populations, nor the course of nature, nor the course of events, that overthrew the throne of Louis Philippe. Amid one of those discontents which are appeased by the sacrifice of a favourite or the change of a ministry, the sovereign and the subjects both in confusion, the king deprived of his wonted energy by a prostrating illness, and the citizens murmuring without convictions, the throne was surprised by the secret societies, ever prepared to ravage Europe.

The origin of the secret societies that prevail in Europe is very remote. It is probable that they were originally confederations of conquered races organised in a great measure by the abrogated hierarchies. In Italy they have never ceased, although they have at times been obliged to take various forms; sometimes it was a literary academy, sometimes a charitable brotherhood; freemasonry was always a convenient guise. The inquisition in its great day boasted that it had extirpated them in Spain, but their activity in that country after the first French revolution rather indicates a suspension of vitality than an extinction of life. The reformation gave them a great impulse in Germany, and towards the middle of the eighteenth century, they had not only spread in every portion of the north of that region, but had crossed the Rhine.

The two characteristics of these confederations, which now cover Europe like network, are war against property and hatred of the Semitic revelation. These are the legacies of their founders; a proprietary despoiled and the servants of altars that have been overthrown. Alone, the secret societies can disturb, but they cannot control, Europe. Acting in unison with a great popular movement they may destroy society, as they did at the end of the last century. The French disturbance of '48 was not a great popular movement. It was a discontent which required nothing more for its solution than a change of ministry; but the sovereign and

his subjects were in sudden confusion; the secret associations are always vigilant and always prepared; they took
society by surprise, but having nothing really to rely upon
except their own resources, the movement, however disastrous,
has been an abortion.

It is the manœuvres of these men, who are striking at
property and Christ, which the good people of this country,
who are so accumulative and so religious, recognise and
applaud as the progress of the liberal cause.

It is very desirable that the people of England should
arrive at some conclusions as to the conditions on which the
government of Europe can be carried on. They will perhaps
after due reflection discover that ancient communities like
the European must be governed either by traditionary influences or by military force. Those who in their ardour of
renovation imagine that there is a third mode, and that our
societies can be reconstructed on the great transatlantic
model, will find that when they have destroyed traditionary
influences there will be peculiar features in their body-politic
which do not obtain in the social standard which they imitate,
and these may be described as elements of disturbance. A
dynasty may be subverted, but it leaves as its successor a
family of princely pretenders; a confiscated aristocracy takes
the shape of factions; a plundered church acts on the tender
consciences of toiling millions; corporate bodies displaced
from their ancient authority no longer contribute their
necessary and customary quota to the means of government;
outraged tradition in multiplied forms enfeebles or excruciates
the reformed commonwealth. In this state of affairs, after
a due course of paroxysms, for the sake of maintaining order
and securing the rights of industry, the state quits the senate
and takes refuge in the camp.

Let us not be deluded by forms of government. The
word may be republic in France, constitutional monarchy
in Prussia, absolute monarchy in Austria, but the thing is
the same. Wherever there is a vast standing army, the
government is the government of the sword. Half a million
of armed men must either be, or be not, in a state of dis-

cipline. If they be not in a state of discipline, but follow different chiefs, it is not government but anarchy; if they be in a state of discipline, they must obey one man, and that man is the master.

England is the only important European community that is still governed by traditionary influences, and amid the shameless wreck of nations she alone has maintained her honour, her liberty, her order, her authority, and her wealth. Yet there is a party among us who yearn for the transatlantic type. Let them remember that in the United States there are no elements of disturbance. Our kinsmen brought the experience of Europe to a virgin soil; they have never had to make war upon tradition, its various progeny and inexhaustible resources. The United States are not even troubled by the perplexity which would seem common to all communities: a surplus population. The United States are a territorial republic; their lands are not yet half appropriated; they are not only a colony but they are still colonising. There may be sympathy of feeling between Great Britain and the United States, but there is no analogy in their social or political conditions. If any party in this country become strong enough to force one and so destroy the existing means of government, that party and their creations will succumb after the usual paroxysms beneath the irresistible law which dooms Europe to the alternate sway of disciplined armies or secret societies; the camp or the convention.

But it is said that it is contrary to the spirit of the age that a great nation like England, a community of enlightened millions long accustomed to public liberty, should be governed by an aristocracy. It is not true that England is governed by an aristocracy in the common acceptation of the term. England is governed by an artistocratic principle. The aristocracy of England absorbs all aristocracies, and receives every man in every order and every class who defers to the principle of our society, which is to aspire and to excel.

Notwithstanding the formal renunciation of the leadership of the protectionist party by Lord George Bentinck, it was soon evident to the house and the country that that renunciation was merely formal. In these days of labour the leader of a party must be the man who does the work, and that work cannot now be accomplished without the devotion of a life. Whenever a great question arose, the people out of doors went to Lord George Bentinck, and when the discussion commenced he was always found to be the man armed with the authority of knowledge. There was, however, no organised debate and no party discipline. No one was requested to take a part and no attendance was ever summoned. The vast majority sitting on the protectionist benches always followed Bentinck, who, whatever might be his numbers in the lobby, always made a redoubtable stand in the house. The situation, however, it cannot be denied, was a dangerous one for a great party to persevere in, but no permanent damage accrued, because almost every one hoped that before the session was over, the difficulty would find a natural solution in the virtual chief resuming his formal and responsible post. Notwithstanding his labours on the two great committees of the year, those on colonial and commercial distress, Lord George Bentinck found time to master the case of the shipping interest when the navigation laws were attacked, to impugn in a formal motion the whole of the commercial policy of Sir Robert Peel, even while the sugar and coffee planting committee was still sitting, and to produce early in March a rival budget. It was mainly through the prolonged resistance which he organised against the repeal of the navigation laws, that the government in 1848 was forced to abandon their project. The resistance was led with great ability by Mr. Herries, and the whole party put forward their utmost strength to support him. But it is very difficult to convey a complete picture of the laborious life of Lord George Bentinck during the sitting of parliament. At half-past nine o'clock there called upon him the commercial representatives of the question of the day; after these conferences came his elaborate and methodical correspondence, all of which he carried on himself in a handwriting clear as print, and never employing a secretary; at twelve or one o'clock he was at a committee, and he only left the committee-room to take his seat in the house of commons, which he never quitted till the house adjourned, always long past midnight and often at two o'clock in the morning. Here he was ready for all comers, never omitting an opportunity to vindicate his opinions, or watching with lynxlike vigilance the conduct of a public office. What was not his least remarkable trait is, that although he only breakfasted on dry toast, he took no sustenance all this time, dining at White's at half-past two o'clock in the morning. After his severe attack of the influenza he broke through this habit a little during the last few months of his life, moved by the advice of his physician and the instance of his friends. The writer of these observations prevailed upon him a little the last year to fall into the easy habit of dining at Bellamy's, which saves much time and permits the transaction of business in conversation with a congenial friend. But he grudged it: he always thought that something would be said or done in his absence, which would not have occurred had he been there; some motion whisked through or some return altered. His principle was that a member should never be absent from his seat.

To Mr. Burn.

HARCOURT HOUSE, *February* 15, 1848.

We have had a witness before the secret committee who has propounded the monstrous dogma that the losses in 1825-26 exceeded those of 1847-48, and he relies for proof on the losses on produce, and especially on cotton. He said : ' There are figures before one's eyes as to some of the prices ; you will there meet with a fall of 1s. or 1s. 6d. upon cotton, whereas 3d. or $3\frac{1}{2}$d. per pound now is the maximum. Cotton was sold at about 2s. per pound in 1825, according to my recollection, and I think it was even still higher ; but it was sold in 1826 at 9d. per pound and 10d. per pound ; but in 1847, when it was highest, and had risen to such a fearful price, it had not risen above 7d. or 8d. per pound. Therefore there was a loss not only of a large amount of cotton, but there was a fall in the price to which the present bears no proportion.'

He was asked: 'Was the stock of 1825 anything like the amount of stock in 1847?'

Answer: 'My impression is that it was larger; the stock of 1847 was remarkably low.'

Now upon referring to your cotton statistics, I find quantities and prices as stated in the enclosed return, which very much differs from the evidence given. Stocks on hand, instead of being larger in 1825-26, proving little more than half those of January 1848, whilst the average fall, instead of 1s. or 1s. 6d. per pound, appears to have been $5\frac{1}{4}$d. or $6\frac{7}{16}$d.—a very wide difference.

But in the export the difference is still more striking, and it is there that England loses the whole amount of depreciation: 207,775 bags exported in 1847 against 68,741 bags in 1826. I believe, too, that bags in 1825-26 scarcely averaged 350 lbs. weight, while in 1847 I believe you estimate them to weigh 400 lbs. Pray tell me how this is, and give me your comments on the evidence I have transcribed.

To Mr. Burn.

Harcourt House, *February* 26, 1848.

I have only a moment before going to my committee to thank you for your admirable and most interesting statistics. The account of the fiats in bankruptcy is one that has been laid before the secret committee, and is of course official. What I want more particularly are the Scotch sequestrations, which the secret committee have not got; and if you could by return of post fill up the bankrupt and sequestration list to the last week of the present year, it would, I suspect, tell a fearful tale.

I think of calling you as a witness before the secret committee and before the sugar-planting committee. In the first to draw the contrast between the distress of 1846-47-48 as compared with 1825-26, with 1837, and with 1839-40-41-42; and before the sugar-planting committee to show the effect upon the manufacturing interests of transferring from the British East and West Indies and the Mauritius to foreign slave-holding countries the supply of this country with sugar.

Before the committee we must begin accurately with the 22nd of August 1846, and bring the period up, if possible, to the 22nd of February, and compare this enlarged period with an equal period under protection. To enable you to do this I propose to call you as late as possible, say the middle of March.

I should wish you also to make a comparative calculation of the proportion in each period which went in wages to operatives, and profits of manufacturers, that I may contrast what the manufacturers and operatives lost by diminished employment with their savings by cheap sugar.

To Mr. Burn.

Harcourt House, *March* 3, 1848.

I thank you for this day's information, but I think we must have the goods reduced; first into money value, and next into wages and profits, and the number of families those lost wages would have sustained. To get accurately at this, we must in each period of eighteen months deduct the value of raw cotton, which I apprehend was far less in proportion in the first period of eighteen months than in the second. I want you then to be prepared with a comparative statement of the gain by cheap sugar and loss by diminished employment and wages to the entire population of the empire dependent upon cotton manufactures for their subsistence.

Take sugar as cheapened 1d. per lb., *i.e.* 9s. 4d. per cwt., and the consumption of sugar at $23\frac{1}{2}$ lbs. per head per annum. This is the true and the telling statement.

To Mr. Burn.

Harcourt House, *March* 8, 1848.

I was so busy all day yesterday I had not time to write to you. I would rather be governed by your opinion than give one in any matter connected with the cotton trade, in regard to which I look with implicit confidence to your universal knowledge of all the statistics belonging to it.

There are two points only that I think require some reflection. First, as regards the number of pounds of cotton assessed to each operative in 1841 and 1846, which you take equally at 823. Now I think you once wrote or said to me that the improvements in machinery and increase of steam power had enabled the same number of hands to work 10 or 20 per cent. more cotton than they did a few years back: I forget the exact percentage. I think this must not be left out of sight. The other point regards the number of persons out of employment in 1847 as compared with 1846. I should like to compare 1846 and '47 with 1844-45; but it seems incredible that 181,341 persons could be out of employment in 1847 without a servile war. I cannot help thinking there must be some mistake about this. I think we could know pretty accurately the number of the twenty-seven classes of operatives dependent upon cotton manufactures for their subsistence employed and out of employ in the Manchester district. I think having got these data to go upon, the safest mode of calculation would be to estimate those out of employment in the United Kingdom in 1847 as compared with 1844-45, as bearing the same proportion to the total number employed that the unemployed of Manchester district in the same period bore to the employed.

I wish you would give me a statement of the average price of cotton in each of the three monthly periods of 1843-44, and first three months of 1845, as compared with the prices of each of the three monthly periods which have elapsed since.

My object is to show that through their entire monopoly of the cotton supply the United States have obtained the entire benefit of the repeal of the cotton duty. Of this I have not the least doubt myself.

I read in the United States papers that so enormous are the profits which the cotton planters have realised in 1846-47 that they can well afford to hold out and starve the English manufacturers into paying such prices as the United States may choose to dictate.

To Mr. Burn.

Harcourt House, *March* 28, 1848.

Do you think if I were to postpone examining you till this day, or Saturday se'nnight, you can manage to make the imports and exports to sugar-growing countries for nineteen instead of eighteen months, thus bringing the period down to the 22nd of this month, and taking another month back in 1845? The larger period of time the comparison embraces the more valuable it will be held as a criterion, whilst I imagine I may assume that the trade to British sugar-growing possessions, instead of getting better, is every month getting from bad to worse.

Mr. Gladstone, in his answer to me the other night, declared that it was not the rivalship of France that Spitalfields was suffering from, but the rivalship of Manchester.

I wish you could find out for me the statistics of the Manchester silk trade from the year 1841 to the present time, viz. :

The number of mills each year employed.

The number of persons each year employed.

Consumption of raw and thrown silk.

Wages of operatives in each year.

I do observe that there appear to be but eight silk mills in Manchester, and 3000 persons employed thereupon, and that all these are working full time. But the question is, were there not in 1845 eight mills and 3000 persons engaged in the silk trade working full time, and working at as high or higher wages and larger profits than they are now working at?

I thought Macclesfield, rather than Manchester, was the head-quarters of the silk trade; if so, perhaps you might be able to obtain some information for me from Macclesfield.

To a Friend.

HARCOURT HOUSE, *April* 19, 1848.

I can hardly imagine, after your great and exciting speech this morning on the mighty concerns of all Europe, in which in an hour and a quarter you taught the house of commons the diplomatic history of northern Europe, of which before they knew nothing, that you can possibly be able to settle down your mind to think of groceries, even on the wholesale scale which involves the sugar trade of the British East and West Indies; but in case you should be able so to distract your mind from European to trading interests, I send you another proof-sheet of the report; this has not been touched at all; it is the original rough draft, and requires even more lopping, methodising, and licking into shape than the last.

To a Friend.

HARCOURT HOUSE, *April* 20, 1848.

I send you all the proofs as far as they are printed. The gap of twenty pages, between pages 55 and 75, arises from the difference between old and new style. No. 1 are new style, viz., the corrected proofs, originally seventy-four pages cut down to fifty-five by being printed all over the sheet, instead of over half the sheet. I have another set coming to-night, which completes the précis, if anything upwards of two hundred pages can properly be so called. I have not looked at these rough sheets.

The chairman of excise with his rule-of-three sum wants some of your attic salt applying to his raw back.

I find our holidays are only a week.

To Mr. Burn.

HARCOURT HOUSE, *June* 11, 1848.

Can you tell me what would be the amount of tonnage required to carry out all the manufactures we export to Brazil, and Cuba, and Porto Rico? Take the average of cotton, woollen, linen, and silk goods exported, what would be the average value per ton of each description of goods?

The point is this, if the navigation laws are repealed, the country which obtains a larger portion of the outward freight must necessarily get the sugar, and coffee, and cotton freights to England. As Cuba, Porto Rico, and Brazil obtain the larger portion of their lumber, grain, rice, and provision from the United States, I think there can be no doubt that the great bulk of the inward tonnage must be from the United States, whilst the great bulk of outward tonnage must go to Europe. Consequently, under the existing law, the great majority of British ships must go out in ballast, and bring home heavy cargoes of sugar to England; whilst the United States ships must enter heavy laden into the ports of Brazil, and return, the great majority of them, in ballast. I judge this must be the case, because I understand that whilst freights are 20s. a ton from New York to Cuba or Jamaica, I observe that they are only 90 to 110 cents from Rio to New York, whilst they are 90s. to Hamburg, and 80s. to London.

PS.—Pray look at the *Economist*, and between this and Friday next do oblige me by dissecting as much of his export statement as you can, especially in regard to cotton manufactures and yarn, the diminution of which he ascribes solely to the disturbed state of the continent, whilst, if I am not greatly mistaken, no mean portion of the diminution will be found in the export trade to the United States, Canada, Brazil, British East Indies, Mauritius.

To a Friend.

HARCOURT HOUSE, *June* 12, 1848.

* * * * * * called here yesterday evening, his object apparently being to prepare me for a general discussion on Friday next upon the sugar question. He said 'the government were prepared with a workmanlike plan, though its details were not finally and irrevocably fixed, which, though it would not give satisfaction to those who looked to protection as the only cure, would take the wind out of Goulburn's and Cardwell's sails.' I could not make out what his plan was, but strongly suspect that loans and assistance in obtaining fresh labour, the repeal of the navigation laws, a reduction of the duty on rum 3d. a gallon, and probably the continuation of the 6s. duty or maybe of the 7s. duty for a limited period, will be the plan.

I cannot say I think the *Times* very complimentary to me, though I am bound to admit they have reported me far better than any other paper I have seen.

The event which seems to have created the greatest sensation is Sir Robert Peel's humiliating reception by his old party. It appears in public opinion to have been the most damaging occurrence which has yet befallen him. A few more such rubs will settle his account.

Have you looked up your figures to see if you are right or Wilson?

My voice is no better or very little than when you last saw me.

To a Friend.

HARCOURT HOUSE, *June* 25, 1848.

I have this moment received the enclosed: the Duke of Newcastle desires your advice thereon. The duke says he will call after morning church. Perhaps you would call and meet him.

The sensation created by your speech in defence of me against ******'s attack is immense. Everybody I meet—man, woman, and even girls—congratulate me on your defence of me.

I enclose you some of my notes which I did not use. Recollect Pickwood was Earl Grey's witness, examined in chief three hours and twenty-five minutes, by my watch, by Wilson. He was sent to prove three things: that free labour was cheaper than slave labour; that absenteeism was at the root of the evil; and that the navigation laws were a great aggravation of it—that their repeal would be a great remedy. I have also sent you an extract of some lines from Tom Moore addressed to George IV., which I had intended to have used myself had the house been in good and listening humour and the debate taken a more playful turn, but I was obliged to shift my ground and take the savage line. I think the house would roar at this appropriate quotation. I also send you some quotations from Peel's speeches on this question.

To a Friend.

HARCOURT HOUSE, *June* 27, 1848.

I send you a very important document prepared by Mr. Greene, showing the pitiful boon that the reduction of the duty on rum will prove to the West Indians. The statement is so clear and irrefragable that it is only necessary to put it in your hands. Divide £47,935 by 160,000 tons of British West Indian sugar, equal to 3,200,000 cwts., and you will find a reduction of 5d. a gallon. Even supposing the planter got the whole and the consumer no part of it, it would only amount upon last year's importation from the British West Indies to 3¼d. and a fraction per cwt. I think it is of great importance to show what a mockery in the way of relief this remission of the rum duties is. I meant to have used it but forgot.

I think it also very material to show that Gladstone's proposal is worse than that of the government. For this purpose I want you to see Blyth and Greene to-morrow or Thursday morning that they may put you completely *au fait* at these matters. They call on me every morning at half-past nine, and I propose if you approve sending them on to you.

I also send you the explanation of the marine picture in the miracle room at the cathedral of St. Bomfim at Bahia, where they 'bless' the sails of the fleets of slavers prior to their departure for what is called 'The Coast.'

I think a religious frenzy might be worked up out of these blasphemous proceedings.

I want to get the picture into the *Illustrated News*.

To Mr. Burn.

Your last return is invaluable. It proves that it is not the disturbances on the continent of Europe from which we are suffering, but the glutted state of the United States, the Brazil, China, and foreign West India markets, together with the ruined condition of the British transmarine possessions. It would be a good thing to take out separately :

1st. Europe ;

2nd. The British possessions in Asia, Africa, and America ;

3rd. Foreign countries in Asia, Africa, and America.

The cotton manufactures appear to be rallying at last. Do you not consider that such is the case? Does the silk trade continue to be as active as you a little while ago described it?

To a Friend.

I am so busy I cannot go out before house of commons time, when I must be there at the meeting, as I have given a notice of amendment to the speaker's leaving the chair to go into a committee of supply. Hawes and Sir G. Grey refused me my motion on Friday night unless I would consent to alter it. I then said I would move it as an amendment on the first supply night, which is to-night.

The session of '48 had been one of unexampled length, having lasted ten months, and as usual under such circumstances the obstacles to the transaction of public business were sought everywhere except in the real quarter. The forms of the house and the propensity to unnecessary discussion among its members were chiefly denounced. Lord George Bentinck did not agree in the justness of these criminations; they were eagerly caught by the thoughtless and the superficial, but it was his habit to investigate and analyse everything, and he found that these charges had no basis. The forms of the house of commons are the result of accumulated experience and have rarely been tampered with successfully, while on the other hand a parliamentary government is by name and nature essentially a government of discussion. It is not at all difficult to conceive a mode of governing a country more expeditious than by a parliament; but where truth as well as strength is held to be an essential element of legislation, opinion must be secured an unrestricted organ. Superfluity of debate may often be inconvenient to a minister, and sometimes perhaps even distasteful to the community, but criticising such a security for justice and liberty as a free-spoken parliament is like quarrelling with the weather because there is too much rain or too much sunshine. The casual inconvenience should be forgotten in the permanent blessing. Acting upon these false imputations a committee was even appointed two years ago of the most eminent members of the house of commons to investigate the subject and suggest remedies, and some votaries of the transatlantic type recommended the adoption of the rules of congress where each speaker is limited to an hour. But an hour from an uninteresting speaker would be a great infliction. The good sense and the good taste of the house of commons will be found on the whole to be the best regulators of the duration of a debate.

The truth is that the delay in the conduct of parliamentary business which has been much complained of during the last few years, murmurs of which were especially rife in 1848, is attributable to the fact that the ministry, though formed of men inferior in point of ability to none who could be reasonably entrusted with administration, had not sufficient parliamentary strength. After all their deliberations and foresight, after all their observations of the times and study of the public interest, their measures when launched from the cabinet into the house were not received by a confiding majority; firm in their faith in the statesmanlike qualities of the authors of these measures and in their sympathy with the general political system of which the ministry was the representative. On the contrary the success of the measures depended on a variety of sections who in their aggregate exceeded in number and influence the party of the ministers. These became critics and took the ministerial measures in hand; the measures became the measures not of the cabinet but of the house of commons; and a purely legislative assembly became in consequence of the weakness of the government yearly more administrative. This was undoubtedly a great evil, and occasioned besides great delay many crude enactments, as will be the case where all are constructors and none are responsible, but the evil was not occasioned by the forms of the house or the length of the speeches. Sir Robert Peel was unquestionably a very able administrator, but if he had not had a majority of ninety he would have fallen in as ill repute as has been too often the lot of Lord John Russell.

Lord George Bentinck was very anxious that there should be a parliamentary summary of this enormous and eventful session of '48, that the conduct of business by the ministry should be traced and criticised and the character of the house of commons vindicated, and he appealed to the writer of these observations to undertake the task. But the writer was unwilling to accede to this suggestion, not only because at the end of August he shrank from a laborious effort, but principally because he did not hold that his position in the house of commons warranted on his part such an interference, since, after all, he was only the comrade in arms of one who chose to be only an independent member of the house. He therefore unaffectedly stated that he thought the office was somewhat above his measure. But Lord George Bentinck would not listen to these representations. ' I don't pretend to know much,' he said, ' but I can judge of men and horses.' It is difficult to refuse those who are themselves setting a constant example of self-sacrifice, and therefore as far as the labour was concerned the writer would not have shrunk from the exertion even on the last day of the month of August, and when the particular wish of Lord George was found to be more general than the writer presumed to suppose, he accordingly endeavoured to accomplish the intention. The reason, which it is hoped will be accepted as an apology, for entering into these particulars is that the following letters on the subject illustrate the character and life of their writer.

To a Friend.

HARCOURT HOUSE, *August* 10, 1848.

I have this morning received the enclosed from a Liverpool merchant.   I have answered him that I am not sufficiently *au fait* at the course of these negotiations (La Plata) to meddle in the matter, but that I have put his letter in your hands.

It strikes me it might constitute an item in the general charge against the government.

I send you the *Chronicle*, which has an article which will afford you a capital brief as regards the health of towns bill.   Six reprints, growing in value from 8d. to 10d., etc. etc.

On this point you would naturally revert to last year's bill; the total metamorphose of the measure from its constitution last year; Morpeth's speech in introducing it last year, when he promised to add God knows how many years to all our lives; calculated that he would by so doing enrich the country by adding to wealth-producing life; and by saving the cost of sickness I know not how many millions a year, but I think £10,000,000 or £20,000,000 a year; whilst the human manure he was to economise was to average I think £3 a man, or £3 a family, I forget which, and estimated by the towns' population, was to realise to the country (an income saved) a sum of £5,000,000 or £10,000,000 more.   I think the speech is worth looking back at.

In treating of the delay in regard to the sugar bill debates, it should be remembered that nearly two nights' debates were created by Charles Wood's dragging in his 'third budget' very *mal-à-propos*, and quite *de trop* with the sugar discussion, in the most wanton way.

To a Friend.

HARCOURT HOUSE, *August* 27, 1848.

I have completed for you the history of the sugar debate.   The 'breach of promise,' in regard to refining in bond, is a most material omission in the other memoranda.   This epitome shows six days' discussion on the sugar bill, entirely created by the ministerial blundering and vacillation, independent of the discussions caused on the 'resolutions.'

Six days' debates and seven divisions of the house.

TO A FRIEND.

HARCOURT HOUSE, *Wednesday, August* 1848,
Half-past four o'clock in the morning.

I am just come home from the house of commons, after a sitting of fifteen hours and a half, the longest but one I believe on record. Late as it is, I send the report of the self-constituted secret committee on savings banks in Ireland, together with the bill that the government have had the audacity to found on it for England, etc., upon their secret Irish evidence. The bill has been awfully cut about in committee, but still it is a monstrous bill, and I should think very likely to put the people of this country in a frenzy. I send it to you, as I think it will afford perhaps your best weapon of attack. The bill was only printed yesterday. The English savings banks are utterly ignorant of its contents, or of the intention of the government to bring forward any such measure. And the chancellor of the exchequer forces us into a consideration of it at eleven o'clock at night, after Lord John Russell is gone to bed, and we are kept at it in committee for two hours after all the reporters are gone to bed too.

I think it perhaps the most scandalous proceeding of which the government have been guilty.[1]

Three or four days after this, the writer, about to leave London, called at Harcourt House to say farewell to his comrade in arms. He passed with Lord George the whole morning, rather indulging in the contemplation of the future than in retrospect. Lord George was serene, cheerful, and happy. He was content with himself, which was rarely the case, and remembered nothing of his career but its distinction and the ennobling sense of having done his duty. Any misunderstandings that may have for a moment irritated

[1] The summary of the business of the session was to be made at noon this very day, and Lord George was in his place at that hour.

him seemed forgotten; he appeared conscious that he possessed the confidence and cordial regard of the great majority
of the protectionist party although he chose to occupy a
private post, and he was proud of the consciousness. He
was still more sensible of the sympathy which he had
created out of doors, which he greatly appreciated, and to
which, though with his usual modesty, he more than once
recurred. 'The thing is to get the people out of doors with
you,' he repeated, 'men like the merchants; all the rest
follows.' It was evident that the success of his colonial
committee had greatly satisfied his spirit. He had received
that day the vote of thanks of the West India committee
for his exertions. He said more than once that with a weak
government a parliamentary committee properly worked
might do wonders. He said he would have a committee on
import duties next year, and have all the merchants to show
what share the foreigners had obtained of the reductions
that had been made of late years. He maintained that,
quite irrespective of the general arrangements of the new
commercial system, Sir Robert Peel had thrown away a
great revenue on a number of articles of very inferior importance, and he would prove this to the country. He said our
colonial empire ought to be reconstructed by a total abolition of all duties on produce from her majesty's dominions
abroad.

All his ideas were large, clear, and coherent. He dwelt
much on the vicissitudes which must attend all merely
foreign trade, which, though it should be encouraged, ought
not to be solely relied on, as was the fashion of this day.
Looking upon war as occasionally inevitable, he thought a
commercial system based upon the presumption of perpetual
peace to be full of ruin. His policy was essentially imperial
and not cosmopolitan.

About to part probably for many months, and listening to
him as he spoke according to his custom with so much
fervour and sincerity, one could not refrain from musing
over his singular and sudden career. It was not three years
since he had in an instant occupied the minds of men. No

series of parliamentary labours had ever produced so much influence in the country in so short a time. Never was a reputation so substantial built up in so brief a space. All the questions with which he had dealt were colossal questions: the laws that should regulate competition between native and foreign labour; the interference of the state in the development of the resources of Ireland; the social and commercial condition of our tropical colonies; the principles upon which our revenue should be raised; the laws that should regulate and protect our navigation. But it was not that he merely expressed opinions upon these subjects; he came forward with details in support of his principles and policy which it had been before believed none but a minister could command. Instead of experiencing the usual and almost inevitable doom of private members of parliament, and having his statements shattered by official information, Lord George Bentinck on the contrary was the assailant and the successful assailant of an administration on these very heads. He often did their work more effectually than all their artificial training enabled them to do it. His acute research and his peculiar sources of information roused the vigilance of all the public offices of the country. Since his time there has been more care in preparing official returns and in arranging the public correspondence placed on the table of the house of commons.

When one remembered that in this room, not three years ago, he was trying to find a lawyer who would make a speech for him in parliament, it was curious to remember that no one in the space had probably addressed the house of commons oftener. Though his manner, which was daily improving, was not felicitous in the house, the authority of his intellect, his knowledge, and his character made him one of the great personages of debate; but with the country who only read his speeches he ranked high as an orator. It is only those who have had occasion critically to read and examine the long series of his speeches who can be conscious of their considerable merits. The information is always full and often fresh, the scope large, the argument close, and the style though simple never bald, but vigorous, idiomatic, and often picturesque. He had not credit for this in his day, but the passages which have been quoted in this volume will prove the justness of this criticism. As a speaker and writer his principal want was condensation. He could not bear that anything should remain untold. He was deficient in taste, but he had fervour of feeling, and was by no means void of imagination.

The writer in his frequent communications with him of faithful and unbounded confidence was often reminded of the character by Mr. Burke of my Lord Keppell.

The labours of Lord George Bentinck had been supernatural, and one ought perhaps to have felt then that it was impossible they could be continued on such a scale of exhaustion; but no friend could control his eager life in this respect; he obeyed the law of his vehement and fiery nature, being one of those men who in whatever they undertake know no medium, but will 'succeed or die.'

But why talk here and now of death! He goes to his native county and his father's proud domain, to breathe the air of his boyhood and move amid the parks and meads of his youth. Every breeze will bear health, and the sight of every hallowed haunt will stimulate his pulse. He is scarcely older than Julius Cæsar when he commenced his public career, he looks as high and brave, and he springs from a long-lived race.

He stood upon the *perron* of Harcourt House, the last of the great hotels of an age of stately manners, with its wings, and courtyard, and carriage portal, and huge outward walls. He put forth his hand to bid farewell, and his last words were characteristic of the man: of his warm feelings and of his ruling passion: 'God bless you: we must work, and the country will come round us.'

CHAPTER XXVIII

THE heavens darken; a new character enters upon the scene.

῏Ω Θάνατε, Θάνατε νῦν μ' ἐπίσκεψαι μολών.

They say that when great men arise they have a mission to accomplish and do not disappear until it is fulfilled. Yet this is not always true. After all his deep study and his daring action Mr. Hampden died on an obscure field, almost before the commencement of that mighty struggle which he seemed born to direct. In the great contention between the patriotic and the cosmopolitan principle which has hardly begun, and on the issue of which the fate of this island as a powerful community depends, Lord George Bentinck appeared to be produced to represent the traditionary influences of our country in their most captivating form. Born a natural leader of the people, he was equal to the post. Free from prejudices, his large mind sympathised with all classes of the realm. His courage and his constancy were never surpassed by man. He valued life only as a means of fulfilling duty, and truly it may be said of him that he feared nothing but God.

A few days after the interview noticed in the last chapter, Lord George Bentinck returned to Welbeck. Some there were who thought him worn by the exertions of the session, and that an unusual pallor had settled upon that mantling and animated countenance. He himself never felt in better health or was ever in higher spirits, and greatly enjoyed the change of life and that change in a scene so dear to him.

On the 21st of September, after breakfasting with his family, he retired to his dressing-room, where he employed himself with some papers and then wrote three letters, one to Lord Enfield, another to the Duke of Richmond, and the third to the writer of these pages. That letter is now at hand; it is of considerable length, consisting of seven sheets of notepaper, full of interesting details of men and things, and written not only in a cheerful but even a merry mood. Then, when his letters were sealed, about four o'clock he took his staff and went forth to walk to Thoresby, the seat of Lord Manvers, distant between five and six miles from Welbeck, and where Lord George was to make a visit of two days. In consequence of this his valet drove over to Thoresby at the same time to meet his master. But the master never came. Hours passed on and the master never came. At length the anxious servant returned to Welbeck and called up the groom who had driven him over to Thoresby and who was in bed, and inquired whether he had seen anything of Lord George on the way back, as his lord had never reached Thoresby. The groom got up, and along with the valet and two others took lanthorns and followed the footpath which they had seen Lord George pursuing as they themselves went to Thoresby.

About a mile from the abbey, on the path which they had observed him following, lying close to the gate which separates a water meadow from the deer park, they found the body of Lord George Bentinck. He was lying on his face; his arms were under his body, and in one hand he grasped his walking-stick. His hat was a yard or two before him, having evidently been thrown off in falling. The body was cold and stiff. He had been long dead.

$$^{\text{ʾ}}\Omega \ \delta\acute{\epsilon}\mu\alpha\varsigma \ o\emph{ἰ}κτρόν. \quad \Phi\epsilon\hat{υ}, \ \phi\epsilon\hat{υ}$$
$$^{\text{ʾ}}\Omega \ \delta\epsilon\iota\nu o\tau\acute{α}τα\varsigma, \ o\emph{ἴ}μοι \ μοι.$$

A woodman and some peasants passing near the spot, about two hundred yards from the gate in question, had observed Lord George, whom at the distance they had mistaken for his brother the Marquess of Titchfield, leaning against this gate. It was then about half-past four o'clock, or it might be a quarter to five, so he could not have left his home much more than half an hour. The woodman and his companions thought 'the gentleman' was reading, as he held his head down. One of them lingered for a minute looking at the gentleman, who then turned round, and might have seen these passers-by, but he made no sign to them.

Thus it seems that the attack, which was supposed to be a spasm of the heart, was not instantaneous in its effects, but with proper remedies might have been baffled. Terrible to think of him in his death-struggle without aid, and so near a devoted hearth. For that hearth, too, what an impending future !

> Ἄγγειλον ἄτας τὰς ἐμὰς μόρον τ' ἐμὸν
> Γέροντι πατρί—

The terrible news reached Nottingham on the morning of the 22nd at half-past nine o'clock, and immediately telegraphed to London, was announced by a second edition of the *Times* to the country. Consternation and deep grief fell upon all men. One week later, the remains arrived from Welbeck at Harcourt House, to be entombed in the family vault of the Bentincks, that is to be found in a small building in a dingy street, now a chapel of ease, but in old days the parish church among the fields of the pretty village of Marylebone.

The day of the interment was dark, and cold, and drizzling. Although the last offices were performed in the most scrupulously private manner, the feelings of the community could not be repressed. From nine till eleven o'clock that day all the British shipping in the docks and the river, from London Bridge to Gravesend, hoisted their flags half-mast high, and minute guns were fired from appointed stations along the Thames. The same mournful ceremony was observed in all the ports of England and Ireland; and not only in these, for the flag was half-mast high on every British ship at Antwerp, at Rotterdam, at Havre.

Ere the last minute gun sounded all was over. Followed to his tomb by those brothers who, if not consoled, might at this moment be sustained by the remembrance that to him they had ever been brothers not only in name but in spirit, the vault at length closed on the mortal remains of GEORGE BENTINCK.

One who stood by his side in an arduous and unequal struggle; who often shared his councils, and sometimes perhaps soothed his cares; who knew well the greatness of his nature and esteemed his friendship among the chief of worldly blessings; has stepped aside from the strife and passion of public life to draw up this record of his deeds and thoughts, that those who come after us may form some conception of his character and career, and trace in these faithful though imperfect pages the portraiture of an ENGLISH WORTHY.

THE END